THE CARDINAL'S COLLEGE

Christ Church, Chapter and Verse

THE CARDINAL'S COLLEGE

Christ Church, Chapter and Verse

Judith Curthoys

First published in Great Britain in 2012 by
Profile Books Ltd
3a Exmouth House
Pine Street
Exmouth Market
London EC1R 0JH
www.profilebooks.com

1 3 5 7 9 10 8 6 4 2

Copyright © Christ Church, Oxford 2012

The moral right of the author has been asserted.

All rights reserved. Without limiting the rights under copyright reserved above, no part of this publication may be reproduced, stored or introduced into a retrieval system, or transmitted, in any form or by any means (electronic, mechanical, photocopying, recording or otherwise), without the prior written permission of both the copyright owner and the publisher of this book.

All reasonable efforts have been made by the author to obtain all necessary copyright permissions for material reproduced in this book. Any omissions or errors of attribution are unintentional and will, if brought to the attention of the author and publisher in writing, be corrected in future printings.

A CIP catalogue record for this book is available from the British Library.

ISBN: 978 1 84668 617 7

Text design by Sue Lamble
Typeset in Photina by MacGuru Ltd
info@macguru.org.uk

Printed and bound in Great Britain by TJ International, Padstow

Contents

	List of illustrations	vii
	Dean's foreword	xi
	Introduction and acknowledgements	xiii
1	Before Christ Church	1
	For 'the keepinge of their horses and cattell and for other occasions': the Meadow	22
2	'This Royall & Ample Foundation': 1546–53	40
	'To perfect the college …': Christ Church and charity	57
3	'Untyll suche tyme that it shall please the Kynge …': 1553–1625	67
	Aedis Christi: *cathedral, college chapel and the choir*	87
4	'The present engagement of the greatest part of them in Armes': 1625–88	97
	Christ Church time	133
5	'With strength of argument and in good order': 1689–1755	138
6	'Learning has been made a duty, a pleasure and even a fashion': 1755–1809	177
7	'Reading as if my life depended on my diligence': 1809–55	201
	'Water coming to the house of office': the plumbing	233
8	'To conduce the welfare and usefulness of Christ Church': 1855–98	238
	'More like some fine castle, or great palace, than a college …': the buildings	282

| 9 | 'Half arsenal, half hotel': twentieth-century Christ Church | 293 |
| 10 | 'Through all the vicissitudes of English history': Conclusion | 331 |

Appendices	334
Abbreviations and conventions	344
Notes	346
Bibliography	390
Index	396

Illustrations

All illustrations are from the Christ Church Archives and are reproduced by permission of the Governing Body of Christ Church except where otherwise indicated.

Photographs by Dave Stumpp as indicated: GeckoGPhotography, www.geckogphotography.com.

Colour plates *(between pages 208 and 209)*

Cardinal Thomas Wolsey by Sampson Strong, c.1610
St Frideswide
Vignette of the college in the corner of Strong's portrait of Cardinal Wolsey
Rudolph Ackermann's early nineteenth century painting of the kitchen
Design of 1803 by G. Smith for a triumphal arch into the Meadow
John Riley's *The Scullion*
The painted ceiling of the first Library
Bennett's plan of the Meadow, 1799
Coloured lithograph of the cathedral, probably from the 1830s
Watercolour of Pusey preaching in the cathedral, 1875
The 'Blenheim Row', 1893
Design for the Memorial Garden by John and Paul Coleridge, 1926
Michaelmas term 1980 intake – with the first female undergraduates
Fell Tower at night *(Dave Stumpp)*
The stairs to the Hall *(Dave Stumpp)*
Engraving of the north prospect of Peckwater Quad
The New Library, begun in 1716

The upper Library, painted by David Gentleman *(courtesy of the Delegates of the Oxford University Press)*
Plasterwork detail by Thomas Roberts, 1752–3 *(Dave Stumpp)*
The new Canterbury Gate, built in the late eighteenth century *(Dave Stumpp)*
The Great Quadrangle *(Dave Stumpp)*
Tom Tower *(Dave Stumpp)*

Black and white illustrations

The statutes of Cardinal College, drawn up in 1525	7
First page of the valuation of Cardinal College	13
John Malchair's 1775 drawing of the medieval gate into Canterbury Quadrangle	20
A plan of the Meadow drawn in 1762 following a dispute over parish boundaries	25
The list of swans owned by the Dean and Chapter	33
Frank Buckland's bear, Tiglath Pileser	35
Oseney Abbey, in an 1820 engraving	41
The foundation charter, dated 4 November 1546	42
A list of the most senior of the 100 Students at the foundation of Christ Church	44
A list of a Scholar's requirements in 1548	50
A page of the records of John Furnivall, manciple in the 1570s	51
Patent entitling John Wilkins to a place in the almshouse, 1698	59
The almshouse	63
Entry from the 1660 disbursement book	65
Mary Tudor's curb on plays and Christmas entertainments	70
Early nineteenth century plan of the site of the chapel of St Nicholas at Wallingford	76
John Bereblock's engraving of Christ Church in 1566, its earliest representation	78
Title page of Nathaniel Torporley's *Diclides coelometricae* (1602)	81
The expulson of Thomas Carter and Samuel Starr in 1610 and 1611	84

Illustrations

Proposal for a military academy in Oxford	100
Financial accounts in connection with Charles I's visit to Christ Church in 1636	101
An appeal by the Dean Chapter for a reduction in contributions to the City	104
The cathedral register	106
John Owen, appointed dean in 1651	110
Documents signed by Oliver Cromwell as Protector	112
John Fell, Roger Dolben and Richard Allestree, by Peter Lely	118
An illustration from Robert Hooke's *A description of helioscopes* (1676)	123
Chapter Book copy of Charles II's demand that John Locke be removed from his Studentship	128
Great Tom bell	134
The sundial on the south face of Killcanon	136
Henry Aldrich, the second great 'builder-dean' and designer of Peckwater Quad	139
Peckwater Quad	142
The list of charges against Augustine Spalding from the Chapter Book	144
Francis Atterbury, possibly the college's most unpopular head of house	148
Documents reconfirming the Dean and Chapter's confidence in the auditor John Brooks	153
Pages from the 'atlas' of the estate left to the college by Edward Careswell	161
Illustration from Charles Boyle's edition of the letters of Phalaris	169
The second 'Classis' in 1727	171
Documents from the papers of William Perrin	173
Regional origins of Christ Church men, 1661–1800	178
Title page from a 1553 edition of Euclid	181
Crime and contrition: an offender's name erased	189
A bill for turtle soup, 1793	197
A letter by George Chinnery	202
From Thomas Vowler Short's notes about undergraduates	206

Three Prime Ministers: George Grenville, William Gladstone and Archibald Primrose	223
Plans to pipe water into Christ Church in the early seventeenth century	234
Henry George Liddell	239
Meadows Building	250
Drawing room or attic? Rooms according to means	267
A member of the Oxford University Volunteer Corps, mid nineteenth century	278
Undergraduates' reading room	280
The old college library	284
Engraving of Christ Church by David Loggan, 1675	285
W. D. Caröe's twentieth-century drawing of Tom Tower	286
William Williams's 1730s ground-plan of Christ Church	287
Early photograph of the Great Quadrangle before Dean Liddell's building and restoration	290
Thomas Banks Strong, dean from 1901 to 1925	295
Beagling and hunting in the Edwardian era	296
Cancellation of Armistice thanksgiving services in the wake of the influenza pandemic	300
Quatercentenary celebrations in 1925	305
Albert Einstein, offered a Research Studentship in 1931	309
Troops marching outside Meadows Building	315
Hugh Trevor-Roper	315
The Christ Church Private Fire Brigade in 1948	319

Foreword
by the Dean

Christ Church has ever been an object of fascination, even among its detractors. Viewed with affection by nearly all those who have been closely associated with it, whatever their role, it marches on, magical and strange. There are few exceptions to a love for the place, but they make racy reading: the fiery egotism of Francis Atterbury (dean 1711–13) did not match college or cathedral well, so he dismissed the place as small-minded and tedious; the victims of John Fell's campaign against 'intollerable misdemeanours' had justification for distance from the House.

Christ Church's past is complex, in part because of the way it was founded, the cathedral and college entwined, the vagaries of royal patronage, the glorious but porous buildings. Judith Curthoys has produced a beautifully excavated mine with style, as a good archivist can. The notes show her workings and we are the beneficiaries of the detail, for good history is in part the knowledge that in the 1540s and 1550s rabbit was eaten in Hall on Thursdays. The wonder of a good institution is the way in which facts and stories which would otherwise have been lost in the wash of time, as it were stick to the place and are preserved. Here we have the material ordered, yet still fresh and appealing.

We also need to know why Christ Church has changed, often rapidly, at times owing to external forces but often on its own initiative. At one time, a dean flees because William and Mary are on the horizon, at another, we discover how learning became 'a duty, a pleasure, and even a fashion', at another, women are admitted; it is almost impossible now to imagine the place without them. Christ Church cannot be said to be isolated from 'the world'.

Judith keeps our feet on the ground, yet our eyes are encouraged to range widely. As she points out, other books have been written about Christ Church but they are either brief or on special aspects of the House. Here we have a book into which everyone can dig, to their hearts' content.

Christopher Lewis

Introduction and acknowledgements

This history of Christ Church is written from an archivist's perspective. It is very personal, based on my own reading of both the primary and secondary sources, conversations with those who know so much about specific areas of college, cathedral and university history, and a certain amount of instinct gleaned from seventeen years work with the archives and their researchers. The principal chapters deal with the history of Christ Church chronologically but, for ease of reading, certain topics which are important but not necessarily a part of the narrative history have been given short chapters of their own. Two larger topics – the architectural history and the history of the college's landed estates – will, I hope, follow as companion volumes.

Christ Church has had only one complete history. Henry Thompson published, in 1900, his often amusing, tremendously useful, but brief contribution to the *College Histories* series.[1] In 1946, W. G. Hiscock, then Assistant Librarian, produced a celebratory volume for the quatercentenary which again has great merit and use but is really a collection of essays, often appallingly referenced, on topics which appealed to him personally.[2] Hugh Trevor-Roper wrote a pocket-book history in 1950 which is still distributed to freshers at their college matriculation but, useful as this is as an introduction, it only scrapes, albeit stylishly, the surface.[3] Specialists have written on specific topics: Geoffrey Bill, Christ Church's first archivist and Lambeth Palace's librarian, wrote a tremendous study of the system of education in the eighteenth century, and with John Mason, Librarian from 1962 to 1987, a further volume on the reform of the constitution and the provision of statutes in the nineteenth.[4] Dr Bill also kept innumerable notes on a wide range of topics, impeccably referenced and always useful. The architectural historian W. D. Caröe wrote an elegant book on Tom Tower, and the building accounts of the New Library were edited by Dr Mason and Jean Cook.[5] Most recently, Professor Christopher Butler has edited the popular *Portrait*, a mixture of history, memoirs of the 'Christ Church experience' and glorious illustrations.[6] Innumerable other volumes and papers on aspects of Christ Church also exist, but it is without doubt time for a new history, to stand, I hope, alongside modern publications from other Oxford colleges.[7]

Clare Hopkins, the archivist of Trinity College, wrote in the preface to her history of that college that she was not intending to write biographies of the great and good, but a history of the institution based on the archives and the records of those who were members of the college while they were students or fellows. Christ Church's membership has been such that any book could be in danger of turning into a mini-*Dictionary of National Biography*, but that would not be a history of Christ Church. I hope that this work follows the path already trodden by Clare, in being a record of the place and its members while they were at college, not of their further careers (unless, of course, these impinged directly on the college or cathedral). Christ Church men have often been heavily involved in the political, religious and cultural life of the nation, and much has been written about their contribution by scholars far more able than I. Rather than attempt to repeat their work, the footnotes will, I hope, direct the curious reader to the right place to learn more. Interestingly, deans traditionally considered to be the 'great' do not always figure quite so strongly when approached from the archive, nor do members whose influence has been, however important, external; less celebrated incumbents, particularly George Smalridge, are far more prominent.

The fact that Christ Church is a unique joint foundation of college and cathedral causes problems for any writer. Once I began, it soon became evident why full histories of Christ Church have not been forthcoming. Its peculiar constitution makes any history complex, and fraught with linguistic danger. To say 'college' alone implies a neglect of the cathedral, but this is not intended. It is impossible for the sake of pleasurable reading to continually say 'Christ Church', and 'the House' is such a personal epithet used by the members that it sounds exclusive. If I use the word 'college' in any way that offends, I apologise. As archivist of both college and cathedral, I am very conscious of the entwined organisations and their importance to each other. The presence of the cathedral in the book is very much as college chapel, rather than as diocesan seat.

Christ Church's odd nomenclature also causes difficulties. A Student, always written with an upper-case 'S', has been, since 1867, the equivalent of a Fellow in any other college, but always stipendiary. This has made it difficult to choose a collective noun for non-stipendiary graduates and undergraduates. Usually called commoners, this term refers to anyone who pays or has paid fees for tuition. Today, undergraduates and postgraduates are usually known as junior members.

There are a few publications that deserve particular mention, in addition to those listed above, without which this book would have been much the poorer. The immense and all-encompassing *History of the University of Oxford*, published in eight volumes between 1984 and 2000, is invaluable. The *Oxford Dictionary of National Biography*, published in 2004 and revised online since, has more uses than one can enumerate, and has provided researchers with more information than we could ever have guessed before its appearance. Over a thousand Christ Church men appear in the pages of the *ODNB*.

No introduction to any book is complete without its personal acknowledgements. Henry Thompson, in his preface, gave due thanks to Thomas Vere Bayne, whose name occurs frequently within the following pages. Bayne's notes and minutes have been a tremendous resource and of invaluable assistance, although it is a century since his death. More immediately, the contribution of immediate friends and colleagues has been immeasurable. This book would never have been possible without the support and continued interest of my colleagues in the Library. First, much gratitude is due to Richard Hamer, the Librarian who took the gamble of appointing me assistant archivist when there must have been many far more qualified people available. I hope he feels I have repaid his trust. Janet McMullin is both friend and classicist without whose Latin and Greek I would be totally lost. Cristina Neagu, James Andrews, Lucy Gwynn and Rachel Johnson have always been cheerful, encouraging and endlessly helpful. Dave Stumpp, Early Printed Books cataloguer and talented photographer, has generously allowed me to use many of his pictures. The late Dr John Mason was always willing to discuss any ideas and to contribute all sorts of information from his phenomenal knowledge of all things Christ Church. I am sorry that the final drafts were unable to benefit from his stern but benign eye. Chris Haigh has been most generous in sharing his understanding of the foundation of Christ Church. Mark Curthoys, my predecessor as archivist, and historian of the university in the nineteenth century, gave much-valued opinions and stylistic help. Without Leslie Mitchell, my still meagre understanding of University politics in the eighteenth century would have been thin to the point of non-existence. His patient and speedy explanations were very welcome. Blair Worden advised on the upheavals of the mid-seventeenth century, and Geoffrey Tyack has been unhesitatingly on call for comment on architecture. Jon Down gave the subtitle, for which I owe him many thanks. Without Adam Sisman, I would never have been lucky enough to encounter the team at Profile, particularly Paul Forty and Penny Gardiner, who have been so encouraging and helpful to me in my first solitary venture into print, and who found me my most generous but anonymous benefactor, to whom my heartfelt thanks. Jonathan Wright, William Thomas, Richard Benthall and Paul Kent – all of whom have known Christ Church for many years – have been kind, helpful and tremendous sources; Brian Young valiantly read the entire text; the Development Office have been wonderfully supportive; and Dean Lewis has been generous to a fault not only in agreeing to write a foreword but in his continuing support for the project. Much gratitude goes to Kathryn Grant who, over and above her usual tasks, agreed to see the book through the final stages with good humour and terrific efficiency. My colleague archivists have been, as ever, wonderful, especially when busy with their own projects. In particular, I would like to express deep appreciation to Robin Darwall-Smith and Michael Riordan, who read much of the text and commented freely, fully and always helpfully.

There remains one to thank, from the bottom of my heart, for his love, support and constant encouragement from start to finish.

1

Before Christ Church

St Frideswide's

The south-east corner of the old Saxon town of Oxford was dominated for over half a millennium by the priory dedicated to St Frideswide, later patron saint to both university and city.[1] By 1546, when that same piece of dry ground just north of the river's flood plain became Christ Church, it had been through several guises and had seen the city grow up around it.

The archaeological jury is still out on the age of Oxford as a settlement, rather than just as a monastic community.[2] In the middle Saxon period, the river marked the boundary between Wessex and Mercia, and the ford from which the city takes its name was the principal crossing point on the upper Thames. Prehistoric peoples found the river gravels a useful and safe place to settle; the Romans had roads passing through the area and settlements in modern north Oxford and south of the Thames; excavations all over Oxford have produced some middle Saxon remains, and in 1998 a skeleton from the seventh century was uncovered in the cathedral cemetery.[3]

The written accounts of St Frideswide were composed some 400 years after her death. A pious, chaste, and noble Saxon lady, Frideswide established a nunnery for herself and twelve virgin ladies despite being pursued relentlessly and increasingly desperately by Algar, Prince of Leicester, for her hand in marriage. Forewarned miraculously of yet another attempt by

> ## St Frideswide's Cartulary
>
> The cartulary of the priory of St Frideswide, which records all the monastery's land transactions up to the middle of the fifteenth century, is probably the only volume at Christ Church to have been on the site since medieval times.

Algar, she and the women fled upriver to hide, staying away for some years at Bampton, where she performed healing miracles. Algar's persistence forced Frideswide to call down blindness on the prince, who repented of his ways and left Frideswide to her devotions.[4]

Frideswide died on 19 October 727 and was canonised in 1480, although pilgrims came to her shrine in the priory church long before this.[5] Catherine of Aragon was one who visited to pray for an heir, the saint being renowned for her gynaecological cures.[6] The shrine was destroyed around 1538 and the saint's remains reburied in some unnamed corner until she was allegedly rediscovered during the reinterment of Catherine, the wife of the reformer Peter Martyr Vermigli, in 1558.[7] Little remains of the Saxon priory; perhaps just a few stones and a single floor tile.[8] The nunnery became a monastery soon after the saint's death, although its history is confused. In 1122 the chancellor formally founded an Augustinian monastery on the site,[9] but it was around the priory, and close to the ford across the Thames, that the town of Oxford began to grow.

Little is known about the priory buildings other than those that survived Cardinal Wolsey in the 1520s. Properties on either side of the city's south gate along the street leading down to the Thames hid the priory, with only a lane running into the precinct from the street.[10] Around the south and west sides of the priory ran the city wall, and the main gateway was probably to the north down another narrow lane from the High Street.

The beginnings of the university and the style of its later colleges were shaped by the monastic communities both in and around the city, St Frideswide's priory being one of only two actually inside the walls of the city.

> ## The Cardinal's Hat
>
> The red felt cardinal's hat (or *galero*) displayed in the Library is said to be that of Thomas Wolsey. Found in a cupboard at Horace Walpole's house, Strawberry Hill, it had been worn by the actor, Charles Kean, when playing Wolsey in Shakespeare's *Henry VIII*.
>
> Although it cannot be proved conclusively that it is indeed Wolsey's own hat, the Worshipful Company of Feltmakers have confirmed that it is of the right period, and made in Italy, where Wolsey would have received it in person in consistory.
>
> The case in which the hat is kept is a Victorian Gothic design, and was given to Christ Church, with the hat, by the Reverend Oxford and his friends who purchased it for £63 soon after Kean's death in 1868.

But its canons were not great contributors to the nascent centre of learning, unlike the monks of Canterbury College (founded in 1363 as a *studium* for the monks of Christ Church in Canterbury), many of whom held degrees.[11]

With the arrival of the Augustinian canons in the early twelfth century, the Saxon buildings of Frideswide's nunnery were gradually replaced with stone monastic buildings, including the surviving Chapter House, refectory and prior's lodgings. Meanwhile, across town to the west, the new and greater abbey of Oseney was founded as part of Henry I's regularisation of the Church in England. St Frideswide's may not have been as influential as Oseney, and did not have the same connections within the early academic body but, being closer to town (and in possession of Oxford's most famous shrine), it was used for sermons and meetings, and to house visitors.[12] The reforms of Thomas Wolsey and Henry VIII, however, meant the end of medieval life and the influence of the monastic houses in Oxford. St Frideswide's priory was suppressed in April 1524, with papal approval, as part of Wolsey's educational scheme, and Oseney, caught up in both Henry's ecclesiastical reforms and in the furore surrounding his attempts to divorce Catherine of Aragon, was surrendered to the administrators of the Dissolution on 17 November 1539.[13]

> ## The arms of Wolsey and Cardinal College
>
> Wolsey's arms are derived from his Suffolk background, and from other influences on his life: the silver cross from the Ufford earls of Suffolk; the four blue leopards from the de la Poles, earls and dukes of Suffolk; the choughs of his namesake Thomas à Becket; the red lion of Pope Leo X, who had made Wolsey a Cardinal; and the Tudor rose of his king.
>
> The arms were granted to the college by Thomas Wriothesley, garter herald, and Thomas Benolt, Clarencieux, on 4 August 1525.

'Bringing upp ... youthe in virtue' – Cardinal College

In 1517, Thomas Wolsey, the son of an Ipswich butcher and graduate of Magdalen College, was Archbishop of York, a cardinal and Lord Chancellor of England. His influence and his income were immense, and his tastes expensive. It is estimated that Wolsey's annual income at the time of his death could well have approached £30,000.[14] A man of his standing needed to make his mark.

Education was one of Wolsey's greatest interests, and he was a great benefactor to Oxford University, his *alma mater*, both financially and in terms of reform. He believed that new schools and colleges were the way forward, that declining monastic institutions should be replaced by young and energetic educational establishments, and that theology and scripture, although still at the heart of the curriculum, should be supplemented by the teaching of Latin, Greek and philosophy.

Wolsey's principal contribution was to be Cardinal College. Concentrating on the humanist teachings already adopted by Magdalen and Corpus Christi Colleges, Cardinal College would take its undergraduates from the grammar school in his home town, Ipswich. Dual foundations were not a new idea: William Wykeham had founded Winchester School as a partner for New College, and Henry VI had designed Eton College to feed King's College, Cambridge.[15] Wolsey, however, did not intend Ipswich to be the only feeder school for his new, grand, humanist and heresy-defeating college; the

> ## Why dean?
>
> A dean is usually understood to be the head of a chapter in a collegiate or cathedral church. After 1546, when Christ Church was founded as a joint institution of college and cathedral, the use of the title 'dean' for the head of house made perfect sense. But why did Wolsey choose to use the title for the head of his college?
>
> A dean could be the head of a group of monks in a Benedictine monastery, but could also be the fellow in charge of the studies and discipline of junior members of Oxford and Cambridge colleges. Wolsey's use of the term demonstrates that he saw his new foundation as a natural successor to the monastery, not a usurper. Wolsey was quietly, but publicly, demonstrating his commitment to the church.

statutes suggest that schools were to be founded in all English dioceses.[16] The king approved his cardinal's plans for the 'bringing upp of youthe in virtue' and for the 'maintenance of Xts chirche and his faith'.[17]

The obvious site for the new Oxford college was St Frideswide's. Wolsey obtained a bull from the Pope for its dissolution in April 1524, and the royal licence for Cardinal College was granted in July 1525.[18] Its chosen arms were those of Wolsey himself; the crest, along with Wolsey's other emblems of office, is prominent on all the buildings.[19] The name St Frideswide's College was used occasionally, and the fellows of the new institution were referred to in the statutes as canons. Wolsey was working within a still-Catholic system, and the statutes of his new college reflected the monastic origins of the site, not least with the requirement that a daily mass be said for the souls of the founders of the repressed monasteries.[20]

Wolsey's constitution for his new college included six public professorships,[21] four private lectors, 100 canons, chaplains, lay clerks, choirboys and music master. The statutes of Cardinal College drew heavily – in many places repeated verbatim – on those of its next-door neighbour, Corpus Christi. But the scale of Wolsey's new foundation was vastly different from anything that had gone before.

The whole institution was to be headed by the dean, a man who was to be honest, of integrity and renown, a clergyman but neither bishop nor a monk, learned in theology and at least a BA. He had to be English, and over 30 years old. The dean could remain in office until his death, provided that he did not accept a bishopric or commit certain crimes. His authority in college was total, but he was expected to consult with the senior canons in all important business.[22]

The first man to occupy the post met all the criteria. John Higden had the right connections and the right background; he had been educated at Westminster School and was elected a fellow of Magdalen College in 1495, becoming its president in 1516. He got on well with Wolsey, his brother was Wolsey's vicar-general at York, and he was probably an obvious choice as dean of Cardinal College. To move from the presidency of Magdalen (with which his relationship was not always smooth) is an indication of the perceived supremacy of the new foundation.[23] A hands-on man, he was evidently active in the building of the new enterprise and the administration of its endowment.[24]

The statutes of the college laid down its administration in minute detail. Under the leadership of the dean, there were 60 canons of the first order, all ordained graduates and considered qualified to teach. They were to be elected from all the dioceses in the country in a given proportion: the majority from Norwich and Lincoln, then York, Durham, and Bath and Wells. Preference was to be given to candidates from dioceses where the college held most property.[25] At least eight of the canons of the first order had to hold doctorates: five of theology, the others of canon law, civil law or medicine. From these eight were selected the sub-dean, who was to deputise for the dean whenever necessary, four censors who were, by and large, responsible for the education and discipline of junior members of the college, and three bursars to manage all financial matters both external and domestic.[26]

Forty junior members, known as petty canons or canons of the second order, were to be elected from the Founder's schools, of which all but Ipswich were still to be established.[27] Most of these would have been undergraduates, and all were stipendiary. The records of Cardinal College are few, and of its

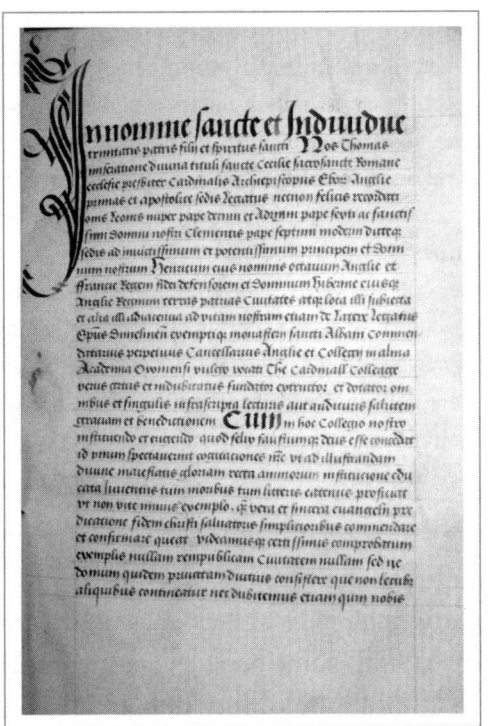

The statutes of Cardinal College, drawn up in 1525, were almost exact copies of those for Corpus Christi and Magdalen Colleges. Although the college was short-lived, its statutes formed the foundation for the administration of Christ Church until 1867.

membership still fewer, but we do know the names of about 32 men who were admitted in the first two years of the college's existence.

After all the serious business of elections, selections, admissions and oaths of the senior members of Cardinal College, the statutes turned to the admission of the priests, clerks, choristers and the master of music. Thirteen chaplains were appointed, three of whom had to be ordained; these were given the roles of precentor (whose task was to ensure that the choir performed its duties), sacristan, in whose charge were all the chapel treasures, and Gospel reader. Twelve lay clerks and sixteen choristers were selected, to be led by the organist and choirmaster. Wolsey, wanting someone exceptional, sent his agent to obtain the services of John Taverner from

> Wolsey had poached from Cambridge a number of studious young men to get his new institution off to a flying start, but was unaware that some, led by John Clarke, had brought with them Lutheran texts. Clarke was a popular canon, and often read with his favourites unorthodox translations of the Bible and commentaries by John Hus, Philipp Melanchthon, Oecolampadius (Johannes Hussgen) and Martin Luther himself.
>
> Although other colleges were involved, Cardinal College was the hotbed of student heresy and, at Wolsey's behest, the university commissary uncovered twenty-two young Lutherans. Several of the young men were incarcerated in the college fish cellars. Some, including Clarke, died in a plague outbreak that year; others escaped to more tolerant parts. Taverner was not considered important enough to be imprisoned or exiled.[30]

Tattershall. Taverner was already well established as a composer when he was approached, and needed some persuasion, including a substantial pay rise, to bring him to Oxford,[28] but under him, by 1528, the choir, some of whom had been poached from Tattershall, had gained an enviable reputation.[29] Taverner was a superlative organist, composer and choir-master; however, he joined up with the cell of Lutheran devotees whose perceived heresy caused major problems for Wolsey and the University.

With so many men studying and teaching in the college, a large staff was needed, all of whom had to be male and unmarried and, like the senior members, had to swear an oath to keep the college's secrets, and to be faithful and honest employees.[31] At the top of the tree was the manciple, responsible for the purchase of all supplies for the whole establishment. Under him were the pantryman, the butler and the cooks. The porter was responsible for ensuring that all the gates were kept closed and locked at all times. Only the wicket gate under the main tower could be left open, and then only at specific times of the day. The barber had to ensure that all members of college looked respectable; he was even given a room to himself in which to ply his trade. The laundryman and a groom completed the line-up, although there must have been a large number of employees not on the foundation, such as gardeners, maintenance men and stable-hands. The dean was granted seven personal servants who were to be funded and clothed from the college coffers, and the sub-dean one.

Once the establishment was laid down, the statutes moved on to daily life at Cardinal College. Special prayers were to be said every day on rising and retiring, and there were innumerable chapel services including seven daily masses and three special ones each week for the commemoration of the Founder.[32] Attendance at the morning mass of the Holy Ghost was compulsory, and expected at most of the others.

There was no rest at mealtimes. Talk at lunch was to be in Latin or Greek, and the Bible was read during dinner with expositions given after the meal. Conversation over a drink after eating was strictly forbidden. Only if a fire had been lit in Hall could students stay behind to benefit from unaccustomed warmth and to enjoy 'temperate recreation'.

Student behaviour was carefully monitored. Good manners were required at all times, dress was to be sober, and arms were not to be carried unless away from Oxford on college business and then only with decanal approval. No dogs, hawks, or other birds (even songbirds) were permitted in college; neither were dice, cards, or any other game forbidden by canon law. As the college admitted gentlemen, moderate hunting was expected when they went home during vacations. Everyone in college was provided with cloth to make a gown once a year, its quality depending on one's rank; the gowns were all of the same colour.

And then there was study. Four private lectors were appointed to teach Aristotle, Plautus, Terence and other orators and poets whose work was considered profitable; and, to ensure that the lectures continued without a break, the lectors were obliged to appoint a deputy should they have to be away from their posts.[33] For the first time all the subjects available at the university, for bachelor and for higher degrees, were taught within a single college.[34] Erasmian teaching had arrived first at Magdalen College and then been embraced at Corpus Christi before Wolsey adopted it at Cardinal College. But these ideas were still new, and he took them on board, creating in his foundation, both physically and intellectually, a great consummation of centuries of college development.[35]

Students were expected to take it in turns to debate daily in Hall, with professors and censors being obliged to attend. Minor canons, especially if seen to be lazy, were to be examined by the dean on the topics of the lectures and disputations, and all canons and chaplains were to have access to the library and could hold keys.[36] It was evidently intended that the library should be stocked by gift, but within certain rules. No material could be put in, or taken out, whether permanently or on loan, without written agreement. At the end of every year, books had to be returned to the library when they could be reissued. There were to be two catalogues, kept separately, and a borrower's ledger. Care of the books and of the library itself seems to have been informally regulated by those with access privileges.

Undergraduates were to take their first degrees at the end of three years' study, certainly within four. Another three years took a man to his MA, six more to a Bachelor of Divinity, and a further four to Doctor of Divinity. In order to continue to hold a canonry, a student had to be ordained, provided he was old enough, within a year of taking his MA. The penalty for not fulfilling this obligation was expulsion. A canonry, but not the deanery, also had to be forfeited if a man was promoted to a position outside college, if he was away for extended periods without leave, or if he received an appointment or ecclesiastical benefice which paid more than £8 per year.

Rooms were assigned by the dean and sub-dean. Each room held two beds: a high bed for a canon of the first order, and a truckle bed for a minor canon. All men over the age of 14 were to sleep in separate beds. No women other than mothers and sisters, with accompanying maids, were allowed in chambers and no 'strangers' could stay overnight. Family and friends dining in college had to be paid for out of the canon's own pocket, unless they were guests of a very senior member and were considered useful to the college in some way, or the friends of noblemen.[37]

Buildings to accommodate all these men and such activity were to be no less impressive. Although the old priory site formed the core of Cardinal College, the whole precinct was much larger. Work began in 1525 at tremendous cost.[38] Portions of the city wall, and all the tenements along St Aldates where the new frontage was to go, were demolished, including two which had belonged to Balliol College (for which no recompense was ever paid).[39] Peckwater Inn, the site of the quadrangle of that name, was acquired and initially used to house workmen,[40] who were led by the architects and master masons, William Jonson, Henry Redman and John Lovyns, and the master carpenter, Humphrey Coke. By July 1525, when the foundation stone was laid, there were 32 masons, 16 rough-layers and 64 labourers on site, overseen by William Staunton. Materials were acquired from several local estates.[41]

Two or three bays of the nave of the priory church were pulled down to make way for the main cloistered quadrangle, the remainder being left as a chapel.[42] Whether Wolsey ever intended to pull down the whole of the old priory church is uncertain; he certainly considered building a new chapel (its roof being made at Sonning in 1528), to rival that of King's College in Cambridge; yet in 1529, while scaffolding was prepared to take down the cathedral spire, new work was still being undertaken in the old church.[43] On the south side of the quadrangle an immense dining hall was erected, its roof designed by Coke but built locally. Lodgings occupied the east and west sides, and the remaining portion of the south. Such was Wolsey's attention to the sumptuousness of his college that he arranged for blue velvet wall-hangings, counterpanes and a bed and bolster from his own private household to be sent to the deanery.[44]

Behind the Hall, but detached, was the kitchen, a 40-foot cube with great fireplaces. Designed to feed a large establishment, it was the first building to be completed – in time for Christmas dinner in 1526.[45] It was sluiced through regularly with clean water, and rainwater was collected into a huge tank in the kitchen so large that a man had to climb right in to maintain it.[46] At the end of 1526, John London, warden of New College, described the ancillary buildings that stretched towards the Meadow: 'larder houses, pastry houses, lodgings for common servants, slaughter and fish houses, with such other necessary buildings substantially and goodly done in such manner as no two of the best colleges in Oxford have rooms so goodly and convenient'.

Although Redman and his colleagues definitely saw and used drawings, and it is said that Wolsey showed his ideas to Queen Catherine as early as 1522, there are no surviving plots or plans and the building was never completed. It would seem, though, that the Cardinal was adding nothing new to the structure of Cardinal College, apart from its sheer size, that had not been seen before in an Oxford college.[47]

There have been long discussions about the design of Cardinal College. Presumably the cloister around the Great Quadrangle would have been completed, with a tower over the Hall stairs providing muniment rooms. If the chapel on the north side had been completed, its frontage might have appeared strangely unbalanced with a turreted tower on the south-west corner and an ante-chapel on the north-west.[48] It was not until the 1660s that Dean Fell chose a symmetrical finish to the frontage.[49]

Its premature end actually meant that Cardinal College, and its successor, Christ Church, were left without elements, such as a library and a muniment room, that one would have expected from a benefactor whose commitment to education and whose talents for administration were so evident.[50] Even so, in the spring of 1528, after only three years' construction, Thomas Cromwell stated that '… the like was never seen for largeness, beauty, sumptuous, curious and substantial building'.[51] But when Wolsey fell from power in 1529, he left his magnificent scheme unfinished. Two sides of the great Gothic quadrangle – which measured 264 by 261 feet, the largest in Oxford – were finished, and most of the west front.[52] Only the foundations and the first row of decorative masonry of the chapel planned for the north side were visible. The cloister was barely begun; just the shafts and springers, heavily restored by Dean Liddell over three centuries later, survive to suggest the intention. Tom Tower did not rise over the front gate until 1681. Of the monastic buildings other than the church, three-quarters of the old cloister, cluttered with the foundations for a bell-tower, the prior's house, which served briefly as the deanery, the old refectory, and the Chapter House, were still standing.[53]

Cardinal College was undoubtedly intended to be bigger than anything that had gone before, both physically and in the size of its foundation. This vast establishment needed an endowment of equally staggering proportions

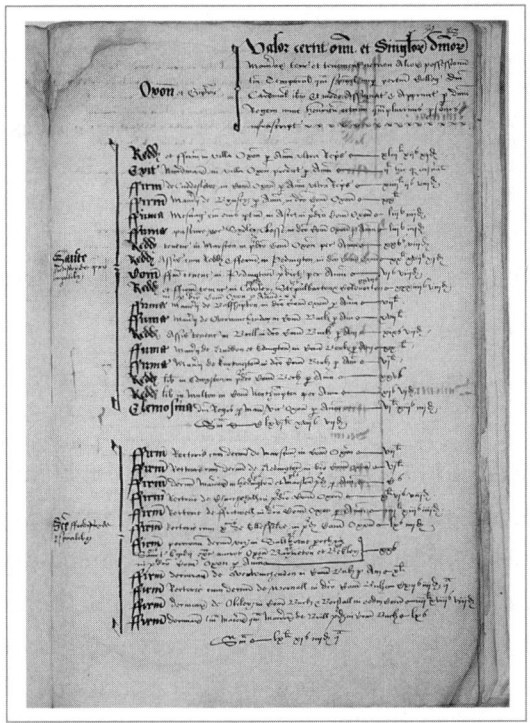

Cardinal College was given considerable property, mainly derived from dissolved monastic houses. This first page of the valuation of the college shows the income due from the lands of St Frideswide's priory.

in order to run. And Wolsey did not stint: along with the lands and revenues that had belonged to St Frideswide's priory, the property of 27 smaller monastic institutions and rectories was acquired to fund the project. He achieved this legally by closing down small houses that had allegedly been founded by a monarch, had fewer than six monks and low revenues, most of which were probably in dire need of reform. These smaller properties, which together had an income of about £1,800, had to be conveyed to the Crown, then re-conveyed to Wolsey by letters patent.[54] Much of the property – which could be manors, tithes or actual land – was local, particularly that from St Frideswide's, but many of the small monastic houses were in East Anglia and the south-east, possibly reflecting Wolsey's own Suffolk origins. The total income expected was just under £2,500.[55]

> ## Robert Amadas
>
> Henry VIII liked jewellery, gold and silver decorations on his clothes, and gold embellishments to his horses' harnesses, and Robert Amadas was court goldsmith to this ostentatious and extravagant monarch. By 1524, Amadas was Master of the Jewels, and a senior official of the Mint. But it was Wolsey who was Amadas's largest client, and one of his biggest debtors.
>
> Glanville, in Gunn & Lindley (1991), 131–148; DP iv.b.2

The estates were administered by progresses. Every Easter, the dean was to go on an extended excursion around all the college lands and holdings, followed by another in the autumn conducted by the sub-dean. All accounts and other paperwork generated by the progresses and the subsequent audits were to be stored in the tower, with the cash received.[56] Although the tower was never built, the statutes were firm in their intentions. Chapel goods and vestments were to be stored in the sacristy, but college items and all records were to be kept locked in the muniment tower behind a secure and strong door with three keys. Inventories and registers of everything were to be kept. Whatever the temporary storage facility, it was clearly considered safe enough for the university's charter of privileges, drawn up in 1523 and read to the congregation in 1528, to be delivered to Cardinal College, rather than the university archives, for safe-keeping.[57]

Perhaps the sacristan took charge of all college treasures, and not just those of the chapel. John Foxe, the martyrologist, suggested that 'this ambitious Cardinal gathered together into that College whatsoever excellent thing there was in the whole realm, either vestments, vessels, or other ornaments, besides provision of all kinds of precious things'.[58] An indication of those precious things is given in an account in the archive of Wolsey's expenditure with Robert Amadas, the royal goldsmith. Wolsey commissioned many pieces both for the chapel and for the table – including a gilt crucifix weighing 117 ounces, and a great drinking horn. The accounts are precise regarding both the weight of the items and their monetary value.

The total for the college amounted to over £300, although Wolsey's total commissions from Amadas, including his New Year gifts to the King, were worth over £5,000.[59]

When Wolsey was charged with praemunire (the assertion of papal authority over that of the Crown), he was left totally dependent on the king for his income and survival. He was permitted to keep some titles and revenues, notably that of archbishop, but the fate of Cardinal College remained uncertain through most of 1530. There were rumours that all the residents were to be evicted and the new buildings demolished, apparently to destroy all the symbols of Wolsey's power that were carved into the stonework.[60] Powerful men – Thomas Cromwell, Thomas More, Norfolk and Stephen Gardiner – sympathised with Wolsey's efforts to save his college, but were either unable or unwilling to act. Dean Higden, through William Tresham, appealed to the king, and was given some hope when Henry VIII declared his desire to have a college in Oxford, but Cardinal College did not survive in the form Wolsey had intended.[61] Ipswich school – the only one of Wolsey's proposed chain of feeder schools that had been established – was dissolved, and the rich possessions of both school and college, including its estates, were taken by the Crown. Wolsey died at the end of 1530 with his great plans in tatters. But his efforts in Oxford had helped to shift the balance of power from the University to the colleges.[62] Christ Church, as the eventual successor to Cardinal College, consolidated this trend, and the statutes of Wolsey's great institution were to form the backbone of Christ Church for years to come.

'The college is undone' – King Henry VIII College

Although it is evident that the full numbers anticipated in the Cardinal College statutes were never reached, there was still a substantial body of canons and servants, as well as all the builders and labourers, and the closure of the college must have been a huge blow to its membership. Thompson remarked that there was no indication of any provision being made for the existing members of the foundation. Certainly, after September 1530, Cardinal College disappeared, with most of its endowment of land

and revenue sold to courtiers or commandeered by the Crown. But Henry VIII evidently wanted a college of his own in Oxford. In August 1530, when the final desperate appeal was made to save Cardinal College, Henry, rather more gracious than his ministers, confirmed to Dean Higden that he had every intention of maintaining a college in Oxford, just not on such a grand scale.[63] In December 1531, he sent Robert Carter and Henry Williams to Oxford with 600 marks for a new college, formally established in July 1532 as King Henry VIII's College.[64] It was a purely ecclesiastical foundation of twelve canons and a dean, with John Higden at its head – a tiny number to find themselves occupying the abandoned building site of the Great Quadrangle.[65]

King Henry VIII College, however small and unsatisfactory, was soon in operation. Higden certainly remained in Oxford throughout 1531, and there were a few men who either stayed or arrived during the interim period before the foundation charter was signed on 18 July 1532.[66] The charter, an unfinished and damaged copy of which is in the Christ Church archives, names Higden as the reappointed dean, and twelve canons, at least four of whom had been at Cardinal College. John Roper, John Cottisford, Richard Croke, Richard Curwen and William Tresham are listed first as theology professors, followed by Robert Carter, John Hastings, Thomas Canner, Edward Leighton, Henry Williams, John Robyns and Robert Wakefield, who are listed as bachelors of theology.[67] Most were Oxford graduates, although Croke and Wakefield, brought specifically to teach Hebrew, came from Cambridge.[68] Nicholas de Burgo, one of only two known appointments between 1525 and 1530, was reappointed as reader in theology at the new institution,[69] and the provision of public lectures, so dear to Wolsey's heart, continued in spite of the collapse of Cardinal College.

Henry's intention was that there should be eight priests, eight chaplains, eight clerks, and ten choristers to sing divine service.[70] The names of only three chaplains are known; John Best, who later became Bishop of Carlisle, Henry Spycer and John Hatley. In 1538, Spycer was denounced by Hatley for maintaining that it was acceptable to pray to images.[71]

The statutes reflect Henry's preoccupations in the early 1530s; under no circumstances was his college to be subject to any power, especially that

> **Thomas Canner** was a demy at Magdalen College before being elected a fellow there in 1517. He was a proctor and keeper of the Langton chest, and sub-dean of Cardinal College. He appears to have held several rectories and his canonry of King Henry VIII College in tandem.
>
> **Robert Carter** was probably the steward of Wolsey's almshouse. He accompanied Higden to London to appeal for the survival of Cardinal College, and was made a canon of King Henry VIII College.
>
> **Edward Leighton** was Censor Theologiae at Cardinal College and a canon of King Henry VIII College before being appointed one of the king's chaplains and clerk of the closet.
>
> **William Tresham**, the only man to have been a fellow of all three colleges (Cardinal, King Henry VIII and Christ Church), had been an undergraduate at Merton College. He was university registrar and vice-chancellor, chiefly between 1532 and 1547. Under Edward VI, Tresham was imprisoned in the Fleet for his Catholic opinions, but he was reinstated under Mary Tudor to serve on the commission examining Cranmer, Ridley and Latimer.
>
> **Robert Benbow,** informator (master of the choristers) at Cardinal College, remained to be a chaplain at both King Henry VIII College and at Christ Church.
>
> *ODNB*; Emden (1974); Foster 1500; Thompson (1900), 9

of a bishop, archbishop, or legate, but that of the king himself.[72] The daily and seasonal round of services was to continue, but in a conservative form, using the Sarum rite; and specific instructions were given as to the style of vestments worn, the duties of the precentor and the sacristan, and the qualifications required of chaplains, lay clerks and choristers.

In the first instance, the canons were granted a stipend of ten marks each, but the dean received the prebendary of Wetwang, in Yorkshire, for his income. There was some dispute in 1533 over the gift when the Archbishop of York gave the same position to a Dr Chamber,[73] only resolved after Cromwell was asked to intercede on the dean's behalf.[74] A year later, the archbishop wrote to Henry VIII reluctantly handing over the prebend to the college (but asking for recompense for Dr Chamber),[75] and by 1535 the dean was receiving £78 per annum. The canons' annual stipends were then £20. Money from revenue was to be set aside each year for building maintenance, stipends and essentials, and the post of treasurer selected from among the canons. It was not a popular job; William Tresham, writing to Cromwell on a personal matter, apologises that the college accounts for 1530 are incomplete, blaming one of the canons: 'Mr Williams alone is in fault. He will not do his duty, though he has been often desired, as Mr Hastings can declare.'[76]

Higden was not dean for long – he died just before Christmas 1532, leaving all his goods to Magdalen, Corpus Christi and New College. There is a touch of bitterness in Canon Richard Croke's letter to Thomas Cromwell:

> His goods are all conveyed to Magdalene, Corpus, and New College, on which he has bestowed large sums, but nothing to this college, where he had his promotion. He had received since its suppression, besides salt and other necessaries, £180 in ready money. Cannore [Canner] is his executor. Long since he had granted away by advowson all his promotions but Witney and the prebend of Melton. On a crafty surmise made by Dr London, that Carter, Leghton, and I should be at London to sue for the avoidance of Melton, he has resigned it to London who is, by common report, an impugner of the King's cause, and an enemy of all that favor it. I have sent my servant to you with this information, forced by my fidelity to the King, who otherwise would be deceived.[77]

But Higden may have felt that leaving his money to King Henry VIII's College was a lost cause.

Croke was angling to be the next dean.[78] As sub-dean and with his academic and diplomatic credentials, he was a likely candidate but he was not successful, and neither were the canons in their wish for an internal appointment. Higden's successor was John Oliver, a prominent lawyer who had worked closely first with Wolsey and then with the king and Cromwell.[79]

Tradition states that after Wolsey's fall, the possessions of Cardinal College were stripped away in their entirety, and the interim institution left with nothing. The statutes suggest otherwise: King Henry VIII College was not impoverished. The *Valor Ecclesiasticus* reveals that, in 1535 at least,

King Henry VIII College had a surplus of around £450 per annum from an income of over £666[80] – tiny compared with that of Cardinal College's proposed revenues of over £2,000, but still substantially higher than that of some of its neighbours.[81] Trinity College, for example, founded just a few years later, had an income of £226, and in the late 1520s Corpus Christi received around £380 with which to support a foundation of 54 men.[82] The property belonging to St Frideswide's priory remained with its site, as well as the lands and revenues of Daventry, Littlemore and Tickford priories (most of which formed part of the endowment to Christ Church in 1546).[83]

Property generated leases and correspondence which had to be carefully preserved, as well as cash from tenants. In the absence of a proper muniment tower, the new statutes decreed that documents be kept in the Chapter House, or a similarly secure place, with a good door and three keys. The buildings in general, and the immense construction site left after Wolsey's fall, must have been problematic for so few men. Unlike the dining hall and kitchen, which were finished and in use before 1530, most of the lodgings were barely habitable.[84] In 1533, the canons appealed to the king for assistance with completing the buildings, and Croke offered twenty nobles to finish his own lodgings 'which will save the King's coffers'.[85] Peckwater Inn seems to have been let or even sold to New College.[86] The statutes of the college required that the buildings be maintained, and it seems likely that the parts of Cardinal College nearing completion were finished and used, along with the remaining priory buildings.

Canterbury College, which is commemorated in the present Canterbury Quadrangle, still survived as a separate monastic hall, but its days were numbered; during the 1530s, the warden and scholars were paying an annuity of 40 shillings to King Henry VIII College, a due which was evidently becoming more onerous as the years went by. In 1538, the warden, William Sandwyche, wrote to Cromwell asking him to intercede with the prior of the mother house in Canterbury for payment of the annuity. He had to pledge the college's plate in order to settle the debt, and without assistance 'the college is undone'.[87]

In 1535, with Oliver still at the head, all but one of the original canons

Canterbury Quadrangle was the site of the old Canterbury College, an outpost of Canterbury Cathedral Priory specifically for its monks. John Malchair's drawing, dated 1775, shows the medieval gate just before its demolition and replacement with the much grander classical structure funded by Richard Robinson, Archbishop of Armagh.

were still in place. John Roper, the first Lady Margaret Professor of Divinity, had died in May 1534, succeeded by Walter Buckler, who came from Merton College and the principalship of St Alban Hall.[88] These men witnessed the destruction of the shrine of St Frideswide in 1538 and prepared for a royal visit in 1543, but the most significant event the dean and canons of King Henry VIII College were to witness was the foundation of the new see of Oxford in 1542.[89]

Oxford, carved out of the huge and ancient diocese of Lincoln, was one of several new dioceses created by Henry across England. The first cathedral was on the west side of the city, the abbey church of Oseney, its first dean, appointed in January 1544, being Richard Cox. Did the canons of King Henry VIII College know that this event would cause the demise of their establishment? Cox, as we shall see, certainly had a hand in the creation of Christ Church, and it seems likely that his close colleagues would have been aware of his participation.

The college continued to function to the end. Wages were paid: at Midsummer 1545, the dean received £25 and four canons £5 each. The schoolmaster, John Candelar, and his usher, Bracegirdle, were paid to care for and educate the grammar school boys who had been moved, with all their possessions, from Oseney to St Frideswide's. Fifty 'exhibitioners' (men in receipt of financial assistance for their studies) also appear in the final closing-down accounts, listed under the names of all the dioceses of the country, men who were part of Henry's commitment to support university education; the old, reorganised cathedrals, and Henry's new ones, were obliged to provide for the education of senior scholars at the two universities. The scheme fell by the wayside when Henry needed revenue for the war with France (the cathedrals provided land for sale, in exchange for funding scholars), but the 50 exhibitions (and three professorships) were transferred to the planned new foundation at St Frideswide's priory. Until the endowment for Christ Church was settled, the exhibitioners were funded by the Crown, and came to form the core of the Student body.[90] There were the cathedral personnel – petty canons, a gospeler, an epistoler, twelve choristers (whose surplices were supplied by the Chapter)[91] – and college staff, such as the manciple, the butler, the barber, the porter, the cooks and the carter. But these were the last days of King Henry VIII College; in 1545, the college was surrendered to the Crown. Only William Tresham was reappointed in the next establishment, the dean and the six remaining canons being given pensions. By Michaelmas 1546, the new foundation of Christ Church was established and ready to fulfil Wolsey's academic intentions.

For 'the keepinge of their horses and cattell and for other occasions': the Meadow

The stretch of land which runs from Christ Church, behind Corpus Christi and Merton Colleges and down to the river came to Christ Church in two pieces. The major part, originally known as St Frideswide's Mead or Stockwell Mead, belonged to the abbey in Abingdon until it was purchased by Elizabeth Montacute, wife of the Earl of Salisbury, and given to St Frideswide's priory on 6 August 1346 to maintain her chantry. The branch of the river Thames – the Shire Lake – which ran through the middle of the Meadow, and divided Oxfordshire from Berkshire, was given to Henry VIII by the City of Oxford in the years between the dissolution of the priory and the foundation of Christ Church.

The smaller area, in between St Frideswide's mead and the river, was called Torald's Ham after the man who had given the land to Oseney abbey. When Oseney was dissolved, Stockwell Mead and Torald's Ham (traditionally an area for the dean to enjoy privately) became part of the 1546 endowment of Christ Church.

Another branch of the Thames, the Trill Mill stream, ran from the city mill on the edge of St Thomas's, then south of the city wall under the present Rose Place, then under the Green Dragon pub into the Meadow. The mill itself, its oak in perfect condition, was discovered under the pub in 1862 when sewers were being replaced, but the sluice gates from this stream and from others needed constant maintenance to protect the Meadow from flood. A new one was erected by John Hudson at the end of the Broad Walk in 1810.[1] The stream, which runs in a tunnel for much of its length, was a favourite for daredevil canoeists.

Flooding on the Meadow was inevitable and, at the right time of the year, was valuable for the growth of new grass. During the Civil War, the tendency of the Meadow to flood was put to good use. The Meadow was bounded by the Cherwell on one side, the Thames on another, the Trill Mill stream on the west, and had the Shire lake through the middle, so it was already waterlogged at times of heavy rain and high water; but the Royalist forces made a cut near Magdalen Bridge to allow the Cherwell to 'overflowe Christch. mede and Cowley landes about Millham Bridge, by the meeting of the Charwell and Thames together, for the defence of the cittie'. Flood potential was reinforced by earthworks.[2] At the wrong time, though, flooding could be a disaster. In 1663, the river waters reached within four yards of Merton College, and in 1809 another flood damaged the Broad Walk to such an extent that major repairs were necessary. Small boats could actually be sailed on the Meadow during the 1852 inundation. In 1705, Edward King, an innholder, was granted the lease of the Meadow for three years at an annual rent of £100 on the condition that he spread 100 loads of dung each year. But his lease stipulated that, if a flood occurred on the Meadow after 10 May in any year, then the Dean and Chapter would agree a rebate.[3] The Tubbs sisters were also granted a reduction in the rent in 1818 because of the Meadow's liability to flood.[4]

Some tenants could cause difficulties, and were handled rather less amicably. During the Commonwealth period, the Meadow was leased to William Adkins, a butcher, who, presumably, kept his cattle there. When the rightful dean and canons returned in 1660, they found the Meadow much damaged and, determined to bring it back to its original condition, declared the lease to be illegal. Adkins believed that he had acquired rights over the land, but the Dean and Chapter were certain he had no justification for such claims. The letter of attorney evicting Adkins stated that the Meadow had always, until recently, been held directly by the Dean and Chapter for 'the keepinge of their horses and cattell and for other occasions'.[5] Adkins promptly took Christ Church to court. His defence lawyer, Mr Crook, failed to settle the case and it went to Judge Edward Hyde, later Lord Chief Justice, who found in favour of Adkins, carrying the jury with him unanimously. Christ Church appealed, and Hyde's judgement was overturned, at which point Adkins tried petitioning the Dean and Chapter directly, 'setting forth his great poverty, and the deplorable condition of himselfe and family'. Christ Church settled out of court, giving Adkins '£500 out of their purses, and forgave him severall years rent then due'. The case may have seen Christ Church considerably out of pocket, but two new judgements under the seal of the Court of Common Pleas confirmed that the whole Meadow, both the part in Oxfordshire and the part in Berkshire, belonged to Christ Church.[6]

In 1761, there was another trial over the Meadow, this time to determine whether or not it was extra-parochial land. On 30 July, the City seized a cart belonging to Thomas Galton, then tenant of the Meadow, to cover his non-payment of £1 12s towards the poor rate charged by St Aldates' parish. Galton insisted that the Meadow was not in the parish and sued the City officers for trespass. Needless to say, the council officials pleaded not guilty, and the case came before the Lent Assizes on 4 March 1762. Mr Justice Noel presided with a special jury of gentlemen of the county, and James Galpin, Christ Church's Chapter clerk, was in attendance throughout the whole trial. Evidence for both sides was given, and irregular record keeping and activity by the City was uncovered. Documentation showed that the Meadow had originally been in the parish of St Frideswide, long swallowed up by the priory. The defence for the council countered with the poor rate books showing that, for a few years either side of the Restoration, rates had been paid by the then tenant, presumably the difficult and now somewhat richer Mr Adkins. However, the rates book was less than useful as evidence, at least for the City; some of the rates were shown as unpaid, others were crossed out, and in 1666 they had stopped altogether, after which the tenant was no longer assessed. The parish perambulations missed out Stockwell Mead completely, but some witnesses tried to suggest that a couple of boys with white wands were always sent along the Broad Walk to meet the parson at the boats and so take in the whole of the Meadow. However, this was

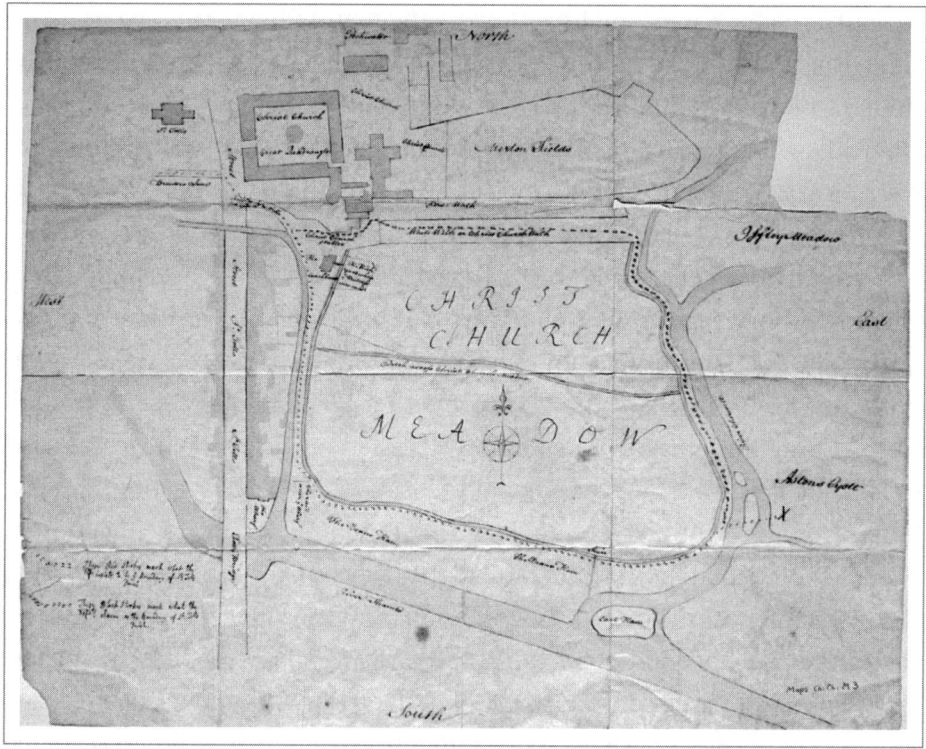

A dispute over parish boundaries and the levying of poor rates in 1762 led to the drawing of a new plan of the Meadow with the defendant's and plaintiff's opinions marked in different colours.

revealed to be a dubious tactic by the council, begun only when the council had first decided it was going to sue for poor rates from the land. Much of the evidence was given by a resident of St Aldates called John Townsend, who had moved there in 1702, when he was four.[7] In the end it was agreed that Stockwell Mead had never been assessed for any rates or taxes, or even tithes, and the jury came down firmly on the side of Mr Galton.[8]

Management of the Meadow, particularly the river banks and the ditches, was a constant theme throughout Christ Church's history. The river remained the major highway into the city until the arrival of the railway, and so the banks had to be kept in good order to allow boats and barges to draw up alongside. In 1689, trees were cut in the college woods in Chandence to repair the water banks and in 1713, the Dean and Chapter agreed that bills signed by the sub-dean for the repair of the Meadow banks should be paid by the Treasurer.[9] In 1805, new posts to moor barges were put down on Earl's Ham and, when the dean had new windows installed in 1862, the old stones were used to reinforce the path by the river. Embankment walls on both the Thames and the Cherwell were erected at the same time.[10]

Keeping the fencing in proper repair was also a major operation. With cattle and horses grazing, and a valuable hay crop to be protected, it was important that fences were not allowed to deteriorate. Merton Meadow was separated from the rest of the Meadow with a post and rail fence. Although Christ Church maintained the longest, southern run, it was the lessee's job to look after the rest. This was usually Corpus Christi College and in 1835, James Norris, the bursar, complained that Benjamin Badcock's revaluation of the property was far too high, and took no account of the cost of repairing the houses, fences or the drains which ran from the city across the Meadow to the river.[11] The condition of the properties was apparently dire; just a few years later, Norris asked Christ Church to help out with the costs of replacing the roof of the stable with slates rather than thatch, but the surveyor felt that the timbers were in such poor condition that they would not support slates. The Dean and Chapter were blunt: they would not assist with repairs that were necessary through neglect rather than through age alone. After some negotiation, Christ Church offered a deal: they would not insist on the repairs to the stables and cottages provided Corpus left the fences in a good condition at the end of their lease. Norris, sensibly, agreed.[12]

The area leased by Corpus Christi lay immediately south of that college and Merton College. Now known as Merton Fields, it was, at least in part, formerly known as the Timber Yard, and had been part of the property of St Frideswide's priory. Until 1649, the Timber Yard was kept in hand, but then was leased out, first to a Mr Dixon, and then to the same Adkins who held the rest of the meadow. It passed from hand to hand with covenants to tend 100 willows and to protect them from cattle, to maintain the pathway through the yard and to scour all the ditches as necessary. It was divided into three parts, one of which had a house built on it just after the Restoration, which was not to be used as victualling house, cheesecake house, ale house or house of common entertainment. In 1771, when Corpus Christi was the lessee, the Dean and Chapter decided that they would take the Meadow back in hand when the lease terminated. After all, it had been part of the college site until the end of the Civil War.[13] But it seems that Corpus Christi hung on to it for many years. For, in 1814, the Timber Yard with its two tenements with gardens and stabling for eight horses, and ten acres free of rates and tithes, was revalued at £66 and leased again to Corpus Christi.[14] In 1835, the thatched tenements were described as having one room on the ground floor, two rooms on the first and two attics. One was occupied by Thomas Macey, the other by Thomas Baldwin and the garden separately by Mr Sheard. One of the stables had been converted into a saddle room. There was also a hovel on posts, two loose boxes and a yard. Thirty years later, Merton Grange, as it had become known, consisted of three cottages – the stables had been converted in 1860 – and was let on a 50-year building lease.[15]

In the same year that Corpus Christi was let off the costs of repairs, a new design was drawn up for Christ Church's portion of the fence, and just a few years later, iron railings and gates were erected at the north-east corner close to the Physic Garden to define the site of St Peter's parochial school.[16] And then, in 1856, another 450 yards of iron post and rail fencing was added to the Meadow. Tenders were received in May from a number of major iron foundries, including Coalbrookdale; the Victoria Foundry in Derby; the Eagle Foundries in both Oxford and Birmingham; Henry Floyd, an ironmonger in Oxford; Gill and Ward, also in Oxford; the Woodside Ironworks in Dudley; Thomas Perry in Staffordshire; and the London Works in Birmingham.[17] The design and the erection of the fence was undertaken by Edward Bruton, with the work beginning at the end of July.

Another area that needed attention was in the south-west corner of the Meadow, across the Cherwell, where the boathouses now are and where many of the college barges used to be moored. Christ Church always charged rent to the colleges for this use of the river bank; boat clubs with barges moored on the Meadow paid £3, and those beyond the Cherwell £5, with an additional, but nominal, rent for the use of the gates leading to them. The

University Boat Club appealed against the quit rent in 1878 but the Governing Body held firm; the costs of erecting and maintaining the iron gates which protected the barges from the general public was high.[18]

A gravel path ran alongside the Thames and, as the numbers of barges grew, so there were applications to extend the walk, with a temporary bridge erected across the Cherwell to allow easy viewing of the boat races. This was not a particularly satisfactory arrangement: the tenant of the Meadow complained that his crops were damaged, and compensation was exacted from the boat clubs. Eventually, it was decided that there should be a permanent bridge over the Cherwell, and a committee was set up to make the arrangements. On 8 May 1878, it was decided to postpone any construction; finances were limited at that moment, and there was a universal desire among the members of the committee that the work be 'done handsomely'.[19] Six years later, decisions were made to build a bridge that was almost level, in wood, and ten feet wide. It was to cost around £250. The specification was sent to Jackson, who submitted a design, Charles Bossom quoted £335 10s 6d, and the bridge was built in the Long Vacation 1884.[20] It was not long after the erection of the bridge that the first proposal came for a boathouse rather than a barge, although it was the 1930s before any building took place.[21] By 1951, the Cherwell Bridge was on the verge of collapse and a new one was soon erected. A new bridge to replace the 1877 hand ferry over to the Iffley Road sports ground is under consideration.[22]

Bad weather and bad luck were always threats to the Meadow. After seven inches of snow and 20 hours of rain on 4 February 1865, anxious measurements were taken of the heights of the Cherwell and the Thames.[23] In 1947, trees were lost in the gales and floods of that spring, and all the elms for which the Meadow was famous had to be taken down as a consequence of Dutch elm disease in 1975.[24] The English elms planted along the Broad Walk by Fell had been interspersed, when the originals reached the end of their natural life, by Huntingdon elms, but neither was immune to the pervasive disease. Mr Burras, the director of the Botanic Gardens, recommended the use of a number of different species to ensure the Meadow would never be so depleted again. Oriental planes were top of the list, to be interplanted with London planes and *Ailanthus altissima* (the 'Tree of Heaven'). The *Ailanthus* was fast-growing and dioecious, and Burras commented that an avenue of both sexes would be unique in Britain. The Cherwell walks were to be treated differently, with much more decorative, medium-sized trees, and beech and hornbeam as occasional large specimens. By the Thames, individual specimen trees were proposed; almost a mini-arboretum. For the walk from Meadows Building to the river, poplar trees, of which there were some already, would complete the avenue with some limes for variation.[25] The Governing Body accepted Mr Burras's suggestions with the exception of the *Ailanthus*.[26]

There were other threats to the Meadow, both natural and human. The Dean and Chapter decreed that the lease of Earl's Ham to its 1757 tenant should never be renewed, as he had planted osiers which were stopping the water and impairing the banks of the Meadow.[27] In 1815 there was a robbery with violence, and Christ Church had to refund the expenses of Mr Vickery, a Bow Street runner, who was sent to handle the case.[28] In order to protect the Meadow, new instructions were issued to the Meadow keepers and constables in 1867: beggars or persons in ragged or dirty clothes were to be excluded, together with anyone who was dressed or behaved indecently; no handcarts, wheelbarrows or perambulators were allowed unless the dean had given express permission. Kite-flying, stone-throwing, ball-games, hoops, bows, arrows and guns were all banned, along with fishing, catching birds or nesting. There was to be no carving of names on trees or benches, no damage to the turf and no fastening of boats or rafts to the river wall.[29] But games were not stopped altogether: a fellow of Merton College, F. H. Bradley, complained in 1890 to his warden about children playing and making 'loud shrieks' under his window. He acknowledged that he had no right to interfere, so the children were presumably not indulging in any of the forbidden activities, but the iron railings ended just by his rooms, making it an obvious place for gatherings. Warden Broderick wrote to the Treasurer, Skene, suggesting that the fence be extended. Alternatively, he quipped, a 'stuffed boy as a scarecrow would probably be effectual'.[30]

In the 1950s, however, there was a real threat to the very survival of

Merton Meadow. Robert Dundas, writing in the Annual Reports for 1942 and 1943, mentioned that the prospect of a relief road across the Meadow had once more been raised. Certainly, in 1941, the Town Planning Committee proposed that the older part of the city should be encircled with a wide tree-planted road directing traffic to a new civic centre east of Magdalen Bridge.[31] It seems an unlikely subject for discussion when the country was in the middle of a war, and Dundas was less than concerned, dismissing the scheme as 'journalistic flannel'.

In 1945, Thomas Sharp was asked by the Council to draw up a report on planning and development of Oxford. Published in 1948 as *Oxford Replanned*, Sharp's work was a comprehensive study of a city growing outside its university into an industrialised area with expanding suburbs and confined by difficult geography; and he made suggestions for its modernisation and layout.[32] The transport system was one of his principal targets. Petrol rationing still artificially suppressed the numbers of vehicles driving through the centre of the city, but there were still more than Sharp thought was manageable. He argued, too, that bicycles, legion in Oxford, were just as guilty of causing congestion, and that some sort of relief road was clearly necessary. One small part of Sharp's proposal was 'Merton Mall', a road which was to run from the bottom of St Aldates, straight through the relatively new Memorial Garden, across Merton Field just to the north of the Broad Walk, and then skimming the edge of the grounds of St Hilda's College and Magdalen College School to the Plain. 'This proposal may cause bitter controversy', he said, prophetically, 'but it is the only possible means of relieving the mad traffic congestion in High Street and of bringing some peace back into the old heart of city.' In 1951, it looked as though the Meadow was safe, newspaper reports saying that the road was not recommended.[33] But after the 1953 Public Inquiry, inner relief roads were back on the agenda.

By 1955, the matter became more serious. Even University men, usually those whose colleges were not close to the proposed road, said that clearing the High of traffic was a top priority.[34] Others said that this was the City taking a good opportunity for a 'swipe in the eye to a rich proud college'. In 1956, the Minister for Housing and Local Government, Duncan Sandys, put Merton Mall firmly back in the picture, even announcing that the five members of the Cabinet who were Christ Church men, including the prime minister, had all backed his decision.[35] The Cabinet was, of course, preoccupied with the more pressing matter of Suez. Christ Church issued a statement declaring that they would resist the road – 'one of the greatest acts of vandalism that could be perpetrated' – by every legal and constitutional means at their disposal. In the first instance, Christ Church issued a writ against Sandys, claiming that his directive was in opposition to the City's development plan which had rejected the Meadow road proposal. Three events turned the tide: the replacement of Sandys as minister by Henry Brooke, a Balliol man; the initiation by Beveridge of a debate in the Lords to move that the whole scheme be investigated by a Royal Commission; and the Ministry's acceptance that the city council was under no obligation to follow its directive.

A traffic survey was advised and duly carried out, reporting in 1959 that an inner relief road across the Meadow was indeed the only solution. After some amendment, the proposal was passed in the city council by 39 votes to 26, the 39 including three University representatives.[36] An inquiry at large was convened, putting forward three principal plans: one which took a relief road south of the Meadow, one which took a road across the northern part of the Meadow and would close Magdalen Bridge to traffic, and a third with a road across the middle of the Meadow. Needless to say, Christ Church, Merton and Corpus Christi were against the second and third schemes. The inspector, Sir Frederick Armer, proposed acceptance of the third idea, a road across the centre of the Meadow, over 300 yards from Christ Church and a quarter of a mile from Merton and Corpus Christi.

A tunnel was mooted as an alternative, which would at least preserve the appearance of the Meadow, but was rejected as being too expensive. The possibility of sinking the road in a cutting was also put forward. Between 1962 and 1964, planning continued but received a setback in 1963, when the Buchanan report, *Traffic in Towns*, was published. Buchanan suggested that restrictions on traffic in town centres was the way forward, and relief roads could be placed anywhere, not necessarily close to the town centre.

In 1964, Congregation (the University's assembly of masters, doctors and professors) affirmed its support of Christ Church, but the road was still very firmly on the agenda. Another inquiry began in 1965 to discuss the sunken road proposal; Christ Church did not give in and with Buchanan siding with the university, discussions continued. Gray, the Christ Church Treasurer, persuaded Lewis Mumford, the American planning theorist, to write to the inquiry, suggesting that to hang a whole development plan on one road was short-sighted. Fresh experts appointed by Anthony Crossman decided that the Meadow Road made no sense, a conclusion that did not sit well with the government, and another outside consultant was brought in. The Governing Body argued through all the inquiries until the local council and the national government both changed and, as Mercurius Oxoniensis suggests, common sense prevailed.[37] The Labour Party won control of the council in May 1972 and duly abandoned the Development Plan as it then stood, including the proposal for a road just to the south of the Meadow. Merton Mall had been finally defeated, and Donnington Bridge, considerably further south, was constructed, connecting the Abingdon and Iffley roads, and reducing the need for at least some traffic to come through the centre of town to cross the river.[38] The government rallied in 1974 with a very short-lived suggestion that the Meadow be used for gravel extraction; if a road could not be run across the Meadow then perhaps it could be used for building more roads elsewhere![39]

The Meadow was always a popular place for leisure, and the walks around its circumference, popular on Sunday afternoons, have been created over many centuries. Deadman's Walk, the path that runs immediately south of the line of the city wall, was the direct route to the cemetery on the edge of town, and there must have been paths of some sort right around the edge for the Rogationtide processions to take place. Dean Fell is credited with the construction of the Broad Walk from the rubble dug out when the Great Quadrangle was lowered. Anthony Wood recorded in his diaries its construction and the planting of 72 elm trees on each side, and the avenue is shown on Loggan's engraving of 1673.[40] In 1726, an estimate of £97 5s 8d was received for creating a walk around the Meadow.[41] The avenue of

The Dean and Chapter owned the 'game of swans' on the stretch of the Thames through Oxford. It was usually leased out on the condition that the lessee provided a swan for the table when the Dean and Chapter requested one. Christ Church swans had their own mark, recorded here in the estates papers.

trees along the Broad Walk was extended by Dean Liddell in 1863, and was planted tree by tree by the whole Liddell family, the sub-dean and his wife, the Jacobson family, and even one by Prince Frederick of Denmark.[42]

An event which must have been quite a spectacle in the sixteenth and seventeenth centuries was the annual census of the swan population, or swan-upping. Christ Church was given a game of swans on its stretch of the Thames with the lands of Oseney abbey, and was permitted to keep ten birds on the Thames and Cherwell. In September 1582, the upping cost 15s 9d, and it was found that the ten originals were now 27 'white game' and three cygnets.[43] The right was leased to John Kirton, the college butler, at a rent of £1 13s 4d plus one fat swan every St Andrew's tide. When Kirton's lease expired, in 1594, the Dean and Chapter were found to have seventeen old swans and nine cygnets, each of which was identified with the college's own mark. The lease of the game of swans disappears from the records during the reign of James I, the last document showing a drawing of the college mark made at the time of the annual swan-upping, when it was borne by 26 swans.[44]

Several pioneering balloon flights from the Botanic Gardens and the Meadow were made by James Sadler, 'the first English aeronaut', his first in 1784. The earliest ascents were in hydrogen balloons, but the one from Merton Field in 1810 was the first hot-air balloon flight. 'Show Sunday' was a particular celebration held in Commemoration Week when Oxonians, dressed in their finest, would promenade around the Meadow. In cold winters, skating was a popular pastime, and ornithologists and botanists always found plenty to study and enjoy all year round.

One nineteenth-century character who strolled on the Meadow's walks and went boating was Tiglath Pileser, a bear cub belonging to Frank Buckland, son of the professor, canon and pioneering geologist. Tiglath Pileser, dressed in a cap and gown, often accompanied Buckland, much to the amusement of the local children. Presumably, the bigger the bear grew, the more of a hazard it became and, in the end, the dean had to insist; either the bear went, or Buckland.[45] Another crowd pleaser was Richard Whately, or rather his spaniel Sailor, whom Whately had trained to climb the trees overhanging the Cherwell, and then plunge into the river below.[46] In addition, since the late nineteenth century Merton Meadow has been used by the cathedral school as a sports ground. Before 1898, when the headmaster asked the Dean and Chapter if there was a means of separating the boys' cricket pitch from the grazing cattle, there must have been a whole new meaning to 'leg before wicket'.[47]

Over the last 50 years, plays and concerts, firework displays, dragon boat racing, Civil War re-enactments, military parades, parachute displays and even a penny-farthing demonstration have taken place. In a recent attempt to find new ways to attract visitors to the Meadow and Christ Church, there was a brief flirtation with the notion of an 'Oxford Eye' to match that on the South Bank.

During times of war – from the Civil War to the Boer War and in two

A very dog-like depiction in a Christ Church window of Buckland's pet bear.

world wars – the Meadow stopped being used for leisure and became a training ground for soldiers. In 1685, the university volunteers gathered against Monmouth paraded there, and again in 1798. In 1891, the University Rifle Volunteers asked permission to drill there and in 1909, the University Officer Training Corps did the same.[48] New's illustration of Christ Church, dated at the beginning of the First World War, shows soldiers marching through the Meadow Gate; and in the Second World War, the Home Guard had a machine-gun post there.[49]

A celebration of Christ Church's history was held on the Meadow in 1968 when a *Son et Lumière* was held. Scripted by James (now Jan) Morris, with a prologue by W. H. Auden, it was narrated by Sir John Gielgud. The theme of the event, remarked Morris in the programme, 'is ostensibly about a set of buildings: but its real theme is the constancy of the Christ Church tradition – the fact that in a way the very same people have been living and working in those buildings through all the vicissitudes of English history'.[50]

The gardens

Christ Church does not have the great public gardens that some other colleges do. As a cathedral, as well as a college, the main quadrangle has been, in effect, a cathedral close, and most of the open spaces that might well have been more secluded quadrangles in other colleges are the private gardens of the canons. Some have become less private over the years, but are still hardly public. The garden behind the Steward's Office and Treasury, once the cemetery for St Frideswide's priory, and then part of a canonry, has now become known as the Cathedral Garden and is used for plays and functions. In the early part of the twentieth century it was laid out with a tennis court, but fell into disrepair when Canon Jenkins had the lodgings – he called it his 'bird sanctuary'.[51] When the canon died in 1959, the property was taken over by the college from the Chapter, initially on a temporary basis, and then more formally and permanently. The garden remained in a poor state until the Friends of the Cathedral took it over in 1961 and, with a grant of £100 from the Chapter, set about restoring it. In the mid-1970s, when the Steward's and Treasury offices moved into the old lodgings, the garden was taken back by the Governing Body.

Also attached to the cathedral is the old cloister which, for many years, displayed the foundations of the old medieval bell tower. In 1985, it was laid out afresh as an authentically planted medieval garden with medicinal plants and plants commemorating the Virgin Mary.[52] It, too, fell into some decay, becoming little more than a rather patchy camomile lawn with a few cowslips, until it was redesigned in 2008 with a new planter containing an olive tree and a fountain representing peace.

The best representations of the canons' gardens are on the engravings by Loggan in the 1670s and, very much more recently, by New in around 1913. In 1673, most of the gardens were laid out in formal parterres. The deanery garden had a summer house on the wall adjoining Corpus Christi College, and there was a long avenue in the next canonry on that side leading to an arbour, probably the bowling alley that was returfed in 1630.[53] The Priory House garden had a viewing mound and the study built for Peter Vermigli. On the north side of the Great Quadrangle, the two plots were in different styles: nearest to St Aldates, the garden was divided into two, with a formal orchard in one half and the other with small beds, some of which may have been for kitchen supplies; the other plot held lawns, hedges and trees in a regular arrangement. Killcanon (the canon's lodgings on the south-west

> ## Claude Jenkins (1877–1959)
>
> Canon Jenkins was one of the most memorable characters of mid-twentieth-century Christ Church. The photographs of his rooms stacked high with books and papers are famous. He allegedly added layers of clothes as the winter wore on, discarding them gradually in the spring to reveal the egg-stains that had been acquired the previous autumn.
>
> His was a broad scholarship, well suited to the role of regius professor of ecclesiastical history at both King's and Christ Church, the librarianship of the Union and of Lambeth Palace, and the editorship of the *Church Quarterly Review*, the files of which were kept in his bath.
>
> In his will, Jenkins left most of his books to St Anne's College, and a sum for the purchase of snuff to the Christ Church Senior Common Room.
>
> Cawkwell, in Butler (ed.) (2006), 176; *ODNB*; *Christ Church 1964*

corner of Peckwater Quad) had a formal garden, with the brewhouse being the only building that looked as if its garden might have been used by small boys playing football. By the time New drew his update of Loggan, most of the gardens appear to have been laid to lawn with a few trees.

The Pococke Garden, a tranquil place set into the crook of the city wall, was once part of the garden attached to the Priory House, and was created in its present form as recently as the 1990s through the benefaction of Miss Page, once college secretary, and the inspiration of Richard Benthall, then Treasurer. Its name derives from the splendid plane tree planted by Edward Pococke, the regius professor of Hebrew.

Between the Pococke Garden and the Meadow is the Masters' Garden, created in 1926–7 by another Treasurer, George Hutchinson.[54] Legend has it that the site was won from Corpus Christi College in a poker match, but that college's only claim to the garden is a view from its own raised walkway along the city wall and a key to the gate. The site had formerly been an orchard belonging to the lodgings of the Lady Margaret professor of divinity, who was then Walter Lock. The name is strange, and seems to have been given to the garden almost by accident; at times in the archives it is simply known as the College Garden, and at others, the Masters' Garden. Even the position of the apostrophe is uncertain. The plaque to Hutchinson's generosity was placed in the wall in 1954, six years after his death, and seems to have sealed the oddity, with plural Masters, in perpetuity. Christ Church has no Master, and there does not seem to have been any intention that the garden was to be restricted to those with MAs. Still, the name stuck, and it has been the Masters' Garden ever since.[55] Planting plans show a regular shape, with a lawn big enough for croquet and, now, for wedding marquees, with large herbaceous borders, a little in the Jekyll style. The walls, gates and drains were all complete by the end of February 1927 in time for the spring planting of the beds by Hillier and Sons of Winchester; and at the same time as the college was laying out the Memorial Garden and the Iris Garden to commemorate those who died in the First World War.[56]

Christ Church's quadrangles have never been gardens. For much of their history none have been much more than gravelled spaces, and the quadrangle between the Old Library and Meadows Building was only planted in order to cover up ugly dustbins and sinks against the walls. In 1884, creepers were planted against the buttresses and the blank walls of the Old Library, shrubs were planted between the Meadows Building and the steps up to Hall, and more shrubs along the base of the wall of the Priory House and its garden. Paving slabs were laid the length of the Meadows Building, probably to keep down the amount of mud brought into the staircases from the Meadow, and to help the scouts.[57] Plans were made to pave the area more decoratively in 1973, but were abandoned.[58] The Great Quadrangle, or Tom Quad, was probably the first to be grassed, possibly by Fell when he completed the quad with its north side and Tom Tower, and only stray plants like the ubiquitous 'Oxford weed' have managed to take hold among the paving slabs.[59] Occasionally it has been suggested that the quadrangle should be softened with flower beds.[60] Even Mercury was not designed as a decorative feature, in spite of the fountain with first its globe and then its statues of Mercury, but as a functional reservoir in case of fire. It has been enjoyed for less prosaic reasons, however. The diary of Mr Borrett, the Head Porter from

For 'the keepinge of their horses and cattell and for other occasions': the Meadow

1936 until 1962, records mishaps such as the painter who stepped back to admire his handiwork on the face of Tom's clock and fell backwards into the pond. Or the swan which, bedecked with bow tie, was found serenely enjoying the water one morning in 1949, an incident not considered at all amusing by the Thames Conservancy people. Much earlier, legend has it that the canons' children were given rides on the backs of turtles that had been purchased for the Chancellor's banquet and turned loose in the pond to keep them fresh.[61] Peckwater Quad was given its lawns in 1936 – 'rather than the present windswept waste of gravel and dust' – and was, for a short period in its history, made more colourful with window boxes and stripy awnings. Perhaps these were considered inappropriate for such a grand site, for they only lasted a short while, and Christ Church's quads remain austerely empty of flowers.[62]

2

'This Royall & Ample Foundation': 1546–53

The foundation of Christ Church, with Trinity, its sister college in Cambridge, was intrinsically bound up with Henry's desperate need for funds after the French and Scottish wars.[1] The site of his new cathedral in Oxford, founded in 1542, was in the old abbey of Oseney, with lands worth over £600 a year. His own college in Oxford was worth about the same. If the two were combined, this would release revenue. In May 1545, both cathedral and college were seized by the Crown; in July, Peckwater Inn was taken back from New College; in September, Tom, along with the other bells, and many fixtures and fittings from Oseney, was moved to the Frideswide site; and in November, Canterbury College was surrendered. Clearly something major was being planned.

But in December 1545, the Chantries Act was passed, devised in part to release money tied up for purposes that Henry had decided were inappropriate. Collegiate revenue was targeted, too, and commissioners, all drawn from Oxford and Cambridge, were sent out to investigate. Fortunately for the universities, two of the commissioners – Matthew Parker, master of Corpus Christi College and vice-chancellor of Cambridge University, and Richard Cox, first dean of Oxford cathedral and tutor to the prince of Wales – were masterly and speedy in their reporting. Much to his surprise, the king discovered that the colleges operated with far fewer resources than he had assumed, and he changed his ideas completely. He decided not only to save

'This Royall & Ample Foundation': 1546–53

Oseney abbey was founded in 1129, and occupied a large site to the west of Oxford. At the Dissolution, it briefly became the cathedral for the new diocese of Oxford. When Christ Church was founded in 1546, Oseney was gradually demolished, with its building materials sold to supplement the new cathedral's coffers, and much of its land formed part of Christ Church's endowment. This engraving is dated 1820.

the colleges as they were, but to create new ones of his own in both Oxford and Cambridge.[2] A draft charter for the new cathedral, which had evidently been in consideration throughout 1545, had been prepared in November of that year. Although stamped on 26 January 1546, nothing more happened; the ageing and ill monarch was considering a unique joint venture, probably inspired by Richard Cox. By October that year, the plans for both colleges were ready, and in fact, building at Trinity College had already begun. Christ Church was formally founded on 4 November 1546, with both college and cathedral, uniquely, being under one head.[3]

The old priory church was re-designated the Cathedral Church of

The foundation charter, dated 4 November 1546, is a rather unsatisfactory and incomplete document. It makes no mention of the academic establishment nor gives any indication of how the unique joint foundation should be administered.

Christ in Oxford of the Foundation of King Henry VIII, and served, in shortened form, as both the college chapel and the cathedral of the new diocese. (Christ Church was also known as *Aedis Christi*, the 'House of Christ', hence the nickname, 'The House'.) The foundation charter, strangely, describes only the ecclesiastical establishment with a mere hint of the academic side of life which was assumed and, to a certain extent, already established.[4] No statutes for either side of Christ Church were ratified, but a new and unique society had been formed.[5]

The absence of statutes was a defining characteristic of the foundation for over three centuries. Henry VIII had died before any serious work on statutes could be started and, although Edward VI tried to set things on a regular footing, with drafts being drawn up – probably by Cox again – the young king, like his father, died too soon.

Several drafts survive in a single bound volume in the archive, the first of which is a copy of the basic statutes issued to each of Henry's new cathedral foundations; the second holds statutes drawn up by Edward VI and collated with those of Corpus Christi, the constitution of which formed the basis for that of Cardinal College. Originally elegantly penned, these have been much over-written and annotated in a number of hands. The third and fourth sets are the same Edwardian statutes without the addition of the Corpus Christi material, and the fifth an even more heavily annotated and corrected version.[6] Although there are some obvious differences with Wolsey's plans for Cardinal College – the intrusion of a cathedral chapter into the scheme is the most significant example – it is remarkable how far Christ Church followed the 1525 scheme.[7]

But all that is written down to describe the form of the new college-cum-cathedral is contained in a few short covenants recorded at the end of an account by the Court of Augmentations. These memoranda, which form an insignificant footnote to a much longer document, deal not with the entire administration of Christ Church but just with additional financial obligations, including the provision of chaplains, lay clerks, and choristers; readers – in Hebrew, divinity, and Greek – appointed by the king and funded by the Chapter; 60 stipendiary scholars or Students; a schoolmaster to teach 40 children; funds for charitable uses; and repairs to the 'most decayed highe wayes within the Countie of Oxford'.[8]

The actual body of men who made up this new establishment – which was, in fact, closer to Wolsey's statutes than to the Henrician covenants – is recorded in the dean's admissions book. On 14 January 1547, 'the following persons were members of this Royall & Ample Foundation ...':[9] after the dean and the eight canons, 88 Students were admitted; a further eight arrived over the next two months, and six more between April and August; thirteen chaplains were sworn in, along with four commoners; and in March, the names of five 'King's Professors' are added: one of Greek, two Divinity, and two Hebrew.[10]

More formally, the first Chapter Book begins with a list of members present in 1549.[11] The eight canons head the list, the first of whom was the sub-dean, William Haynes, who had been a canon of Oseney abbey until its dissolution, a fellow and provost of Oriel College, and a chaplain to King

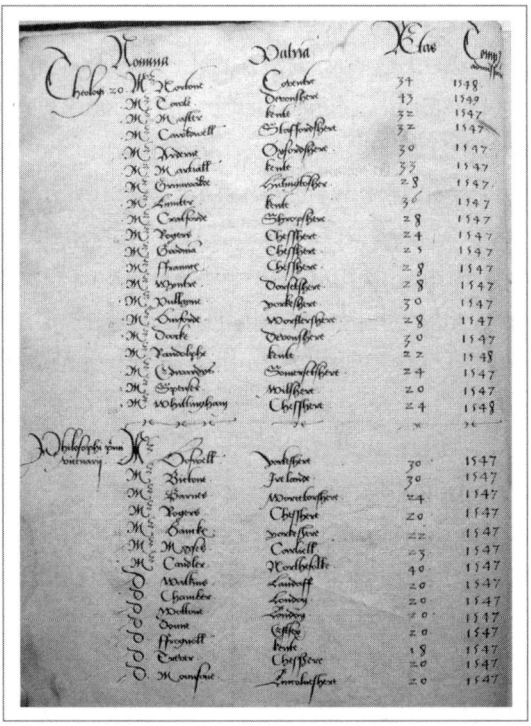

Christ Church was founded with a dean at its head, eight canons and three professors. After these were the 100 Students. This list shows the most senior – the theologiae *and the* primi philosophi *– with their ages on admission, and their counties of origin.*

Henry VIII from 1539. He was probably a significant cog in the machinery that founded Christ Church. William Tresham, the sole survivor from both Cardinal and King Henry VIII colleges, was appointed canon of the second stall and given lodgings in the Priory House.[12] Thomas Day, in the third stall, resided in the centre of the east side of Tom Quad, directly opposite the great gate. Day had been a canon of Oseney and sub-warden of All Souls College. Alexander Belsyre had come from a fellowship at New College, and would later become the first president of St John's College. The fifth canon was James Curtoppe, a fellow of Corpus Christi College. Thomas Bernard was from King's College, Cambridge; he was appointed, almost simultaneously, to the seventh stall at Christ Church (residing in Peckwater Inn), to

> ## Students
>
> The terms 'Student' and 'alumnus' have always caused problems at Christ Church. A Student (always with an upper-case 'S') is now the equivalent of a Fellow. Before 1858, Students were stipendiary members of the academic establishment, whether graduate or undergraduate. Only the Dean and Chapter were the Governing Body. The remainder of the Students could be tutors, or studying for higher degrees, or just pupils. Non-stipendiary undergraduates were called noblemen, gentlemen commoners, commoners, or servitors. 'Alumnus' was the Latin equivalent for Student, and did not mean an old member of the college as it is commonly used today.

the rectory of Pyrton in Oxfordshire, and as chaplain to Thomas Cranmer.[13] Robert Banks, the eighth canon, had the poorest lodgings in old medieval Canterbury College.[14] The final man in the list, Henry Siddall, described within his own college as somewhat 'inconstant in religion', went on to become an effective college treasurer.[15]

Following the canons were the three public lecturers (the regius professorships) who continued, on a reduced scale, Wolsey's proposed scheme. Peter Martyr Vermigli held the position in Divinity; Thomas Bruarne in Hebrew, and George Etheridge in Greek. Both Bruarne and Etheridge were Oxford men, but Martyr was a renowned Italian evangelical reformer who had been forced to flee his home country for more sympathetic company. Driven further and further across Europe, Martyr was invited to England by Cranmer. The hoped-for respite was not, however, forthcoming in the conservative University, and Martyr's life at Christ Church was dogged by protest.[16]

The largest portion of this 1549 list is that of the fellows, soon to be known as Students or *alumni*. The first 20 were the *theologiae*, senior men, all Masters of Arts who, on admission ranged in age from 20 to 43. Beneath them were two further ranks, the senior and junior *philosophi*. The eldest of these was 40, and the youngest 13. At the top of the list were 7 MAs, then 23

BAs, and finally 40 undergraduates all of whom were to progress upwards through the ranks as they achieved their degrees, and as new and younger men arrived after them. All were stipendiary, as the 100 senior and junior canons of Cardinal College were to have been. It was obviously intended that Christ Church, too, should have 100 in its academic ranks. Each man's name is supplemented with his age on admission, his county or country of origin, and the year in which he was admitted. Preceding many of the names are an 'M' or a 'D' signifying that a man had proceeded MA or BA already. Men at the top of the list would soon be prefixed with Dr, or *doctores*. Undergraduates were recorded merely by name. Progression through the ranks depended on examination success, as well as seniority, and was formalised at an annual election ceremony held as close to Christmas Eve as possible.[17] These stipendiary Students could stay at Christ Church indefinitely provided they passed their examinations within a given time frame, took holy orders (it was only necessary to become a deacon), remained single, and took no additional post that paid a living wage.

By 1550, although the numbers still stood at 90, an inserted word divides the junior *philosophi* into two uneven groups. The top third remained *philosophi* and the rest became the *discipuli*, the most junior of the stipendiary academics.[18] A year later, the *discipuli*, too, were divided into junior and senior groups.[19] The earliest surviving disbursement book, from 1548, supports the Chapter Book list, person for person.[20] Everyone was in residence by the second week of the year.[21]

Commoners – fee-paying undergraduates – were at Christ Church from the start. Four were admitted in 1546, before some of the stipendiary body, although their exact status is uncertain. Certainly two became chaplains, and one may well have been a college officer, rather than a student. Whatever the role of these very early non-foundationers, it was only a matter of a few years before a fee-paying undergraduate body was well established at Christ Church.

Chaplains, lay clerks, and choristers – eight of each – are recorded next, and then the list is completed with the *famuli*, or college servants. There were the sacristans (*editui*) and vergers (*vergibaiuli*) in the cathedral, and then butlers (*promi*), the manciple (*obsonator*), the auditor, porters (*janitores*), cooks (*coqui*), the scullion (*lixa*), and maintenance men (*operarii*). In 1550, a barber (*tonsor*) joined the ranks, and in 1552, a clock keeper (*custos horologie* [*sic*]). That year, the first list of college officers was appended to the annual election list. Siddall was elected as sub-dean, with Belsyre, Curtoppe and Francis the treasurers (*prefecti erarii*). Rogers and Banks were Censors, Elcock and Calfhill the lecturers in dialectic, Donne the lecturer in rhetoric and Nowell mathematics lecturer.[22] And things remained much the same throughout the rest of the sixteenth century.

The size of the establishment followed almost exactly the statutes laid down by Cardinal Wolsey in 1525, including bedesmen lodged in the almshouse across St Aldates. Wolsey's scheme had allowed for 13 poor men with a female servant, and Henry had provided for 12 honest paupers in his first foundation. Christ Church's charter, however, appointed 24 almsmen in common with Henry's policy for all his new cathedral foundations.[23]

This was a substantial establishment which needed to be paid, fed and lodged. If further proof were needed that Henry had planned a new and large institution, an assignment of property – lands, rectories, tithes and other profits – was made to the Dean and Chapter on 1 October 1546, before the formal foundation.[24] The net value of the gift was £2,273 3s 3¾d. On 11 December 1546, a month after the signing of the foundation charter, Christ Church was given its Charter of Dotation. This massive document, which far exceeds the foundation charter in grandeur and importance, granted to Henry's new creation an endowment which almost matched in value that of Cardinal Wolsey. The property that had been retained by King Henry VIII College was re-granted, and a whole new tranche given, including much of the endowment that had been provided for the Oseney cathedral in 1542. The work of the receivers of the Court of Augmentations is evident in the early leases of Christ Church property. The Court was administered by region – the estates in Norfolk, for example, by the Crown Surveyor, Sir Richard Southwell, whose name appears in the titles to the property there.[25]

The geographical bias of the new estate was completely different from that of Cardinal Wolsey's benefaction. Whereas Wolsey had given property in the east and south-east, Henry's gift was predominantly in the west Midlands. Much was from the dissolved abbeys of Oseney and Eynsham, with a substantial proportion in Oxfordshire and the surrounding counties, but the distribution spread from Devon to Yorkshire, and from Wales to Norfolk. In total, the Dean and Chapter had a financial interest in 183 parishes across England and Wales.[26] The expected revenue, of over £2,000 per annum, greatly exceeded that of any other college.[27]

* * * * *

Barely was the ink dry on the charters before Christ Church was functioning. In fact, progress was under way before November 1546; New College had surrendered the site of Peckwater Inn in September, ready for it to be included in the new endowment, and the last few inhabitants of Canterbury College vacated their premises in November. The dean and canons bought new keys for both properties, and had surveys made. Oseney abbey was already being stripped of its fixtures and fittings, and these were all being directed to Christ Church. (Shifting everything across Oxford evidently took its toll on the college cart, which was constantly being repaired with new clouts, grease, hoops and ropes.) King Henry had said that he was

> pleased and content that the said Deane and prebendaries shall have all the ornaments plate and jewells and all the stone Tymber glasse Iron belles and leade which remayned at the late Cathedral Churche of Osney and Colledge of Frideswides ... together with such sommes of money as were dewe and owinge unto the said late Cathedral Church of Osney at the tiyme of the Surrender thereof.[28]

Much work was needed to the buildings of the college itself. Little had been achieved between 1529 and 1546 apart from making the canons' residences habitable. A glazier was employed to complete the kitchen and the chapel windows; weeds growing between the flagstones were pulled; furniture was made and the buildings cleaned from top to bottom. A shovel even had to be purchased to clean out the drains. The five walnut planks costing 5s 4d may have made a table. Carpenters, masons, glaziers, lime mixers, carters, sawyers, ditchers, cleaners, joiners and labourers were paid throughout 1546.[29] Timber was recycled from Oseney or purchased new from Sugworth and Abingdon.

The first formal activity was the oath-taking. Everyone on the foundation swore to obey the dean and officers, to follow the statutes and ordinances, and to be 'faithful and kind unto this Church, ready at all times to profit and honour this Church and in no manner of means to hinder or hurt the same'.[30] How the oath was taken is unknown, but it is likely that the whole assembly would have gathered in the Hall; the dean and the censors probably at High Table, and maybe the canons, although the records throughout Christ Church's first three centuries usually indicate that they occupied a separate table.

The oath was just one of the requirements a Student needed to fulfil on becoming a member of Christ Church. 'What everie scholler owght to have before he enter into Christe churche' included:

1. Fyrste a Tutor one of the Divines or one of the philosophers primi vicenarii
2. Honeste apparrell mette for a scholler
3. Bedding sufficiente and mett for one man
4. A Psalter of Leo Judas translation wrytte or prynte
5. Oth to the kyngs majestie
6. Hys Catechisme sett forthe in the boke of common prayer by harte
7. Grace accustomed to be sede in the hall in lyke manner by harte.[31]

A grace to launch the great new enterprise was not formally said for some weeks; 14 January, the day on which the dean made his first list of members, was a Friday, so there was no meat, and no big celebration. Instead, just fresh fish and cheese was served, costing 19s 6d.[32] A foundation feast, which cost a far more celebratory £21 10s 2d, did follow at some point in the first few weeks, along with a special service of celebration, but the date is unknown.[33]

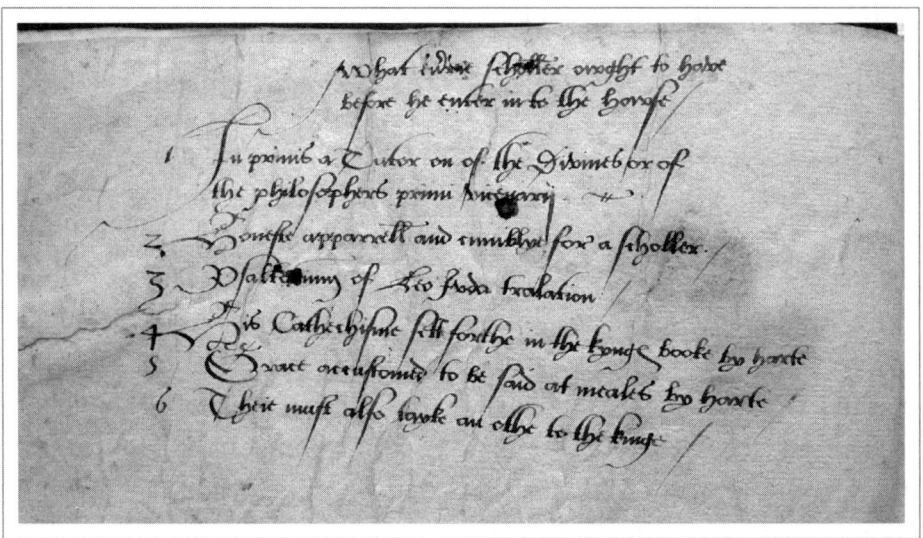

A Scholar's requirements in 1548. This short list shows the very basic things that a new undergraduate was expected to have organised before he matriculated: a tutor, suitable clothing, a psalter, his oath to the king and his catechism and grace by heart. An earlier list includes bedding.

As the week progressed, the foundation members were fed a rather dull diet of boiled beef and mutton; leavened by a little wine with supper on Tuesday, and some rabbit on Thursday. However, as the stock cupboard was filled with essentials such as salt, vinegar, flour, spices of all kinds (ginger, cinnamon, cloves, mace, pepper, saffron), oil and suet, things began to improve. Butter, eggs and milk were bought in frequently and, as the winter turned to spring, the diet expanded to include roast beef, pies, and chickens on Candlemas day. Onions and leeks were the first vegetables to appear, with figs and raisins often appearing in the accounts. But it was fish that predominated. A wide variety was offered to the establishment in the first few weeks: including pike, salmon, conger eel, chubb, crayfish and oysters to name but a few. And these were being bought in vast quantities: on Thursday 16 March 1547 alone, 6d worth of unspecified fresh fish was purchased, along with 3 ling, 8 stock fish, 360 whiting, 36 New-land fish (cod), 6 congers, 10 salted salmon and 180 red herring. This was all accompanied by beer, between

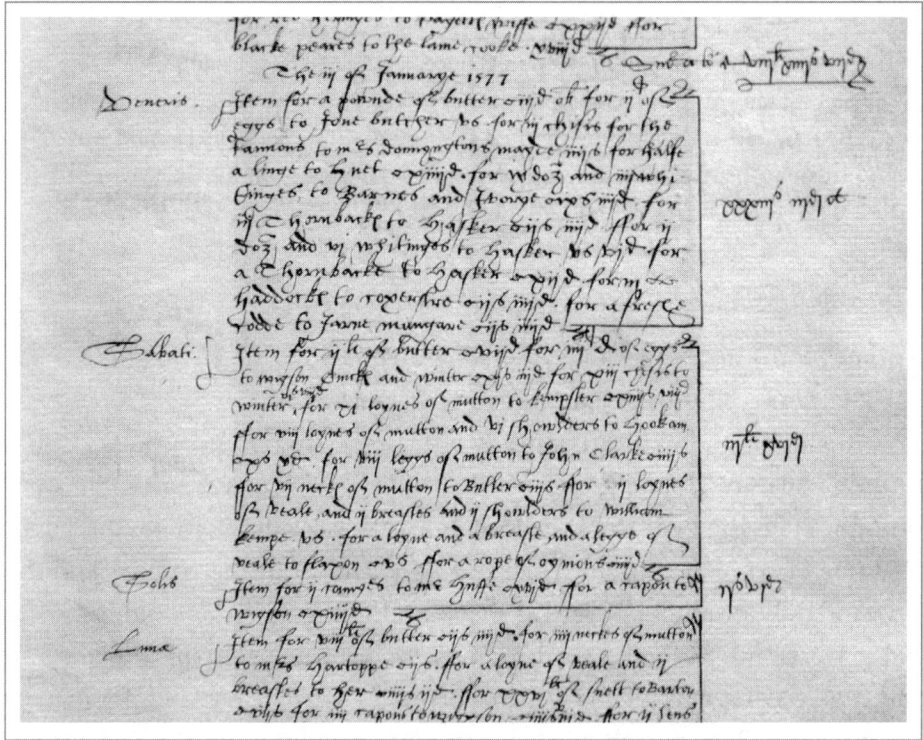

John Furnivall was the manciple at Christ Church in the 1570s. He was a meticulous record keeper, and this page shows each item purchased, the price paid, and often the supplier, from Friday 3 January 1577/8 to the following Monday. Friday being a fish-day, whiting and ling dominate the menu, but on Saturday it is mutton and veal.

10–30 kilderkins each week (a kilderkin being a cask holding between 16 and 18 gallons). The cost was about £8 a week to feed and water an establishment of around 130 men.

On top of the costs of feeding the foundation and making sure that the buildings were in a fit state for accommodation, everyone had to be paid. Stipends in the first year cost over £458, a quarter of Christ Church's predicted income. Alexander Belsyre's accounts for the first year record rents coming in from all over the country, but Foundation Day came too late for the Michaelmas rents to be collected.[34] Dean Cox was given an allowance to cover the interim period between opening the doors and the first rent collection, so

> **Alexander Belsyre** had come from Gloucestershire to New College in 1519. He became sub-warden there in 1537, before being appointed a canon in the new cathedral at Oseney, and then to Christ Church in 1546, and was probably one of the three treasurers right from the beginning. Belsyre was elected the first president of St John's College in 1555.

income for the first year looked high, a total of £3302 0s 16¾d plus the use of 72 fothers[35] 221 lbs of lead recovered from Oseney.

Income came in from sources other than rents and grants. Christ Church had its own slaughterhouse for a while, and sheep in particular were brought in on the hoof from the local markets at Wallingford or Abingdon. The sale of wool in that first year put an extra £5 in the coffers, and the unwanted by-products from the sheep and cattle, such as offal, fats and hides, were sold.[36] Woods and meadows also provided valuable income and raw materials. It was just as well, for expenses were heavy, and not just for the buildings. The church needed vestments mending, the clock repairing, and all its daily requirements of communion wine and wafers, candles and service books which came to £11 that year; the Hall and Buttery expenses were an enormous £406, and those for the kitchen were £414. There was the barber, David Jenkinson, who had his own office and was paid 40 shillings a quarter as well as being provided with all his equipment. The almshouse, across the road, had to be tidied up and made suitable for the pensioners, who were also entitled to a small annual stipend.[37] And then there were administrative expenses: legal costs, progresses to check on the newly acquired estates, auditors and charitable giving. Dean Cox and his treasurer, Alexander Belsyre, were careful men, however, and the year ended with a surplus of over £1,000. There was even a stock account: nearly £6 worth of wood and coals had been accounted for but was still available for use, £19 worth of salt fish was ready in the cellar and £6 worth of spices was stored safely in the larder. And 164 sheep still grazed somewhere close by (after the sale of 24 and the death of 19), along with 10 oxen.[38]

The majority of income, however, came from the landed estate. The foundation estate, given by the Charter of Dotation in December 1546, was extensive and its management, had the Dean and Chapter attempted a 'hands-on' approach, would have been burdensome. But the vast majority of the estates were leased out, often to noble tenants, who could sub-let and reap the profits from manors, farms and tithes. Only a few things were 'reserved' for Christ Church – usually timber or the right to present to a living. From the beginning, leases for all types of property were signed, sealed and copied into the estates registers, which continued the medieval tradition of the cartulary.[39] Rents, which were fixed, came in automatically; the existing tenants were unaffected by the change of landlord, although the local bailiff, who held the responsibility for bringing in the rents from a geographical group of estates, may well have been a new face. The system of beneficial rents, by which the annual sum due to a landlord was fixed almost in perpetuity, had been in operation for many years, and meant that there was no fear of a sudden rise. Only the seven-yearly survey and the subsequent entry fine could cause difficulties, but this was a long way off and tenants seem to have been content to carry on as before.

The administration of Christ Church's estates continued on similar lines to those laid down in the statutes for Cardinal and King Henry VIII colleges: canons who had family connections or a particular interest in an area of the country appear to have taken responsibility for that portion of the estate. Progresses were still part and parcel of the land management strategy, and the responsibility of tenants to pay for the provision of bed and board for college officials and their horses was often written into deeds. On a day-to-day basis, senior men and messengers travelled backwards and forwards between Christ Church and the estates; the 1548 disbursements record Alexander Belsyre's trip to Wallingford, with companions, to take possession of a new house there and to sign all the documentation.[40] Expenses for 'law and journeys' soon become regular entries in the disbursements.

Once the living-in arrangements were settled, the real business of the college began: the education of young men. Although the curriculum was laid down, and the reading necessary to pass examinations was accepted by everyone, the arrangement between pupil and tutor was largely private. The

Chapter Books include lists from 1550 showing the names of the senior men who were qualified and entitled to take pupils, and the men they were teaching. Those considered able to teach had to sign a formal agreement.[41] Most tutors had one or two pupils but a few attracted a greater following. Richard Marshall, soon to be vice-chancellor of the university and dean of Christ Church, had six pupils, and Christopher Goodman, the active reformer who had to flee England on the accession of Mary Tudor, had five. The most junior of the tutors – Edward Beaumont, who was 19 and only just in receipt of his own BA – was well down the list of second-class *philosophi*, breaking the rule, almost as soon as it was written, that tutors should be either a *theologus* or one of the first order of *philosophi*. Young graduates were expected to take pupils very quickly. Many needed to, in order to fund their own progress towards their Masters degrees and beyond. But there were complaints, almost from the start, that some of the Students were idle, funded by the estates, and that those who had incumbencies provided by the Dean and Chapter were ignoring their responsibilities and living out their lives at ease.[42]

Although there are very few records about the teaching and examination process in these early days, there are a few clues that the central business of education was under way. On 5 October 1550, a dozen scholars at the end of their second year were examined by Censors Edward Cratford and Christopher Goodman. Only one, Herbert Westphaling, appears to have shown any real proficiency.[43] Lectures in Hall and disputations for all degrees above BA were a daily occurrence. These were laid down in the statutes for Cardinal College and seem to have been instituted by Dean Cox in much the way that Wolsey had intended. Pupils were expected to come prepared to answer questions on the previous day's lectures[44] on subjects that included theology, philosophy both moral and natural, rhetoric, law, mathematics and dialectic.

The subjects for discussion were often topical and at the cutting edge of religious and scientific reasoning. In its early years, Christ Church was full of notable and scholarly men from all disciplines and from both sides of the religious divide, so lectures and debates must have been lively and inspirational. Peter Martyr, for example, was an extraordinary scholar from Florence, the son of a shoemaker, who learnt Latin from his mother, taught himself Greek, and studied the Aristotelian and humanist principles that were to be so influential in Oxford. Martyr was a man of renown. Coming to England at the end of his flight across Europe, he was appointed, in 1548, regius professor of divinity and went head-to-head with William Tresham, that sole survivor from both Cardinal and King Henry VIII colleges. Their point of disagreement was the Eucharist, Tresham holding out for the Catholic view of the real presence of Christ in the sacrament, and Martyr for the more Protestant doctrine that the ceremony was symbolic. The debate, both the formal occasion and the inevitable talk it must have inspired in the quads and tutorials of Christ Church, had a less than satisfactory outcome for both men. Martyr left Oxford to escape the backlash of the 1549 Prayer Book rebellion, and in 1551 Tresham found himself in the Fleet prison, unpopular with Edward VI for his conservative views.[45] Bernard Gilpin, the 'apostle of the north', was another clergyman who, like Martyr, had read and thought his way out of Catholicism. A powerful preacher, he lectured against clerical abuses and against anything that he saw as an injustice against ordinary men such as rack renting, engrossing and enclosure. Christopher Goodman, part of Martyr's circle and Lady Margaret professor of divinity, was another radical thinker who spent Mary's reign either on the continent or in Scotland.[46] Laurence Nowell and George Etheridge were the first natural philosophers on the foundation; Nowell was lecturer in mathematics, and went on to be a renowned cartographer and antiquarian, while Etheridge published a text book of medicine and pharmacology.[47]

The only book that new undergraduates were required to bring with them was Leo Judas's translation into Latin of the Psalms. This was part of the Zurich or Zwingli bible, printed by Christopher Froschauer between 1525 and 1531.[48] It was assumed that 'essentials', such as the catechism and the basic order of service, had been learnt by heart as children, and the basic premises of the discussions raging around them would have been familiar even to the youngest undergraduates. There was no library at Christ Church until the early 1560s, so texts needed for their studies had to be bought, new or second-hand, or borrowed from tutor, friend or home. Booksellers and bookbinders were prolific in the university town, but the names of Oxford suppliers appear in relatively small numbers in college accounts. Magdalen

College, for example, appears to have made most of its purchases in London.[49] The cathedral, which had, of course, been operating as a priory church for many centuries, had to adapt to its new role and new books were purchased, including ten new psalters. In 1549, chains were bought for a 'paraphrasis'. Mr Hether was paid for 'prycking [or copying] of the buriall service eight tymes in sundry places', and Mr Gore supplied two new service books.[50]

Expectations of decent behaviour were as high at Christ Church as they had been at Cardinal College. Moderation in attire had been addressed both by Wolsey and by the University.[51] The rules, which seem to have been honoured more in the breach, were part of the Crown and Court's obsession with status and rank, and the ordering of society. The regulations laid down for Cardinal College were, no doubt, continued, with strict stipulations about the colour and cost of a Student's dress. Every year, the disbursements conclude with the payments for liveries.[52]

Although chambers were provided – rarely did members live outside the walls – it was expected that men bring their own bedding. Wolsey had evidently intended that a senior and a junior member would share a room, but whether this was ever necessary at Christ Church is unlikely, as its large site included Peckwater Inn, the buildings of Canterbury College, the remaining priory buildings, the three-quarters of Tom Quad that had been completed, and the use of Broadgates Hall (now Pembroke College) as an annexe for commoners. Certainly, by the end of the sixteenth century, only the canons in their large residences would have taken in pupils as lodgers.[53]

By 1550, therefore, the college and cathedral were operating much as they would for the next 300 years. Men were taught and examined; the estates were being administered by the dean and canons, and by their agents in the field; and some pupils, like William Whittingham, were already taking leave of absence to travel to broaden their horizons in universities overseas.[54] Even the buildings stayed much the same for at least 50 years apart from tidying up and running repairs; the Great Quadrangle remained three-sided with no gatehouse tower, the medieval Peckwater Inn continued to be used as undergraduate accommodation, the cathedral stood peculiarly truncated and isolated behind the east side of the quad, and the old priory and Canterbury College buildings remained in use for years to come.

'To perfect the college ...': Christ Church and charity[1]

When Wolsey founded Cardinal College in 1525, he began to build a hospital on the other side of St Aldates for thirteen poor men with one female housekeeper. Each resident was to receive 20 shillings each year with clothes, commons and fuel. After Wolsey's fall, Henry VIII continued the plan, first making provision for 12 honest paupers and then, in 1546, increasing the number to 24, each receiving £6 per annum. It was part of Henry's wider plan that all his new cathedral foundations, and Trinity College in Cambridge, should maintain a body of almsmen, and this was laid down in the covenants for his new college, written in October 1546, just before the formal foundation of Christ Church. The almshouse across the road accommodated around half of the men, probably the thirteen that Wolsey had first envisaged. The others lived out, in town, often with wives and families.[2]

Traditionally, the men were retired soldiers or sailors, their patents of admission often detailing service in the conflicts of early modern and modern Europe.[3] Thomas Brickland, admitted in 1720, had received wounds as a corporal in the regiment of Major-General Evans; John King (1736) served in eleven campaigns in Flanders and had 'grown ancient and uncapable of further service'. Charles Lewis, whose patent is dated October 1873, had served 20 years and 27 days in the 68th Regiment of Light Infantry, and had been awarded the Crimean Medal with clasps for the battles at Alma, Balaklava, Inkerman and Sebastopol. One or two men had performed other

> The form of the almsmen's patent has remained the same for 450 years. The earliest surviving is that of John Brassard, dated 15 December 1622, although there is an earlier version, dated 1604, transcribed into the sub-dean's book. Each patent is signed by the monarch and by the Principal Secretary of State (to 1782) or the Home Secretary. Brassard seems to have been one of the unfortunate men who died before a place became available.

forms of national service, notably William Gates and John Bresson, who had worked in the royal kitchens of Elizabeth I.[4] Not all the men were dependent on charity; in the wills of some were inventories including household possessions such as furniture, linen, kitchen equipment and tableware. One of the earliest almsmen, Nicholas Padgett, left a property of at least six rooms, two horses and a cow.[5] John Wykyns bequeathed his fire-irons to the dean, and a length of worsted to one of the lay clerks, John Scott. Everything else he possessed was divided between the other resident almsmen, a poor woman living in 'St Owles church house', and various Christ Church servants including Sylvester Tennant, the Porter and Wykyns's executor.[6]

The almsmen were granted their places by the Crown, usually on the recommendation of the dean. Francis Atterbury, that notoriously difficult and absentee dean, received a complaint from the Chapter in April 1712 concerning his neglect of college business, including his failure to fill two vacant places in the almshouse.[7] Until the nineteenth century, it was common for men to receive their patents before a place was actually available, and a waiting list was kept by the sub-dean at least from 1551 until the Civil War. If their need was particularly great, some men received alms in the meantime, and some unfortunately died before a room was free. Waiting time was usually around three years, although this could be much longer; John Norris, for example, was given his patent on 17 December 1563; finally admitted in 1570, he stayed in the almshouse for 28 years. Poor William Bodington, who was admitted in 1561 after an eight-year delay, died within a few months.

During the Civil War, nomination to almsmen's places was conducted

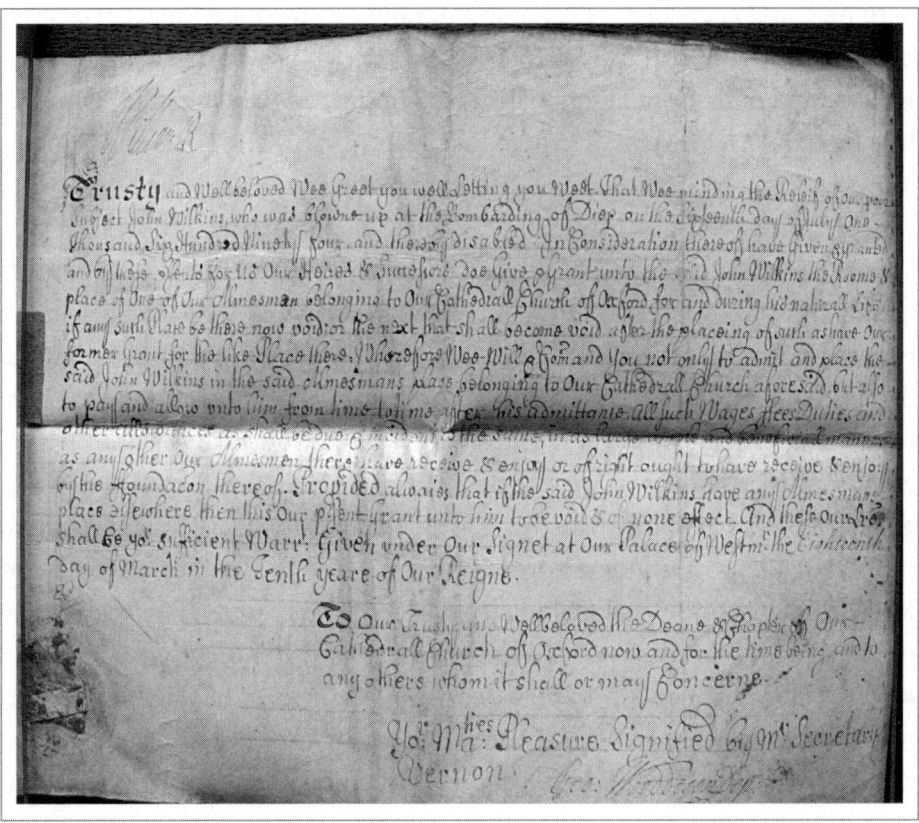

Each man nominated for a place in the almshouse received a patent from the monarch. John Wilkins had received injuries at the bombardment of Dieppe in 1694. He had to wait four years for a vacancy but, once in, Wilkins remained here until his death in 1751.

by the Committee for Public Revenue, and men who served the parliamentary cause were, unsurprisingly, given preference. In 1660, however, Charles II directed the Dean and Chapter to purge the almshouse of those occupants who had been improperly installed, and to return any evictees to their rightful places. His letter alleged that rooms had been given to men 'that either are noe Souldiers at all, or if they be Souldiers, they are such as never served either the King our Father or is, and are neither impotent or wounded persons; whilst others that have lost their blood and their Limbs in our Fathers and Our owne service, goe begging up and downe the streets both here and at Oxford.'[8] Everyone claiming an almsman's place was summoned to the Audit House on 15 October 1660 to prove their right. It must have been a difficult meeting, with every man who held a patent, whoever had signed it, feeling that his room had been earned. The Dean and Chapter drew up a report, and expelled sixteen men. Eight were allowed to stay, six restored and a new group of eight chosen to make up the numbers.

How the men who lived in the almshouse occupied their time is difficult to say. In other cathedral foundations, the men often worked as cleaners or bell-ringers, and their uniforms served to identify them and encourage diligence. At Christ Church, though, no such tasks were allocated. There were rules, of course, the first set of which can be found in the draft Henrician statutes. All the men were to come to all services, begowned and in one group. They were to do anything that the dean or college officers required of them. Quietness and good order were expected at all times. A curfew of 8 pm in winter and 9 pm in summer was to be kept, and when they did go out it was to be in pairs at least (unless they were visiting their wives) and only to honest places. At no time were the almsmen to be idle. But no specific tasks were ever given to the men to do and abuses were rife almost from the outset. When tenures were very long – nineteen men were resident for over 26 years, and three of those for over 50 – it is hardly surprising that some of the bedesmen found use for their idle hands.[9] In 1723, part of the almshouse was being used as a brewhouse. Although the Dean and Chapter gave the entrepreneur six months to cease his trade, he was evidently still working out of his rooms six years later. At about the same time, John Crozier and Christopher Taylor were caught selling strong liquor, and were severely reprimanded but avoided expulsion. Charles Pritchard, however, was less fortunate. By some fraudulent means, he had actually persuaded one of the commoner undergraduates of Christ Church, Robert Hacker, to marry his daughter. The censors seem to have discovered the plot in the nick of time, and Pritchard was expelled from the almshouse with only a week to clear out his belongings and find new accommodation. Both Pritchard and Hacker soon left Oxford. The affair must have prompted a review of the almshouse, for two more residents were reprimanded on the same day for 'selling jeneva and other strong liquors'.[10]

By the nineteenth century, Pembroke College, on to whose property the almshouse backed, were finding their neighbours less than appealing. New rules were laid down by the Dean and Chapter in the hope that behaviour and cleanliness could be improved, but it became increasingly obvious that the place was an embarrassment. It was also rather dilapidated. Debates raged about the future of both the building and the almsmen. Some argued that the house should be sold to Pembroke College, who made overtures in 1829 about purchasing the site for their new college chapel. John Bull, the Treasurer, thoroughly approved. The almshouse, he said, 'with the exception of two or three apartments all are very filthy, and despite of repeated orders company of a very questionable character are to be often found there'.[11] A new almshouse could be built on the site of the stable block on the Christ Church side of St Aldates. Others wanted to see the whole idea of the almsmen abandoned altogether. In the end, neither happened, the first as it was too expensive, the latter because the Charity Commission said no. Legal advice was that the almshouse could not be sold, and that the consent of the Crown would be required to remove the almsmen, even if new rooms were provided. As the expense of an Act of Parliament made the whole exercise prohibitive, the Dean and Chapter decided to repair the building. The total cost of the work done by John Hudson – including a new north front, new plumbing, repairs to the roof, new chimneys and new gables – came to £1,346 6s 11½d. Fourteen new kitchen ranges were installed and new rules laid down about keeping the rooms and staircases clean.[12] Although the restoration may have made the building more respectable and acceptable to the neighbours, it did nothing to make a decision over the almsmen themselves any easier. In spite of suggestions by the Cathedrals Commission that bedesmen be integrated more into the lives of their cathedrals, the relationship of the Christ Church almsmen and the college became increasingly distant. By 1867, a proposal was on the table to increase the almsmen's pension in exchange for their vacation of the premises.

Canon Payne Smith was practical: no lodgings could be found in town for less than £14 a year and it would be wrong to evict the almsmen with neither compensation nor the ability to support themselves. But only £10 was offered; not a generous offer in the light of the stipends paid to other almsmen in other cathedrals.[13] The paltry offer prompted the almsmen to petition the queen, an action that achieved little. The Charity Commission now decided that they had no jurisdiction over the almshouse as it was part of a cathedral foundation. If Christ Church had been a conventional college, things would have been different, but as it was, the almsmen lost their case. In 1868, a new stipend of £16 per annum was agreed for all new almsmen, all of whom would live out, and rooms were gradually shut up as the resident almsmen either died or moved out. Seven years later, the few men remaining successfully negotiated the £16 allowance for themselves with the proviso that they vacated the premises by March 1876.[14]

Thomas Vere Bayne, Student and diligent college administrator, objected violently, but in vain, to the loss of the almshouse. He argued, in a printed document sent to the Governing Body, that the proposal was as bad for Christ Church as had been England's loss of Calais, and that every Christ Church man passing through Tom Gate would be reminded of the cession of one of its foundation properties.[15] At first, the building was converted into a residence for Faussett, the Treasurer, and then, just a few years later in 1888, was finally sold to Pembroke College.

Today, almsmen are still appointed, usually to honour long service to the college or cathedral, and the patent is still issued by the Crown. Efforts are in hand to change the rules so that women may be appointed, and to ensure that the tradition that almspeople are from the forces is not a rule.

* * * * *

The almsmen were not the only recipients of the Dean and Chapter's charity. All through the disbursement books, the Chapter Books, and the Governing Body minutes, there are entries recording donations to a tremendous variety of causes. The covenants attached to the terms of the foundation, require the Dean and Chapter '... to distribute yerelie for ever in almes emongest the povertie within the towne and universitie of Oxforde the some of £20 unlesse the[y] shalbe commanded and appointed to the contrarie by the kinges majestie as [sic] suche as his highnes commissioners as shalbe

The provision for almsmen was part of Henry VIII's plan for all his new cathedrals. One of the covenants made in 1546 stipulated that 24 men, traditionally old soldiers or sailors, would receive lodgings and a small stipend from the college's endowment. They lived in the almshouse opposite Tom Gate until the late nineteenth century when the building was converted first into a residence for the Treasurer, and was then sold to Pembroke College in 1888.

any tyme appointed for that purpose'.[16] The fragmentary first disbursement book records the distribution of £6 18s 2d in 1548 to 'pore folke' who were chosen by the 'churchmen' or two honest men in each parish in the city: Marjorie, who worked in the kitchen, received a new frock, hose and shoes; Mother Frye who was bed-ridden was given some financial assistance; and medical aid was provided for a poor boy whose arms were out of joint 'by chyming' – presumably bell-ringing in the cathedral.[17]

The earliest almsgiving was relatively domestic, but it gradually began to extend far beyond the boundaries of Oxford and the University, occasionally to quite exotic locations and people, others local but no less intriguing. In 1578, a mariner from Yarmouth with a passport to Cornwall was given 2s 6d, and an 'outlandish gentleman' was granted 6s 8d in 1600.[18] Three servitors in the same year were given £1 for being 'troubled in conscience for hanging a dog on the Sabbath day,' and it seems to have been common in the late sixteenth century for the poor to stand at the bottom of the Hall stairs hoping for alms.[19] Educational establishments were frequent recipients: in the 1660s, students from Piedmont were given a few pounds each term by arrangement with the university, and a donation was given to the University of Aberdeen.[20] Much later, in 1828, a contribution of £250 was made towards the establishment of King's College, London.[21] Frequent contributions were made for the building of new schools in Christ Church's parishes, partly as aid and partly to uphold the influence of the Anglican church in an increasingly non-conformist country. Almost as rewards, converts to Anglican Protestantism were helped, too; Beta Shemuell, a converted Jew, was given £1 in 1664, and Solomon Franco £2 just two years later.[22] Signor Dandalo, presumably a convert from Roman Catholicism, was granted £5.[23]

The deserving poor were high on the list for donations, too. One lady received a gift towards the bonding of her son to an apprenticeship in 1662, and a poor tailor who had a sick wife and children to support was assisted. The harshness of particularly cold winters, such as those in the early nineteenth century, was eased by contributions to special funds.[24] The Irish were sent donations to help them through the potato famine, and in 1854 the 'Patriotic Fund for the Widows and Orphans of Soldiers and Sailors who may fall in the present War' received £100 from the dean and canons' private account.[25] A pauper lunatic asylum in Denbigh was sent £50 in 1843.[26] Victims of disasters received help, such as the cities ruined by earthquakes in Syria in 1823, and churches abroad, as well as those at home, were also beneficiaries. In 1660, £10 was sent to the churches of Lithuania, and the same for the relief of the Strasbourg Protestants.[27] An appeal for an English church in Amsterdam was received in 1827 and benefited to the tune of £46 8s 6d, not long after a contribution had been made for a church in Rotterdam.[28]

Even the possibly non-deserving – the prisoners in the castle jail – received regular doles of meat. In 1849, the magistrates asked the Dean and Chapter to commute the benefaction into money so that the strict regulations concerning the diet of felons could be met. The Chapter was reluctant at first; the origin of the dole was uncertain, and they were unsure how a

'To perfect the college ...': Christ Church and charity

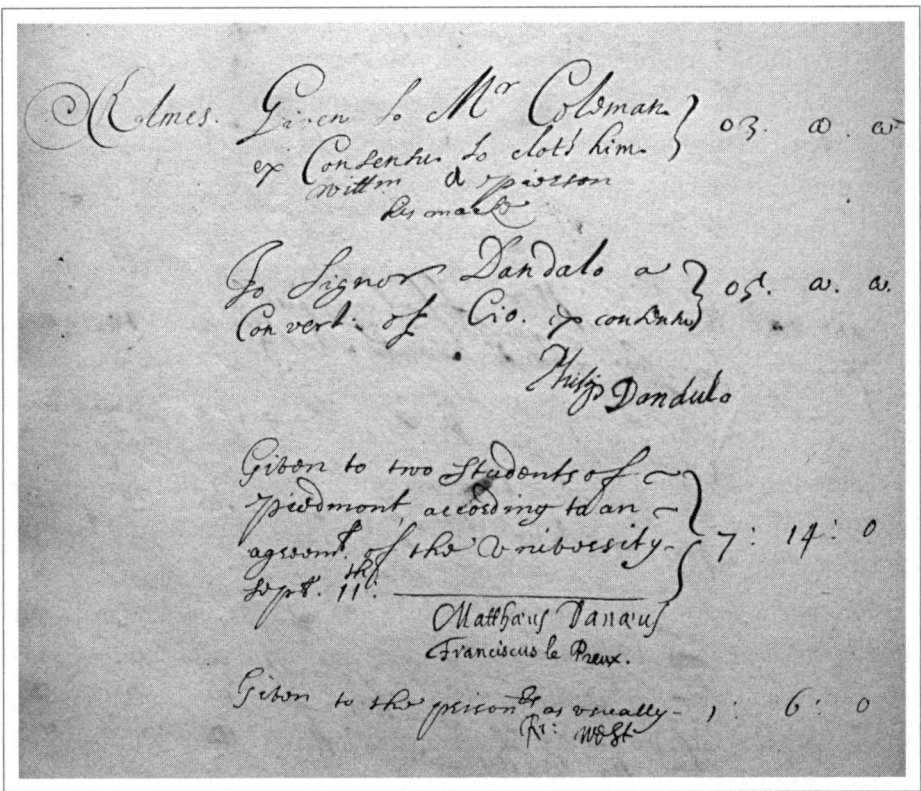

Aside from the almsmen, the Dean and Chapter regularly gave to deserving, and sometimes not-so-deserving, causes. This entry from the 1660 disbursement book records donations to Mr Coleman for new clothes, to Signor Dandalo, a Catholic convert, to students from Piedmont, and the regular dole to the prisoners in Oxford castle.

money gift would be used. But they agreed to the commutation on being assured that it would be paid to the governor and entered into a book called 'the commuted benefaction book'.[29]

In modern times, charitable giving continues, focusing still on causes within Oxford and the University, but benefiting people further away, too. The educational theme is followed with donations to local schools and playgroups in Christ Church parishes as before, but also to research foundations, overseas ventures, academic institutions, youth clubs, museums and libraries. Hospitals, hospices and charities working with victims of illness or crime are in the list of bodies assisted, and organisations working for the preservation of buildings, manuscripts and even wildlife.

But it is not just the Chapter or the Governing Body that have worked for charity. The junior members have always played their part, too. In 1961, for example, a spectacular concert was held in Tom Quad in aid of famine relief. The City of Birmingham Symphony Orchestra, the trumpeters of the Blues and Royals, the Oxford Society of Change Ringers, the band of the 15th/19th the King's Royal Hussars and the Christ Church organist all came together in an outdoor performance commencing with the march from *Aida* and culminating in the *1812 Overture* complete with cannon loaned by Sandhurst.[30] Less noisily, in 1971, nine undergraduates made an expedition from Oxford to Cambridge by punt to raise £1,000 for Shelter, travelling along the Thames, the Thame, the Grand Union Canal and the Ouse, arriving, nearly two weeks later, on the river Cam.

In recent years, one of the main focuses of giving is Oval House. Beginning as the Poplar Mission in the East End for boys from poor families, Oval House now concentrates on music, dance and drama, and works with young people who have been excluded from school to help them back into education or training.[31]

3

'Untyll suche tyme that it shall please the Kynge ...': 1553–1625

Just as Christ Church had settled down into some sort of routine, despatching overseas its more troublesome members such as William Whittingham, the young Edward VI died, his attempts to ratify statutes for the foundation floundering in red tape, and his reforming appointments short-lived. It was not just Peter Martyr who caused controversy; his wife, Catherine Dampmartin, once a nun before her conversion and marriage, also became the focus of anti-Protestant opinion in the city. The citizens of Oxford disapproved of women in the colleges, and there were still doubts about the legitimacy of clerical marriages. When the Martyrs' lodgings, overlooking St Aldates, were pelted with stones and the couple subjected to continual disturbance, they moved to the Priory House, deep inside the walls of Christ Church. But soon after, in February 1553, Catherine died and was buried in the cathedral. On Mary's accession, in July 1553, Martyr fled to the continent, and Catherine's remains, buried close to those of revered St Frideswide, were thrown on to the Deanery dungheap by order of Cardinal Pole.[1] A new phase had begun for the young college.

A college founded by Henry VIII and brought into being by his still more radical son was full of reformers, so Mary's accession saw a change in personnel: ardent Protestants like Cox and Martyr departed, passing others on their way back in. George Etheridge, the Catholic professor of Greek, who had left after the visitation of 1550, returned. Thomas Bernard, however,

> ## St John's College
>
> It was during Mary's reign that the Dean and Chapter drew up an agreement granting Bernard College to Sir Thomas White – for a rent of 20 shillings – so that he could found a college for the maintenance of virtue and good learning. It was the 'hartelye desire' of the Dean and Chapter that the heads of the college should be either members of Christ Church or at least fellows approved by the Chapter. White was given three years, until the feast of St Andrew 1557, to erect his college, after which time, if the conditions were not fulfilled, the site would revert to Christ Church. By this date there had to be at least six persons in the new college, and an endowment of 300 marks.
>
> The quit rent of 20 shillings was redeemed in 1876, and St John's choice of president no longer requires the approval of Christ Church.
>
> MS Estates 121, ff.204–16

who had demonstrated his reformist leanings by whitewashing the walls of his church in Pyrton and by replacing the altar with a communion table, was ousted and replaced by Richard Marshall, who took not just Bernard's living but Cox's place as dean, too.[2] James Calfhill, a Student deprived of his place in 1554, described Marshall as a man of drunken habits and a fanatical temper fit, no doubt, to perform both the exhumation of Catherine Martyr and the degradation of Archbishop Thomas Cranmer in or near the cathedral on 14 February 1556.[3]

However unpleasant Marshall may have been as a person, Mary's relationship with Oxford and with Christ Church was generally good. To ensure that the university stayed faithful, she invested both money and good will, and turned, if not a blind eye, then certainly an unseeing one, to the sudden absence of many academics.[4] Christ Church benefited financially when Mary finally settled the long debate with Edward VI over the shortfall in his father's promised endowment, the rectory of Tring being granted by Letters Patent signed on 7 July 1554.[5]

Under Edward's sister, although everyday administration continued in spite of the religious turmoil, statutes for an Oxford college, already apparently running quite smoothly, were not high on the agenda. Without doubt, Mary intended to complete her father's and brother's work. A letter dated 1 September 1554, from John Mason, chancellor of the University, admonished the Students for their disobedience to the dean and the sub-dean, and obliged them to 'kepe and observe as Statutes (decrees made by the Dean and Chappiter) untyll suche tyme that it shall please the Kynge and the Quenes hieghnes to sende you statutes Indented according to the foundac[i]on of that Churche'.[6] A further letter from Reginald Pole, Mason's successor as chancellor, confirms the intent.[7]

The statutes never did appear, but Mary was evidently determined to keep control. New, or confirmatory, decrees were laid down concerning all aspects of Christ Church life: for the ministers in the church, for the conduct and attendance at services, on disputations and lectures, on conversation during meals, on academic exercises, on residence and absence and on ordination.[8] An inventory of the elaborate vestments of embroidered velvet and damask kept in the cathedral was drawn up in July 1556, which included, at the end, silver items such as crosses, verges, cases for the corporal cloth and a thurible.[9] Even the plays that were performed at Christmas were controlled: there were to be only two comedies, for which no more than 20 shillings each was permitted, and two tragedies at 40 shillings per play. One of each had to be in Latin, the others in Greek.[10] But it was not all doom and gloom: at Christmas 1554, the dean dined in Hall and was entertained by four pipers, and on New Year's Day following, when Sir Thomas White and Alderman Atkins were guests, the meal was accompanied by four pipers and a trumpeter.[11]

No minute survives to record the accession of Elizabeth; one assumes that the bells were rung and a general celebration held, as there would have been for any new monarch. But just five years since the last, there was yet another round of personnel changes. At the top of the tree, the drunken Marshall was replaced by George Carew. Carew seems to have been a man who could play the game: having been chaplain to Edward VI, it looked as though he would suffer under the Marian regime but, after a rocky start, he

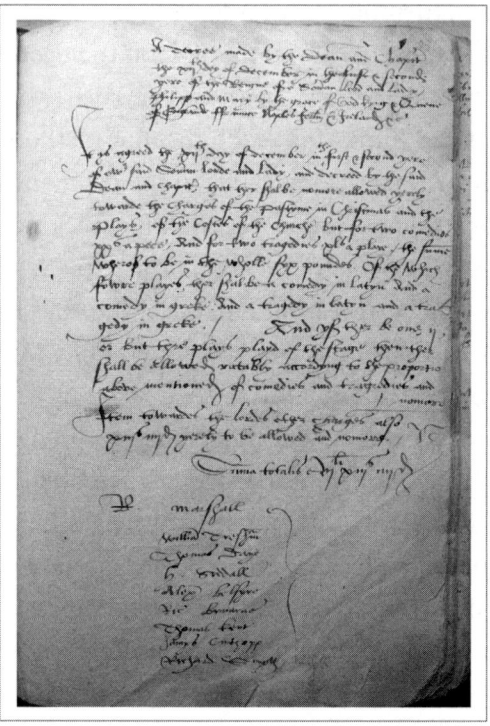

Expenditure on plays and Christmas entertainments was curbed by Mary Tudor. There were to be two comedies and two tragedies at the most, one of each in Latin and one in Greek. Comedies were to cost less than tragedies.

managed to persuade Mary that his loyalty was always first to the Crown. Elizabeth saw Carew as a safe and untainted pair of hands, and placed him at the head of Christ Church, gave him the deanery of the Chapel Royal, and restored to him his deanery in Bristol.[12] Little is recorded anywhere in the archive about this period; the results of the annual elections are not written into the Chapter Books between 1555 and 1561, and only two Chapter decrees are recorded, one confirming the teaching of Greek, and the other ensuring a pay rise for John Blithman, a loyal and hardworking chaplain in the cathedral.[13] But, after the resignation of Carew in 1561, soon after his appointment as dean of Windsor, his replacement by the rather more Protestant Thomas Sampson, and with the appointment of Robert Dudley, Earl of Leicester, as chancellor, in December 1564, things began to progress.[14]

> ## Students
>
> Of the Students elected to Christ Church each year only four or so were Westminster Students. The remainder were **Canoneer** Students, nominated to their positions by a member of the Chapter. The dean had two nominations per year, and the canons one each, a form of patronage that was well used and much cherished. It was not uncommon for young men to be nominated long before there was a place available, and many came up as commoners first, sometimes for a few months, occasionally for several years, before they could receive their stipends. Thomas Torporley, who came up in 1571, was desperately worried about his financial position before his Studentship came through (MS Harley 416, f.189). A new roll of nominees was drawn up regularly, and recorded, particularly during the eighteenth century, in the chapter books.
>
> Four of the 100 Students were known as **Faculty Students** who were permitted to hold their positions without the need to be ordained. Two were lawyers and two physicians. A fifth was added in 1665 – the **Thurston** Studentship – which increased the number of Students to the famous 101.
>
> One other 'named' Studentship was the **Vernon**. In a dispute over the right to present to the living of Rostherne in Cheshire, Christ Church allowed the Venables family, from 1601, to nominate to a Studentship in exchange for the presentation of Christ Church men to the parish.

Sampson's deanery underlined Christ Church's position as a centre for reforming thought. One of his first acts was to remove all surviving traces of Catholicism from the cathedral. He refused to wear clerical vestments, a decision that would cost him, in 1565, his position at Christ Church and for a short while put him in prison.[15] Sampson was, however, a good administrator and a scholar, and one of the most significant and long-lived results of his period of office was the creation of the Westminster Studentships. Links with Westminster, and other schools, had been laid down in the draft statutes, but never truly established.[16] Other colleges had links with specific schools – New College with Winchester, for example – but it was not until 1561 that Elizabeth I set aside awards from Westminster School to be tenable at Christ Church and its sister college, Trinity, in Cambridge. A number of Students, usually four each year, were chosen on the basis of an oral examination, held on the second Monday of Easter term, before the dean of Christ Church, and the master of Trinity College.[17] Candidates were allowed to express a preference for either Oxford or Cambridge by addressing, in Latin, the head of whichever college he had selected. If an election was in dispute, then the other members of the electoral panel – the dean of Westminster, the headmaster of Westminster School, and, occasionally, the regius professor of divinity – had casting votes. Studentships were often given to those in financial need, but there was no real advantage to being a Westminster Student, as opposed to an ordinary or 'canoneer' Student, until the eighteenth century, when various trusts were set up in these Students' favour.[18] There were irregularities from time to time, however. Westminster Students were often chosen in the summer but were not formally admitted to their places until the Christmas election. In 1594, it was noticed that some had been receiving their stipends before Christmas. An order was immediately given that 'every one of these hereafter to be admitted shall both pay for his commons and receive nether wages nor liverye untill the Christmas following his sayd admission excepted only those that shall be admitted at Christmas time'.[19]

At the same time as Elizabeth was establishing the Westminster Studentships, Christ Church began to create a library for the burgeoning academic body. There is no documentary evidence in the archives for the foundation of the library, either in the Chapter books or in the accounts. But there is evidence that an appeal was made at some time around 1561 or 1562 for funds or donations.

The new library was set up in the former refectory of St Frideswide's priory, a late fifteenth-century hall which stands on the south side of the cloister, close to the cathedral. It was fitted with wooden lecterns, like others of its period, which Christ Church, with its eye for a bargain, purchased second-hand at some time in the late 1550s or early 1560s from the derelict medieval University library.[20] The books were chained, and were mostly large Latin folios on theology and patristics. There were very few books in

English, it would seem, until Tobie Matthew, probably on his appointment as dean in 1576, presented a copy of John Foxe's *Acts and Monuments* (or the '*Book of Martyrs*'). Matthew was an ardent supporter of the library, giving several books himself, and encouraging others to do so.[21]

Sampson was credited with keeping Christ Church solvent, but the archives only show a few minor financial decisions, including a new payment for the Censor Theologiae for his office, and an allowance for the auditor.[22] It was under his headship, too, that Catherine Martyr was re-interred in the cathedral, as were the newly discovered bones of St Frideswide.[23] Decrees were made concerning absence from Oxford, and fines – usually a month's commons (the cost of one's keep) – were put in place for those who defaulted on their exercises or declamations.[24]

Throughout the 1560s and 1570s, there was a constant battle in Christ Church and across the whole University to bring behaviour into line. Leicester, even before his appointment as chancellor, had strong links with the university, and particularly Christ Church, supporting Sampson's appointment as dean. Two matters worried Leicester mightily: the conduct of academic exercises, and the standard of dress among members of the university.[25] In Christ Church, new regulations were laid down, or old ones re-stated, on these two problems, and on many others.[26] Fines and sanctions were put in place for not attending church, or learning one's catechism, and for misbehaviour in Hall. The butler, manciple and cook were given strict rules about stock control, the sourcing of foodstuffs and the numbers of staff they could employ. It would seem that backhanders and nepotism were rife.

Absenteeism may have been common, too; 'Often there is doubt between the officers and the company about the dates of term ...', said the Dean and Chapter in May 1577. University term dates were to be followed, with the Natural Philosophy Reader giving his lectures on Mondays, Wednesdays and Fridays, and the Moral Philosophy Reader on Tuesdays, Thursdays and Saturdays. Masters were to begin their disputations and lectures in the first week of full term. The Bible must be read by masters every Monday, Wednesday and Friday, and the rhetoric readers must begin to read on the first day of every term continuing to the last. Any default was liable for removal from office.[27] Any leave from college had to be recorded by the sub-dean.[28]

Overdue payment of battels bills (costs of lodgings and provisions) was evidently just as much of a problem in the sixteenth century as it has ever been. In 1577, it was laid down that no commoner was permitted to take commons unless his debts were cleared, and no bachelors could add to their debts without the bond of either a senior college man or 'some substantial person in the towne'.[29]

These, although not minor concerns, were not where Leicester's real influence lay. His closeness to the queen gave him tremendous scope to recommend his men for positions either of power or value. At Christ Church alone, Sampson's and William James's appointments to the deanery (in 1561 and 1584 respectively) were the result of Leicester's influence, and it was through Leicester that the controversial Spanish theologian Antonio del Corro was eventually granted his doctorate (notwithstanding his alleged heretical views), and appointed to a lectureship with the Censorship Theologiae.[30]

Leicester died in 1588, but his successors were equally active. He was replaced first by Christopher Hatton, during whose short term in office the frequency of Chapter meetings was regularised, and then by Thomas Sackville, Lord Buckhurst, in 1592.[31] Buckhurst, Archbishop Whitgift, and the Lord Keeper of the Great Seal, Sir John Puckering, used their considerable powers to reprimand misbehaviour. In 1595, the Students of Christ Church complained that their daily ration of bread had been reduced to a mere nine ounces a day, but their petition received short shrift. The Students were required to apologise to the Chapter for their disorderly conduct during the controversy and were told to be content with their lot:

> ... during this dearth of Corne, and untill upon consideration of the fall of Corne, their Lordships shall otherwise determine, everie of the Students of the said Cathedrall Church shall hereafter at everie meale been allowed onlie and soe content themselves with the rate of nyne ounces weight, as it cometh furth of the Oven, of well baked wholsome bread of wheat for one man ... [32]

The dispute prompted another reciting of orders, especially with a view to frugality in a difficult economic period. On 11 April 1595, the Dean and

> ## Eedes v. Ravis
>
> Although his name appears in the archives on occasions as the queen's representative in the University, it is in the choice of William James's successor as dean that Buckhurst is probably best known. Buckhurst's rivalry with Essex, the Queen's new favourite, reared its head even in this arena. Buckhurst wanted Thomas Ravis, but Essex preferred Richard Eedes. Either man would probably have been acceptable: both were academic, senior clerics and courtiers. Ravis was probably the better administrator whereas Eedes had the jollier reputation of playwright and poet. Eedes was also related to Essex. Only Cecil, Elizabeth's long-standing and trusted adviser, probably with the support of Archbishop Whitgift, saved Buckhurst from an ignominious defeat. Ravis was duly appointed in June 1596 with Eedes receiving the deanery of Worcester.
>
> ODNB

Chapter issued 'Orders revived and published for the better government of Christchurch in Oxford'. The decrees reiterated that old orders concerning church services, academic exercises and domestic arrangements were to be 'executed as they were entended'. Thrift and frugality were encouraged; leave from college was regulated, whether just into town or on longer absences; and the costs of alterations to the canons' lodgings had to be approved by Chapter. Perhaps most significant, however, was the acknowledgement that the Students' protests might have had some justification. The seventh decree announced that:

> for the better encouragement & maintenance of the students, whose commons is not so sufficient as is to be wished, yet much better then it was in former tymes, in manner doubled, it is voluntarily yeilded unto and agreed uppon by the deane and Chapter that all the improvements of rents by vertue of a statute & all the rents of the grounds of Bynsey with all such provision of beefe and mutton as shall feede in the tymber yard & Chandons (saving such as shalbe for the necessarie use of the Canons table) shalbe wholly remployed in the students

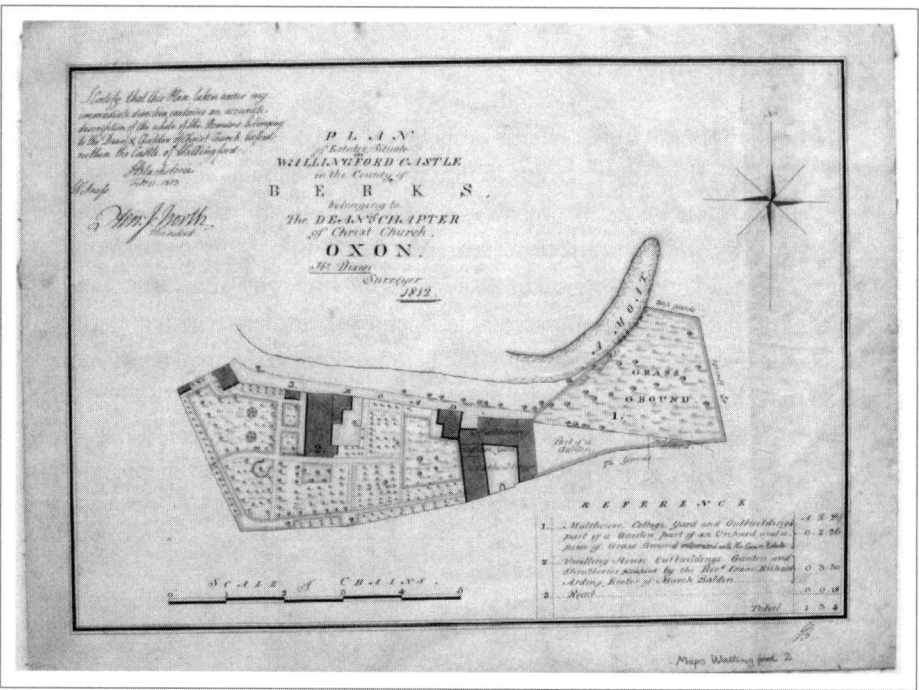

The site of the chapel of St Nicholas within the bounds of Wallingford Castle was purchased by the Dean and Chapter in 1548 as a refuge from plague, far enough away from danger, but close enough to allow business to continue. This plan is early nineteenth-century, drawn just before the sale of the property, and clearly shows the extent of the buildings.

commons, untill such tyme as by vertue of the saide statute or otherwise the commons of ancient tymes allowed shalbe doubled at dinner & supper throughout the yeere and then a convenient portion to be allotted to the deane and the prebendaries table and other uses as especially to save decrements.

Item it is also ordered that yeerly hereafter the Treasurer provide in Aprill or the beginning of May 8 or 10 steeres to be fed in a ground at Chandons to serve until grasse beefe come in the market and ever at Michaelmas or at before his discretion 20 or 24 oxen to be fed in the tymber yard & Chandons to be spent in the deerest times of the yeere, as also as manie sheepe as the said grounds can beare.[33]

By the end of the year, fresh orders increased the ration of bread back

> **John Furnivall** must have been part of the furniture of Christ Church in its early years. He was appointed barber in 1552, and then received the privileges of the University in 1561 when he became a verger in the cathedral. By 1577, Furnivall was manciple, running all the catering and domestic activities. He continued to hold all three positions until his death in the summer of 1580, when his wife, Dorothy, received 40s 2d of back pay and an additional £19 9s ¾d for his expenses.

from eight to nine ounces a day, but the quantities served were still to be carefully monitored and recorded.[34]

A side issue of the poor harvests was poor health. Plagues of all sorts, including influenza, malaria and typhus, as well as the terrifying bubonic plague, were common in sixteenth-century England, and Oxford suffered no less than London.[35] The house in Wallingford, purchased in 1548 as a refuge, was far enough away from Oxford to be safe, but close enough to continue business as usual.[36] It was quite substantial, with three separate residences: the Dean's Lodging had a hall, two parlours, various other rooms, a gallery, a buttery, kitchen, and more than one 'house of office'; the Priest's House was similar, and included the cloister of the old St Nicholas's college; and the Clerk's Lodging had its own kitchen and a stable. There were also gardens and orchards. The manciple was responsible for keeping the house ready. Between 1563 and 1565, Robert Boote claimed expenses for candles, coals, wood, communion wine, a cleaver and a branding iron, as well as the hire of a horse so that he could travel between Oxford and Wallingford.[37] During these years, it would seem that fifteen weeks during the summer of 1564, and twelve weeks of Michaelmas term, were spent away from Oxford.[38] Substantial as the property was, it was not large enough to accommodate the whole foundation; presumably only the Dean and Chapter went to Wallingford, and maybe the senior officers of Christ Church; the rest of the college and cathedral had to remain behind, in spite of the risks. In the particularly pestilential year of 1577 – at the same time that rules and standards were being reiterated – the then manciple, John

John Bereblock, a graduate of St John's College, is best known for the engravings of the Oxford colleges and University buildings that he made in conjunction with the visit of Queen Elizabeth I in 1566. His picture of Christ Church has a rather odd perspective but it is the earliest representation of the college.

Furnivall, was paid £10 for catering costs in Oxford on 13 September, and a further 56s on 25 October. At the same time, he received £20 on 13 September and 39s on 25 October for catering in Wallingford. The two houses were evidently functioning simultaneously.[39] Mr Bernard had laid out 24s 3d for butter for use at Wallingford, and repairs were undertaken at the house during December of that year.[40]

In spite of the dangers of sickness, or possibly because of the increased risk in London, Elizabeth visited Christ Church twice during her reign, as part of her progresses around the country. Her first was in 1566, during the short deanery of Thomas Godwin (1565–7). Elizabeth, by all accounts, had a soft spot for Godwin, who was tall, good-looking and a scholar.[41]

> **Tobie Matthew**'s appointment in 1576 was not popular 'in-House'. The internal preference was for William James, once Student and then Master of University College, and an administrator of some reputation, particularly of financial affairs. Matthew, it was said, was merely more accomplished at currying favour. He had, however, held both University positions and the presidency of St John's College. He was, too, a man of his time, a conforming Elizabethan Calvinist.
>
> James, whose opinions on church government had probably moderated as he grew older, followed Matthew into the deanery in 1584.
>
> ODNB; Darwall-Smith (2008), 112

The east side of the Great Quadrangle was made into a residence for the queen – a part of the college which seems to have been designated in Wolsey's original plans as a royal lodging house – with direct access to the Hall created specially. She attended plays, which cost £148; Bereblock wrote that 'nothing more costly or magnificent could be imagined than its staging and arrangement.'[42] Disaster occurred at the beginning of one play when part of the stage collapsed, killing three men and injuring five more. The queen dispatched her own surgeon to tend to the needs of the wounded, and then apparently enjoyed the plays hugely.[43] She was also treated to a splendid oration by a young MA Student, Tobie Matthew. Her attention was caught, and Matthew would soon become dean of Christ Church and later Archbishop of York.[44]

Elizabeth came again in 1592, but not before she had taken advantage of her position as Visitor (the ultimate authority in a college) and sent, in June 1583, one of her diplomatic guests, Prince Alasco of Siradia (Sieradz) in Poland, to be entertained by the House.[45] On his first night, being too tired to indulge in anything too cerebral, the prince remained in his rooms to watch fireworks in the Great Quad. On the following two evenings he was entertained with plays and pageants, hailstorms of confectionery, rainstorms of rose water, and swirling artificial snow, hunters and hounds, and Mercury and Iris descending from and ascending to the roof of the Hall.[46] William

Gager, who famously disputed with John Rainolds of Corpus Christi over the morality of play-acting and particularly over men dressing as women, wrote the plays for the prince's pleasure, including one based on the story of Dido from the *Aeneid*. Produced by George Peele, a friend of Shakespeare, who was paid £18 for his services,[47] the staging required trees to be cut down on the college estate at Chandence to build the 'heavens' and other parts of the stage and scenery.[48]

The monarch's second stay in Christ Church was managed by a committee of Christ Church men, the vice-chancellor and the proctors. College autonomy within its own walls was temporarily suspended, and the university took control. Junior members were closely supervised so as not to cause an outrage in the presence of the queen.[49] There was also a sharing of the costs of the royal visit. In 1566, the costs had fallen completely to Christ Church, and the Dean and Chapter were reluctant to accept the responsibility again. A scheme was drawn up to spread the cost according to the revenue of each college. Christ Church still ended up carrying most of the cost as it was valued at more than twice Magdalen, the next in the table.[50] One of the plays performed was Gager's *Rivales*, described by Hiscock as 'a rich pastoral' with 'rustic love-making, drunken songs, speeches, and gestures'. That it was performed before the queen was the ultimate defeat for Dr Rainolds and his Puritanical objections to stage plays, made even more emphatic by the queen's own admonition of Rainolds for his 'obstinate preciseness'.[51]

* * * * *

There is little in the archives about the undergraduate and graduate curriculum during the sixteenth century. Classical texts continued to be popular, taught perhaps with a more humanist leaning. A few very new books were introduced for arithmetic, by Cuthbert Tunstall and Gemma Frisius, but the course for a BA was, in effect, a medieval one.[52] Two boys who were at Broadgates Hall in the 1570s, Richard and William Carnsew, left diaries in which they recorded their reading and teaching.[53] They read classical history, practised logic, tackled translations from Latin of Caesar's works and into Latin with Foxe's sermons. Mathematics, anatomy, Jewish

Science flourished at Christ Church. Nathaniel Torporley came up to Christ Church in 1581. He devised a new system of spherical trigonometry and published his book Diclides coelometricae *in 1602, of which this is the title page.*

history, natural philosophy, Aristotelian logic and Valerian rhetoric were also part of their studies.[54] There was even an element of modern history and politics. The combination of texts covered much of what would have been expected under the university's statutes. Tutoring was a private matter between teacher and pupil, and tutors – once approved as capable by the dean – were often selected by parents. Philip Sidney, newly returned to Court from Europe, placed the education of his brother Robert into the hands of his friend Robert Sackville. Sackville promised to take great pains to teach Robert, in fulfilment of Philip's wishes. The young Sidney was also tutored by John Buste, who had been Treasurer of Christ Church a few years before, and had just been proctor to the University. Sackville assured Sidney that Buste was trustworthy in all things.[55] A tutor's care extended beyond education;

he was, to all intents and purposes, *in loco parentis*, especially as undergraduates were often much younger than they are today.[56] When plague broke out in Oxford in October 1575, Sackville took the precaution of sending Robert, with his friend Edward Montague, to Montague's home at Boughton in Northamptonshire. Buste went too, so that the boys' tuition could continue unbroken. There were occasions, though, when a tutor admitted defeat; one of Sackville's other charges, John White, had eyes only for Court. On 21 March 1576, Sackville pleaded with Sidney to find John a place – as 'nature had not intended him for the discipline of higher learning'.[57]

In the last year of Elizabeth's reign, John Howson, one of the canons of Christ Church, was appointed vice-chancellor by Buckhurst. The choice was both religious and political. Howson preached against the evangelical puritans in Oxford, urging conformity with the prayer book and support for royal supremacy. Although there were arguments against, and had been for a decade or so, Howson and Buckhurst managed to defeat the most outspoken element of non-conformity, particularly John Rainolds of Corpus and Henry Airay of Queen's. As a consequence, Oxford did not suffer the same scrutiny to which Cambridge was subjected in 1604–5. However, Buckhurst evidently had misgivings about the protagonists on both sides in the debate, and reined in Howson by trying to persuade Airay to become his next vice-chancellor, in the hope that the appointment would demonstrate that conformity reaped rewards.[58]

The beginning of the seventeenth century saw still more consolidation, in spite of the fast turnover in deans during the first 25 years. Thomas Ravis was the dean in place when Elizabeth was succeeded by James I.[59] He was at once identified with the new monarch when he was appointed one of the translators of the Bible at the Hampton Court conference in 1604. There was some concern among the canons as, soon after James's accession, there were rumours that Ravis was to be permitted to hold the bishopric of Gloucester along with the deanery, and it was generally felt that the dean ought to be resident. Ravis did indeed receive a licence to hold both posts (and two additional livings) but he resigned the deanery soon after, and his place was taken by John King in 1605.[60]

James I's choices of dean were interesting. All three men – John King, William Goodwin (appointed in 1611) and Richard Corbett (1620) – were renowned preachers. Corbett was also celebrated as a humorist and poet. All three, as their sixteenth-century predecessors had been, were good Protestants but perhaps increasingly less Calvinist. All three were royal chaplains.

King was a popular choice at Christ Church, and was, by all accounts, a brilliant preacher.[61] No sooner was he in place than James I came to visit.[62] Arriving at Woodstock on 21 August, James moved on to Langley three days later. On 27 August, the royal party, which included Queen Anne and Prince Henry, was received in an Oxford newly scrubbed, polished and painted for the occasion. On the ringing of the bell of the University church, all graduates were to come out, appropriately dressed, to line the streets until the king's entourage had entered the gates of Christ Church. The king had already heard sermons in St Mary's, speeches at the Town Hall, a Greek oration at Carfax, and seen a drama outside the gates of St John's College. In the cathedral James heard verses (in Latin for the king and English for the queen), a performance by the choir and musicians for whom two new treble cornets were bought by the Dean and Chapter for the occasion, and prayers.[63] Unsurprisingly tired, the king and queen retired to the deanery, and the prince to Magdalen College. The following day, plays were given for the royal party, including a pastoral called *Alba*, in which there were five or six near-naked young men, much to the disapproval of the queen, and rustic music and dance which was thought very tedious.

After two days of more formal and academic business, while the king was visiting the Bodleian, the poet and court favourite, Samuel Daniel, performed his *Arcadia* for the queen and prince, and was rewarded at Christ Church with a place on the canons' table in Hall.[64] The bill for the king's visit amounted to £177 6s 6½d, of which £105 was received from the University to help defray the costs.[65] Under James, Christ Church continued to play to visiting dignitaries, particularly when the monarch was lodging at Woodstock. The Spanish ambassador, Gondomar, stayed briefly in September 1605, leaving his room in such a state that it needed fumigation.

William Goodwin was next in line, taking up residence in Christ Church in 1611. He seems to have taken a strong line on discipline.[66] Numbers had

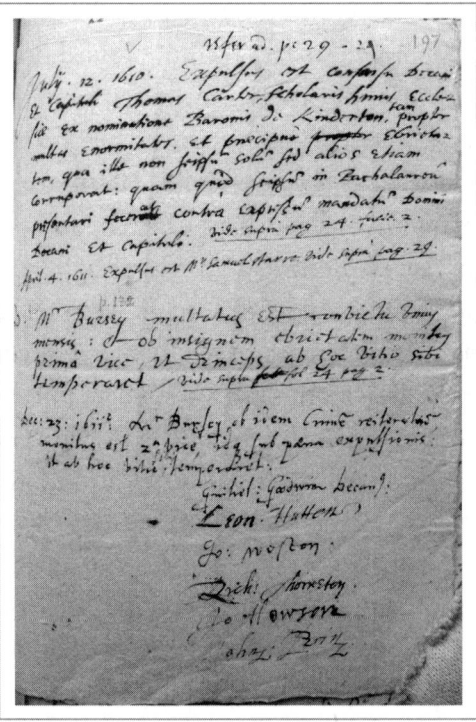

Thomas Carter and Samuel Starr were expelled in 1610 and 1611 for being drunk and disorderly. Carter had completed his BA and Starr, who was 27, his MA. Maintaining discipline was an on-going concern of the Dean and Chapter.

begun to grow in the late Elizabethan and early Stuart period, and Peckwater Quad was altered to accommodate new arrivals. As well as formal appointments and elections, the Chapter Books began to record everyday administrative and disciplinary matters, such as the expulsions of Thomas Carter and Samuel Starr in 1610 and 1611 for being drunk and disorderly.[67] But it was not just individuals who were subject to the harsher line under Goodwin. On 27 August 1611, at a Chapter meeting, it was decided to abandon the entertainment for incoming Westminster scholars which had 'grown to an intolerable excess'. Even the censors' supper was to be abolished, and the censors' breakfast and the supper for determining bachelors were restricted for their 'very scandalous' nature, with no BA being permitted to spend more than 10 shillings on entertainment to celebrate his

'Untyll suche tyme that it shall please the Kynge ...': 1553–1625

> ## Professorships at Christ Church
>
> It was under James that the regius professorship of divinity was annexed to a canonry at Christ Church in 1604, followed by that of Hebrew in 1630.
>
> The oldest professorship in Oxford is the Lady Margaret professorship of divinity. Founded in 1502, the chair was formally attached to a Christ Church canonry in 1840.
>
> The first five regius professorships – divinity, civil law, medicine, Hebrew and Greek – were founded by Henry VIII in 1546. The stipend laid down by the king was £40, and Christ Church paid those of the divinity, Greek and Hebrew professors. The Greek professor's pay remained at £40 per annum until 1865.
>
> The regius professorships of pastoral theology (now moral and pastoral theology) and of ecclesiastical history were not created until 1842 and were attached to canonries from the start.
>
> Many of the reforms of the mid-nineteenth century revolved around professorships, their role and their attachment to colleges. At Christ Church, their attachment to canonries created an additional problem.

degree.[68] Matters evidently did not improve, however, and the suppers were abolished in 1620.[69]

The king, like monarchs before him, was happy to act as patron to those he felt were worthy candidates for both senior and junior positions, but also to favourites, or the sons of favourites. Under James, the system was formalised, as requests were often passed on as commendatory letters under the signet.[70] The king's choices for the deanery were made to ensure the continuation of Elizabethan Puritanism, but there were requests for less exalted places. James Bandinell, for example, was put forward for a Studentship in April 1618.[71] His father was a minister on Jersey, soon to become the island's first Anglican dean. The king's letter told of the poor state of education there. The Dean and Chapter were evidently slow to respond, for another letter from Fulke Greville, one of James's councillors, arrived in December reminding them to do their duty.[72] Although the Scots-born James made efforts to ensure his countrymen could receive positions in Oxford colleges, there is no overwhelming evidence that there was a marked increase in the numbers of men from north of the border into Christ Church.[73] The only certain Scottish member was Lord Roxburgh, who had accompanied the king from Scotland in 1603, and was appointed a canon commoner in 1605.[74]

James also intervened for current members. One of the rules for holding a Studentship was that a man should not receive a living wage from outside college. Henry Devick, perhaps through a recent inheritance, owned land worth over £40 per year. The Chapter had, as a consequence, told Devick that he must surrender his position. James requested, in the summer of 1620, that an exception be made in the case of this 'forward student' in spite of the fact that he had already received his BA. Devick was granted a short reprieve, and was allowed to stay until 1622.[75]

The relative calm of the later Tudor period and the early Stuart years allowed Christ Church to stabilise. Its administration and customs had settled into an established routine, in spite of the lack of statutes. The Students had made their first tentative protest – a foretaste of the future – but the college and cathedral were in a secure position to cope with what was to come later in the seventeenth century.

Aedis Christi: *cathedral, college chapel and the choir*

The nucleus of ancient priory buildings – including the church, Chapter House, cloister, priory house and monastic refectory – is all that escaped demolition when Wolsey set about his ambitious scheme for Cardinal College.[1] Its architecture is early, with surviving medieval features such as the windows in the Latin chapel, the 'watching loft' and St Frideswide's shrine, yet the old priory church of St Frideswide, while also Oxford's cathedral, is essentially a college chapel writ large. Nearly all the monuments are to Students or canons, most of the windows were commissioned by the Dean and Chapter or are gifts from alumni, the reconstruction of the nave was the brainchild of George Gilbert Scott and Henry Liddell, its arrangement being more for collegiate than diocesan use.

Until relatively recently, the world outside Christ Church only once made any real impact on the cathedral architecturally. During the English Civil War, when the king and court were based in Oxford, the burials of soldiers and courtiers took place there.[2] A grand monument in the Lucy chapel to Sir Peter Wyche, Comptroller of the King's Household, is one of several. The grandest of all, perhaps, is to William Villiers, Viscount Grandison, who died from wounds received at the siege of Bristol, and was buried in the cathedral in October 1643.[3]

In 1542, Henry VIII created the new diocese of Oxford, carved out of the huge medieval power-base that was Lincoln, and made the abbey church at Oseney the new cathedral. But Henry really preferred his new cathedrals to be central to their cities,[4] so with the refoundation of King Henry VIII College as Christ Church, he moved the cathedral here, and in so doing founded an extraordinary and unique institution. The church's diocesan function has often been secondary, however, and sometimes substantially neglected. Unless a member of college, the bishop was barely welcome.[5] Indeed, in the early days the Dean and Chapter must have been accustomed to working without a bishop as, from 1558 until 1604, the see was largely vacant.[6]

This independence, combined with the odd physical relationship of having a cathedral within a college, meant that the bishop was often isolated. Richard Corbett, who had been dean before becoming bishop, felt it his right to ordain and confirm in the cathedral without asking consent of the Chapter, and confronted Brian Duppa, his successor in the deanery, on the issue. Duppa sensibly insisted that asking to use the cathedral was just a courtesy and that any request would not be denied. Corbett, however, was affronted, and announced that he would perform his duties elsewhere and not be beholden to the Dean and Chapter for the use of the church.[7] In 1783, when Bishop Butler asked if he could use the Chapter House to prepare his candidates for ordination, the Chapter refused permission.[8] The bishop was less than amused and wrote a letter complaining that: 'I shall be driven to the necessity of meeting candidates for orders in the church on the day before Ordination and of putting on my episcopal habit the next morning at the church door ... I shall hope to bear both the inconvenience and the apparent humiliation.' The bishop's letter is endorsed by an irritated dean 'Foolish answer'.[9] Unlike other Chapters, though, the Dean and Chapter of Christ Church were also the Governing Body of a large collegiate establishment, with many young men requiring education, care and discipline, a task which evidently occupied a considerable portion of their time and energies. The bishop's need for a dressing-room was a long way down the agenda.

* * * * *

Services, apart from the installation and enthronement of canons and bishops, are ill-recorded, although rules for attendance were laid down frequently. In the 1570s, a new decree was made that Students, chaplains and singing men were to be fined 12d for every unauthorised absence from church on Sundays and holidays, a penalty shared by every servant and member of the house.[10]

Holy Communion was compulsory, as was learning the catechism. In 1761, when William Holwell replaced William Jane as catechist, a new termly lecture in the catechism was introduced to be read in the Latin chapel. Other lectures were given in the cathedral, such as the Challoner divinity lectures – on the Thirty-Nine Articles – which were read, in English, in the Latin chapel at 11 o'clock on the first and last Thursdays of full term. All undergraduates and bachelors were obliged to attend.[11] The junior chaplains who read the Latin services had their stipend increased to £10 each year in 1772.[12] Latin was abandoned in college services in 1861 when Charles Sandford, later to be Bishop of Gibraltar, and George Kitchin, later the Dean of Durham, were censors.[13] Communion was held once a month after choral matins and before breakfast, a two-hour service that was less than popular with a hungry student population. Weekly communion was introduced in 1865, and then another on Thursdays a few years later. There were no college sermons, only those delivered when Christ Church hosted the University sermon.[14]

In 1860, the Ecclesiastical Commissioners drew up a scheme to allow 24 honorary canonries in each cathedral, partly to compensate for the reduction in the numbers of residentiary canons. Eight could be appointed in the first year, and two more in subsequent years. These men could preside over a service in the absence of the dean and canons, and there would be a rota drawn up for preaching. At first the scheme was not popular at Christ Church, and there was considerable to-ing and fro-ing between the Dean and Chapter and the commissioners about seniority, seating and processional arrangements, and general 'interference' in the authority of the Chapter. Only one member of Chapter, Richard Jelf, attended the installation service for the first honorary canon on 23 July 1866.[15]

* * * * *

After Duppa's time, little work seems to have taken place on the building itself until the nineteenth century, except in 1794, when the cathedral was closed from 14 July for the whole of the long vacation, in order for it to be whitewashed and the organ pipes regilded.[16] The spouts on the north side of the Chapter House were repaired in October 1806, and the organ loft fitted up for the choir.[17]

Most recorded decisions made for the cathedral were on minor matters: for example, the choir was to be lit by wax tapers from 1762 onwards, and the treasurer was ordered to supply velvet covers for the communion table, the litany desk and for the canons' and noblemen's seats, and to arrange for a new marble font with a silver gilt bowl.[18] New Greek testaments were purchased for chapel use in 1785, a new Bible in 1748 and two copies of Jackson's church music in 1822. A drawing of St Frideswide's shrine by Roberts was purchased for ten guineas in 1791.[19]

The cathedral must have been bitterly cold during the winter months. In January 1821, the Treasurer was instructed to buy stoves, an installation hastily completed by the end of February, with a stock of coal laid in. Richard Keys, the verger, was paid £10 per annum for his additional labours attending to the stoves, and he and his colleague were given new gowns.[20] Keys, a long-standing employee, lived in a 'cottage' constructed within the south transept of the cathedral, where a chimney from the bedroom fireplace poked unceremoniously through the tracery of one of the windows.[21] He acted as a dog-whipper, keeping in check the dogs belonging to the gentlemen members of Christ Church who liked to bring their pets with them to chapel, and was renowned for keeping his beer in a cupboard in the chancel.[22]

Until the changes in the constitution of Christ Church in the 1850s and 1860s the cathedral was funded as the college chapel, its costs being met like any other expense. A chest was purchased in 1731 to hold the church's money, but this meant the cash of the whole institution.[23] After 1867, the cathedral was given an annual grant with which to manage its affairs. The Chapter Fund was set at £17,000, of which £13,500 was reckoned to be the emoluments of the dean and the seven canons. The remaining £3,500 had to meet the costs of the then six chaplains, the organist, the lay clerks, the choristers – including their education – the vergers and other staff, pensioners, almsmen, and charities, plus the maintenance of the cathedral and the Chapter House, and the costs of services. When the seventh stall was finally suppressed in 1871, after the death of Richard Jelf, the grant from the Governing Body dropped by £1,500, the sum that each canonry was permitted to receive by the Cathedrals Commission.

Out of that £3,500 came fixed costs that the Chapter could not alter: there was the annual £144 due to the almsmen, and the aggregate stipend of the chaplains was not permitted to fall below £660. In 1868, the six chaplains each received £110 per annum, with one receiving an additional £4 as precentor, and another an extra £110 as schoolmaster to the choristers. The organist was paid £300. The lay clerks, of whom there were eight or nine, received stipends between £40 and £90. Eight choristers each received £40 per annum and the two vergers £30. With such fixed commitments, it was astonishing that the Chapter still managed to reserve money for the building fund (£500 in each of 1870 and 1872). Routine expenditure in the early 1870s was around £2,700. In 1876 the Chapter begin to stock the wine cellar, not just for enjoyment during Chapter meetings, but as a profit-making venture. Within a decade, in spite of fixed costs and extraordinary expenditure, the canons had managed to build up a surplus of nearly £3,000. Although legally this could have been distributed among the canons as part of their stipends, it was decided instead to restore the Chapter House. But those fixed costs were beginning to creep up: from £2,836 in 1873 to £3,457 in 1882, only £43 short of the £3,500 allowance.

* * * * *

The biggest drain on resources was the choir school, and despite one suggestion that the boys be sent to Magdalen College School, a new school was opened in 1894, the Governing Body granting the site but offering no contribution towards the costs. The bill came to £5,132 with an additional £260 for the architect. The dean and canons had little choice but to meet this themselves. Stock valued at £3,481 was sold, the wine cellar fund was raided for £877, Dr Ince generously gave £500 and the other canons £50.

But by 1894, fixed costs had risen to £3,617, and the Chapter were beginning to worry; they could only keep their heads above water when canonries stood vacant. Towards the end of the First World War, the Chapter acknowledged that they would have to ask the Governing Body for a grant to keep the choir school afloat. The Governing Body responded, giving £1,000 in each of 1919 and 1920, and then £1,500 in 1921 and 1922. The following year, after a threat that the school would have to close in 1924, financing was changed so that the school operated on a separate budget with contributions from both Governing Body and Chapter. By the end of the Second World War, regular payments stood at £3,782, but Dean Lowe was not sure how long things could continue.[24] By the early 1960s, the school was building up a considerable deficit which could only be met by increasing both fees and numbers. The first was possible, but the second out of the question; the old buildings on Brewer Street were not only too small but desperately in need of overhaul. Amalgamation with Magdalen College School was suggested again and, by 1968, things seemed to be progressing well. A new preparatory/choir school was proposed on a Christ Church site on the Iffley Road, but negotiations floundered, not least because of the uncertainty of the future of direct grant schools but also because it turned out that funding a new school would probably cost more than funding the deficit. Fees went up, a grant was received from a charity, and an appeal was launched to endow the choral foundation. By the early 1970s, the appeal, combined with Dean Simpson's bequest, ensured that the school did at least have a working profit.

The choir has been an essential part of college and cathedral life from the start, and it would be hard to imagine an English cathedral without their wonderful sound. The first list of members recorded in the first Chapter Book lists not only the academic establishment and college servants, but the sacristan, vergers, eight chaplains, eight singing men or lay clerks and the eight boy choristers.[25] A school was established for the choristers at the foundation, and their education was the responsibility of the schoolmaster and organist. The choristers met first in the rooms under the Hall, their playground being the area to the south of the Hall near the kitchen.[26] The school developed during the nineteenth century from an establishment solely for young choristers into an independent preparatory school. Its premises moved first to a new building to the south of School Quad (probably the building now known as Mrs Potts's cottage – the Clerk of Works' office), with a playground where the workshops now stand, and then from the main site to buildings on Brewer Street. Initially, the boys and their master squeezed into 1 Brewer Street, which had a tiny backyard used for a squashed and novel form of cricket. It was a noisy and smelly site, over the old city ditch and next door to the stables for the city's tram horses. It was not until the mid-1890s that the boys were given Merton Field as their sports ground.

By 1892, when Henry Sayers (headmaster 1884–97) was about to marry, space became a major issue and a new site was considered. A building on the Meadow was considered but rejected after complaints, and the new school was begun just a little further along Brewer Street. The building was completed in the spring of 1894, with a service of blessing held on Easter Saturday. A new building was constructed behind it in 1992, expanding and improving the facilities, and allowing for the opening of a pre-prep school.

In around 1850, the daily routine for a chorister started after breakfast with lessons for an hour between 9 and 10, a cathedral service for an hour, and then more school lessons until 1 pm, including Latin and Greek as well as writing and arithmetic. Choir practice was held in the organist's house between 1 and 2 pm three times a week, followed by dinner in the Chapter House. There was meat every day except on Wednesdays and Fridays when there was pudding only, and water was shared in a communal quart cup. Every Friday at 5 pm the choristers were given a jam tart as a special treat. Between 3 and 4 in the afternoon there were more lessons, followed by another cathedral service, and prep in the evenings until bedtime. Cricket and football were popular, and the boys had six weeks' summer holiday and four weeks at Christmas. Every saint's day was a whole holiday, and Wednesdays and Fridays were half-holidays. Clothes were provided and other living expenses met.[27]

Thomas Gaisford was rather against the choir, and the cathedral services generally met with some disapproval during his deanery. In 1847, a visitor proclaimed that the services at Christ Church were the 'most slovenly and irreverent ... in any English cathedral'.[28] Soon, though, with Liddell's approval, Charles Corfe revived the choral services.[29] In 1873, the three choirs of Christ Church, Magdalen College, and the Chapel Royal at Windsor brought Bach's St Matthew Passion to the cathedral for the first time.[30] The boys and adult singers of the cathedral choir entered festivals, and sang at the reopening of Worcester cathedral in 1874.

* * * * *

In 1545, just before the foundation of Christ Church, a joiner was paid for repairs to the organs, and more repairs were undertaken by a Mr Borough in 1591. Two new organs were set up by Mr Dallam, the London organ builder, one in 1608, another in 1624.[31] In 1680, Henry Aldrich – a man who loved music of all genres – set about making good and replacing the instrument that was moved during the Commonwealth, and it was then that the organ made by Father Bernard Smith was installed.[32]

Originally, the organ stood further east, blocking the chancel from the nave. But during Billings's restoration work on the cathedral in 1856 it was shifted to the south transept. Just under 30 years later, in 1884, it was moved to its current position at the west end, and the much rebuilt and altered Smith instrument was restored by Henry Willis, the appeal for which was administered with great efficiency by Liddell's wife. John Stainer, soon to be professor of music, had advised Lloyd, the Christ Church organist, and commented in a letter to the dean that Willis had spared no 'pains to produce an instrument of the highest excellence'.[33] By 1970, though, it was time to start again, and Dean Simpson's bequest to the choral foundation allowed for a new organ to be commissioned. Originally the contract went to an American company, Lawrence Phelps and Associates, but the company went into liquidation and the organ was never supplied. There was considerable discussion over the costs of this setback, and the ethics involved in the use of the bequest to pay for something that had not appeared. Eventually, the Austrian firm Rieger took on the task, and the new instrument was inaugurated on 15 December 1979.[34]

The last move of the organ deprived Christ Church of any real nave, the area east of the organ giving the impression of being all chancel. Scott's arrangements allowed for the undergraduates to be seated immediately east of the organ, with freshmen under the tower, then the canons, with Students and graduates furthest east. Any of the public attending services have to sit around the edges, almost invisible and unable to see the progress of the liturgy at all. The censors have their stalls almost under the organ, the dean's throne is just east of the tower and the bishop's is in the sanctuary. The vice-chancellor also has a throne opposite the pulpit.[35] The predominance of college over cathedral here is evident.

* * * * *

But recently, the diocese and city have slowly begun to regain a foothold in their cathedral, not least in the Military Chapel, dedicated in 11 November 1931 to St Michael, in memory of the men of the Oxfordshire and Buckinghamshire Light Infantry who had died in the First World War. It is a corner of the cathedral which is truly of the town rather than the gown.

Services, too, are no longer just college functions; quite the reverse. Baptisms, weddings and funerals have always been conducted in the cathedral, although burials inside the cathedral ceased in August 1855.[36] Musical events and exhibitions are held; and the cathedral welcomes large numbers of tourists from all around the world, some of them staying for choral evensong. Links with the diocese and with the incumbents of college livings are encouraged, not least through the Friends organisation, formed in 1936 under the caring eye of Dean Williams with the deliberate aim of fostering relations between the cathedral and individuals, and to raise money to maintain the building and its treasures.[37]

In 1942, during the celebrations for the 400th anniversary of the foundation of the diocese of Oxford, the bishop, preaching in the cathedral, said that 'our heritage was menaced today as never before. Its visible beauty was threatened; but still greater and graver was the threat to our invisible inheritance.' [38] Oxford survived the war relatively unscathed, but although the passage of time has been less kind to a cathedral built of soft local stone, its invisible heritage has been vigorously maintained.

4

'The present engagement of the greatest part of them in Armes': 1625–88

Succeeding William Goodwin, the first dean to die in office, was Richard Corbett, who took office in 1620 and in 1625 hosted a visit from Parliament at a time of plague in London. A cheerful and talented man, popular with both James I and Charles I,[1] Corbett was soon elevated to the bishopric of Oxford, principally to make way for a new man, Brian Duppa, who had been nominated by his patron, the powerful Edward Sackville, Earl of Dorset.[2] No sooner had Duppa arrived – his installation was on 28 November 1628 – than he began preparations for a formal state visit in 1629 by Charles and Henrietta Maria.[3]

At Christ Church, Duppa is best known for his alterations to the cathedral, but he was also heavily involved with William Laud's overhaul of the University's administration. The first moves to reform the University's statutes had taken place in June 1629, but Laud, as Chancellor, made sweeping changes, supported by the unusually named Accepted Frewen at Magdalen and by Duppa. New University statutes, generally known as the Laudian Code, were promulgated in June 1636, formalising the relationship between the University and the colleges, confirming the authority of the Chancellor, and establishing the Hebdomadal Council – the weekly meetings of the heads of houses. The Code also set down all sorts of miscellaneous rules including some concerning the general deportment of Students. When Charles I visited soon after, in August 1636, he was greeted by serried ranks of silent members in gowns, showing, at least outwardly, their adherence to the new regulations.[4]

Goodwin and Corbett had already attempted to tighten up discipline, and Duppa followed suit.[5] Even before Laud's measures were approved, he was issuing new decrees and correcting inappropriate behaviour. In 1630, One King (another unusual Christian name) was required to make a public recantation of his sedition against the church and a few months later, Richard Mylls was reprimanded for 'most intemperate language and notorious drunkenness at supper in the audit house'.[6] A verger was admonished for not performing his duties properly.[7] Dress codes were reiterated; on 28 July 1632, all members were directed to come to all formal occasions wearing proper academic caps rather than more fashionable hats. To ensure compliance, caps were shortly provided for everyone, to be worn daily thereafter. Fresh rules were issued about the payment of battels and the use of the buttery, and students were reminded that they must not leave college without permission.[8]

On 2 August 1636, following the promulgation of the Code, further decrees were issued by the Dean and Chapter on a variety of matters, and this continued for the next two years. The numbers and behaviour of college servants and servitors (the lowest rank of undergraduates who were expected to work for their keep and education) were carefully monitored; mulcts, or punishments, were put in place for Students missing disputations; those who were permitted to hold livings alongside their Studentships were told that they must attend at least two meetings a year; Students were restricted in the income they could receive from their livings, and these could be no further than 30 miles from college. Old decrees concerning the choir were revived and new ones added requiring certain anthems, such as the *Te Deum*, the *Venite Exultemus* and the *Benedictus*, to be sung every Sunday and holiday. A regular meeting was to be held so that the Chapter could check on the choir to encourage or correct the boys. Even the Westminster supper, which must have replaced the rowdy entertainment banned in 1611, was abolished.[9]

In January 1641, the Students finally began to fight back. Resentment was always simmering over their relatively lowly position compared with that of their stipendiary colleagues in other colleges and the richer commoner members, and occasionally it boiled over. The Students presented a petition to the Dean and Chapter questioning particularly the rule limiting the value of a living (to 20 nobles) that could be held alongside a Studentship. Many Christ Church livings were valuable, and to restrict Students to just the poorer ones was, they felt, unfair. Although the Dean and Chapter could be lenient from time to time (George Aglionby, for example, was granted permission in 1632 to hold the valuable living of Cassington as he was unmarried and had no other income),[10] on the whole, the Students felt unfairly treated.

The Students also requested that the revenues from wood and coal, butter and spice, and from the 'home' farm at Chandence, from Binsey and from the Meadow be added to their income, rather than the revenue from inflation-bound corn rents, tied to the price of grain in the market. It would seem, too, that Students were not always getting rooms in college: if easy money could be earned by leasing out accommodation to fee-paying members of college who could afford rents, or even to outsiders, then the opportunity was taken. The petitioners insisted that accommodation be reserved for them.[11] As if in some recompense, old rules about the conduct of commoners were reiterated, but these murmurs among the Student body were the beginning of over two centuries of discontent.[12]

Life was not all orders and control. Theatricals were always popular, culminating in the performances given for royal and diplomatic visitors, and proposals were made for a school to teach riding, fencing, and instrumental and vocal music. Students had long taken classes in music in the town, and sports of all sorts were encouraged as healthy pursuits. Such skills were a must for any young man wanting to make his way in society. Only games that might lead to gambling were frowned upon. The proposed school would also teach the 'practical part of Mathematicks that is of measuring at distance of Militarie architecture and of drilling' – perhaps a sign of times to come, but another indication of the expectations of young gentlemen.[13] Men of rank were often destined for the court, and from the middle of the 1630s, increasing numbers of Students undertook official journeys abroad. Young

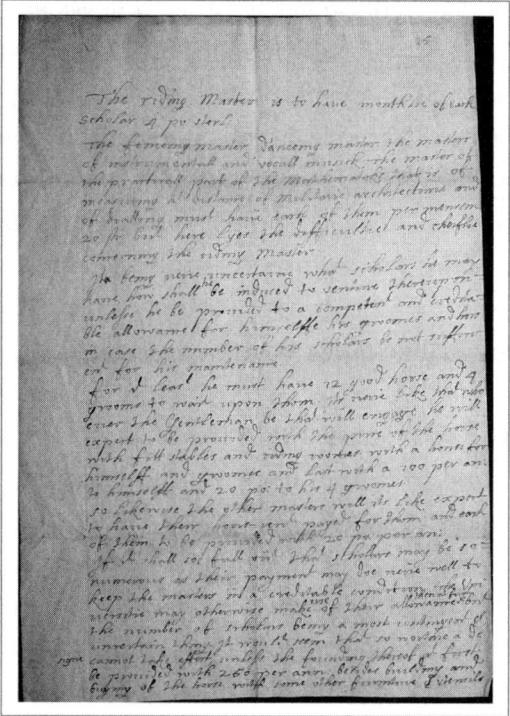

Proposals to set up a military academy in Oxford show not only the expectations young gentlemen had of their university career, but possibly the political uncertainty of the period. Students were to be educated in the mathematics necessary for military architecture and drilling, in riding and fencing, and in the more genteel pursuits of instrumental and vocal music. The academy was evidently thought too expensive, and it never made it off the drawing-board.

men had taken leave to travel since the foundation, often on diplomatic missions, but suddenly there was a rush. In February 1635, Henry Killigrew was permitted to be absent for an unprecedented three years on employment for the queen.[14] The following year, Thomas Lockey was granted his full allowance while working in France, and in 1637, Maurice Berkeley, too, was allowed a complete stipend during his time abroad.[15]

Charles I visited Oxford in August 1636, the high point of Laud's chancellorship. More plays were produced at Christ Church for the court's entertainment. The costs were again astronomical. Inigo Jones was principal designer, and spent £260 on the scenery and staging alone. The stage

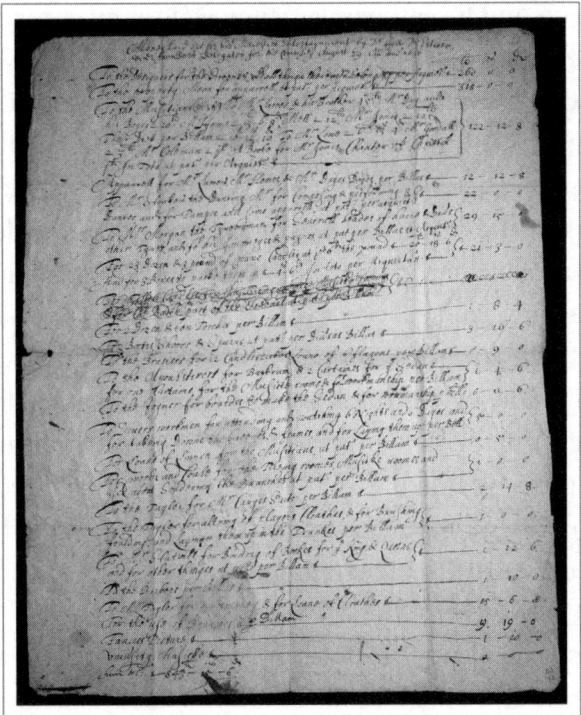

Charles I's visit to Christ Church in 1636 was not a cheap event. The costumes alone cost over £300, around £40,000 today based on the Retail Price Index.

stretched from the upper end of the Hall, almost to the hearth in the centre of the room, and the scenery was sumptuous. Many of the staging effects were pioneered for the occasion, and the 'variety bred very great admiration', said Anthony Wood.[16] Props men were paid over £300 for the costumes, and the musicians received £122 12s 8d.[17] The plays were in English, and all comedies – nothing too heavy for Charles.[18] But the college and the University were to pay dearly for their loyalty to the Crown.

In 1640, after the debacle of the Scots Wars, with increasing concern about popery in the disguise of Laud's high-church Arminianism and the disenchantment of the newly called Parliament, Oxford found itself at the centre of the political crisis. The University met Parliament's demands as far as it felt able to do so, and defended themselves as one against accusations of Catholic leanings while sending petitions supporting the episcopalian

Anglican church and its cathedrals. Many Oxford men, including William Cartwright, Christ Church's eminent and talented poet, saw Parliament's attack on the Church as an attack on the University itself, of the same seriousness as Henry VIII's on the monasteries.[19] Clerical support for Charles within the conservative University met head-on with the town's increasing anger against the power of the gown in the city. Dissident academics encouraged the townsmen in their riotousness. Although opinion remained divided, the ever more radical views voiced at Westminster brought a natural conservatism to the surface. Charles, always in need of funds, reminded the University of his support for the seat of learning and asked for a loan to go to war against Parliament.[20] It was a mark of Oxford's allegiance that over £10,000 was raised within a week, Christ Church possibly contributing up to £4,000. Parliament, needless to say, was less than pleased, and required the Heads of Houses to place their monies and plate somewhere safe so that it could not be used against them.[21]

On Thursday 18 August 1642, all men with arms of any sort were called together at the Schools at the Bodleian Library, and then marched to Christ Church and arrayed in the Great Quadrangle for exercises. It began to rain during the afternoon, so they marched back to Schools and went home.[22] In spite of this rather damp and ignominious start, they marched again on Saturday and soon began to resemble a reasonable fighting force. Undergraduates, Masters of Arts, and even Doctors of Divinity skirmished together to improve their technique, and the Cooks Corporation provided the drums and trooped the colours. The city was gradually barricading itself against attack with defences under the gates and over the bridges. The first of the Royalist troopers arrived late in August 1642. But in September there were rumours that the City was about to declare itself for Parliament, and the University attempted, unsuccessfully, to negotiate with the Parliamentary forces at Banbury. The Royalist soldiers left Oxford on 10 September, taking a number of loyal scholars with them, and just two days later, Parliamentary troops under Colonel Goodwin marched in from Aylesbury, billeted themselves at Merton College and pastured their horses on Christ Church Meadow. All the defences, so laboriously constructed by the students in between their studies and devotions, were pulled down, and the students of Christ Church, Magdalen, Merton and Corpus Christi were disarmed.

A fresh attempt was made to purloin the college's plate, with soldiers being sent into Oxford to conduct a thorough search. Fell's personal plate, hidden in the house of Emme Weekes in St Ebbe's parish, was discovered and taken away under guard. Legend has it that Mrs Fell buried the University's plate in the deanery garden. If she did, it was never recovered.[23] More troops, maybe those stationed on the Meadow, searched the buildings during the night, finding still more treasure behind wainscotting and in cellars. Storing it in the deanery overnight, they were enraged the next morning to find everything gone. Richard Allestree, having been entrusted with a key to the deanery, had moved everything, including the contents of the college chest.[24] Were it not for the urgent call for the Parliamentary soldiers to leave Oxford to join the Earl of Essex, the consequences for Allestree would have been dire.[25] Essex's troops departed, without garrisoning Oxford, and after the battle of Edgehill at the end of October, the king entered the city with the princes Rupert, Maurice, Charles and James. The city presented the king with a sum of money, and Richard Gardiner, canon and orator, celebrated Charles's arrival at Christ Church.[26]

At some time early in the Civil War, probably in the winter of 1642/3, the Dean and Chapter wrote to 'the Right Honourable the Lords and others the Commissioners for the Fortifications':

> The humble petition of the Deane and Chapter of Christ Church in Oxford humbly sheweth that whereas towards the Designe of new fortifying the Citty of Oxford, the said Church is taxd at a 4th part of the charge, which is allotted to the University, upon a pretended antient value, never yet submitted unto, as being, in divers consideracions very unequall, & especially at this tyme when this Church hath been & yet is continually charged with many extraordinary expenses to a greate value for his Majestie's accommodations, to which no other society in this University contributes anything at all.
>
> May it therefore please you to order that either this taxe maybe rated and leavyd as heretofore per Capita or els to take some such other Course for the releife & ease of your peticioners as to your wisdome & equity shall seeme good.

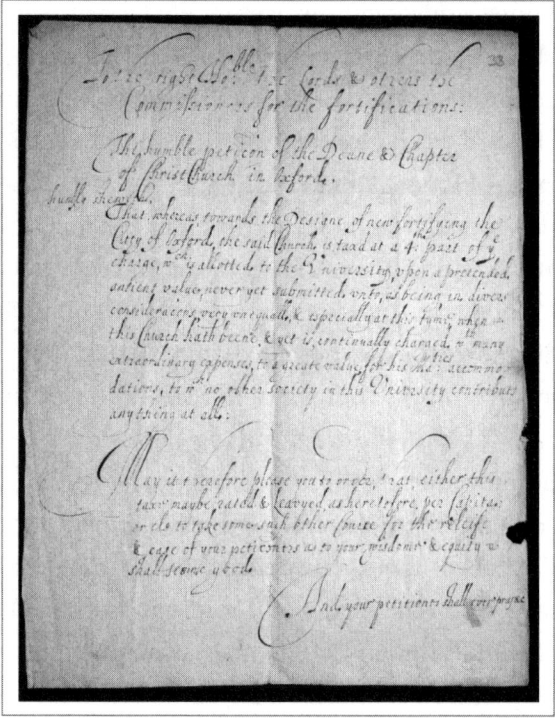

The Dean and Chapter, whose finances were rather depleted as a result of the King's residence at Christ Church, appealed for some leniency in their contributions to the fortification of the City.

This letter and the response, which reduced Christ Church's contribution from £10 per week to £7, are the only two documents in the archive which specifically mention the residence of the king. And yet it is universally acknowledged that the king stayed regularly at Christ Church over a period of some four years.

Charles I made Christ Church his capital; he resided in the deanery for at least half his time between 1643 to 1645, his 'parliament' assembled on occasions in the Hall, his privy council met in the south-west canonry, and the cathedral was the scene of the weddings and funerals of members of the court and senior military men who were accommodated in student rooms, vacated by those who had either joined up, or just remained at home for the duration of the hostilities. The Great Quadrangle continued to be used as a parade ground for soldiers, and a cannon foundry was set up on site.[27] To allow private visits between the king and his queen, who was resident at Merton College, a gate was cut through to Corpus Christi College in the wall at the end of the canons' garden beside the cathedral, and another through from Corpus to Merton.[28] There is no written evidence of the extra costs – for alterations to buildings, or even just the board and lodging expenses of so many new residents – but they were definitely being accrued. In the final pages of a ledger kept by the sub-dean, which generally recorded leaves of absence and other daily administrative affairs, there is a single account showing that the Treasurer was settling bills for things definitely not of an academic nature. These included a pound of powder, three yards of match, three girdles of bandoleers, eight staffs of whole pikes and ten of half pikes, five weeks training for 'our men', and the costs of Rankling the smith, who was mending and making armoury.[29] These new financial demands prompted another complaint from the Students: on 12 July 1643, they wrote that their commons had been reduced to one meal a day, which they considered 'farre below what they conceive their due as also below ye exigencies of these Times looke they either upon the smalnes of their Comins or the present engagement of the greatest part of them in Armes'.[30] Evidently, the college suffered the intrusion of the court, but not always quietly.

Slowly, the number of undergraduates and bachelors in residence dwindled as men either went home or to war. At the end of Michaelmas term 1642, nearly every man in college went home for Christmas, some taking just a few days off, others a month or so. Those remaining became soldiers. At least a fifth of the Students were officers in the Royalist army, and others were involved with protecting the city and colleges.[31] At Easter 1643, however, nearly every man left on 17 March and few returned for the summer term. By 1645, the place was almost empty of students. Permission for leave, usually given to individuals, was on this occasion granted to the remainder of the student body in its entirety.[32] Unsurprisingly, admissions had reached rock bottom: in 1641, 28 men had been admitted to Christ Church; in 1645, only five.[33]

Throughout the Court's residence, however, Dean Fell tried to keep

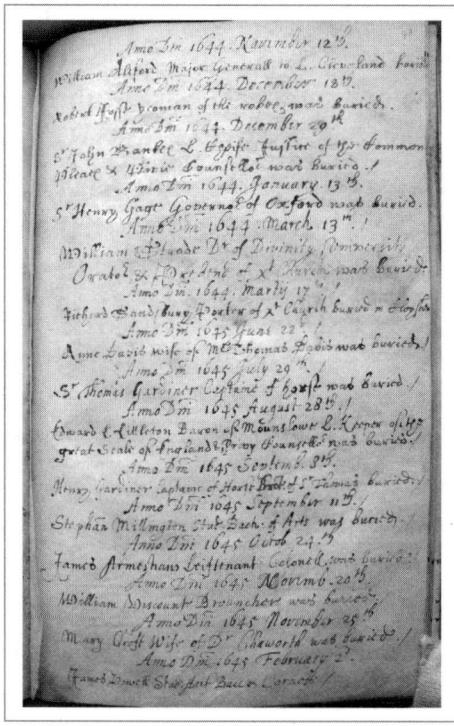

The cathedral register is one of the only documents in the archive which show court, cathedral, and college living, working, and dying together. In 1644/5, soldiers, courtiers, college servants, Students and canons were all buried in the cathedral.

business as usual. It is the cathedral register which uniquely shows Court, college and cathedral attempting to live, or die, together. William, the son of Sir Peter Wyche, Comptroller of the King's Household, was baptised in the cathedral on 14 April 1643, just before the daughter of one of the canons, but it is in the lists of burials that we see most clearly the presence of the Court at Christ Church. Paul Pert, servant of the Counting House, was buried in April 1643, followed shortly by Anthony Brown, Clerk Controller. Interspersed with members of college, and their families, are two yeomen of the wardrobe, two Garter Heralds, Peter Wyche himself, three army captains, two major generals, two lieutenant colonels, the Lord Chief Justice of the Common Pleas, the Governor of Oxford, and the Keeper of the Great

Seal. The register confirms the devastating effects of the 1643 typhus and the ensuing plagues in the city: in 1642, only two people were buried in the cathedral; in 1643, nineteen; in 1644, fourteen; in 1645, ten. No wonder the students were staying away.[34]

Just as war was breaking out, Dean Samuel Fell installed one of the most beautiful features of Christ Church, the delicate fan tracery above the stairs to the Hall; but soon the college was falling into financial difficulties. There were far fewer commoners paying fees, the king continued to 'borrow' money and plate, and, whether through real difficulties or opportunism by tenants, rents were not coming in as regularly as they should from the college's estates.[35] By the end of 1649, rents had fallen so far into arrears that it was impossible to meet allowances and charges due to members of college and cathedral. Dr Mills, the Treasurer, was granted *carte blanche* by the Dean and Chapter, and promised all the assistance he needed to deal with the problem. He was given £100 towards expenses, an instrument of agreement with the Chapter, and a Letter of Attorney, giving him all the powers he needed to gather in rents, to hold monies and to distribute them as he felt best.[36]

Charles returned to Oxford for the final time in October 1645 in the wake of the battle of Naseby and his subsequent attempts to rally support across the country. He stayed in Christ Church until the end of May 1646 when he left, initially for London, but eventually heading towards the north where he surrendered to the Scots. Immediately after the king's departure, Parliament prohibited the University from making new appointments or from issuing new leases of its properties. A band of new ministers was sent in to ensure that preaching was 'reliable', and the University once more fell under the control of Parliament.[37]

However, the old regime was not prepared to lie down and surrender, and had gathered together a powerful body of men, led by Fell as dean and vice-chancellor, to argue for the University against the Parliamentary victors. Fell's position as one of the leading Royalists in Oxford had been established back in 1642 when he took the Protestation only reluctantly.[38] An order had been given for his arrest then, and Fell had fled Oxford, only returning late in the year to play host to his king. After the monarch's departure, Fell continued his resistance, this time against the Parliamentary Visitors (or commissioners) who were imposed by ordinance on 1 May 1647 to reform and deal with 'abuses' in the University. He arranged, or so the Visitors alleged, for the clock at the Schools to be put forward a few minutes, thus making the Visitors, who had been at a service in the University church, late for their first meeting with the senior members of the University. Fell left the Convocation House at the hour the meeting was scheduled to begin, passing the tardy Visitors on his way out. In the end, drastic action was taken.[39] Fell was imprisoned in London in October, having refused to appear before the Visitors, and others of the opposing delegacy were removed from their posts.[40] He was permitted to return to Oxford later that year, but he and his family were ordered to leave the deanery, a command that they defiantly ignored. Pembroke, the new Chancellor, sent in soldiers. Margaret Fell and the children were forcibly removed, carried out into the Great Quadrangle on their chairs, an experience which can only have ensured that the 22-year-old John Fell followed in his father's Royalist footsteps. Edward Reynolds, one of the preachers sent to Oxford after Charles's departure, replaced Fell as vice-chancellor and then as dean, and, in spite of the king's constant efforts to make Parliament's advances very difficult, the academic rebels were slowly brought into line.[41]

It was then the turn of the general population of the University. Of 379 fellows recorded by the Visitors, over a third refused to submit to Parliamentary reforms and orders, with a further fifth failing to turn up for their interviews with the commissioners. Christ Church seems to have roughly equal numbers of those expelled and those allowed to remain.[42] Sixty-one men suffered expulsion as a result of the Visitation, or very soon afterwards, of whom 46 were Students. A few were soon allowed back, and others, such as Robert Lowe, a young commoner who had only arrived in 1647, were permitted to retain their rooms in spite of officially losing their places. Some were obvious candidates for expulsion: Robert Meade, for example, who had served as a captain in the Royalist forces.[43] Or Richard Geale, who, in the middle of the Christmas holiday, no doubt a bit the worse for wear, drank the

'The present engagement of the greatest part of them in Armes': 1625–88

> ## Christ Church men of the Commonwealth
>
> **Edward Pococke (1604–91)**, the regius professor of Hebrew, is best remembered at Christ Church for the huge and vigorous plane tree which has grown in the garden behind the Priory House since the 1640s, as well as his skills in oriental languages.
>
> **Ralph Button**, a professor at Gresham College who became a canon of Christ Church in 1648 only to be replaced by Fell in 1660. **Nathaniel Hodges** was given a Studentship at Christ Church by the Parliamentary Visitors. An eminent physician, he bravely stayed in London during the 1665 plague.
>
> **Robert Foulkes**, who matriculated as a servitor in 1652, was one of Christ Church's only two known murderers, and was hanged at Tyburn in 1679.
>
> **Joshua Hoyle**, Student and regius professor, was appointed to the Mastership of University College, and **Henry Langley**, canon from 1648, to the Mastership of Pembroke College.
>
> **Anthony Radcliffe**, elected to a Studentship in 1648 by the Visitors, remained in place after the Restoration, received a canonry in 1681. He left his money to Christ Church for the rebuilding of Peckwater Quad. **John Temple** trained as a barrister, and became Solicitor-General in Ireland, and Speaker of the Irish House of Commons.
>
> ODNB

king's health. In spite of submitting to the Visitors in 1648, he was deprived of his Studentship.[44] Not even the almsmen were immune. Those who had fought on the Royalist side were expelled and replaced by loyal Parliamentarians, such as Matthew Brown, who had served as a soldier in the Regiment under the command of Colonel Samuel Jones and Major General Skippon.[45]

In some ways, in spite of yet another change in personnel, things quickly began to return to what looked like normality. Numbers immediately soared, with a new intake of 35 in 1647 in addition to the returning students, a situation echoed much later in 1919. In other ways, though, change was very evident.

John Owen was appointed dean in 1651 after his predecessor, Reynolds, refused to take the Engagement. Under his moderate rule, Christ Church was managed with great efficiency, and survived the Commonwealth relatively unscathed.

In July 1649, the organ was removed from the cathedral, the first real evidence of the new Puritan regime, although Captain James Wadsworth – pursuivant of the court of high commission and the privy council – had petitioned Parliament for the removal of 'divers Reliques of Superstition of Popery ... and Massinge Stuff' as far back as January 1647.[46] The main damage to the fabric was the destruction of the beautiful van Linge windows.[47] By a decree issued in June 1651, 'all Pictures representing god, good or bad Angells or Saints shall be forthwith taken downe out of our Church windows'. Henry Wilkinson, an outspoken Puritan appointed a canon by Parliament, in an iconoclastic outburst of which there appear to have been few, jumped on the windows as they were removed, destroying most beyond any repair. Only one window survived intact.[48]

The Visitor's first choice of dean, the moderate Edward Reynolds, appointed in 1648, had been removed in March 1651 for having refused to take the oath of loyalty to the Commonwealth known as the Engagement. He was replaced by the Independent, John Owen.[49] In Owen, a protégé of Oliver Cromwell, Christ Church was given a remarkable dean who valued tranquillity, possessed the art of turning a blind eye, but who also knew when to put his head over the parapet. Serving as vice-chancellor and dean – as Reynolds had before him – Owen outwardly defied the Puritan stereotype; he dressed flamboyantly, raised and led his own troops from within the University when necessary, and showed tolerance with the University's Anglicanism. He handled small irritations, like positions of seniority, swiftly and effectively, and allowed grand events like the Act Supper to take place.[50] Christ Church also owed to Owen's friendship with Cromwell the retention of its landed estate. Student numbers remained stable throughout the Commonwealth, and the canons who ran the college and cathedral were able men. Tutors and officers like Richard Lower maintained the educational vigour. Life in 1650s Christ Church appears to have been relatively peaceful; and evidence suggests that Christ Church came through the Civil War and the Commonwealth relatively unscathed. But not all was harmonious.

It was in the dining hall that the niggles of discontent between the established members of the House and the newly intruded men made their presence felt. Usually, at Christmas, the annual election took place which established all the Students in their places according to their seniority for the following year. The traditional progress up the scale of seniority, represented by the movement from table to table in Hall, had been muddled by the change of men and no one knew where they stood. In July 1649, the Chapter had to intervene when a place was misappropriated.[51] The canons decided that there was no way forward except to conduct a 'remend' early to 'satisfy both parties and take away doubts and differences amongst them'. An election therefore took place in August 1649, followed by another in January 1650.[52] The new and 'old' Students soon settled in together; so much so, that by 1651, they were united in a revisitation of the old complaint of a shortage of dues and low stipends.[53] No doubt an almost universal voice

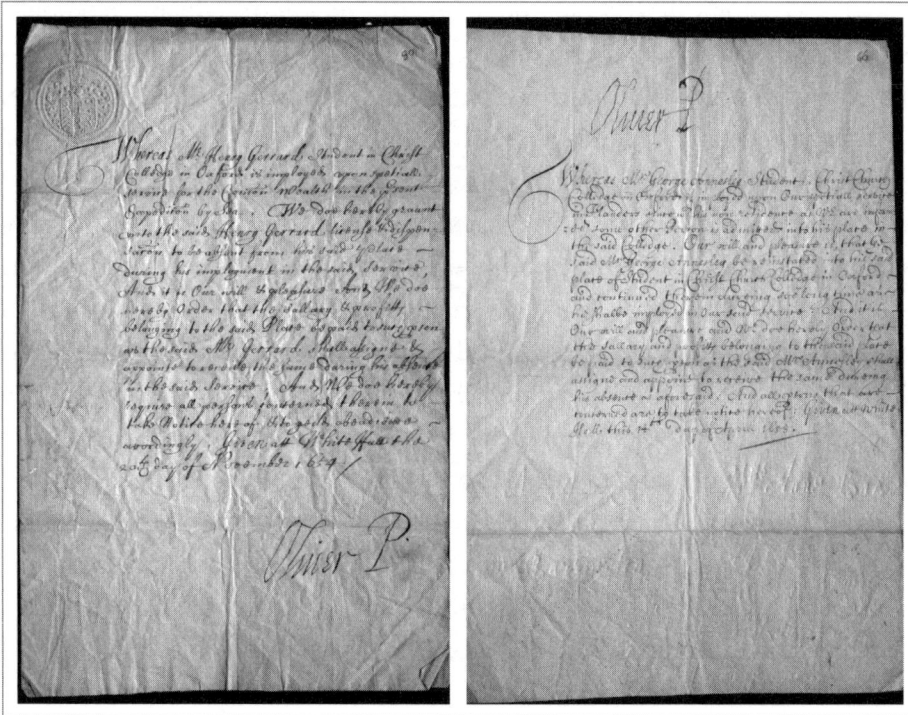

During the period of the Commonwealth, Students continued to travel on official duties for the government. Henry Garrard was permitted to keep his Student's stipend while on service overseas, probably to the Caribbean, in 1654. George Annesley served as a major in the Parliamentary army and was granted leave of absence to go to Flanders in 1658. He drowned in the Thames just 40 days before the Restoration of Charles II. These are the only two documents in the archive signed by Cromwell as Protector. The change in his signature shows his increasingly poor health.

was raised against the 1653 decree by the Visitors that every undergraduate must give account to a suitable person, every Sunday, of the sermon heard in chapel or of the religious exercises performed. Certainly George Annesley, later to be sent abroad on special services, was admonished for 'affronting' the Dean and Chapter when they entered Hall to observe the new rule.[54]

Even so, life was, at least on an everyday level, much the same as before. Men were still being sent abroad on special service, but now the orders were signed by 'Oliver P' rather than by a monarch; Henry Garrard was guaranteed payment of his stipend while away on the disastrous expedition to Hispaniola (designed to attack Spain in the Caribbean while avoiding war in Europe), and George Annesley was sent to Flanders.[55] Undergraduates still misbehaved and paid the consequences: William Devereux was publicly whipped and rusticated for twelve months for 'divers grosse and scandalouse Acts', and Knight, for 'divers disorders and misdeameanors' and Annesley, already an MA, was reprimanded for being seen in a tippling house on the Lord's Day.[56] Even the staff were not immune to the increased vigilance: Hawkes and Wilkins, under-butlers, were mulcted an immense 20 shillings each for 'drinking health and committing other misdemeanours lately at one Gregorie's house'. Their fines were distributed among the poor of the local parishes. Both men were also suspended from all profits of their posts until Lady Day, seven weeks later.[57]

Rules were tightened still further. The Visitors required the Dean and Chapter to ensure that 'Cavalier' fashions, such as long and powdered hair or extravagant clothes, were discouraged, and excessive spending in the buttery was to be reported by the butler every week. Gentlemen commoners were not expected to spend more than five shillings per week, and commoners no more than three shillings.[58] Students were not to let out their chambers to anyone without permission, or to have guests stay for any extended period. Ingress and egress was carefully controlled by the dean, who ordered that new gates be set up near the stables and the meadow, and any keys not held by the porter be handed over to his care.[59]

Men were still taking degrees and in many ways the academic standards were higher than in pre-war days. The use of Latin was enforced, as was the standard of tutors. No one was permitted to be a tutor in the House without the dean's approval, and those excluded by the Visitors were definitely not to teach. They were to read constantly to their scholars from approved classical authors, and cause them to come together to pray privately. Chapel, at which the Directory had replaced the Prayer Book, was compulsory every morning and evening, and senior men were expected to set an example to juniors in religious duty.[60] Every man was expected to study properly towards his degree, and time that was spent in ways other than study would not count towards the residence requirement. Degrees were to be received in person, and all bills had to be paid on pain of losing one's degree.[61] There were some dispensations; because of the war, Richard Russell, Samuel Ward, Lewis Atterbury, William Carpenter and William Crompton had not achieved the full residence requirements but were all granted grace for their BAs in December 1649.[62] All five had been appointed to their Studentships by the Visitors. Honoured men, such as Thomas Silsby, Jeremiah Clarke, Nathaniel Dunbavin and Vincent Denne, were still given MAs of the House.[63]

Everyday business continued as usual. If anything, administration was more efficient than it had been before the war. Contact with estates was common, and actions to right wrongs occurred frequently. When, for instance, the parishioners of Marcham complained vociferously to the Dean and Chapter about the quality of their new vicar, Mr Read, and requested that he be replaced (not through any fault with his doctrine, but because his voice was too soft), the Chapter suggested that Read be given a slightly longer settling-in period to see if he improved with practice.[64] There was evidently some disagreement over the use of Abbots Wood in South Stoke, and a progress and court were planned to take place as soon as legal advice had been obtained.[65] In 1656, the vicar of Great Bowden, in Leicestershire, complained that his stipend was far too small, and a decision was made to include an increase in the next lease of the estate.[66] Internal problems were also dealt with quickly, such as the inflationary effects of the Civil War on domestic bills. Hudson, the cook, for example, had his allowance raised from £28 to £30 a quarter, to cover the 2d a sack rise in coal prices.[67]

Owen was removed as dean in March 1660, having actively stood against George Monck and accused him of almost single-handedly toppling Cromwell. Reynolds, who advocated a moderate episcopacy acceptable to the major parties, returned briefly during the spring and early summer of 1660.[68]

The Restoration was greeted by bell-ringing and a celebratory bonfire, and then Christ Church, with the rest of Oxford, began to pick up the pieces.[69] George Morley, a middle-of-the-road Christ Church veteran who had been evicted from his canonry in 1647, was made dean in 1660 to great

'The present engagement of the greatest part of them in Armes': 1625–88

> ## The canons in July 1660
>
> 1st stall: Jasper Mayne, once a Student, replaced Henry Wilkinson
>
> 2nd stall: John Fell, once a Student, replaced Ralph Button. When Fell took the deanery, his canonry was occupied by Sebastian Smith
>
> 3rd stall: Richard Gardiner returned and replaced Christopher Rogers
>
> 4th stall: John Dolben, once a Student, replaced John Poynter
>
> 5th stall: William Creed, elected to a Studentship by Dean Owen in 1656, replaced Henry Cornish
>
> 6th stall: Edward Pococke returned and replaced John Mills
>
> 7th stall: John Wall, the one canon who made it through the Commonwealth
>
> 8th stall: Richard Allestree, once Student, replaced Henry Langley

acclamation.[70] Entering the college on 26 July, the first act of the new dean and his Chapter, on 27 July, was to return the canons' table to its accustomed place in Hall.[71] Fourteen Students who had been ejected by Parliament were restored to their places.[72] But there was a problem with those who had been intruded; Christ Church was restricted, if not by statute then by custom, to 100 Students so, in order to return some to the rightful places, others had to go. Charles II appointed a commission to review the situation, and to expel those who had been improperly elected or who were particularly factious. By the end of 1660, only five of the Students appointed by Parliament in 1648 or elected by the Visitors remained. Two, Richard Russell and Thomas Vincent, resigned before the commission questioned them. Two more were interviewed: William Segary was deprived of his place, but Anthony Radcliffe was allowed to remain and, on his death, bequeathed over £2,000 to the rebuilding of Peckwater Quad. The fifth man, George Atherton, was not examined and retained his Studentship. Six more were expelled, and a further three resigned. Why some Students were permitted to remain is unclear, but it may have been dependent on the religious leanings of the nominating canon. Bringing men back meant that another reorganisation of the Student roll became necessary; the restored Students were placed with some ceremony at the top of the list, with those who had submitted to the Parliamentary Visitors back in 1648 moved down to make room.[73]

Morley was, by all accounts, abstemious but kind and generous. His character is reflected in the new decrees which were issued by the end of his first month as dean, and passed to ensure that governance was restored to a sure footing. The new rules limited the number of servitors to 20, reduced the number of scouts who had been 'retained unto this House upon pretence of goeinge on errands or the like', and raised the minimum age of bedmakers to 40. Christ Church was a college more used to the presence of women than any other, as the dean and all the canons were entitled to marry, and most had families resident within the walls, but the maintenance of the morality of the junior members was considered paramount; an old rule, laid down initially by Wolsey in 1525, that laundresses were not even to enter the college but were to collect and deliver their work at given times to the gates, was resurrected. At the same time, the porters were charged with ensuring that no 'seamstresses, stocking menders and applewomen or any suspicious persons of any kind be admitted'. Both fasting nights and gaudy nights were limited to the original number permitted by both church and college, Latin prayers were to be held at 8.30 every night, and monthly communion was to be revived.[74] Last, a new survey of chambers was to be drawn up, to check that residents were those who were really meant to be there.[75]

Such rules were evidently necessary. In January 1664, Anthony Wood recorded that one of the chaplains, Richard Berry, 'one much given to the flesh', had called an apple-seller to his rooms to 'coole his passion',[76] whereas other chaplains were interfering with the choirboys. Christ Church was, according to Anthony Wood, notorious for venereal disease – the 'pox' – which was rife thanks to the bawdy houses, and unscrupulous businessmen were taking advantage of the naivety of youth, selling their potions to deal with such unspeakable diseases. Gambling was commonplace, drunkenness frequent, extravagance was encouraged by salesmen all too keen to make a quick profit, atheism was spreading and disrespect to one's elders was on the rise – all because, said Wood, the MAs were not setting an example.[77]

> ## College officers under Fell
>
> **Catechist: Richard Howe** matriculated in 1631 but was expelled during the Interregnum.
>
> **Senior Censor: Thomas Vincent** was first appointed catechist in 1654. A zealous non-conformist, he was renowned for staying in London during the 1665 plague to attend to the dying.
>
> **Junior Censor: Henry Bold** was elected during the Commonwealth but later became secretary to Arlington, Charles II's secretary of state.
>
> **Rhetoric lecturer: Henry Bagshaw**. Another Commonwealth Student, Bagshaw was chaplain to the English ambassador in Spain from 1663.
>
> **Greek lecturer: John Locke** matriculated in 1652, and was recognised with the lectureship in 1661.
>
> **Praelectors:**
>
> **Samuel Jackson** was expelled during the Interregnum, but permitted to keep his rooms while he studied medicine.
>
> **Thomas Martin** matriculated in 1654 and worked his way quietly through the Commonwealth, only showing his colours when he contributed to the celebratory poems published at the Restoration.
>
> **Benjamin Woodroffe** held a Studentship from 1656 and a canonry from 1672. He was chaplain to the King and was offered the deanery in 1688.
>
> **Francis Eedes** came up in 1656 and followed a career in medicine.

Keeping a rising undergraduate population in check was never easy, and efforts to do so account for the constant repetition of regulations both in the colleges and across the University at large.

Morley remained dean until October 1660, when he was appointed Bishop of Worcester. John Fell, who had been made a canon in July at the same time as his friends Richard Allestree and John Dolben, stepped into his shoes. Fell was a Christ Church man through and through, and he embraced the task of rebuilding it, both academically and physically. He had arrived at

John Fell, John Dolben and Richard Allestree, Christ Church's Restoration triumvirate, by Peter Lely.

Christ Church from Lord Williams's School in Thame as a Student in 1637, just short of his twelfth birthday, and just before his father, Samuel, was appointed dean. Obviously an astonishing intellect, Fell took his MA at 18 and, with Allestree and Dolben, rode out the dramas of the Commonwealth. Then, during Morley's brief period in the deanery, the three men effectively ran Christ Church. Allestree was Morley's proxy, standing in while the dean was away carrying out his diplomatic business in London, so the decrees laid down in July were as much the work of the rulers-in-waiting. Once Fell was officially in place, Allestree became sub-dean and Dolben was elected Treasurer. The allowances paid to the college officers were increased; the sub-dean was given £20 per annum, and the Treasurer £40.[78] John King was returned as auditor by order of the vice-chancellor's court, in place of Samuel Bedford, the Commonwealth man.[79] All the absentee Students were called home, and ordered to arrive back before 1 January 1661 or to risk losing their places.

Fell continued and expanded on Morley's restoring labours. The first of the great 'builder deans', he immediately put into action a plan for the completion of the Great Quad, placing on the site of Wolsey's proposed chapel, in the same early sixteenth-century style, a north range. He built a new, eponymous accommodation block, and commissioned Christopher Wren to build Tom Tower. In 1667, the Chapter Clerk was given the unenviable task of surveying all the estates documents in the archive – apparently in an abominable state – to ensure that the full extent of Christ Church's property was recorded and understood.[80] The maximisation of income was vital if the place was to be made the greatest college in Oxford. Dolben's efforts as Treasurer are immediately obvious in the audited accounts: in 1660/61, receipts were £4,026 10s 8d with a balance of income over expenditure of £587; the following year, receipts were up to £9,057. It was just as well, for with the increased expenditure on Fell's building projects, outgoings totalled £8,750.[81]

One of the reasons for the building scheme was to seek new undergraduates among the rich and influential.[82] But Fell was not entirely seduced by the wealthy. Statistics show that he evidently had an eye for the talented, too – men like Thomas Bennet, the grammarian, who had come up to Christ Church as a commoner, but was soon elected to a Studentship. The dean ensured that he received the position of architypographer at the University Press, where he proofread Fell's own books. There were the usual future senior clergymen and politicians but Fell also nurtured colonial administrators such as Christopher Codrington and William Penn, medics such as Edward Hannes, entrepreneurs such as Richard Newdigate, playwrights and poets such as Thomas Otway, lawyers such as William Banister and Thomas Trevor, the antiquarian and naturalist Robert Davies, and John Berkeley, a naval officer.[83] During the decade of the Commonwealth, 91 gentlemen commoners had been admitted and 82 servitors; in the following decade to 1670, Fell admitted 93 gentlemen commoners and 115 servitors. Unsurprisingly, no noblemen had been admitted during the 1650s.

Fell immediately put that right, but even though the numbers arriving were much higher than they had ever been, still only 27 – about 5 per cent of total admissions – were entered during the first ten years of Fell's deanery.[84]

Undoubtedly, there were some exceptionally wealthy and high-born men among the newcomers at Christ Church: Lord Thomas Leigh, for example, had a personal servant and paid for a college servitor, too. But the claims of John Percival to have had a bedmaker, a laundress, a barber and other servants in his employ may just have been a young man's boast that he could afford to make full use of the college's staff. The rather odd benefaction of William Thurston, another donor apparently unconnected with Oxford, also demonstrated that the college was attracting the attention of the wealthy. In 1664, Thurston bequeathed £800 to the 'King's College in Oxford'. There was debate for a while over which college Thurston had intended to benefit; both Oriel and Brasenose felt that they had a claim, but the judgement of the Archbishop of Canterbury in the Court of Arches awarded the gift to Christ Church. From 1665, when a new Studentship was formally introduced and funded by Thurston's bequest, there were 101 Students, and Tom began to chime an extra note each evening.[85]

Fell ruled Christ Church firmly, closely supervising the work and conduct of undergraduates. Behaviour was as strictly monitored as ever. William Okell, for example, was found guilty of 'enormous misdemeanours for which he deservedly ought to be removed and expelled'. He was granted a small reprieve, however, and was confined to the library for three months to complete any exercises given to him by Sub-dean Allestree. Should Okell absent himself from the library during that period, or misbehave again, his Studentship was to be declared void. Some crimes, though, were less sympathetically handled: William Levett, elected to a Studentship in 1663, was expelled just a year later for climbing over the college walls after curfew in the company of his accomplices, Thomas Ackworth and Alexander Morison, killing a sow belonging to a poor woman, and stealing a bundle of laths.[86] Although it was Levett who was sent down, it seems to have been Morison who led the others into trouble. Just a few months later, in November 1664, this 'person of notorious and incorrigible debauchery' was discovered drunk and fighting in Merton College. To this charge, other 'intollerable misdemeanours' were to be added: he disturbed the peace in Christ Church by 'shouting loud and uncivil clamours and hootinge', drank in his chambers, debauched with a gentleman commoner late at night, and was also found to have been an accomplice in the robbing of the Dean of Westminster's hen roost. Unbelievably, he seems to have got away with everything. He raised a petition among the undergraduates and bachelors, requiring the dean to bring evidence against him. The dean was effectively blackmailed – produce evidence or Morison would create sedition and faction throughout the House. A compromise was reached: Morison's expulsion was suspended, but he was refused any promotion up the election list and the grace to take any further degrees.[87]

Occasionally, college rivalries broke out physically. In 1652, Edward Fowler of Corpus Christi was deprived of his commons for throwing bread at the Students of Christ Church and provoking them to riot.[88] Six years later, a party from Christ Church, 'fild with mighty valour and potentiall ale', took the battle the other way, storming Corpus and beating them all 'great and small' into their chambers.[89]

Students were ever the same, however. Fell was a disciplinarian, without doubt, but he also tried to encourage the lighter side of undergraduate life. In January 1664, he actively supported the premiere of Richard Rhodes's *Flora's Vagaries*, but was careful that only those men he considered suitable could see the play. He guarded the doors, and for his pains was treated to vandalism and vocal scorn by those who were not allowed in. The actors, all undergraduates, evidently saw themselves as special – after all, the dean had given them supper and Allestree had presented each of them with a book worth seven shillings – and supper lapsed into a drunken and wanton occasion. Fell never allowed a play to be performed again at Christ Church.[90]

Cases of misbehaviour by the Students were always carefully heard by the Chapter. In the same year that Morison's behaviour was censured, John Locke, then Senior Censor, was called before the Chapter to answer a claim that he had sconced a college servant. Perhaps unsurprisingly, he was found not guilty.[91] Not all hearings concerned bad behaviour. Lapses in

> ## Robert Hooke (1635–1703)
>
> Hooke came up to Christ Church in 1653, and was soon working as assistant to Thomas Willis and Robert Boyle in their experiments. He studied astronomy, which led to the development of clockworks, and the invention of a spring-regulated watch. His most famous work, *Micrographia*, revealed life in all its minutiae.
>
> ODNB

protocol could prompt disciplinary action; when William Ellis took his MA and Isaiah Ward his DMed from Cambridge without first obtaining grace from Christ Church, both were dismissed from their Studentships. And, in 1667, Fleetwood Sheppard was expelled for not making sufficient progress in his studies. This was a brave move; elected a Student in 1652, Sheppard had both his BA and MA within the expected period. He should have taken orders, but in 1664, Charles II had written to the dean asking that he be given a faculty Studentship.[92] Sheppard spent most of his time at Court, and the Chapter evidently felt that his place could be better filled by someone else.

On the whole, however, the religious upheavals of the mid-seventeenth century seem to have promoted studies rather than suppressed them. All through the Commonwealth period, Christ Church men had continued the earlier work of Nathaniel Torporley and Edmund Gunter, notably Peter Turner, who lectured on magnetism and electricity, and whose position as Savilian professor of geometry was brought to an abrupt end when he was forced out of the University by the Parliamentary Visitors in 1648.[93] Certainly, science was at a peak of inventiveness during this period and at Christ Church, men like Robert Hooke, Thomas Willis and Richard Lower were spearheading experimentation. Willis was a doctor, practising out of his rooms at Christ Church and engaging both Hooke and Lower as his assistants.[94] All three men, pushing the boundaries of science in Oxford in the 1650s and 1660s, and active in the newly founded Royal Society, must have imbued the college with a sense of excitement and forward thinking.

'The present engagement of the greatest part of them in Armes': 1625–88

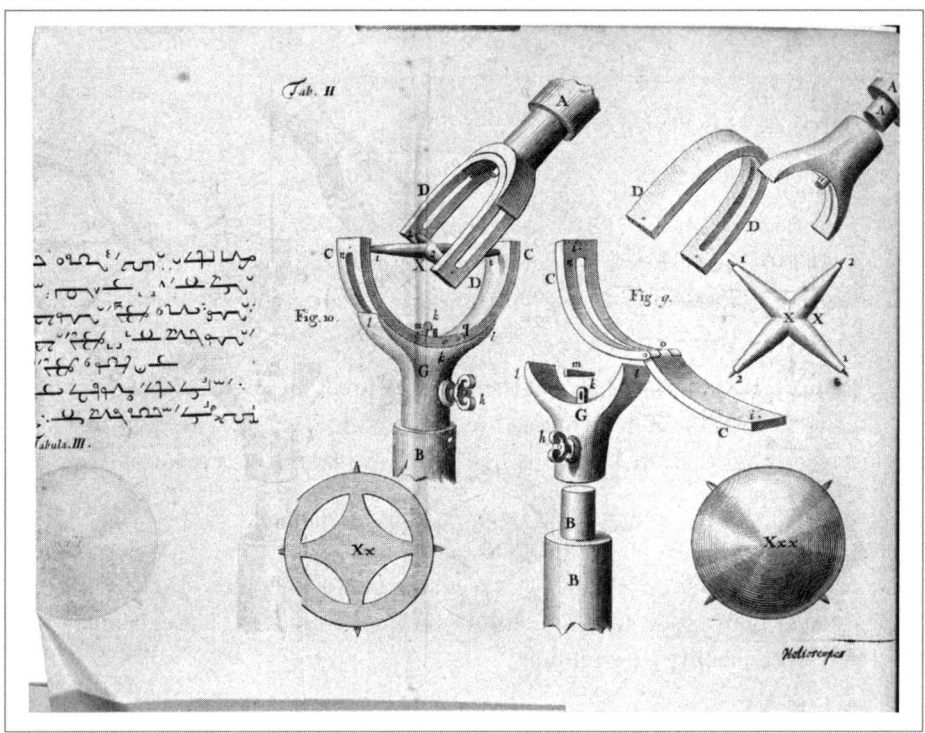

Robert Hooke matriculated from Christ Church in 1658. He and his colleagues, members of the nascent Royal Society, brought tremendous originality of thought to natural philosophy. His universal joint, illustrated in A description of helioscopes *(1676), is still in use today.*

Other subjects were also flourishing. Mathematics and astronomy were taught as practical subjects. The extraordinary career of the young Edmond Halley may well have been a driving force behind Fell's desire for an observatory in Tom Tower; an idea which Christopher Wren, himself a student of astronomy among all other branches of science, successfully blocked. Edward Pococke had fostered the study of Arabic and other Middle Eastern languages, particularly during the 1650s when, although deprived of his canonry, he retained his professorships in Arabic and Hebrew. Although not the greatest teacher, Pococke doubtless inspired young men with tales of his travels to Syria and Constantinople, and he certainly brought to Oxford, and to Christ Church, the benefit of his huge learning.[95]

Trusts, 1625–1688

Bostock

Joan Bostock left, in 1633, three houses in Peascod Street, Windsor, the income from which was to be distributed between four needy Students who held out the 'towardliest hope for learning and conversation'.

Morris

John Morris, regius professor of Hebrew, gave funds for seven exhibitions of up to £3 per annum to encourage Students to study Hebrew. They were first awarded in 1693. In 1830, the number of exhibitions was reduced from seven to two.

Gardiner

Richard Gardiner, who funded the construction of Mercury, also gave an estate in Bourton-on-the-Water to fund awards to servitors. Each exhibition was worth about £7 per annum.

Busby

Richard Busby's estate at Willen paid for the foundation of the Common Room, and various lectures.

Paul

Rachel Paul, widow of the Bishop of Oxford, bequeathed a few acres in Eynsham to assist three Bachelor servitors, preferably the sons of clergymen.

Cotton

Edward Cotton, a canon of Exeter, left the tithes of land in Ottery St Mary for the support of servitors from Devon, Cornwall and Oxfordshire.

Fell and Hill

The Fell and Hill trust, created by Dean Fell and Canon Richard Hill in 1685, gave a small donation to two Westminster Students. The award was first made in 1714. Fell's estate around Bampton and Standlake, gave £15 a year to the vicar of Spelsbury, and the remainder to 'ingenious and indigent' members of Christ Church, after examination.

'The present engagement of the greatest part of them in Armes': 1625–88

In 1667, Richard Busby, then headmaster of Westminster School, proposed that the low room under the Hall be set up for mathematical and oriental lectures. His benefaction was not a success; the lectures never really took off, and the only immediate result of Busby's gift was the foundation of a common room at Christ Church. Part of the agreement between Busby and the Dean and Chapter was that the room would remain a common room in perpetuity; should the room ever be used for anything else, then the monies spent in its conversion should be reimbursed to himself or his descendants.[96] It must have been a novel addition to college life, and one that was being adopted by other colleges, too; up until this time, sitting around an open fire for sociable evenings was rare, as most men were expected to return to their own rooms after dinner. Even so, in the early years the Common Room was not the most comfortable of places, particularly from 1720 when it was rather encumbered by the vaulting installed after a fire in the Hall.[97]

Studies could be interrupted by disease: in October 1683, just as students were returning to Oxford after the summer break, there was an outbreak of smallpox. Some turned around and went straight back home. Perhaps they were wise to do so, as Wood records that, on 6 November, four men fell ill at Christ Church on the same day. By the middle of the month, the city had ordered the churches to stop tolling their bells for the dead, as it was scaring people away and ruining trade.[98]

John Fell was the only man ever to hold both the deanery and the bishopric simultaneously, and his influence across the university, both during and after his period as vice-chancellor, was immense. So much so, that he could inspire rancour, as shown in the famous rhyme:

> I do not love thee Dr Fell,
> The reason why I cannot tell;
> But this I know and know full well,
> I do not love thee Dr Fell.

An energetic achiever, it was Fell who encouraged the building of the Sheldonian Theatre in which to hold university ceremonies, and Fell who pushed the development of the University Press. Anthony Wood suggested that he grasped at too many public affairs, 'few of which he thoroughly effected'.⁹⁹ He used his power to ensure that his own college and cathedral were protected and enhanced. One notable dispute occurred when Fell insisted that, when it was the canons' turn to preach before the University, their sermons could be given in the cathedral rather than in the University Church of St Mary's, as they had always been before. The vice-chancellor, then Ralph Bathurst, president of Trinity College, the proctors, and the heads of houses, reacted angrily, writing to the Dean and Chapter that they were going against the University statutes in insisting that *all* their sermons should be given at the cathedral. They complained, too, that the cathedral was not as convenient as St Mary's: it was further away; it was difficult to hear anything, particularly in the north transept; the seats were uncomfortable, and the bell could not be heard from any distance away. The canons were most put out at the suggestion that they would break their oaths to the University merely to maintain a 'punctilio of grandeur' and responded with a clause from the Foundation Charter that exempted members of Christ Church from 'appearing at the public conventions of the University, whether sacred or civil'. Thompson suggests that the Chapter knew they were on weak ground here as they recited an earlier agreement with the rest of the University that, while the cathedral was used as a college chapel, the members of Christ Church, with as many others who wish to attend, would go to the cathedral. On occasions when other members of the University were preaching, Housemen would be encouraged to go to St Mary's.¹⁰⁰ Fell and the canons were also determined to repudiate the charges of inconvenience. The cathedral was not so far beyond St Mary's as to cause a wearisome journey and, as for the bell not being loud enough, what else was happening in town to hinder it being heard at those hours of the morning and evening? The battle raged, in the manner of things apparently not so important, and eventually the king had to intervene. Charles pronounced that when a canon was preaching as a canon, then the service would be at Christ Church, but when he was preaching in another capacity, then the service would be held at St Mary's.¹⁰¹

Fell was a Royalist, and entertained the monarch and his family on several occasions. Charles and Catherine visited twice, once in 1663 and again from September 1665 until February 1666 when the plague was rife in London. On the first visit, the royal couple were accompanied by Lady Castlemaine, newly delivered of a baby, who was discreetly put up by Dr Gardiner on the other side of college from the deanery. Sturgeon appeared on the dinner menu.[102] The second occasion was in the company of the Duke and Duchess of York, who were accommodated by Richard Allestree in the brand-new north side of the Great Quad. The Duke of Monmouth came too, unaware that in 20 years' time, just before his death, John Fell would summon a troop of Christ Church undergraduates to fight against him for James II. The queen, like her predecessor, resided at Merton College. Fleetingly, in May 1669, the Duke of Tuscany, Cosimo de Medici, passed through on an official visit and was treated to a couple of speeches, one by Canterbury Gate and the other in Hall given by William Wigan.[103] Over in the Bodleian, among presentations by many students, the duke heard two Christ Church undergraduates disputing eloquently, and 'Crispin,' probably Stephen Crespion, singing.[104] The following year, just before Christmas, William, Prince of Orange, lodged at Christ Church, spending only two days in Oxford but visiting much of the the University. Five dozen torches were purchased to light his way around the college.[105]

In 1681, Charles's fifth Parliament descended on Oxford, necessitating the clearing-out of all undergraduates from Christ Church, Corpus Christi and Merton just to accommodate the Court. Other colleges were commandeered for the Privy Council and Parliament. Preparations began in January, with the Lord Chamberlain's men arriving on 11 February to check on the accommodation. The king arrived in Oxford on 14 March with great ceremony. When he entered Christ Church, the cathedral bells began to ring, and the whole atmosphere was one of great celebration. Parliament was a short-lived affair this time, however. Much to everyone's surprise, Charles dissolved Parliament before the end of the month, and left immediately for London, followed shortly by the queen.[106] He did not return to Oxford, but the cessation of royal visits did not stop the procession of dignitaries. The Duke of York came in 1683 with his wife and his daughter, Lady Anne, later to be queen. The duke noted that his name had been on the books since his

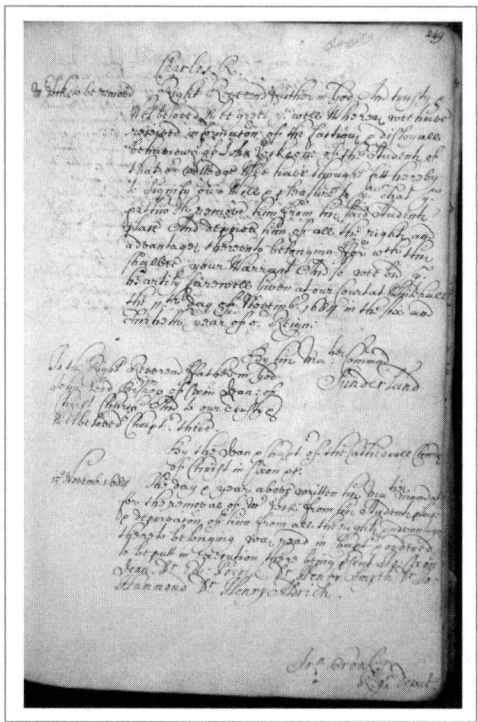

John Locke, celebrated philosopher and author of An Essay concerning Human Understanding, *had come up to Christ Church in 1652, and held various college offices. After the Restoration, his politics became increasingly radical and his views made him less than popular. At the monarch's request, recorded here in the Chapter Book, Locke was expelled from his Studentship in 1684.*

visit to Christ Church in 1642.[107] In May 1682, the ambassador of Fez and Morocco dined in the deanery only to have his visit interrupted by a hurricane, and later that year the nephew of the king of Sweden was entered a canon commoner of Christ Church, and presented with an honorary DCL.[108]

Fell's loyalty to the Crown was tested when he was required to dismiss John Locke from his Studentship. Locke had come up in 1652, and may have been the most distinguished thinker ever to have entered through Tom Gate. After the Restoration, he was immediately appointed Greek reader, reader in rhetoric, and then Senior Censor. He held a Faculty Studentship, exempting him from taking holy orders. Locke had, though, outside interests and became increasingly involved in politics during his time as secretary to Lord Ashley, whom he had taught as a child. Locke was suspected of conspiracy on Monmouth's behalf, and the Christ Church Students tried hard to trap him into confessing. Locke was far too clever, and Fell had to admit there was no real evidence against him, but, in an increasingly Tory university, the rumours and suppositions, combined with Locke's leanings towards Whiggism, made him an object of suspicion. The royal mandate for Locke's expulsion was issued on 11 November 1684, and Locke was formally deprived of his Studentship on 15 November.[109] There was no dramatic removal of Locke from his rooms, however. Locke was abroad at the time of his expulsion, and did not return to England for another five years. It is ironic that, during the eighteenth century, when Locke's writings were less than popular across the university as a whole, Christ Church made them an integral and important part of the curriculum, and his statue, by Roubillac, was placed with some honour in the New Library.

Fell's death on 10 July 1686, just a year after the accession of James II, caused a crisis at Christ Church which tested the solidarity of the Chapter.[110] Jonathan Trelawney, Bishop of Winchester, writing to Archbishop Sancroft, said that he could not see who might take Fell's place in either the deanery or the bishopric.[111] He remarked that he wouldn't contemplate taking one without the other, but Trelawney was never considered as a candidate. Sancroft was less perplexed: 'For Christ's Church, it is a most flourishing society and hath bred vast Numbers of Worthy persons fitt for any Station in the Church. But I am a stranger there ... And yet I will be bold to say with some confidence, yt there are not in yt great Multitude 2 more excellent persons better qualified to suit any Vacancy yt is or may be yn Dr Hooper of Lambeth and Mr Wigan of Kensington.'[112] Neither of Sancroft's choices were in the running either.

There was a six-month gap between Fell's death and the appointment of his successor as dean. In between, a new bishop had to be found. In spite of doubts that a headless Chapter could actually make any real recommendation, Henry Aldrich, the sub-dean, took a firm hand and conducted procedures. The general feeling was that Robert South, who had been holding out

> ## Allestree and Dolben
>
> Fell's greatest friends, who might well have been considered likely candidates for the succession, were no longer in the field.
>
> Dolben, through family influence, had been made Dean of Westminster in 1662, bishop of Rochester in 1666, and finally archbishop of York in 1683. He died on 11 April 1686, just three months before Fell.
>
> Allestree had remained in Oxford, becoming regius professor of divinity in 1663. A dedicated scholar, he was probably the author of *The Whole Duty of Man*, a devotional work in a High Church tradition, published in 1658. He died in 1681, leaving his library to the University.

for the bishopric of Oxford in spite of offers of other high church positions, would be a natural choice, but he damaged his chances twice, first upsetting the Royalists by writing a vicious letter opposing the blatant Catholicism of Obadiah Walker, the master of University College, who was, from August 1686, openly conducting mass in his own chapel. Second, perhaps more significant, was his ambivalence towards William of Orange, which upset those on the other side of the fence. Instead, Archdeacon Samuel Parker, unpopular and a fervent supporter of James II, was enthroned in November.

As the Catholicism of the king became more evident, so decisions were made which greatly disturbed the University and the colleges. University College was the rallying point for Catholicism in Oxford, and its Master cultivated a small group of young protégés (although most of the membership did not convert). Within a short space of time, the heads of All Souls, Magdalen and Christ Church all died, and Walker was ready with his band of loyal disciples. Soon rumours abounded that John Massey, a fellow of Merton College and a servitor of Walker's, was to be given the deanery. The gossip proved to be true, and Anthony Wood expressed his opinion vociferously, hinting that the canons of Christ Church were affronted at the prospect of having not only a Catholic imposed upon them but also a man so relatively junior in the University. But no word was apparently spoken at

Christ Church. Massey was installed on 29 December at a ceremony that was both farcical and awful. The undergraduates treated the whole affair as a joke, talking and pulling faces throughout, but the canons were serious in the extreme. During the service, a dispensation was read which, in effect, relieved Massey of conducting any Anglican ceremony at all.[113]

From the archival point of view, Massey's period is poorly documented. Only everyday business, alongside a few formal documents, is recorded in the Chapter Books. Admissions dropped from 43 during 1686 to only 15 in 1687 (one of whom, Hugh Boulter, would be dean).[114] There are no apparent similarities, or Catholic leanings, between the young men who came up that year. They were, no doubt, just those who were destined to come anyway and whose parents had weighed up the pros and cons of sending their sons to a reluctantly Catholic Christ Church.[115]

Thompson, in his 1900 history of Christ Church, described Massey as a 'very insignificant person', and suggested that the government of college and cathedral was managed by Aldrich. This may have been true; certainly Christ Church, both in the latter years of Charles's reign and into James's, was at the forefront of resistance against Catholicism in the University. So much so that the vice-chancellor, Halton, begged the canons not to openly preach against Catholicism in case they were called to account by James's new ecclesiastical commission.

But Massey was the king's man, and his appointment could have been seen as a disciplinary action against an anti-Catholic, Protestant, cathedral foundation.[116] As a consequence, he lacked any internal support among the canons and Students, and appears not to have tried to gain it. He continued his association with Walker and the other Catholic notables in Oxford, converted the old refectory of Canterbury College into a chapel for his private use, and appointed a Jesuit priest as his chaplain.[117] He relied entirely on those outside Oxford, not least the king. Meanwhile, Aldrich and a dedicated team of academics worked hard to counter every pro-Catholic document that was published by Walker and his acolytes, and life within Christ Church was made very difficult for Massey. The Declaration of Indulgence, issued in April 1687, was the final straw. The Indulgence appeared, at first glance, to be an attempt to widen religious toleration, but instead was seen by the academic clergy as a means to split them. Parker's request that the University send an address thanking the king was refused. Both academics and clergy stood together. The tension must have been palpable, and the watchful Catholic contingency were all too ready to pounce on any sign, however small, of dissent: a Christ Church undergraduate merely smirking during a mass in Walker's chapel was arrested and imprisoned, only to be released by his Protestant gaolers.[118] Undergraduates treated Massey with contempt and insolence, and the canons had little incentive to reprove them. In spite of the pomp and circumstance afforded the monarch during his visit to Oxford in September 1687, the relationship between king and University deteriorated to such a point that the University came out as one in support of William of Orange's invasion.[119] On the landing of William, on 5 November 1688, there were tremendous celebrations in Oxford, and by the end of the month Massey had made good his escape to France.

Christ Church time

In 1546, the chief carpenter, John Wesburn, was given the awesome responsibility of taking down the bells of Oseney abbey and reinstalling them in the tower of the newly designated cathedral. The eight bells – Hautclere, Douce, Clement, Austin, Marie, Gabriel, John and, largest of all, Great Tom – were carted through St Thomas's parish into the city by a Mr Willoughby of Eynsham.[1] No doubt they rang at the foundation feast, and then for the accessions of Edward VI and his half-sister Mary, in whose honour Tom was rechristened for the five years of her reign.[2]

The bells were much used, marking not just services and celebrations, but the daily timetable. As early as 1583, new bell wheels were needed, and there were frequent payments for clappers and baldricks. The ringing of the bell 100 times each evening, representing the original number of Students on the foundation, probably started soon after 1546.[3] But Tom, no longer Mary, was not a happy bell. It was recast in 1612, possibly to rid it of a 'papist' inscription, then again in 1654 by Michael Darby of Whitechapel, who had worked on the bells at both Merton and New College.[4] His work was less than satisfactory. The Merton bells were recast by another London founder, Christopher Hodson, but Christ Church tried a local man, Richard Keene of Woodstock. After three unsuccessful attempts, the Dean and Chapter finally turned to Hodson, not just to recast Tom but also to make new bells.[5]

In October 1680, ten bells were rehung in the cathedral tower, with

Great Tom came to Christ Church from Oseney Abbey, and originally hung, with the other bells, in the spire of the cathedral. When the tower over the main gatehouse was built in 1683, Tom was recast and rehung. The '101', the chime representing the original number of Students plus the extra one created by the Thurston bequest, has rung from Tom Tower at least from that date at 9.05 pm every night.

Tom set aside for a new home.[6] Tom's last recasting coincided with Fell's decision to build the new tower at the Great Gate. The bell was installed and by May 1684 was ready to ring out in celebration of the anniversary of the Restoration.

Tom has been rehung three times since then: in 1692, when the bellfounder and two carpenters were kept busy for ten days; in 1847, when the bell was fixed and first operated by a hammer; and then once more in 1953.[7] Ringing the 101, which involved tying a rope to the clapper and just pulling it against the bell, was causing considerable damage and urgent repairs were necessary, including the replacement of the wooden headstock with a modern cast-iron one.[8] Mechanical ringing of the '101' was considered too expensive, but an arrangement for the bell to be rung by rope directly from the Porter's Lodge was to be rigged up, all the work to be completed in time for the coronation of Elizabeth II.[9]

The ten bells of the cathedral peal were originally rung from the floor, but in 1624 three lofts were built: the ringing loft, a further loft above it and the organ loft.[10] Estimates were received in around 1840 for rehanging the cathedral bells (although there is no evidence that this was done), and repairs were made to the frame during work to the cathedral in the 1850s. Gilbert Scott, however, found the spire to be unsafe, and the bells were moved to the Wolsey Tower in the 1880s.[11] Two new bells were added in 1897 to celebrate Queen Victoria's Diamond Jubilee, and mufflers were bought for all twelve on her death in 1901.[12]

Over the years, the ringing of Great Tom has become synonymous with great events. A regular muffled toll was heard after the two-minute silence every Armistice Day until the outbreak of the Second World War.[13] Then, after a six-year silence, along with bells across the nation, Tom celebrated the end of the war on VE Day. It has tolled, with the clapper muffled, on the occasions of royal and decanal funerals. When Edward VII died in 1910, and on the deaths of George V in 1936 and George VI in 1952, Tom was rung for half an hour at half-minute intervals. It would have been a difficult thing to do; the normal toll, once every four or five seconds, was reasonably easy once started, but for a 30-second toll it would have been necessary to start the swing for every strike.[14] In 1984, on its own anniversary, the bell was rung 300 times.

Time, marked by Tom's chime, has always been important in a place where meetings, lectures, meals and curfews governed the day. There was a sundial on the cathedral, illustrated in Loggan's engraving of the college, and another on the south side of the Hall. A new one was made on Kill-canon at some point in the eighteenth century, and a modern one installed in the Pococke Garden in 1997. Tom Tower had a clock from the start, and there was probably a mechanical clock in the cathedral before Christ Church days.[15] In the 1830s, it was proposed that a new clock be installed in the

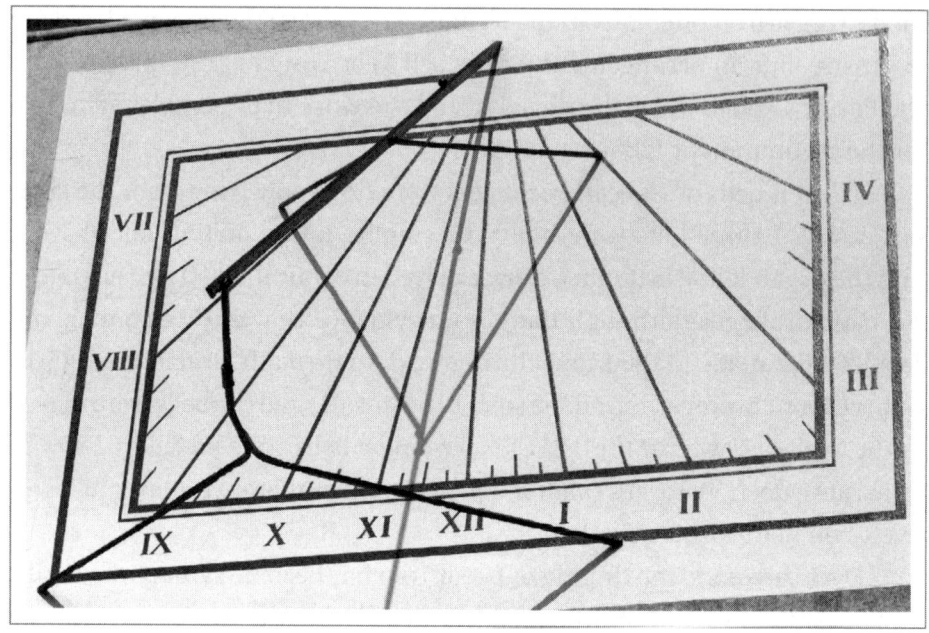

No record of the painting and installation of the sundial on the south face of Killcanon survives. It is very accurate, as long as one remembers to adjust to Greenwich Mean Time.

cathedral, and Benjamin Vulliamy, the famous clockmaker, estimated that it would cost £283 and take six months to produce something suitable.[16] The Dean and Chapter baulked at the price, but Vulliamy responded 'it will be a work that will hand my name down to the latest posterity as a clock-maker'. Vulliamy's reputation won the day and the work went ahead. Over budget and over time, the maintenance and management of such a complex mechanism caused problems. The adjusting swivels were unique to Vulliamy and seemingly beyond the skills of poor Mr Souter, who was dismissed from the daily care of both the cathedral and the Tom Tower clocks.[17] In 1904, Rowell's, who had always maintained the clock in Tom, commented that, while the cathedral clock was well constructed, it would be a better time-keeper if it were given a gravity escapement and a compensated pendulum.[18] Vulliamy, never one to shy from giving an opinion, was quite complimentary about Rowell's work on Tom, but suggested improvements to the spring and the pendulum.[19] Before 1841, the clock on the tower had only one hand, and so showed only the hours. It had to be wound and set daily, and an accuracy of within three to four minutes was considered sufficient until the railway arrived in Oxford.[20] Vulliamy offered to make a new clock for the tower, saying that nothing 'would gratify me so much as making a clock to that Bell capable of fetching the tone out of it'. By way of recommending himself to the Dean and Chapter, he noted that he was currently making a clock for Calcutta cathedral. It would seem, however, that Vulliamy's second offer was not taken up by the Chapter. A new spring and pendulum top were made, and by February 1842, the clock was said to be working well.[21]

In 1852, Greenwich Mean Time was formally adopted nationwide, but Christ Church steadfastly retained 'Oxford' time, five minutes behind GMT. Cathedral services still begin five minutes after the advertised time; dinner, which the statutes say should begin at 7.15 pm, actually starts at 7.20; and, most famously, the ringing of the 101 commences at 9.05 pm.[22] For a short while, there were two minute hands on the Tom Tower clock, one showing local time, the other GMT.[23]

In 1886, another company, T. Cooke & Son, investigated the clock and found it not worth repairing. Its dials, dialwork and hammerwork were all in good condition, and a new clock could be made, incorporating these parts, for £300. Cooke's advised against installing electricity to run it. The Governing Body sought advice from Lord Grimthorpe, architect and horologist, who recommended either Potts of Leeds or Joyce of Whitchurch.[24] Both companies, and a third, E. Dent & Co., submitted specifications along with Cooke's. Grimthorpe stuck with his two original choices, and the Governing Body came down in favour of the cheaper, J. B. Joyce.[25] The clocks were repeatedly cleaned; according to the Porter's log, in 1896, 1901 and 1906. Both the Tom Tower and cathedral clocks were overhauled in 1926, and Tom clock again in 1937 when the figures were repainted – an occasion made memorable by the painter, who, having coming down from his scaffolding, walked backwards to admire his work and fell into Mercury.[26] The painters who redid this work most recently were more careful – and less wet.

5

'With strength of argument and in good order': 1689–1755

The late seventeenth and the early years of the eighteenth centuries saw Christ Church basking in the sunshine of the 'new Fell', Henry Aldrich, before being plunged into Stygian gloom under Francis Atterbury. Their four successors may be less well known, but each played his part in maintaining and enhancing Christ Church's reputation as the place to be for young gentlemen and aspiring academics.

Aldrich's installation as dean was celebrated with a feast to which all heads of houses and doctors were invited. Aldrich was a polymath – interested and skilled in art, music, architecture, science, logic – as well as being pleasant and convivial. He was, perhaps, Christ Church's most 'Renaissance' dean.[1] Appointed on 4 April 1689 and installed on 17 June, he made his first appearance in Hall on 25 June, and was treated, as was the custom, to speeches by two young Students, James Harrington and Edward Wells, who were granted their degrees in recognition.[2] Aldrich's inauguration papers stated that he was chosen dean in John Fell's place, and a fresh Chapter Book was opened to mark the new beginning.[3] The inconveniences and irritations of Massey's rule were swept away in what must have seemed like the dawning of a new age. King James made one last-ditch effort to hold sway over Christ Church; on 8 December 1688, after Massey's flight and just three days before his own from Whitehall, he nominated his long-term friend and ally Benjamin Woodroffe to the deanery. But no one appears to have taken the slightest notice.[4]

'With strength of argument and in good order': 1689–1755

Henry Aldrich, the second of the great 'builder-deans', was popular and accomplished. He designed Peckwater Quad, which he would just have seen completed before his death in 1710, and left to Christ Church his collection of manuscript and printed music, engravings, and books.

Immediately after his installation, Aldrich set to work; his first task seems to have been to sort out odd problems with the leasing of estates, but there was far more to do – not least reversing the decline in admissions under Massey.

Aldrich had been actively against the Catholicisation of the University during the reign of James II, and although numbers never reached the heights that they had under Fell, his stance was probably a factor in the steadily rising admissions among all the fee-paying classes of undergraduate after his arrival in the deanery.[5] Aldrich, like Fell, encouraged noblemen and gentlemen commoners to come to Christ Church. In 1704 alone, Aldrich admitted 39 men, of whom an unprecedented third were gentlemen commoners.[6]

> ## Admissions, 1691–1710
>
> **Servitors** – 118 (19.4 per cent of total admissions)
> (3.9 per cent between 1561 and 1660)
>
> **Commoners** – 236 (39.1 per cent)
> (40.2 per cent between 1561 and 1660)
>
> **Gentlemen Commoners** – 145 (24 per cent)
> (15.2 per cent between 1561 and 1660)
>
> **Noblemen** – 38 (6.3 per cent)
> (0.71 per cent between 1561 and1660)
>
> **Students** – 67 (11.1 per cent)
> (38.4 per cent between 1561 and 1660)

The Tory leanings of Aldrich's Christ Church did not sit comfortably with everyone. Humphrey Prideaux, who had supported comprehension (the inclusion of non-conformists into the Anglican communion), refused a canonry when it was offered, stating that 'I nauseate Christ Church ... and will never live more among such people who now have the prevaileing power there'.[7] The reluctance of men such as Prideaux to take a place in the Chapter meant that Aldrich and his colleagues were able to present a united front to both University and national politics. Christ Church had a huge presence in Convocation (the legislative assembly of the University); between 55 and 60 men could be mustered when necessary. Only Magdalen College could approach such numbers. Nationally, Christ Church's presence in Parliament was significant, not least because any noblemen who came up to Oxford were almost exclusively Housemen.[8] And in the Church it was greater still; in the lower house of the newly recalled Convocation of Canterbury, there were 96 Oxford graduates in a membership of 135, and 25 of those were from Christ Church.[9] Tory Oxford was pre-eminent, and continued to be so into the reign of Queen Anne.

When the queen visited Oxford in 1702, Aldrich and the young gentlemen of Christ Church were full of enthusiasm, expecting the relationship between University and the Crown to continue undisturbed and fruitfully. Queen Anne, however, was a moderate, determined to put the strife of the seventeenth century firmly into the past, and to balance the Tory/Whig powers in her government. Christ Church was drawn into the struggle, not least over the appointment of the successor to William Jane as regius professor of divinity. Candidates were put forward by both sides for Crown approval: George Smalridge, who had effectively been Jane's deputy, was the choice of both Anne and Christ Church.[10] Anne's ministers, including Marlborough and Archbishop Tenison, preferred the Whig-inclined John Potter. Anne held her ground for as long as possible, but in the end was forced to compromise. She filled the vacant bishoprics of Chester and Exeter with her candidates, but lost the professorship, Potter being created regius professor and canon of Christ Church in January 1708.[11]

This period also saw an increase in both the numbers and status of undergraduates. Much renovation and reconstruction of the buildings was therefore deemed to be necessary to render the accommodation suitable for the needs of gentlemen. Peckwater Inn was the first to be tackled and, with the arrival of a gift from Anthony Radcliffe, Aldrich could start work. The rebuilt Peckwater Quadrangle was opened in 1707, with the south-west end assigned to a canonical stall. The grandest sets of rooms, on the first floor, were designed for gentlemen and noblemen. The next task was to fill the south side of the quad. Aldrich probably designed the building to provide more accommodation, but just after his death, the plans were altered to create a fine library equalling the grandeur of Peckwater. Work began under Dean Smalridge, and was accelerated under John Conybeare, dean from 1733 to 1755, who recognised just how desperately the new building was needed. In the 1720s and 1730s, there were three major gifts for the library: Lewis Atterbury's pamphlet collection in 1722; Charles Boyle's legacy of his vast collection of notable scientific and medical books, complete with his scientific instruments, in 1731; and Archbishop William Wake's several thousand books and manuscripts in 1737. The old library was packed to the rafters, and residential chambers had been commandeered for temporary storage.

Peckwater Quad was designed and its building supervised by Dean Henry Aldrich in the first decade of the eighteenth century. The grand Palladian style replaced the more homely Tudor of its early seventeenth-century rebuilding, and provided accommodation for gentlemen and their servants.

But it wasn't just high-status students from influential and powerful families who interested the eighteenth-century deans; Aldrich and his successors were equally determined that academic quality was to improve. On his appointment as vice-chancellor of the University, Aldrich had announced that discipline and academic exercises were his priority.[12] And Christ Church was the focus of his attention.

Most of the deans entered Christ Church determined to do something about the state of student behaviour; Aldrich was no different. Unlike the earlier Chapter Books, those of the late seventeenth century onwards give much more detail about individual cases. In May 1690, two new decrees were issued against absentee Students: if a Student was absent from his exercises, he would be fined, lose half his allowance and lose his place in the seniority.[13] The first Students hauled before the Dean and Chapter under

Charles Boyle

Charles Boyle, 4th Earl of Orrery, was an extraordinary man: MP and soldier, politician and courtier, scholar, scientist and collector. His son, John, however, was less talented; he was admitted to Christ Church in Michaelmas term 1723, but despite his father's hopes, John was no great achiever and Boyle senior evidently considered him a waste of time. The relationship was further soured by the son's disapproval of his father's mistress. John inherited the Orrery title and estate (heavily in debt, and with a large bequest for the mistress and her children), but not the collections which included the orrery, a moving model of the solar system, designed by George Graham and made by the celebrated instrument-maker John Rowley. The model was given Orrery's name in honour of its patron.

the new regime were Benjamin Dod and Anthony Alsop.[14] Both were new Students, almost at the bottom of the 1691 election list, and their misbehaviour must have been relatively minor, perhaps some breach of protocol. However, their entry in the Chapter Book demonstrates how the disciplinary procedure was conducted. Dod and Alsop were admonished *prima vice* (for the first time) and moved even further down the list of *discipuli*, with a cross placed against their names.[15] Similarly, Thomas Woodward received his first cross for 'having been notoriously Scandalous for Some years, for neglecting all the duties and exercises of the College And going frequently out of Town without leave of his Proper Officer And for his remarkable non proficience in Learning'.[16] Many men gained a first cross against their names and a fair few received a second, but when a Student was called up before the Dean and Chapter for a third time, discipline became very serious.[17] Woodward escaped being demoted, possibly because of a far more scandalous case; just two weeks after Woodward's hearing, Augustine Spalding, a much more senior Student, in the second rank of *philosophi*, was called before the Dean and Chapter on 29 March 1693 to answer a list of horrifying charges:

1. that he had accused George Smalridge of opening his letters, assaulted

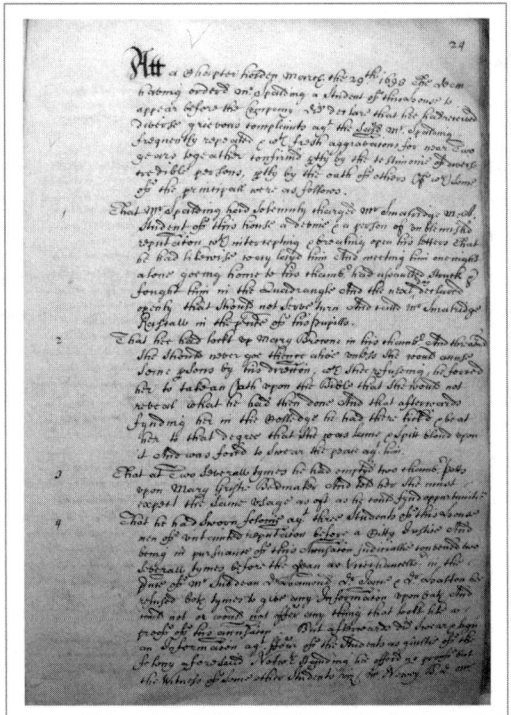

The list of charges against Augustine Spalding recorded in full in the Chapter Book, along with the witness statements and decisions made.

him in the Quadrangle, and then called him a rascal in the presence of his pupils;[18]

2. that he had locked up Mary Browne, one of the bedmakers, in his chamber and threatened that he would not release her unless she accused various people at his direction, and when she refused he beat her until she was lame and spat blood;

3. that he had twice emptied chamber pots on Mary Gristie, another bedmaker and mother of Mary Browne, and told her to expect it as often as he found opportunity;

4. and that he had sworn feloniously to a city justice against seven Students of previously unblemished character.

Earlier that month, John Wallis, one of the City Justices, had issued a warrant demanding that the vice-chancellor – then Aldrich, of course – deal with all these charges forthwith, calling all the relevant persons to give testimony. Spalding made a statement that his room had been broken into several times by a number of different Students, and papers had been taken. The crimes of which he was accused were retaliation. Witnesses were called to court, but all denied any knowledge of the 'facts' laid out by Spalding and hinted that there had been some intimidation. Smalridge, accused of intercepting and opening one of Spalding's letters, had been violently assaulted. Spalding did not help his case by boasting of the attack in Hall, publicly announcing that he felt he should have done more. Both the bedmakers repeated the charges against Spalding, Browne accusing him of imprisoning her for five hours, berating and threatening her, and all the while eyeing a hatchet. Although Browne had been forced to take an oath of silence on the Bible, someone informed the dean and, before long, Spalding was seeking his revenge. He attacked Browne so viciously that she was unable to work and in fear of his 'doing her great mischief'.

Spalding did not stand a chance. In addition to his crimes, his academic achievement was well below par. He himself confessed that he was not able to perform the exercises and felt that there was not really any hope for improvement. The Chapter tried confining him to his room, but his behaviour showed no sign of improvement at all.[19] He had written contentious letters to the vice-chancellor, slept outside his own chamber, been caught by the Proctors in alehouses in bad company, and was often 'conversant with a woman of ill fame'. When left in charge of a fellow Student's room, Spalding sold all the contents and told the victim that his room had been burgled. Drunken and disorderly behaviour – which would have earned just a rap over the knuckles for any other Student – was the final charge against him, and his immediate expulsion was unanimously agreed.[20]

Spalding's case was exceptional, but other men with 'two crosses' against their names were in equal danger of being sent down. When John Addenbrook received his second cross he was given nine months to improve his ways, but nothing changed. He was given one last chance, kept down in the lowest group of Students, and told to reform his manners on pain of expulsion.[21] Just seven months later, in July 1706, having 'continued in a most notorious irregular life', Addenbrook was expelled. But others survived two crosses: George Beaulieu, admonished the same day as Addenbrook in December 1705, went on to receive his BA and MA and remained a Student until his death in 1736.[22]

Some crimes seem to have been bad enough to bypass the crosses system. John Richardson, a Student on the verge of receiving his Doctor of Medicine degree, was summoned to answer an accusation that he had fathered a bastard child, presumably during the frequent noctivagations with which he was also charged. Expulsion was the only option. Richardson confessed to his nightly wanderings, but was saved from being sent down by the mother of the child, who insisted under oath that the accused was not the father. Both Richardson and the girl were evidently convincing, for he was granted grace for his degree at the same meeting.[23]

The threat of degradation and expulsion was not the only recourse open to the Dean and Chapter. Confinement to the Library for intensive study was much used. John Pelling, having been convicted of assaulting the head porter after coming in late one night, was deprived for six months of the privileges due to him as a Student, and required to report to the Dean and Chapter on his reading of Suarez's *Disputationes Metaphysicae*.[24] Pelling must have thought the punishment effective as, some years later, one of his pupils, William Dockwra, suffered a similar fate. Accused of drinking and revelling in a tavern all night and then ignominiously falling out of a chamber window into the street, Dockwra was confined to the Library 'at all the usual hours of Study there And that therein hee read Grotius de jure pacis et belli And all such other Books as the Subdean shall from time to time appoint him'. As if this open-ended punishment were not enough, he was gated indefinitely.[25] For both men, the method worked: Pelling later became Senior Censor and most senior Student before he left in 1710, and Dockwra took his BA and MA, and remained a Student until 1735.

It was not just the junior members of Christ Church that needed keeping in check. When, in 1707, a would-be dean, Benjamin Woodroffe, ran into terrible debt, the Chancellor approached the Treasurer to pay Woodroffe's share of the profits from the renewal of leases directly to two of his creditors. Woodroffe, horrified, cited the custom whereby profits were always paid directly to the canon, not through the Treasurer. The Chapter, concerned that Woodroffe's canonry might be sequestered in its entirety to pay the debt, put the money into a strong box, paying neither debtor nor creditors until they had sought advice. Their lawyer thought it safest for the college to keep the money until the plaintiffs' case was better understood or until Woodroffe had discharged the sequestration, to avoid an apparent sanctioning of the non-payment of a debt.[26]

The college otherwise ran smoothly, and the relationships between members of the Chapter were generally genial. There was, however, a brief setback early in the century when Aldrich – who had followed in Fell's footsteps in the education of the junior members of college, in his position in the University, and in his passion for building and embellishing – died on 14 December 1710. The view of Thomas Hearne, antiquarian and diarist, that, 'as a Christian scholar and gentleman, he was one of the most eminent men in England', seems to have been universally held. Canon Stratford, writing to his regular correspondent, Edward Harley, commented that, although 'miserable ... as we have lost our old head', Christ Church was full, at peace, and continued on an even keel – thanks largely to the character of its late dean.[27]

That late dean's successor, Francis Atterbury, was less of a triumph, in spite of his politics, which should have endeared him to the Tory college. Stratford was concerned at the appointment; although he was sure that the Chapter would do their best to be accommodating, he was surprised that anyone would 'have desired to come to where he knows so many stories of former failures are yet fresh, and where no one can have the authority that is requisite to this place whose youth was not without blemish in it'.[28]

Atterbury had been a protégé of Aldrich as a Westminster Student, and then praelector and tutor, notably to Charles Boyle, whom he defended during the Phalaris affair (see p. 168 below). But he was soon disillusioned with Christ Church life. Increasingly involved with politics, both secular and ecclesiastic, he became the clerical ally of rising stars, Robert Harley and

Francis Atterbury was dean from 1711 to 1713, and was possibly the most unpopular head of house in all of its five centuries.

Simon Harcourt.[29] His high-church manner, outspokenness and obsession with personal power made Atterbury less than popular and, on Aldrich's death, prompted a Court battle over the succession. Queen Anne and the Chapter once again favoured the mild-mannered George Smalridge, once a close friend of Atterbury when they were both Students. Nothing happened for some months, and the rumour circulated that the queen was waiting for a vacancy to which she could appoint Atterbury which would satisfy everyone. But it was not to be, and at the end of August, nine months after Aldrich's death, the queen, under pressure from Harcourt (recently appointed Lord Chancellor), reluctantly signed the document declaring Atterbury's appointment.[30]

Even before the installation ceremonies, Atterbury upset the college. Aldrich had been modest, and had forbidden any attempt to laud him into

Oxford as the new head. Atterbury, however, made every effort to encourage it. Careful notice was sent ahead, requesting that every man with a horse should ride out to Shotover to greet the new dean as if he were royalty or a visiting dignitary; the Chapter, hedging its bets, advised compliance, and many men spent the afternoon of 24 September 1711 rushing around trying to find horses for hire.

Atterbury's installation was a grand event, attended by Harcourt and the most influential Tories.[31] In his inaugural speech he began well, extolling the virtues of both Fell and Aldrich, and admitting that, although he would try, he could never match the achievements of these great men. But the good impression he tried to give had been ruined even before he stood up. Atterbury had no intention of addressing the whole establishment, just the most senior or most influential. As the canons pointed out, to invite some to the dinner only, rather than to include all in the full ceremonials, was a grave error in protocol which caused terrible offence.[32]

The dinner was immense and expensive, costing over £200. Inauspiciously, the customary ringing of Tom to celebrate the arrival of a new head was abandoned as the tower was deemed not strong enough, and so Atterbury was greeted by Little Tom, ringing from the cathedral spire.[33] The fragile peace that accompanied Atterbury's arrival did not last.

Appointment to Christ Church was a chance to exert influence, particularly as so many of its young men went on to become stalwarts of the state and church, whether in the higher echelons of the 'establishment' or at parish level. Both Fell and Aldrich had intended Christ Church to become powerful, and it was the significance of Christ Church in the affairs of the nation that had attracted Atterbury back to his alma mater.[34] But in contrast to Fell, whom Atterbury himself described as one who 'stretched the authority of the Dean to the utmost', the new dean had no subtlety, operating through the subversion of old methods of management. He refused to learn or adapt to the traditions of college and cathedral or to established methods of governance, and claimed sole responsibility for the appointment, punishment and dismissal of college officers, the exclusive right to present college livings and to control Chapter business.[35] This was unprecedented and within a month was causing uproar. Needless to say, the canons reacted. Stratford pointed out to Harley that if Atterbury continued in the manner he had started 'we shall all be better known in the Court of Chancery or at the Council Board'.[36] Stratford worked hard with the new dean, trying to convince him that Christ Church's security against attack from outside had always been the unanimity of the Dean and Chapter, but his words fell on deaf ears. Atterbury's vanity, too, caused eyebrows to be raised; although only arriving back at Christ Church in time to see the finishing touches put to Peckwater Quad, he decided to erect a statue of himself, holding a model of the building, in the centre of the new quadrangle. However, as an earlier proposal to erect a statue of Marlborough in the same place had been refused by Aldrich, despite it being backed by a donation of £100, the dean, in a rare moment of wisdom, pursued the idea no further.[37]

Atterbury was evidently irritating beyond belief: Stratford recalled an occasion when a tenant arrived at Christ Church to pay his rent, accompanied by a neighbour who was laying claim to part of the land leased. Stratford, then Treasurer, despatched the tenant with Mr Brooks, the auditor, to the audit house to have dinner and to sort things out. No doubt other canons were at the meal and the dean, seeing the men in conversation, sent Stratford an angry note asking how long he had taken it upon himself to call Chapter meetings without the dean. Stratford, exasperated, responded that handling disputes in this manner was perfectly standard practice and was in no way an attempt on the dean's authority. 'Guess what a comfortable life I lead,' moaned the treasurer. 'Somewhat or other of this nature is started every day.'[38] Canons were understandably reluctant to take on offices under Atterbury's deanery. John Potter was expected to take Thomas Burton's place as sub-dean, but he refused the post, saying that Roger Altham was more senior and should have the place before him; but it was common knowledge that Potter just did not want to work with the dean.[39] When Atterbury was claiming such petty things as payment of his stipend from the date of his patent, rather than from the date of his installation as was usual, it is hardly surprising that he was not a popular colleague. The year 1711 ended, three very long months after the arrival of Atterbury in the deanery, with the annual election of new Students; Atterbury, finding that he had forgotten to bring a Bible, swore in the boys on the University statute book instead, much to the dismay of his colleagues. Potter, eventually persuaded, was elected sub-dean.[40]

Atterbury's deanery continued in swathes of dissent and outright mutual dislike. His attempts to take sole control were not restricted to Christ Church, but to the University as a whole. With the support of Lord Keeper Harcourt and Henry Sacheverell, a Fellow of Magdalen College, he tried to establish a new ascendancy based on Christ Church and Magdalen, in spite of the traditional antipathy between the two colleges, and to overrule the more moderate college heads.[41] Relationships with former friends at Christ Church broke down and enmities worsened. A trumped-up charge of embezzlement and theft was made against William Stratford, John Hammond and Thomas Burton. The three were accused by Charles Aldrich, the late dean's nephew, of stealing papers and money from Henry Aldrich's study in the days following his death. Stratford believed that the younger Aldrich was being used as a pawn in Atterbury's game against the Chapter, and had been coerced into signing the paper in which 'every one word [was] by the Dean'. At the Chapter meeting called to resolve the matter, the dean refused to allow the canons to take notes, and stormed out, declaring to his senior colleagues, 'I despise you!' Stratford, behaving with calm dignity, reminded Atterbury that he, the dean, had once had a key to Stratford's house in Westminster, and mused whether Atterbury remembered everything that he had done or touched in the house at such a distance of time. Partly because Atterbury realised he was on shaky ground, and partly because other events took over, the matter died away.[42]

There were discourtesies that rankled among the Chapter, such as Atterbury's failure to visit Lord Pembroke, who, on a brief visit to Oxford, had contributed £100 to the Peckwater building fund; and ridiculous situations such as the imposition of a room-mate on Samuel Palmer, a newly appointed praelector. Custom dictated that the Chapter decided which rooms should be doubles and which singles, and the dean then allocated the rooms accordingly. Palmer had been given his single room in the new

Peckwater Quad by Dr Hammond, Aldrich's proxy, but Atterbury arbitrarily decided to turn the chamber into a double.[43] Palmer appealed to Stratford who, with Hammond, revisited the room, decided that it could not be conveniently converted into a double, and then took advantage of one of the few occasions when the dean was calm in a Chapter meeting to spell out the usual manner of dealing with rooms. All appeared to be smoothed over. But Stratford was under no illusions; he was certain that the decision to double-up the chamber had been a deliberate attempt to undermine the Chapter, and himself in particular.[44]

He was proved right. Atterbury then took it upon himself to dismiss John Brooks, acting auditor and Chapter Clerk.[45] Stratford had heard rumours that Atterbury was plotting this as a deliberate attempt to goad the Chapter into an action which would allow the dean to appeal to his friend and sponsor, Lord Keeper Harcourt (who also represented the monarch as Visitor), and underline Atterbury's authority in the House. But it was December, and if Atterbury dismissed Brooks before the election of officers, then the division of entry fines, from which the dean would be paid around £400, would not be made.[46] The dean was quite aware of the potential loss to his pocket, so deviously appointed his own clerk, Charles Perrott, in Brooks's place. The canons' response was to point out that the dean was not entitled to appoint a new clerk or auditor without their consent. Atterbury refused to hold Chapter meetings without his man, and the canons refused to attend unless Brooks was there. The stand-off meant that no business could be done, and the Chapter was at a loss as to how to proceed. In time-honoured tradition, they sat and waited. All the entry fines were in, about £1,000 in total, waiting to be distributed among the dean and canons. Atterbury had assumed that the canons would be so anxious to receive their own dues that they would give in, but the Chapter stood firm. Things were working against Atterbury, and in desperation he demanded his money with threats and even violence towards Francis Gastrell, a co-Treasurer with Stratford and once close friend of the dean.[47]

Things were still not resolved when, much to the relief of the beleaguered Chapter, Atterbury's deep involvement with state and church politics

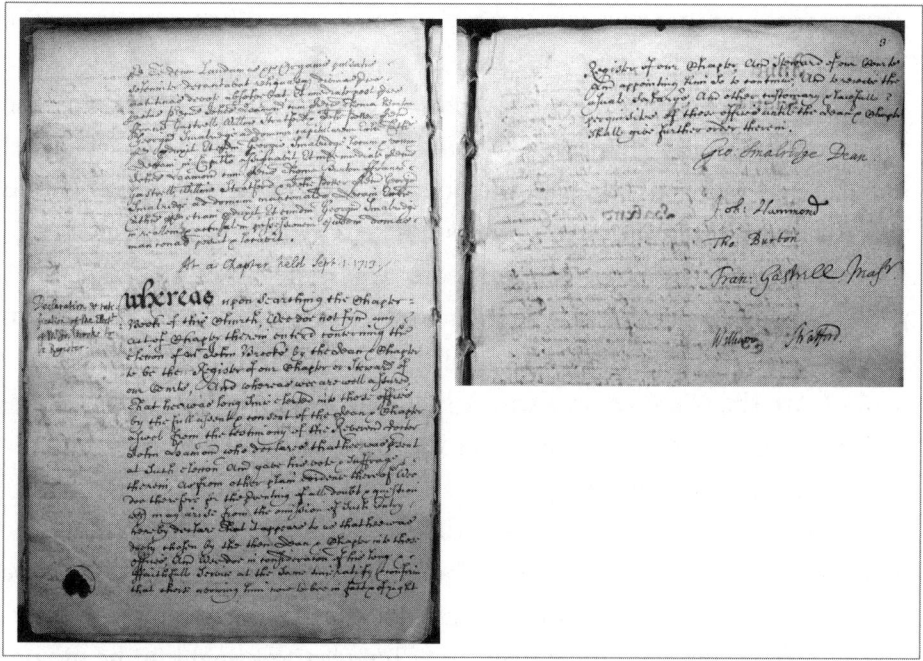

John Brooks, the auditor, was a victim of Dean Atterbury's extraordinary behaviour. As soon as Atterbury had departed for Rochester, the Dean and Chapter reconfirmed Brooks's position and their confidence in him.

led to his nomination to the bishopric of Rochester, to be held together with the deanery of Westminster. Stratford expressed his surprise at the appointments, saying: 'It is lucky for the fellow that he has got off; that proud soul would have been humbled had he stayed here longer; he is talked of no otherwise in this place as a common rogue.'

Atterbury left Oxford in the summer of 1713.[48] But not quietly; even after his installation at Westminster, Atterbury tried to appoint a new chorister and a new chaplain. He also demanded his entitlement of hay from the Meadow, coming down to Oxford to make sure that the mowing was done before his consecration at Rochester, after which even Atterbury might have felt awkward about claiming his alleged dues. Having been told by the canons that the order to cut would not be given before the grass was ready, he attempted to bribe the mowers with the promise of extra pay if they assured him that they would not go off to do any other work before the Christ Church Meadow was finished.

At the next Chapter meeting, on his soon-to-be successor's advice, the canons agreed to pay Atterbury all that he was due according to the usual practice, and requested that all the documents relating to Christ Church business that were in the dean's possession be returned to the Treasurer. To make it look less personal, a general decree was issued requiring all persons holding Chapter records to return them or, at the very least, to make a list, in their own hand, of the papers they kept. The patent confirming the appointment of Atterbury's successor was desperately awaited; that it was George Smalridge, who had been waiting in the wings since 1709, was already known and greatly welcomed.[49]

All sorts of usurpations of the Chapter's role were discovered in the weeks after Atterbury's departure. The bailiff of Binsey revealed that the dean had tried to appoint a gamekeeper on his own authority, but on requesting that Brooks drew up the patent, the Chapter Clerk said that he did not know how to do such a thing (meaning, of course, that this was the wrong way to go about things). He had also drawn up a document, with his own seal, rather than the official Christ Church seal, claiming sole proprietorship of all the college's copyholds, again swearing the local bailiff to secrecy. Last but not least, Stratford calculated that Atterbury's profits from his short time in the deanery amounted to £1,300, but still he walked off with the locks to his residence which had been paid for from the corporate purse.[50]

There were no great ceremonies to mark Smalridge's move from one side of the quad to the other. He was installed on 18 July 1713, but there were no long speeches or a great feast, partly because he was rather ill, and partly because tradition dictated that the incoming dean give a speech extolling the virtues of his predecessor, which would have been an unpalatable task.[51] Smalridge's promotion was greeted with calm relief.[52] Another new Chapter Book was begun, in spite of the many pages left in the old one, drawing a very definite line under the unfortunate period of Atterbury's governance. Atterbury was, at least, mentioned in the installation papers of his successor, unlike Massey just a quarter of a century before.[53]

Smalridge did not stay in the deanery for very long, but he held the post during a period of turmoil in Oxford. Queen Anne's death, the succession of the Hanoverian George I and the return of the Whigs to government set Oxford and State in direct confrontation. The University was powerful, producing half the country's clergy and being full of non-jurors. Between 1714 and 1717, troops were stationed in the city to control the outbreaks of rioting that had been fuelled by Jacobite and Whig agents whipping up youthful firebrands.[54] However, whatever the politics of nation or University, Christ Church was a fashionable place to be. From Smalridge's appointment until Bagot's arrival in the 1770s, Christ Church sat back from University politics, became increasingly Whig, or at least less Tory, and concentrated on its academic standing.[55]

Apart from his overhaul of the system of internal examinations, known as collections, Smalridge's short deanery was unexceptional. Needless to say, he had to deal with his fair share of mishaps and miscreants. No sooner had George Smalridge arrived in the deanery in July 1713, than he was faced with the sad case of Francis Bayly, who drowned in the 'house of office' in Peckwater. Bayly was last seen, in his nightgown, heading that way at around nine in the evening of the Monday before Smalridge's installation. He was a young man prone to disappear for a day or two at a time, so no one worried about his absence the next morning. In fact, it was Thursday before anyone commented to Thomas Terry, Bayly's tutor, that he was not to be found. When they did search, the poor boy was found completely smothered, having evidently leant back too far and fallen into the pit beneath the lavatory seats. Canon Stratford noted, too late, that he had often complained that the seats were too big and had no backs. The sorry Bayly must have died rather slowly; another young man had visited the lavatory at eleven on the Monday night but had been scared away by the groaning noise issuing forth. John Wainwright had assumed that the noise he heard, a full hour later, was someone being sick in Bear Lane, and Richard Jenkinson, who at least peered in, thought it was just a dog. Terry was in a state of the 'utmost affliction', and the affair must have been a discouraging start for Smalridge.[56]

He also had to cope with James, Duke of Hamilton, a young Student who was very conscious of his social position and used it to full advantage. Hamilton was about to leave Christ Church, and was in town to receive his honorary degree in Civil Law. But his battels were six months in arrears and, although he had been given six weeks to pay, he had still not settled up and his commons had been stopped. This was of no great consequence to Hamilton, who was more than able to manage without his meals in college. Whilst in Oxford, the young man, still only 16, dined with the vice-chancellor, William Delaune, and the warden of Merton College, John Holland. After a few drinks, the two men found Hamilton's situation rather funny and decided to allow him his doctorate, bills paid or not.[57] The Dean and Chapter must have felt that Hamilton was rather thumbing his nose at them. Trying to be fair, they had decided that it was not right to single out Hamilton when so many other men were also in arrears, so decreed that all men who were three months or more in debt would suffer loss of commons until their battels were paid. Even then, men were given a full quarter to pay and so could be perpetually three months in arrears. In theory, the caution money (a deposit paid against damages or default) that was paid on admission would be set against unpaid bills but, in practice, it was never enough.[58] For the richer students, arrears could add up to several hundred pounds. Hamilton was approached before the decree was posted in Hall, in the hope that he would pay his bill and that others, less well-off, would not have to suffer. He saw the reason behind the approach, but still failed to settle in time to save his friends. To add insult to injury, the Chapter could not even withhold Hamilton's caution money, however inadequate; Hamilton had not paid this either, and the Dean and Chapter, conscious of Hamilton's social status, had been just too polite to ask.[59]

Smalridge died in September 1719, leaving his family in straitened circumstances.[60] Immediately after the funeral, the canons who were in Oxford approached first John Potter, the once reluctant sub-dean and now bishop, to ask if he would be the next dean. When Potter refused, they tried Henry Egerton, who was much keener to allow his name to be put forward.[61] In less than a month, however, Hugh Boulter was named as dean.[62] Boulter, the king's chaplain, was travelling with George I in Hanover when Smalridge's death was announced, and was immediately offered both the deanery and the bishopric of Bristol by the king.[63] Like Smalridge, and comfortingly unlike Atterbury, Boulter was installed quietly and privately on 6 November.

> ## Bishops of Bristol
>
> It was not uncommon, during the eighteenth century, for the bishopric of Bristol to be given in conjunction with the deanery of Christ Church; the richness of the latter appointment effectively paying for the former. In his history, Thompson commented that the consequence of both positions being held simultaneously often meant that neither was conducted properly.
>
> Thompson (1900), 169

Rather than holding a big feast, he donated £100 to the building fund. It was a peaceful start.

Quiet and relatively trouble-free Boulter's deanery may have been, but it does not appear to have been particularly happy or successful. He was only just gremial (a member of Christ Church before appointment), having been a commoner for only a short while before moving to Magdalen College.[64] He was often away from Oxford, and Stratford was as jaundiced about Boulter as he was about any dean after Aldrich other than Smalridge. His letters to Harley during the early 1720s are despondent. By April 1722, after only 30 months of Boulter's residence, Stratford wrote that 'our Governor is as weary of us as we can be of him, and that he will leave us as soon as ever he can, for a bare equivalent, without any advantage'. As it happened, Boulter was made Archbishop of Armagh in 1724 and Stratford's fears that his place would be taken by 'that scandalous man Baker of Wadham' proved unfounded.[65] The next appointment did not meet with much more approval, certainly not from Stratford, who decided that the new dean would be no better than the last, but that he might 'have more bustle'. Fourth in a succession of short-lived deans, William Bradshaw had been appointed as a canon of Christ Church in 1723, and had immediately set off on the Grand Tour with the son of the William Cavendish, Duke of Devonshire. Stratford expected nothing but dullness.[66]

• THE CARDINAL'S COLLEGE •

* * * * *

Bradshaw's deanery saw the efforts of the Wesley brothers give rise to a new fervour in religious adherence.[67] John Wesley was concerned both by the rather woolly Anglicanism that was prevalent in the University at the time and by deism, a philosophy popular with students which acknowledged a supreme being but rejected faith in favour of reason. His moderate piety began to attract a small group of men which became known as the 'Holy Club'. Soon after taking his BA in 1724, Wesley was elected to a fellowship at Lincoln College, where he was accused of preaching 'methodism' to his pupils. Although he denied the charge, his influence was evident. At Christ Church, the cause was quietly continued by John's younger brother, Charles, but small groups sprang up all over the University, each making practical efforts to demonstrate their faith, not just by preaching and taking regular communion, but also by distributing food, medicine and fuel to prisoners, to the workhouse and to local almshouses.[68] The Holy Club waned somewhat after 1732, when criticism of the Methodists reached its height, and even more so after 1735 when John and Charles left for America, but still the impression of a University riddled with religious apathy and over-indulgence was tempered by the piety and moderation of a significant group of young men.

* * * * *

But it wasn't all boredom. Early on, Bradshaw's appointment had irritated the sub-dean, Thomas Terry, who had hoped for the deanery himself; he took his frustration out on poor Bradshaw, saying to anyone who would listen that he could not serve as deputy to the new man. Things looked awkward for a few weeks, but Bradshaw exercised some diplomacy and, over a glass or two of port, brokered peace. In fact, it became common for the sub-dean to visit the dean after nine o'clock prayers and he was often seen leaving after one in the morning.[69] The tranquillity in the relationship between the two top men was not transmitted to the rest of college, however. Bradshaw was essentially a Whig in a Tory Chapter, and non-gremial at that. Within two years, Stratford was writing that things were bad, and that the dean was held in real contempt; so much so that Bradshaw was said to have been driven to drink, a vice which was believed to have shortened his life.[70]

In spite of the danger of a political divide between the members of the Chapter, Stratford remained bemused about what it was that Bradshaw had done to generate quite the hatred he received.[71] Within two more years, the friendship with Terry had deteriorated and the two men were once more at loggerheads. There was a public battle between them when Terry asked to have a new coach-house built at the college's expense, which provided sport for everyone within Christ Church. The rules were quite strict about what could be paid for from corporate funds, and the dean refused to give permission until an estimate had been drawn up and more of the canons were in town to give the matter some consideration.[72] Terry was incandescently angry, and his temper gave way just after dinner one evening, when he began to shout obscenities at the dean. Bradshaw responded in kind, and insults were hurled between them 'which they should not have given to each other [but] it is likely both might in some measure deserve'. The battle raged for some weeks, much to the amusement of the young men of the college.[73] Some sort of compromise must have been reached, and some odd jobs were done, including the reroofing of the privy, but the Chapter did not approve the funding of the coach-house.[74]

However unsatisfactory Boulter's and Bradshaw's deaneries were to the members of Christ Church who witnessed them first hand (so much so that Stratford wrote that 'the aspect of the planets seems not favourable to Christ Church at present'), daily business continued normally, with the Chapter pulling together when necessary.[75] They stood as one in 1720 when the vice-chancellor expelled a Christ Church exhibitioner so that he could put in a candidate of his own. Allegedly, the young man, who was a servitor, had spoken against the church, but no evidence was produced to back up the charge. The matter was taken by the boy's tutor to the Visitor, in the person of the Bishop of Lincoln, Edmund Gibson, and he was immediately restored to his rightful place.[76]

Bradshaw died in December 1732, leaving £300 for the Library fund,[77] and his place was filled by John Conybeare, a man who had no connections with Christ Church at all, having been educated at Exeter College and elected its rector in 1730. His appointment had the appearance of being purely political, pushed by Gibson, that powerful and influential clergyman who, allied with Prime Minister Walpole, was determined to show that the church was safe in Whig hands.[78] Conybeare was a member of the whiggish Constitutional Club and an orthodox Anglican.[79] A noted theologian,[80] he proved to be an energetic dean with a bent for administration.

* * * * *

Benefactions were always welcome, and the eighteenth century was a period of real generosity by old members of Christ Church, and those seeking to commemorate others. During Conybeare's 20 years in the deanery there were some valuable gifts. One in particular was completely unexpected and unsought. Early in 1746, the common seal was put to 'proposals for admitting the Shropshire exhibitioners in pursuance of the last will of Edward Careswell'.[81] Why Careswell, a wealthy Shropshire landowner, chose to leave six farms to Christ Church for the funding of eighteen exhibitions is still a mystery. Careswell had not been educated at Christ Church and, as far as is known, had no connections with Oxford at all. He may have been friendly with men from Christ Church who held livings or who came from the area, possibly even William Wake, but nothing is certain. His will, dated 1690, bequeathed the farms in Shropshire and Staffordshire with the intention of funding boys from grammar schools local to his home all the way through Christ Church from their undergraduate years to three years after their MA.[82] It was some years before the bequest benefited the boys. Careswell had left his estate first to his sister and then to Andrew Charlton, who was the king's housekeeper, and then to Thomas Lloyd of Whittington. In 1736, the reversion finally fell to Christ Church, and the first proposals for the scheme were put forward to the Attorney General in 1741. Skeins of red tape meant that it took at least a year for all the necessary parties, including the Lord Chancellor, to accept the terms of the trust. Even then the farms needed some improvement before they could produce the income vital to administer

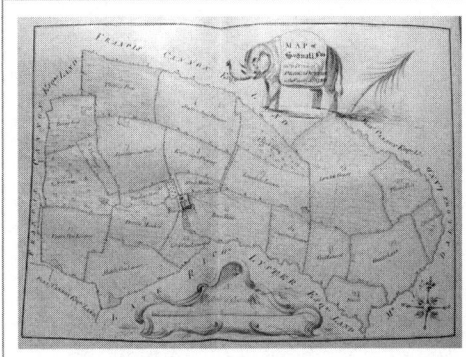 

Edward Careswell left several farms in Shropshire and Staffordshire to Christ Church to fund exhibitions for boys from Shropshire's grammar schools. The Dean and Chapter commissioned an 'atlas' to enable them to plan improvements to the estate.

the exhibitions, and it was 1746 before the first young 'Careswells' arrived at Christ Church.

The Careswell trust was just one that Conybeare made an effort to organise or reorganise. As far back as 1620, Robert Chaloner had left a property in Garsington, just south of Oxford, to fund a lectureship in divinity.[83] The property came to Christ Church in 1638, but something went awry with the application of the rents from the farm – the lands had been intermixed and confused with those of other farmers, and it was not until 1750 that Conybeare and the Chapter swung into action to sort it out.[84] It was decreed immediately that a lecturer was to be nominated every year at Christmas and to take up his office on Lady Day, receiving the rents from Garsington as his stipend. Every term, the lecturer was required to give two lectures in English on the subject of the Thirty-Nine Articles. These were to be given in the Latin chapel of the cathedral, at 11 am on the first and last Thursdays of full term. All bachelors and undergraduates were obliged to attend.[85]

Administration of all the trusts and bequests, a task that usually fell to the under-treasurer, was evidently becoming something of a chore. In 1748, John Richardson was paid an extra £5 per year for managing William Stratford's benefaction with a bonus of 50 shillings, and another £3 per year

> ### Trusts, 1688–1755
>
> **Careswell**: Edward Careswell's will gave farms in Shropshire and Staffordshire to fund exhibitions at Oxford for boys from Shropshire grammar schools . Although the will was dated 1690, the fund was not finally set up until 1741.
>
> **Wood**: Thomas Wood, Bishop of Coventry and Lichfield, left £7,000 in 1692. An estate in Chatteris was purchased, the profits from which benefited the Senior Masters. In 1756, it amounted to an extra £6 annually on top of the usual stipend.
>
> **South**: In 1714, Robert South left the reversion of his estates in Kentish Town and Caversham. There was to be an annual supplement of £10 to twelve Christ Church livings, donations to six poor Westminster Students, and any surplus was to be added to new building work.
>
> **Holford**: Lady Holford gave a legacy in 1717 in memory of her son to fund an exhibition for scholars from Charterhouse School.
>
> **Stratford**: Canon Stratford's benefaction was for the augmentation of small livings, and was used in conjunction with monies from Queen Anne's Bounty.
>
> **Frampton**: Robert Frampton, Bishop of Gloucester, left a small estate in Eynsham to benefit undergraduate servitors.
>
> **Pauncefort**: Edward Pauncefort died in 1726 leaving sufficient money to fund awards for ten servitors and six Students to receive around £5 a year.
>
> **Nash**: In 1754, Richard Nash bequeathed sufficient money to pay a Bachelor to give a commemoration speech each June.

each for his work on Dr South's and Fell's trusts. Another 30 shillings came his way for managing Smith's benefaction to found Portsmouth Grammar School. Just three years later, he was rewarded again. His administration of the Fell trust would now pay another £3 per annum, and the 30s for looking after the Smith money was increased to a bonus of 20 guineas. His basic annual salary went up threefold, from £5 to £15. Richardson was evidently highly regarded as a man of talent and diligence, for the Chapter minuted that these payments were purely for him, and were not to be seen as standard for any successor.[86]

Throughout Conybeare's deanery, small organisational matters were tightened up, including the regulation of the payment of caution money by all commoners and the hearing of disputations – if men were away or sick, then those below them in the list would move up. Those who missed their place joined the end of the queue once they returned.[87] The timetable for taking degrees was laid down:

> Students and chaplains when standing for MA are, by ancient custom, to be presented in the house on the first Monday of full term … They must also proceed the next Congregation together, otherwise they are not to be presented until the last week of term. All undergraduates who are standing in Easter term or before Michaelmas shall speak their speeches in the Hall on the first Tuesday in Easter term. Those standing in Michaelmas term or in Lent term shall speak on the first Tuesday in full term after Michaelmas. Only those two days have been allocated.[88]

In the cathedral, junior chaplains were given the task of reading Latin prayers every morning and evening, instead of the senior MAs or members of Chapter, and the times of morning prayers were established at 7 am from Michaelmas to Lady Day, and at 6 am in the summer. No variation was allowed, even during vacations and especially not on 'sleepy mornings'.[89] Rules were stipulated in the library; every book borrowed had to be returned two days before the annual Visitation by the Chapter, no one could take Library books out of town, and the Librarian was not permitted to deliver volumes to anyone without prior permission from the dean, the sub-dean or the Senior Censor. All visits to the archives had to be supervised by the Librarian. The Librarian was, however, granted permission to hold a college living in conjunction with his Studentship, on the condition that it was no further than 30 miles from Oxford.[90]

The constant striving by the Chapter to encourage better behaviour among the Students was allegedly a fundamental reason for Conybeare's appointment. But although some notorious cases were heard during his 20 years, there is no evidence that the college was in a particularly bad way. One of these cases was that of undergraduate Richard James, Conybeare's response to which met with approval on all sides – not only demonstrating his wisdom in the handling of ill-disciplined undergraduates, but also demonstrating his loyalty to the Whig government of the time.

Richard James had matriculated in June 1748, was always in trouble for irregular behaviour and showed no signs of reform. The final straw came in 1750 when he gave a dinner to celebrate the birthday of the Pretender. This might have been passed off as youthful folly, however indicative of any underlying Jacobitism in the University, were it not for James's behaviour after dinner, when he forced his way out of college, threatened to kill the Porter, and then failed to respond to the Censor's notice requesting his appearance before the Dean and Chapter. He was promptly expelled. Two of James's dinner guests, William Sealy and Ralph Barnes, were spared expulsion but had to give penitential speeches in Hall after dinner, and were confined to college for the remainder of the year. Barnes, accused of particular violence against the Porter, was further confined to the Library for as long as the dean directed.[91] But Conybeare used not just stick, but carrot too. One young undergraduate benefited from James's stupidity; it was decided that good behaviour should be rewarded, and William Pemberton, who had come up as commoner in 1748, was elected to a Studentship:

> Whereas for the support of wholesome discipline the Chapter hath found it necessary to Expell some irregular members of this house, and Whereas it hath been thought conducive to the same good end to distinguish some exemplary young man by Electing him into one of the vacant places ... It is therefore agreed that on this occasion the Course of the Roll be suspended for one Turn and that William Pemberton a Commoner of this house be elected into one of the Studentships of the same.[92]

Most of these problems were part and parcel of college life, however; the same sorts of disciplinary matters had come before previous deans, and would do so again. Like all deans before him, Conybeare was adamant that behaviour would improve, and that the House would not be brought into disrepute during his tenure: 'There have been of late several disturbances in Christ Church at unseasonable hours to the prejudice of discipline and the reputation of the house, young men are therefore cautioned against any such excess. Any found guilty will be severely punished.'[93] It is evident that he was particularly hard on anyone whose misdemeanours involved violence.[94]

On the whole, Conybeare's time in the deanery was peaceful and productive, but there was one small rumble which anticipated a future need for a more formal constitution. In 1737, Thomas Lamprey, a chaplain at Christ Church since 1714 and curate in Cowley, was given notice to leave on the grounds that he was a married man. Lamprey had never tried to hide this; he had been married for seven years, and lived quite openly with his wife and children, so his sacking must have come as quite a shock. Lamprey appealed to the Earl of Hardwicke, Lord High Chancellor and the representative of the monarch as Visitor. Affidavits were made, documents produced, and evidence heard. The canons stood up in court all affirming that a chaplain's place was void after marriage, in the same way that a Student's place became invalid, but there was plenty of evidence that chaplains before Lamprey had been married. There were, of course, no statutes to produce; Christ Church's constitution remained one of custom, a problem that the dean's barrister pointed out could be an 'utmost hazard to our side of the question'. As it was, it worked in the Chapter's favour; if the custom was held that Students must resign their positions when they married, then the dean's plea that the same custom applied to chaplains could be equally upheld. The Lord Chancellor's decision was made in favour of the dean, and the case was dismissed, along with Lamprey.[95]

* * * * *

Politics, discipline and money were not the sole interests of the Dean and Chapter, however. The eighteenth century is often seen as a period of severe academic decline, and the behaviour of a small number of miscreants could easily disguise the quieter but greater achievements of the many. At the end of the previous century, Aldrich's aim, continued by his successors, particularly Smalridge, was not just to improve discipline, but also to raise academic standards. Along with the decrees issued in 1690, not long after Aldrich's installation as dean, there was a further pronouncement in 1706 that:

> It has been noticed that for some years there has been a great neglect in the performance of divinity exercises both in lectures and disputations. It was ordered that for better compelling of such exercises in future, if any Master shall neglect to appear and perform his exercises when and so often as his turn shall happen, the sconces for every such neglect shall be raised (viz, when the same was heretofore used to be 6s 8d, it shall be 20s, and when it was 13s 4d, it shall be 40s).

In addition, entertainments and treats were curtailed, as bad behaviour and hangovers were clearly having a detrimental effect on studies.[96]

Under Fell and Aldrich the system of education remained much as it had been since the foundation of the college.[97] The Scriptures and Anglican doctrine were core subjects and each year group, or Classis, received a set course of lectures from the praelector for that Classis, and had to sit examinations each week on the previous week's teaching. The books read by each Classis are recorded in the Collections books with the names listed beneath of those undergraduates who passed each year.[98] In the first instance, undergraduates must have received notes on the texts from their praelectors, but as printed books became increasingly available at prices that were affordable, Students had access to the works themselves. Four times a week, undergraduates had to attend lectures in rhetoric at 9 am, and Greek at 1 pm. Once a fortnight on Saturdays, they were expected to declaim in Greek. After successfully completing his four years, a pupil asked for grace to receive his BA. Once a Bachelor, a graduate, heard by the sub-dean and moderated by the censors, declaimed in Hall twice a week. Each man had to give six satisfactory lectures on Aristotle before he could take his Master's degree. (The emphasis on Aristotle was supposed to increase a student's power of logic and reasoning.) Masters were required to dispute on theological matters, in Latin, every Friday, moderated by the Censor Theologiae, and to lecture twice a week.[99] Although every undergraduate was obliged to have organised a

> ## Collections
>
> 'Collections' were originally the notes compiled, or collected, by undergraduates on authors they had studied and lectures attended. The origin of Collections as college examinations at which notes were presented for inspection is unknown, although in 1638 the Dean and Chapter were rebuked by Laud for introducing their own internal examination to be taken before a degree. The first real evidence of the expansion of such examinations at Christ Church is the survival of the Collections books. These begin in 1699/1700 with notes of books studied by individual pupils. From 1717, under Smalridge's reorganisation, the format changed, and the books for each Classis or year are listed and then followed by a list of men reading those books. Usually, each man's name is marked, presumably showing a successful Collection, or at least attendance.
>
> In 1768, under Dean Markham, the Classis system appears to have been abandoned, and the Collections books record again the individual reading of each man each term. In 1769, Edward Wortley Montagu was the first to be punished for not offering Collections. In 1774, Collections became compulsory for Noblemen and Gentlemen Commoners as well as Students and the lower ranks of commoners.
>
> Collections remain today as internal termly written examinations.
>
> Bill (1988), 210 – 19; li.b.1

tutor before matriculation, until the end of the seventeenth century tutors were less important than the praelectors in education, their role tending to be *in loco parentis*; one of moral guidance. Tutors had been included in the Laudian statutes but only as a part of the already established teaching mechanisms of the University and colleges.[100] Slowly, as the books became available, and with the steadily increasing age of matriculands in the early years of the eighteenth century, oral instruction began to give way to a tutorial system which would develop into more modern teaching methods.[101]

Outside the formal teaching programme, Fell and then Aldrich encouraged learning in other ways. Fell instigated the New Year gift book soon after his appointment as dean.[102] These books were new editions of patristic texts, often by Fell himself, and often with the assistance of another member of college, with the intention of producing still more learned clergy. Printed by the University Press, the editions were bound and distributed to all members of the House at the dean's own expense. Fell aimed for a clean text, without excessive notes or commentary, and with a translation in Latin if the original were in Greek. Aldrich preferred classical authors, and it was he who began to assign the editing to a pupil, including his nephew Charles Aldrich, who came up to Christ Church as a Westminster Student in 1699 and was elected praelector to the first Classis in 1703 as soon as he had taken his BA.[103] Many of the editions, simple texts designed for undergraduate use, unsurprisingly found their way on to the curriculum. Less well-off pupils must have found the gifts a real boon. The books were not, however, intended to be great scholarly works, so the row that surrounded the edition of Phalaris's *Epistles* demonstrates not just how the gift book scheme was an encouragement to young men in their classical studies, but also the prominence of Christ Church in the world of learning.

Phalaris was a sixth-century BC Sicilian tyrant who was renowned for shutting his captives into a bronze bull, lighting a fire beneath and enjoying the screams of his prisoners as they roasted alive. Letters, supposedly by Phalaris, but probably written some four centuries later by Adrianus of Tyre in an attempt to rehabilitate Phalaris as a man of philosophy, humanity and learning, survived in a manuscript at the King's Library, in the care of Richard Bentley, keeper of the Library.[104] In 1692, William Temple, diplomat and author, had published his *Essay on Ancient and Modern Learning*, giving particular praise to Aesop and to Phalaris. Temple had argued that the letters were genuinely written by Phalaris, and Aldrich suggested that Charles Boyle should tackle them for the next gift book.

A particularly talented young man, Boyle, unusually for a nobleman, had received his BA by examination, rather than by gift of the dean and canons. Boyle employed a scholar to collate the text for him before he began on his edition, and then produced a typical New Year text: the Greek with a Latin translation, a preface and some notes. It was the preface,

Charles Boyle, later Earl of Orrery, was given the task of editing the letters of Phalaris as a New Year Book. Boyle's publication caused a furore for a short while, and helped to establish Christ Church as pre-eminent in influence and in the academic world.

rather than the edition itself, which made the book infamous. In it, Boyle accused Bentley of not allowing his colleague sufficient time to study the manuscript. Bentley denied the charge, but Boyle refused to withdraw. His slight prompted Bentley to a retaliation in which he not only cast doubts on the authenticity of the Phalaris letters, but also on Boyle's scholarship. Bentley's serious academic attack, tearing holes through both Boyle's and Temple's scholarship, was perceived not just as a personal attack on Boyle, but also on the concept of a liberal education which aimed to train men for life rather than for academe. Christ Church rallied to Boyle's defence, and several members, including Francis Atterbury, George Smalridge and Anthony Alsop, wrote a spirited response under Boyle's name. For a while, the wit and humour of the Christ Church response made Bentley a laughing stock. But Bentley, biding his time, eventually produced a new essay in which he proved his case against Boyle and the Phalaris *Epistles*; by then, however, the case for liberal education had been squarely won.[105]

The ready availability of printed books meant that the texts that were suitable for the undergraduate curriculum had to be more carefully prescribed. But the course of studies was still not precise, and could include some really unusual texts, notably the Koran, which appears just once, in 1703.[106]

George Smalridge, picking up the pieces after Atterbury, continued Aldrich's work, making his own attempt to take the educational standards at Christ Church to a new height. Just a couple of months after his installation, the Chapter reviewed the requirements and exercises for higher theological degrees, and Smalridge devised a list of books for each Classis, and collections, compulsory for all Students, commoners and servitors, and designed to impose a minimum level of achievement rather than foster any sense of competition between undergraduates.[107]

The system of Classes, well-structured in theory, was not as straightforward as it seemed. The ordered progress from one Classis to the next was frequently broken as some men were held back and others sped forward. Some progressed from one Classis to another within a single year. Only about a half the undergraduates moved smoothly through all four. Oral exercises, which had been such a signal part of the curriculum for centuries, were also failing. At least twice during Aldrich's deanery Chapter orders had been made to tighten up their performance.[108] By 1706, matters had deteriorated seriously; several young men were reprimanded for neglecting their exercises, and the Chapter, evidently in a state of some despair, trebled the fine that could be imposed for so doing.[109] This appears to have worked. Certainly, no more decrees were passed in the remainder of the first half of the eighteenth century, and very few undergraduates were disciplined for lack of achievement. By the middle of the eighteenth century, however, although disputations for bachelor degrees were to struggle on for a while longer, those for Masters degrees had been abandoned, to be replaced by extra-curricular speeches such as the Fell and Gaudy Orations.[110]

'With strength of argument and in good order': 1689–1755

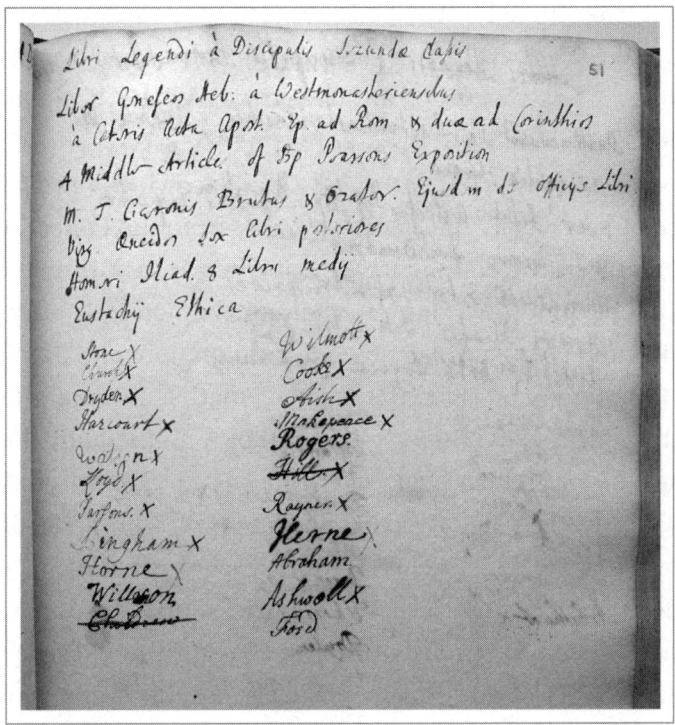

The second 'Classis' in 1727 studied Genesis in Hebrew, the four Apostles and the letters to the Romans and Corinthians in Greek, the middle four Articles from Bishop Pearson's Exposition on the Creed, Cicero, Virgil, Homer, and Eustachius's Ethics.

The availability of texts and the rise in the age of matriculation, together with the improvement in the quality of education in schools, meant that the need diminished for large classes and lectures, and allowed a gradual expansion of the curriculum. The focus was on five main topics: logic, mathematics, classics, ethics with metaphysics and religion, and science or natural philosophy. Logic was always an important part of a liberal education, and disputation was considered essential.[111] John Wallis, Savilian professor of geometry, considered that the study of logic taught men to 'manage our reason to the best of advantage, with strength of argument and in good order, and to apprehend distinctly the strength or weakness of another's discourse'.[112] Throughout most of the eighteenth century, logic, particularly

Aristotelian, was studied in the first year. The standard text, until at least 1826, was Aldrich's *Artis Logicae Compendium*, published by the University Press in 1691.[113] Logic was seen as a deductive exercise, useful in the study of law, morals and divinity.

Maths was often studied as a sub-set of logic, which probably explains the absence of specifically mathematical texts from the Collections records until much later in the eighteenth century, and it took time for maths to develop as a topic in its own right. In the years immediately after the Restoration, maths and geometry were read in conjunction with astronomy. The Dean and Chapter encouraged the study of maths: although it was never established, they accepted Busby's proposal of a mathematical lectureship in 1667, and Aldrich's own book on Euclid was going through the Press at the time of his death. David Gregory, Savilian professor of astronomy, proposed a course of lectures in 1703 which included Euclid, trigonometry, algebra, mechanics, 'catoptricks and dioptricks' and astronomy.[114] Euclid was to become the most studied author at Christ Church during the eighteenth century. Dean David Gregory, 60 years after his father's innovations, brought the maths lectureship to actuality, making provision for four Westminster undergraduates to learn maths and study natural philosophy. The Lee lectureship led to an immediate take-up of mathematics in Collections: courses of mathematical lectures – in mechanics, optics, hydrostatics, pneumatics and astronomy – are mentioned in the papers of William Perrin, who was at Christ Church in the early 1760s.

Classical texts were originally studied not for their content but for the skills they could teach; and construing fostered logical thinking, fluency, clarity, brevity and even virtue. They were considered useful in developing an understanding of contemporary affairs, and the curriculum embraced classical studies even more enthusiastically with the growth of empire. Latin authors predominated until Greek – beginning with Xenophon – was introduced to the undergraduates by Dean Gregory with the support of William Markham, the headmaster of Westminster School.[115]

The dominance of Aristotelian influence in the curriculum continued into the study of ethics. The most popular text, used by second-year

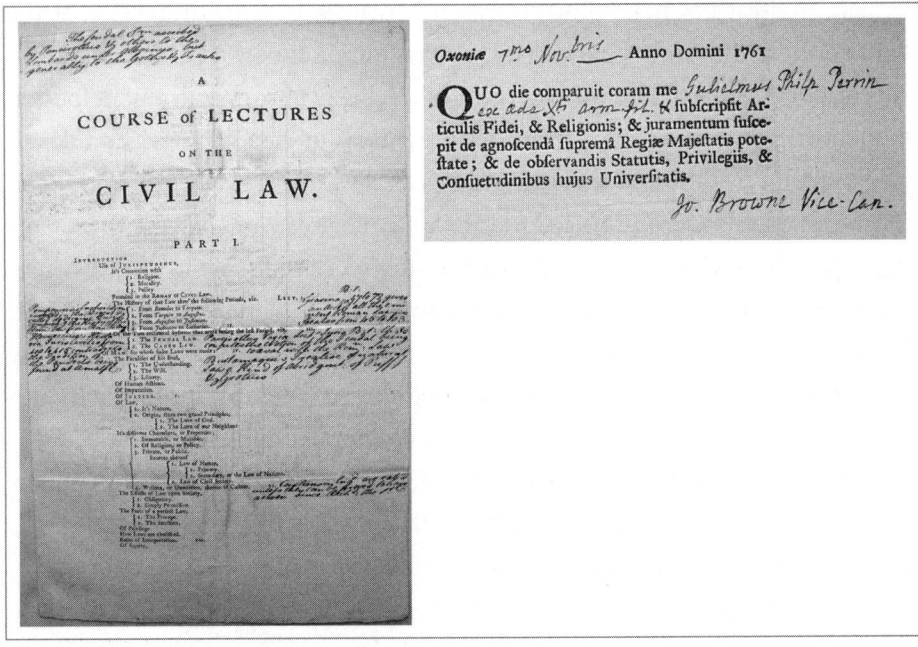

William Perrin came up to Christ Church in 1761. His papers reveal much of the life of a gentleman undergraduate in the mid-eighteenth century, including bills for dinners, often cooked by chefs from other colleges who went 'freelance' for extra money, and for essentials such as wigs, table ware and stable expenses. But there were also lecture lists in both law and mathematics.

undergraduates until 1743, was Eustachius's 1658 treatise. It was replaced by *Ethicae Compendium*, a collection probably published in Oxford in 1743. Metaphysics was a topic to which an undergraduate came in his final years of bachelor studies. Burgesdichius, whose *Institutiones Metaphysicae* was published in 1653, was the standard author. He was studied alongside others, notably Locke's *Essay on Human Understanding*, which superseded Burgesdichius completely by 1743.[116]

Theology, or at least a fundamental knowledge of Christian doctrine, was considered essential until the nineteenth century. The scriptures were studied in their original languages, forming a crucial element in the teaching of Greek and Hebrew. It was not uncommon for students to be required to translate large chunks from Greek or Hebrew into Latin and then into

English. Hebrew at Christ Church was encouraged by the annexation of the regius professorship to a canonry, the creation of Busby's Oriental lectureship, and the bequest of John Morris of his Hebrew library and a benefaction to encourage the study of the language. Busby, as headmaster, had developed a strong tradition of Hebrew studies at Westminster School, and Westminster Students were required to take up collections in Hebrew once they arrived at Christ Church. All undergraduates were required to attend oriental lectures. After the Bible, the Thirty-Nine Articles were an important part of the curriculum. The catechetical lectures given to prepare every young student for ordination must have included the Articles, and John Pearson's *Exposition on the Creed* appeared on everyone's collections record.

The history of the Church in England was not studied, although patristics found their way on to the curriculum for a brief period between Fell's and Smalridge's deaneries. The book which, according to Bill, 'more than any came to represent the tolerant and unenthusiastic religion taught at Christ Church' was Grotius's *De veritate religionis Christianae*, which set out a 'code of Christianity irrespective of sectarian belief'.[117]

Natural philosophy floundered somewhat after the Restoration. The subject had flourished throughout the early part of the seventeenth century and during the Commonwealth, but its teaching stagnated with Fell's opposition to science generally and, more particularly, to the new Royal Society. It was not until the deanery of David Gregory that Aristotelian principles began to lose ground, and a more practical science was promoted. An already crowded curriculum meant that this could still only be accommodated through professorial lectures. Throughout the eighteenth century, probably beginning with the appointment in 1702 of John Keill, once a student of Gregory in Edinburgh, Christ Church was the only college until the mid-nineteenth century that required its students to follow a course of lectures in natural philosophy.

It has often been said that it was the benefaction of Matthew Lee that distinguished Christ Church as a place for the study of natural philosophy. When Lee died in 1755, he left his estate to Christ Church to found lectureships in anatomy and mathematics, and the Anatomy School was built to fulfil the terms of his will. But it seems that Lee was simply advancing studies that already had a thorough grounding at Christ Church. Although medicine and science were not offered as part of the curriculum towards a degree, and few of those who went to lectures in the Anatomy School were destined for a medical career, the work of those seventeenth-century scientists – Hooke, Willis and Lower – continuing experimentation, and a new emphasis on the teaching of science as a practical subject by Gregory, Keill and his pupil Desaguliers must have had some influence on Lee's decision to make such a generous gift to his college.

* * * * *

By 1755, the year that both Lee, the great benefactor, and Conybeare, the great administrator, died, Christ Church had begun to come out of its political torpor. For some years, post-Atterbury, the college had continued to bring up young men destined to lead the country in all walks of life, but had stayed out of university and national politics. It was still naturally Tory, as was the whole University, in spite of Queen Anne's moderation and the Hanoverian succession. In the 1751 election for the University's member of Parliament, Christ Church backed Robert Harley – definitely Tory, but moderate and well-connected. The other candidates were Roger Newdigate, a solid Independent country gentleman with strong Tory connections, and Sir Edward Turner, a Tory with Whig contacts and friends. Most of the other colleges voted for Newdigate as a safe pair of hands; a man whose background reflected that of most of the young men coming up, and he won the day.[118] Within a couple of years, however, the Whig or 'New Interest' camp began to gain ground, and even at Christ Church, support for the Whig cause slowly began to predominate, which rendered the college suspicious in the eyes of the rest of the University. By the local election in 1754, heavily influenced by three local Whig peers – Marlborough, Macclesfield and Harcourt – the battle between Whig establishment and Tory gentry had become aggressive. On this occasion, Christ Church nailed its colours firmly to the Whig mast, even appointing to the vacant position of under-treasurer a strong New Interest supporter, Richard Hanwell, to aid relations between college and city.[119]

Conybeare was absent from Oxford through much of this period, although his Whig leanings may have influenced the gradual change in the political outlook of his Chapter. He had been appointed to the bishopric of Bristol in 1750 and, rather ill, spent much of his time there until he died in 1755. Although most of the last two decades had been energetic, filled with administrative zeal, during his last few years his deanery was apparently as impoverished as the man.[120] He left little, and it was only the publication of his sermons that would fund the care of his two surviving children. Apart from a skirmish over the principalship of Hertford College in 1753, little of note appears in the Chapter Books.[121] Christ Church seems to have been holding its breath.

6

'Learning has been made a duty, a pleasure and even a fashion': 1755–1809

It was the deans of the later eighteenth century who put Christ Church firmly on the academic map. Continuing the reforming programme instigated by Smalridge in the 1720s, David Gregory, William Markham and Lewis Bagot, followed by the great Cyril Jackson, made Christ Church a place where 'learning has been made a duty, a pleasure and even a fashion'. Largely through the hostile writings of Edward Gibbon, the eighteenth-century University has always been characterised as a place in considerable academic decline or, at the very least, lassitude. This indictment has been modified in more recent years. If there were students who could be tarred with the brush of dissipation, it was the noblemen and gentlemen commoners whose post-university lives were already mapped out and who could enjoy the social elements without worrying too much about the inconvenience of study. But, in spite of Christ Church's aristocratic reputation, its academic standing was unmatched – although other colleges were also going against the alleged trend, notably University College where, under Nathan Wetherell, teaching was transformed and new academic heights achieved.[1]

Young men were coming from all over the country. Unlike many colleges, Christ Church was better able to draw its pupils from a wide background, having no overwhelming affinity with any particular school or any regional bias.[2] Most, between 1660 and 1800, came from London and the West Midlands, but there were significant numbers coming from less predictable regions.[3]

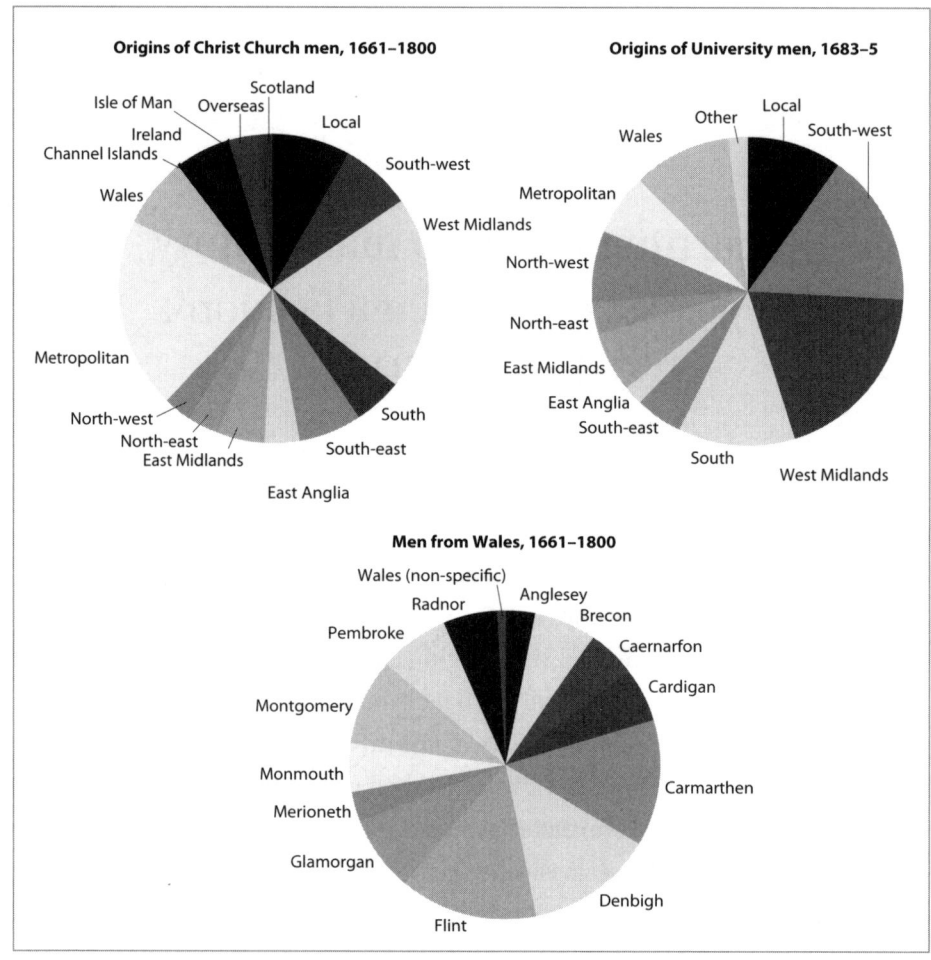

Christ Church men came predominantly from London, Middlesex and the counties of the West Midlands, but there was always a considerable number from Wales from the earliest years of the foundation.

Around 20 per cent of men came from London and Middlesex (a higher proportion than in the university at large), and roughly the same number from the West Midland counties, with Shropshire sending the most (6 per cent), even before the creation of the Careswell exhibitions.[4] There was a distinct westward leaning even beyond the Marches and West Midlands, with a surprisingly large number from the south-west. Nearly 8 per cent came from Wales and another 6 per cent from Ireland. Very few came from the north or East Anglia.

'Learning has been made a duty, a pleasure and even a fashion': 1755–1809

As these young men from across the country left college, many headed for Parliament. The middle of the eighteenth century saw Oxford, and Christ Church in particular, flourishing in the Commons. From 1754 to 1761, 170 Oxford men served in the House, of whom 44 were from Christ Church: 30 on the government benches and 14 Tories.[5] Gregory, and his successors, were determined that Housemen would continue to be influential. A good grounding through a complete overhaul of the curriculum, with termly collections and weekly declamations, was essential.

It was David Gregory – linguist, educationalist and Whig – who stepped into Conybeare's shoes. He had been heavily involved in administration for the previous few years, working closely with Conybeare, particularly on the buildings, so the ten-month gap between Conybeare's death and Gregory's installation was unlikely to have been one of particular difficulties. He had come up to Christ Church as an undergraduate at the beginning of Smalridge's deanery, and adopted many of Smalridge's ideas; he also brought in, as we have seen, some of the ideas proposed by his father, particularly in relation to the teaching of maths. His plans were encouraged by the bequest of Matthew Lee, whose death coincided with Gregory's appointment.[6]

Lee, a contemporary of Gregory, had been physician to Frederick, Prince of Wales, from 1739 to 1751, and a fellow of the College of Physicians. Over the years, he had amassed quite a fortune, from which his old school and his college were to benefit greatly. The first sign of his generosity appeared in the summer after Lee's death when his wife, Sarah, sent a silver soup tureen as a gift to the Dean and Chapter, which was duly inscribed.[7] But this was just the beginning. After the life interest of his wife, the majority of Lee's estate reverted to his old college, a bequest which amounted to about £30,000. It was to fund an anatomy lectureship, four mathematical exhibitions for Westminster Students, an annual prize which was known as the Lee Certamen, and more general exhibitions for Westminster boys.[8] It took ten years of administration, but a decree was finally passed in Chapter announcing that the exhibitions and the Certamen were to commence from 10 October 1765. The under-treasurer was granted £25 a year to manage the trust.[9]

Gregory did not live to see the purchase of the estates in Warwickshire which were to ensure the continuation of the Lee Trust, or the opening of the Anatomy School, both of which took place in 1768, but he was instrumental in, if not crucial to, the negotiations.[10] He certainly took a lead in the building of the theatre, which was begun long before the money from Lee had come through, financed initially by a bequest of £1,200 from John Freind.[11] John Parsons was appointed a medical faculty Student in 1765, before the theatre was completed and, with the new lectureship in his sights and a grant of £120 in his pocket, he set about finding and preparing specimens and other materials that would be useful. On 29 February 1768, Parsons was elected anatomical lecturer. It being impractical, according to the regius professor of medicine, John Kelly, to attempt dissections without help, John Grosvenor was promptly made assistant dissecting surgeon.[12] The numbers of medical students at Christ Church had been high all through the first half of the eighteenth century, but the opening of the new school rendered unnecessary the *Schola anatomica* in the Bodleian Schools Quad and the Ashmolean anatomy room. Students from other colleges were encouraged to sit in on lectures and demonstrations. Parsons's successor, William Thomson, even advertised his lectures in the *Oxford Journal*.[13] From this date on, the Chapter Books include references to young men being granted leave of absence to attend medical lectures in London or Edinburgh.[14]

Thomson's lectures were popular, particularly those on mineralogy and anatomy, but his management of the School was less successful. After his ignominious departure from the University in 1790, things were discovered to be not quite right.[15] The Dean and Chapter remarked, in February 1791, that 'considering the state of the Anatomy School, Mr Pegge [the new lecturer] was to draw up an accurate catalogue of all the preparations and to write to his predecessor for all necessary information'.[16] It took two years for matters to be sorted out, for the college finally to pay compensation for all the preparations that had been purchased by Parsons, and to set up a regular payment from the Lee Trust to pay for new specimens and books. Nothing more was to be placed in the school that had not been purchased by the Fund.[17] William Stephens was appointed as the new assisting dissecting surgeon at the usual salary of £40 per year.[18] Christopher Pegge climbed the academic ladder, becoming regius professor of medicine in 1801. Like

'Learning has been made a duty, a pleasure and even a fashion': 1755–1809

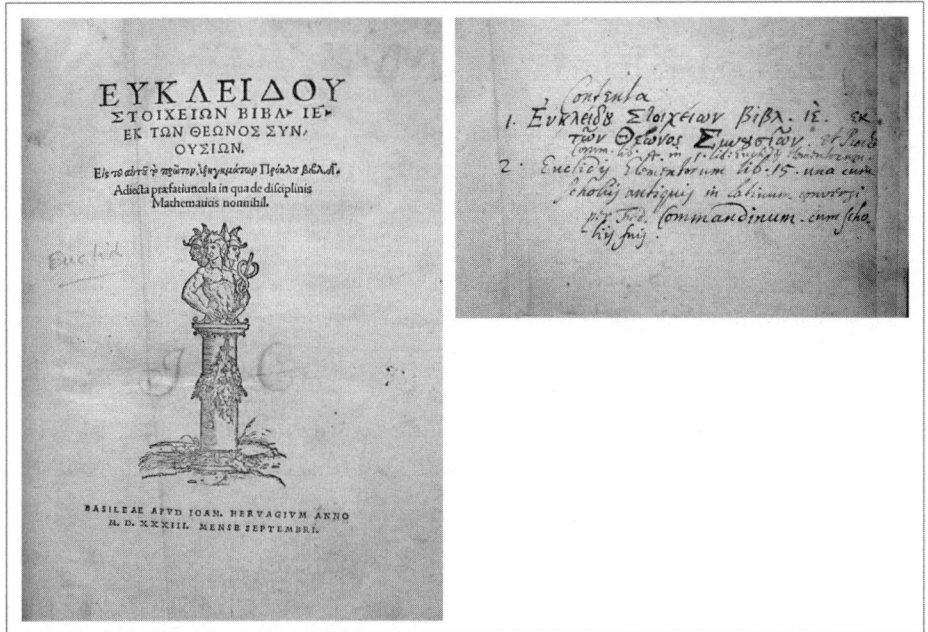

It was under Dean Gregory that Euclid became one of the most widely studied works at Christ Church. Mathematics saw a huge rise in popularity after the establishment of the Lee lectureship. This title page is from a 1533 edition in Charles Boyle's collection which was given to the Library in 1733.

Parsons, he added to the School's collections, including, rather exotically, anatomical preparations made by Signor Clementi Susini in Florence, which cost £50.[19]

It was under Gregory that Euclid, soon to be the most frequently read of all works at Christ Church, was added to the reading lists along with Maclaurin's *Treatise of Algebra*. The study of maths, perhaps unsurprisingly given the dean's scientific background, progressed rapidly, especially once a new mathematical lectureship, first proposed a century before by Richard Busby, was established.[20] The Lee lectureship led to an immediate take-up of mathematics in collections. Markham and Bagot continued the crusade for better and wider teaching of mathematics, which went hand in hand with the expansion of classical studies; more Latin works were introduced and were studied faster, and Greek texts were introduced for the first time.

> ## William Markham (1719–1807)
>
> Markham had matriculated at Christ Church in 1738 as a Westminster Student. When only 33, he was appointed headmaster of Westminster School having already been tutor, praelector rhetoricae, and Junior Censor of his college. His time at Westminster was evidently successful, although the boys were apparently in awe of the tall, portly man. He encouraged classical plays, and gave the school a set of scenery which was used for nearly a century.
>
> Two years before his installation as dean of Christ Church in 1767, he was made dean of Rochester cathedral, and then in 1771, Bishop of Chester, holding both positions in conjunction with his deanery until 1776 when he resigned all three on his enthronement as Archbishop of York.

William Markham had worked closely with Gregory while he was headmaster at Westminster School, altering and expanding the curriculum at the school so that the reforms continued seamlessly once he became dean in 1767.[21] The study of law became increasingly popular, too, with many young men asking permission to 'enter the law-line', to the extent that, in 1759, an old law insisting that pupils take an MA before beginning a law course was revived.[22]

The reforms of Gregory and Markham were popular, and a Studentship was much sought after.[23] Learning at Christ Church, according to Gibbon, had become a pleasure, and effort was rewarded; in 1763, William Weller Pepys was presented with a book for his much approved dissertation on the third book of Apollonius Rhodius.[24] Even so, work was evidently hard and lack of it punished readily. In 1769, only two years after Gregory's death, Markham imposed the first punishments on Edward Wortley Montagu and Alexander Akehurst for not taking up collections.[25] Collections could induce some panic; Henry Fynes Clinton admitted that his reading had been less than structured and the arrival of the end of term saw him unprepared: 'I was obliged to get through it by a hasty application of a few days or nights.' This experience evidently caused Clinton to turn over a new leaf;

he exchanged his lodgings for a room in Fell's Building – 'a situation better adapted for study' – and settled down to 'a more useful habit of study and literary occupation'.[26]

Prizes were not only given to encourage pupils; tutors could also be awarded bonuses for special attention to their duties. In 1777, Thomas Pettingal, John Randolph and William Jackson were paid £50 each for their services in promoting the public lectures and carrying on their courses with 'uncommon diligence and ability'.[27] James Chelsum's course in theology was so admired by the Dean and Chapter that he was permitted to hold a living – although not one in the gift of Christ Church – for as long as he continued to teach.[28]

Once the new Library was in operation, the books became much more easily accessible. Almost unheard of, on 4 August 1784, a commoner, James Blackstone, was granted permission to use the Library, the dean vouching 'that the indulgence would be advantageous to him and would not be abused'.[29] William Thomson was granted permission to use any plates that might be of use in his classes, and Abraham Robertson, then one of the chaplains, who would become Savilian professor of geometry, was given leave to borrow a manuscript of Pappus on the condition that he did not blot or damage it in any way.[30]

But it was not just scholars within Christ Church who were granted wider access to the Library. John Parsons, from Balliol College, was permitted to borrow Xylander's translation of Strabo so that he could correct the edition to be published by the University Press, and Burgess from Corpus Christi was granted leave to use an edition of a work by Curtius.[31] Dr Pett, the principal of St Mary Hall, was granted permission to use the Library as he wished.[32] Robert Holmes, who had been a canon, was even given his own set of keys.[33]

Outside the curriculum, pupils and tutors alike were reading widely. Poorer students tended to confine their purchases (from stationers' shops such as Blackwell's) to books that they were required to read for their studies: in 1797, Jones and Williams, both servitors, bought copies of Euclid, Xenophon and Demosthenes, together with Watson on confirmation

> The rapid growth of the Library's collection was matched by the development of the college's collection of portraiture. There seems to have been a conscious effort to increase this collection and, by 1749, pictures of nearly all the deans were hanging in the Audit House. On at least five occasions between 1760 and 1789, the dean of the time had to write to donors to thank them for portraits that had often been painted by the most fashionable artists of the day such as Joshua Reynolds. In 1785, a Mr Jones gave a portrait of William Bradshaw, and Lord Stormont sent his own picture. In 1790, a painting by Copley of Sir Francis Bernard, governor of Massachusetts, was given by his son. It was rare for the college to commission a portrait; instead the Chapter approached ex-Students to 'enable' their portraits to be hung in Hall.

and Aldrich's *Logic*. Gentlemen commoners, though, were definitely reading more widely, perhaps with an eye towards their Grand Tours. William Mitford's *History of Greece*, the first volume of which was published in 1784, and other travel books covering Paris and Rome, as well as atlases and maps of the British Isles, were frequently ordered.[34] Literature, unknown in the curriculum, and making no appearance in the Library's collections until the twentieth century, often made its way into the pockets of gentlemen. Charles Atterbury purchased a Sicilian romance, and other young men bought poetry and Shakespeare.[35]

Geography, mineralogy, British history, botany and modern languages – particularly German – were all new subjects, unstudied in the normal course towards a BA, but devoured by all and sundry. Canon Hay, in just one shopping expedition, bought maps of Scotland, the West Indies, the 'British Channel', Switzerland, Prussia, Poland, China, Italy and Wales, together with Charles Marshall's *Introduction to the Knowledge and Practice of Gardening* (1796), Edmund Burke's letters on the French Revolution, Thomas Bewick's *History of British Birds* (1797), and texts with the intriguing names of *Bloody Busy* and *Reform or Ruin*, this last written by John Bowdler, appealing for moral reform to protect the British gentry and upper classes from a fate similar to that of their French neighbours. Lord Webb Seymour, one of the noblemen up in the last years of the century, demonstrated a gentlemanly interest in science: his purchases included Richard Walker's work on artificial cold (1796), Kerr's translation of Antoine Lavoisier's *Elements of Chemistry* (1796), Priestley's 1796 edition of *Experiments and Observations relating to the Analysis of Atmospheric Air*, Smith's *English Botany* (1790–1814) and Richard Kirwan's *Elements of Mineralogy* (revised 1794–6). He leavened his selection with a collection of Welsh poems and a guidebook to Wales by Aikin and Evans.

The new academic regime encouraged not only broader reading, but also competition for various prizes, including the Latin verse and prose prizes, introduced through the legacy of Matthew Lee.[37] These were judged by the dean and the college officers, successful entries being read out in Hall. All entries were then commented on, in public, by the panel. Failing to win a prize could generate considerable bile. One unsuccessful candidate, William Shipley, wrote a pamphlet against the judges, entitled *Comparative Observations on Two of the Poems ... in a late Certamen*, in which the senior members of the Chapter 'are maliciously asperse with equal insolence and injustice'. Considered a dangerous influence on the younger members of Christ Church, Shipley was accused of libel and expelled.[38]

The Lee bequest, which had raised scientific study at Christ Church to new levels, was not the only one that came into effect during the later eighteenth century. Fifteen years after his death, and some 30 years after Hugh Boulter had left the deanery of Christ Church for Armagh, the first elections were made to his eponymous exhibitions. Those for commoners were gifted after examination, to help young men through their first years at Christ Church from matriculation to BA. His exhibitions for servitors were in the gift of the Dean and Chapter and worth about £4 per year, a significant sum when a servitor's usual expenditure on battels in 1757 was between one and two shillings a week.[39] Nash's 1754 bequest prompted the amalgamation of the Ascension Day and Lady Day gaudies, to be held in June to coincide with the Commemoration speech, a tradition which has continued ever since.[40]

It was in this period that investment in the financial markets began, bringing another strand of income alongside the traditional revenue from agricultural, urban and industrial estates. Surpluses from trust accounts were often put into bonds or shares, such as the £1,200 worth of new South Sea annuities purchased with surplus from the Fell estates and the £2,000 invested in 1775 from the sale of the Ramsbury estate given by Richard Frewin.[41]

Another destination for surpluses was new buildings. The anatomy theatre, and the consequent erection of a new house for the college organist, were two of Gregory's contributions to Christ Church's architecture, but it was the finishing of the New Library in Peckwater Quad in which he took greatest pride. Gregory's interest in the Library never waned; in his will, he left many of his books to Christ Church.[42]

Gregory tried to tighten up the use of college funds for building and repairs to canonries. He was certainly not the first to do this, but the row between Bradshaw and Terry over the coach-house (see p. 159) must have persuaded him that rules needed to be tightened. It must have been commonplace for small bills to be passed quietly through the Treasury for all sorts of odd jobs. From now on, however, only external work would be paid from the corporate purse and, even then, the canons had to pay for the removal of any mess generated. To be fair, Gregory applied the same rules to himself. It was therefore quite an unusual and somewhat ironic occurrence for Philip Barton, one of the canons, to be given a grant to build a new coach-house in 1763, a dispensation which may have been connected with Barton's gift to the college of valuable English coins in that year.[43]

Throughout the eighteenth century Christ Church had at least one corner under scaffolding, whether for major work or simply for maintenance. Markham oversaw the final details to the Library, the conversion of the old library into rooms for the Westminster Students and its ground floor into lecture rooms, and some minor projects such as renewing the sashes of the Peckwater windows.[44] Under Bagot, the rebuilding of Canterbury Quad began, a project that was just about complete as Cyril Jackson was appointed to the deanery.[45] Jackson was probably the first dean to reside in college and not commission or inherit construction. Instead, he looked forward, anticipating work that would be required in the future, and in 1791 he set up the building fund that would eventually pay for the demolition of Fell's Buildings and Chaplains' Quad, and the erection of Meadows Building in the 1860s.

Alongside the improvements in the curriculum and their interest in the college's buildings, the four deans of the second half of the eighteenth century were just as interested as any of their predecessors in ensuring that discipline was maintained. There were the usual misdemeanours: Edward Taylor Ludford, for example, was put back a year for idleness and disorderliness, and Thomas Penrose was rusticated for 'his long course of irregularities and particularly for his getting out of the College in the night by the help of ropes after having been refused going out of the gate by the porter, and for abusing the porter, breaking the Censors windows, and for his impertinent rudeness to the subdean'. Penrose already had two marks against his name when the Chapter's patience finally ran out. For continued irregularities and for absenting himself without leave, he was expelled.[46] Another man, John Davis, was confined to college for a month for gambling and was required to write and deliver an English speech against a vice which was commonplace among the better-off undergraduates.[47] Another, John Hume, was confined to college for a month while he translated three of Dr Barrow's sermons on industry into Latin.[48]

A name that kept cropping up was one that the Dean and Chapter would probably have preferred not to hear again. In 1759, just after he had taken his BA, Francis Atterbury, grandson of Dean Atterbury, was punished for not 'burying' the censor.[49]

For a while he settled down, but at his own 'burial' ceremony, nine years later after a period as Senior Censor, Atterbury made some remarks, unrecorded but concerning the monarch, that shocked many of those present. Markham felt obliged to censure him, and demanded that Atterbury hand over his speech. Atterbury said that he had burned it, at which point he was summoned before Chapter 'as though', said Thompson in his recounting of the event, 'he were an undergraduate in disgrace'. Destroying the document was considered tantamount to admitting its inflammatory content:

> ### Burying the censor
>
> Every Christmas, it was customary for Bachelor Students to give complimentary orations to 'bury' the outgoing censor. Originally, these orations may well have been more academic disputations, and failure to 'bury' the censor appropriately resulted in a reprimand by the Chapter. There is still an annual censors' dinner at which a speech is given.

'It was at best very indiscreet to meddle with matters which were foreign to the business of your speech … You are to understand, therefore, that we consider that part of your speech as very disrespectful to the Chancellor, as very offensive to your hearers, and in every view highly improper.'[50]

Markham also had to deal severely with one particularly nasty case of the 'most flagrant act of lewdness and immorality within the walls of college'. Whatever the actual offence, it was judged to merit immediate expulsion, but the officers of the college came in person to the Chapter to appeal on behalf of the accused, giving accounts of his former good behaviour. Whoever he was, and whatever the exact nature of his crime, he escaped sending down, but was rusticated for six months, his degree put back by two terms, and he was set a long list of exercises to perform including the abridgement of the whole of Herodotus, drawing out schemes and enunciations. He was to master the fifth, sixth, eleventh and twelfth books of Euclid, and to write down and work out all the examples in the first part of Maclaurin's *Algebra*. In addition, notes had to be taken on all of St Paul's epistles and of the last 100 psalms in Hebrew, and the ninth discourse of Sherlock's sermons was to be translated into Latin. Once the sixth-month rustication was completed, he could return to college, but would be confined for a further three months after which he would be expected to stand before the Chapter and the officers of the college to ask pardon. His father was to be informed, and his sentence made public to all members of the House. Nine months later, having 'acted in full conformity to the injunctions specified, and also given entire satisfaction to the sub dean and other officers of

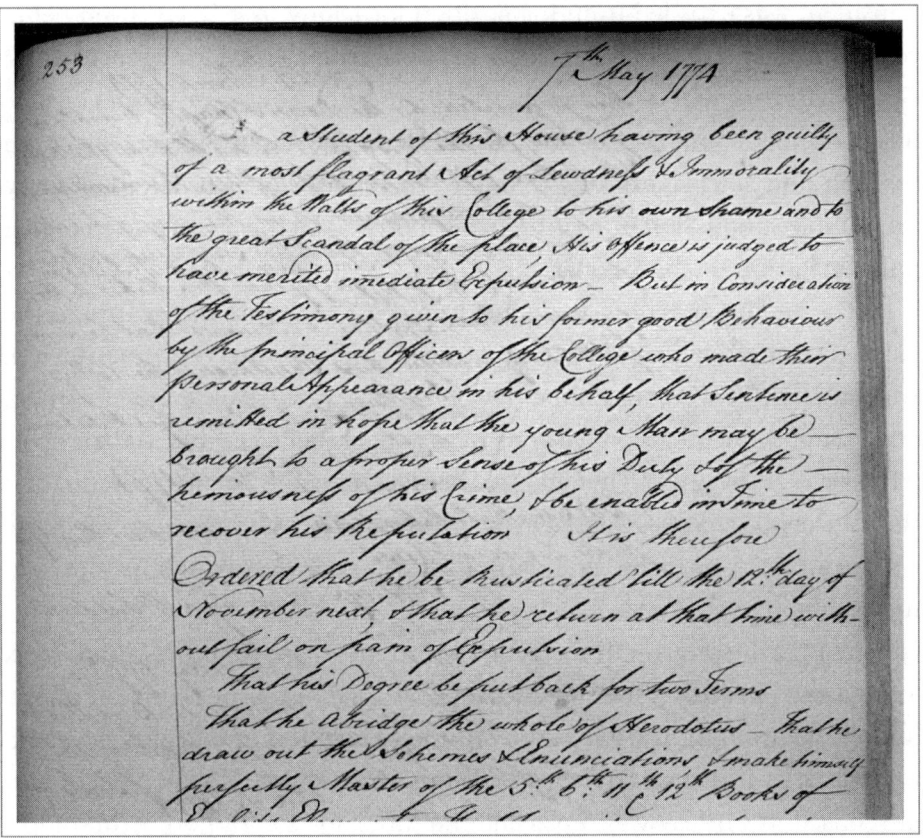

The man responsible for the 'most flagrant act of lewdness and immorality within the walls of college' was so diligent in carrying out his punishments and so obviously contrite that the Dean and Chapter decreed that his name should be erased from all record of the offence.

the college since his return to college [he] is hereby declared to be released from all remaining parts of that censure, and his name to be erased from all orders relating to the matter'.[51]

Most of the disciplinary cases that came before the deans were much more commonplace. John Swinney was punished for turning up in the Latin chapel in a 'grotesque habit', John Scriven was reprimanded for acting as second in a duel between two gentlemen commoners, John Soley for his non-attendance at his mathematics lectures, and John Brodrick was admonished for contempt to college officers and his tutor. John Kimber, one of the almsmen, was expelled from his position for felony in 1781.[52] Even being related to a senior member of college did not exempt a man from reprimands: George Gregory was called before the Chapter to answer for his negligence in his exercises and chapel duties, and David Markham, having given an insolent and abusive exercise to one of the canons, was ordered to 'carry an humble submission in writing to be approved by the dean' and to read it publicly in Hall on the following Saturday.[53]

The small Governing Body at Christ Church – just the dean and the canons – generally meant that administration, both internal and external, was efficient. Meetings of Chapter were usually attended by at least five men, and for important decisions canons were either recalled or sent in their opinions and votes by proxy. The Chapters of Markham and Bagot – more so than that of David Gregory – were heavily involved with the administration of the college estates. The records suddenly filled with decrees about land management, tenancies and college livings. The period of these two deaneries coincided with a huge growth in the enclosure of the agricultural landscape. Trees were purchased for the enclosure of Bledington in Gloucestershire, and the petitions for the enclosure of Butlers Marston in Warwickshire and East Garston in Berkshire were sealed by the Chapter.[54] A new farm was purchased in Cutteslowe to provide the funds for the Holford exhibitions, and the prizes were given for the first time since Lady Holford died in 1720.[55]

More local properties were also subject to close attention. The turnpike road from Oxford towards Botley was widened and, as it crossed Christ Church land, payment was received and duly invested in the name of the Chapter; the profits from the sale of a fee in St Michael's parish in Oxford were to be applied to the College Fund; and it was decided to keep the Meadow entirely in hand by not renewing a long-standing lease of the Timber Yard to Corpus Christi.[56] All new leases of houses and buildings had to include a covenant allowing the Dean and Chapter to enter the property and assess for repairs. Any work not undertaken would nullify the lease.[57]

Finances were always to the fore, with investment traditionally and primarily in agricultural estates. However, as we have seen, the growth of banking from the end of the seventeenth century encouraged investment in

> Lady Holford, who was the daughter of a coachman from Stanton St John in Oxfordshire, founded five exhibitions in memory of her only son, Henry Harbin, who had come up to Christ Church in 1696 and who had died young. The exhibitions were granted by examination and were specifically for boys from Charterhouse School. The estate left by Lady Holford was only sufficient for three-quarters of her legacies to be met, so the Dean and Chapter accepted a lump sum of £1,500 which was duly invested until it reached £2,200 and was sufficient to purchase the farm.

stocks and shares and government bonds.[58] The interest and dividends were regular, but banks were not always safe, and were at risk from national and international affairs (from which they could also benefit). It had always been the case that the Treasurer took personal responsibility for funds but, in the early 1770s, after numerous bank failures, it was decided that it was not fair to allow him to carry such a load. It was decreed that, in the case of any such failure, the debt would be covered by the Public Account of the college.[59]

Getting junior members to pay their bills was always a problem. A new rule was laid down in 1767 that all arrears were to be paid within a month of each quarter day, but although this was a real tightening up of the regulations, it seems to have had little effect. The 1770s therefore saw further changes to internal finances. Caution money was raised, gentlemen commoners found their bills brought into line with those of the noblemen, room rents were increased on the recently refurbished 'Siga' chambers in Peckwater, and yet another order was issued requiring the settlement of all bills quarterly, within six weeks of the expiration of the quarter. The penalty was a reduction in allowances and stipends.[60] Some of these changes were effected because the butler, Hanbury Humphreys, had died in 1772, and his executors had announced that the butler's accounts with the college could not be settled until all the arrears due on battels were paid. Every debtor was urged to pay immediately to avoid the indignity of the executors suing. The under-treasurer and the new butler, George Hunt, were given permission to deduct the arrears of chamber rents and commons from stipends.[61]

But even these threats were unsuccessful; just a year later it was noted in the Chapter minutes that 'great inconvenience having been found from the long arrears incurred on account of commons, battels, cook's bill, chamber rent, bedmakers and scouts, it is hereby ordered that all such arrears now due be discharged by 1st January next [it was then 16 November 1773]. Anyone found, after 1st January, to be two quarters in arrears on any of the above accounts will have his name crossed out and will then be out of commons and battels and be disabled from keeping term.' Things were evidently no better four years later when the butler was ordered to bring a list of all arrears into the Treasury on the first day of every term.[62] It was not all bad news, however. It was found that the trusts set up to help servitors were at an all-time high. It was decided that sums not exceeding £5 could be paid from time to time to particularly deserving cases.[63]

It is possible – though unlikely – that the inaccessibility of the Treasury was the cause of such problems with payments, for at the same time and in the years following, there was a major overhaul of the offices of Treasurer and sub-dean. With effect from Christmas 1775, new rules were put in place. All canons were obliged to serve the two offices, but the positions were a burden; so in order to prevent one or two diligent souls from being coerced into excessively long service, it was laid down that no man had to take a position for the first year of his canonry or be obliged to serve for more than six years, although a minimum of three was preferred. The more senior men were expected to take on the offices before the younger ones. The rules covered every eventuality including the resignation period, death in service, death *before* service, deposits to discourage avoidance, and extra pay for those who took on the role again if no one new was available. The rules, written down in the Chapter Book, were signed by all the canons.[64]

Fourteen years later, when a new under-treasurer was appointed, the opportunity was taken to restructure both that role, and the general running of the Treasury. It may have been necessary; just a few years before, the Dean and Chapter had decreed that the under-treasurer was to be considered an agent of the Chapter, rather than of the Treasurer, so that the Treasurer should not be liable for any mistakes by his junior. But the under-treasurer's job was getting more onerous; as more and more trusts were established, so his administrative burden grew.[65]

John Bennet was appointed under-treasurer in 1789, and the bank notified. The Chapter then made sure that everyone understood how the Treasury should run. Opening hours were set from 10 am until 3 pm every day, except during the first two weeks of every quarter, when it would open at 9 am. Students, chaplains and commoners were to have preferential service, especially those who were officers and tutors.[66] The under-treasurer was required to keep a list in his office of everyone in college, to be corrected regularly. The tutor of each undergraduate had to be named on the list and, before payment was due each quarter, was sent a list of the amounts owed by his pupils. It then fell to the tutors to collect the dues and deliver them to the Treasury. Exhibitions could not be paid before a pupil had proved that he had fulfilled any residency requirements. A printed table of requirements for each exhibition was provided by the Chapter for the under-treasurer to use, and he was expected to 'strictly and invariably observe the orders of the Chapter'.

Bennet's cash book had to be balanced every day before he left his place of work, and was examined and signed off every week by the Treasurer, the dean, or one of the senior canons before the necessary cash to pay expenses was banked.[67] The tightening-up of the management of the Treasury evidently created extra work for the under-treasurer for, in 1799, John Bennet junior was taken on at a salary of £40 per annum to assist his father.[68]

It was not uncommon for servants' pay to be raised when new expenses or responsibilities were incurred. In 1774, sixpence per quarter was added to the battels of all members, except servitors and choristers, to pay the laundress an additional sum for washing the Hall linen, and threepence per quarter was added to everyone's battels bills in 1776 to pay the messenger who collected the post from the Porter's Lodge and delivered it to the Post Office in town.[69] In 1800, for example, the laundress received still more, and in 1802 the schoolmaster's salary was raised to £20.[70] Sometimes, changes were made just to make administration easier: in 1808, the Chapter Clerk's stipend was increased by £12 10s, replacing his usual annual charge of ten guineas for extraordinary expenses.[71] And there were bonuses, too, on special occasions; a gratuity of ten guineas paid when his Royal Highness, the Duke of York, 'condescended to place his name on the books of the college' in 1799.[72]

But there were less honourable ways of supplementing income. George Colman, the younger of the father-and-son dramatists, described how the scouts could easily add to their incomes by fleecing the naïve fresher:

> my two mercenaries [scout and bedmaker], having to do with a perfect greenhorn, laid in all the articles for me which I wanted ... with many useless et caetera, which they told me I wanted; charging me for every thing full half more than they had paid, and then purloining from me full half of what they had sold. Each of these worthy characters, who were upon a regular salary, introduced an assistant (the first his wife, the second her husband), upon no salary at all. Hence I soon discover'd the policy of always employing a married Scout, and Bedmaker, who are married to each other; – for, since almost all the college menials are yoked in matrimony, this rule consolidates knavery, and reduces your ménage to a couple of pilferers, instead of four.[73]

In 1791, the Bread and Beer butlers were allowed candles and profits from dinner victuals; Radge, the Head Porter, received the profits from showing visitors the Hall and Great Tom; Showell, Radge's deputy, showed guests the pictures in the Library; and Banting was a guide in the cathedral. The manciple, Attwood, received profits from meat purchases, and second butler Mott was allowed the profits from the canons', the noblemen's and the gentlemen commoners' tables.[74] It was this method of giving a basic salary which could then be supplemented with profits that was to cause a major row in the middle of the next century, and alter the management and structure of Christ Church dramatically and permanently.

Alongside salaries and stipends, there were always extraordinary expenses. War and affairs further afield often required the Chapter to make payments, and charitable giving or donations to good causes of all sorts were common: over just three or four years, major gifts were given, including the complete cost of the restoration of the memorial to John Locke in his home church of High Laver, £100 for repairs needed at Southwell minster,

'Learning has been made a duty, a pleasure and even a fashion': 1755–1809

> ### Servants' pay in 1791
>
> Attwood, the manciple, received wages of £40 p.a. plus bonuses and additional profits, bringing his income to £65. (His recorded wage in the disbursement books was £6 13s 4d p.a.) He also worked as a bailiff for the college, for which he received an additional £12 16s 6d.
>
> Parker and Martin, the vergers, were paid around £12 in total, and Banting, the first sacrist, received nearly £40, of which only £20 were actual wages. Hownam, the first butler, received £41 with perks. Cluff, the cook who would prepare the sumptuous banquet for the Duke of Portland in 1793, was paid in total over £93. As there was no third cook at the time, Cluff received his wages and bonuses too, an extra £10. The second cook, Smith, was paid almost as much.
>
> In addition to the profits from showing visitors the Hall and Tom, Head Porter Radge had a salary with perks of over £73.
>
> MS Estates 125, ff. 1 & 2

£100 to the Scottish episcopal clergy, and £50 for the support of immigrants fleeing post-revolutionary France.[75] The fear of invasion from across the Channel prompted the University and the colleges to do what they could for the defence of the nation. In 1795, the dean placed a levy on all members to meet the college's quota for raising men for the Navy, raising £49, and in 1807, £100 was contributed to the Oxford Volunteers, a serious force funded by subscription from the colleges and the University.[76]

However, in spite of the somewhat dire political situation in Europe, and the expenses of war that filtered their way into college accounts, there was always time for a celebration over and above the usual gaudy dinners. The war itself gave some party opportunities, such as Admiral Duncan's victory over the Dutch at Camperdown, which was celebrated with special illuminations.[77] Closer to home, the college paid 30 guineas to the vice-chancellor as its contribution to the University's commemoration of the king's golden jubilee in 1809.[78]

The biggest event to take place at Christ Church during this period was the banquet in honour of the Duke of Portland's appointment as Chancellor of the University in 1792. The choice of Bentinck was a political move to appease Prime Minister Pitt, and he was soon active in University affairs, maintaining close contact with Cyril Jackson and the Bishop of Oxford, Edward Smallwell.[79] His installation ceremonials in 1793 caused great excitement both in the city and at Christ Church. Although the formal installation took place at a private ceremony in October 1792 at Bulstrode Park, his home in Buckinghamshire, a great party was held over a full week in July the following year. The streets of Oxford were full of light-fingered characters hoping to make a quick profit from the crowds who had come to watch the ceremonies, but 'every precaution had been taken to prevent their depredations'.[80]

In addition to his official business, the chancellor attended a concert with performers such as Signors Bruni and Monzani, Mr Cramer, Mrs Billington (who drew much admiration), and Madame Krumpholtz.[81] Events at Encaenia[82] the next day were almost disastrous when the doors to the Sheldonian Theatre were opened too soon, and crowds poured in, filling the place to bursting point. It was the chancellor himself who stopped proceedings to protect the spectators.

But it was Thursday 4 July when Christ Church, the duke's own college, laid on a huge banquet in Hall. The kitchen was already renowned for its munificence; a visitor in 1772 noted that 'we saw in the great Kitchen not the least symptom of scarcity'.[83] Preparations had been going on for weeks, and costs were huge. Sixteen pineapples and six melons cost £15, and the turtle for the soup, for which Christ Church was famous, cost £25 10s alone. Extra provisions were brought in from local suppliers and from London by Ephraim Ward's Flying Stage Wagons, and temporary staff were employed by the dozen, including police constables to ensure that order was maintained, not just outside the dining hall, but inside as well. Two tables were laid for the special guests: one from side to side of the dais, and the other right down the centre of the Hall. The dean and the sub-dean took their places at the ends of the high table, with the newly installed chancellor and the high steward of the University either side of the dean.

The chef, Mr Cluff, assisted by his own staff, and a visiting chef, Lizeron,

'Learning has been made a duty, a pleasure and even a fashion': 1755–1809

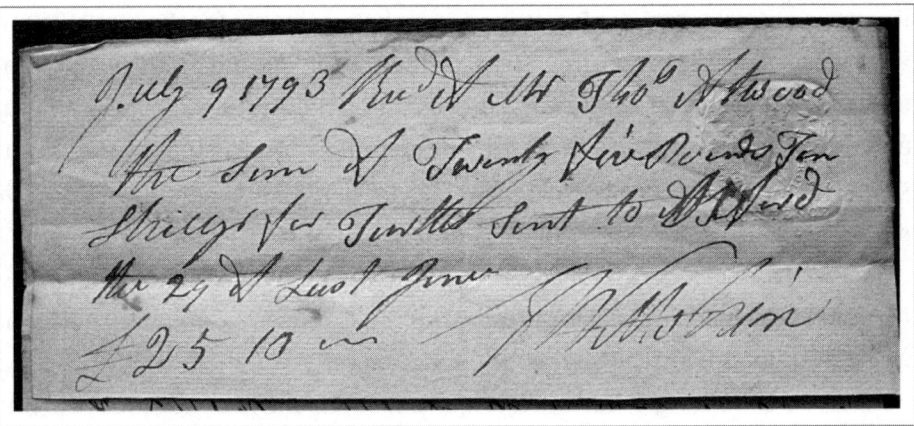

The Duke of Portland was appointed Chancellor of the University in 1793. The huge banquet, held on 4 July, included Christ Church's famous turtle soup.

prepared dozens of dishes. The high table began their meal with turtle dressed with brandy, and then continued with turbot and lobster, salmon, trout, pigeon, crayfish, chickens, ducks, geese, guinea fowl, turkey, lamb, veal, pork, sweetbreads, cucumber salad, beans, potatoes, root vegetables, peas, beef, venison, hare, pineapples and melons. Cluff was paid £30 for his labours on the day, a bonus of about four months' pay. At the end of the meal, the chancellor proposed a toast to the prosperity of Christ Church, and was greeted with loud and enthusiastic applause.[84] A few days later, the Treasurer paid out £205 2s 10d in costs.

However, one regular celebration was curtailed. Back in 1611, the festivities surrounding the annual election of the Westminster Students were abolished, and its successor, the Westminster supper, was abandoned in 1638 at the request of Charles I. But still the customary greeting of the new Students continued. Every year, the previous year's election rode south to Nuneham Courtenay to meet the new boys and bring them back for a welcome meal. Evidently, things often got out of control, and in 1788 Jackson made an attempt to deal with this once and for all. On 21 May, five Westminster Students – Osborn Markham, Arthur Paget, Charles Chester, Thomas Warren and William Rutton[85] – set out as usual to meet the new boys against the specific orders of the Junior Censor, Charles Sawkins. All five were severely punished; confined to Hall and Chapel for the rest of term, they were obliged to maintain strict residence for the next four terms from the first day until collections, to ask pardon of the Junior Censor in a Latin epistle within the day, and to perform such impositions as the dean thought proper. The censure was pinned up in Hall to 'demonstrate publicly that this practice is to be abolished absolutely and not to be revived'.[86]

Whatever else was going on across the University and in college, education never stopped, and yet more academic reform was enforced throughout the University during the later eighteenth and early nineteenth centuries. As early as 1715, changes had been proposed, particularly about the tenure of fellowships, and then Nicholas Amhurst, in his *Terrae-filius*, criticised both heads of houses and the examination system. In the middle of the century, there was a fresh attack by Richard Newton, the founder of Hertford College, on the standards of behaviour and lack of discipline, not just among the undergraduates, but also among the senior members of the colleges. It was also at this time that it was first suggested that subscription to the Thirty-Nine Articles, one of the anchors of the undergraduate curriculum, should cease to be a criterion for membership of the University.[87]

It was a radical proposal. Most senior men in Oxford, including Christ Church's Lewis Bagot, found it unacceptable, fearing that, if subscribing to the Articles ceased to be compulsory, the University could go, in one jump, from being an upholder of Anglicanism (seen as vital to the stability of the nation) to a breeding ground of divisive opinions.[88]

The parallel discussions about reform of the examination system, proposed in the 1770s by John Napleton, a fellow of Brasenose College, were more cautious.[89] Nothing appeared to happen as a result of Napleton's work, but seeds had evidently been sown. His recommendations were picked up by Vicesimus Knox, a fellow of St John's and then headmaster of Tonbridge School, who had radical views on education and trumpeted rather more loudly than Napleton. The horrific situation in France also alarmed everyone; if the universities there were unable to repress revolution, were the English ones any better? A new examination statute was prepared in 1800 under the guidance of John Eveleigh of Oriel College and Cyril Jackson (appointed dean in 1783), introducing the concept of an Honours degree.

> ## Lewis Bagot (1741–1802)
>
> Bagot was educated at Westminster School but was not elected as a Student. He came, instead, as a Canoneer Student through the nomination of Fanshawe. He was made a canon in 1771, and then appointed to the deanery in 1777 after Markham left for York.
>
> Bagot was refined and genteel, but had a keen eye for discipline, particularly for curbing gambling. He presided over a college that was full to bursting, and oversaw the rebuilding of Canterbury Quad.

This proposal was sufficiently conservative to receive widespread approval. Candidates for the BA were to be instructed in the same subjects as before – grammar, rhetoric, logic, moral philosophy, mathematics and physics – and for the MA, mathematics, physics, metaphysics, history and Hebrew. In addition, every candidate had to be proficient in the elements of religion and the Articles. Six examiners were appointed, of whom at least three were to examine six candidates each day. Pupils who wanted to take Honours had to sit a viva with the whole panel of examiners, on a wider range of books than those for pupils seeking only a Pass degree. Needless to say, committees took hold of the suggestions and debated them for six years. The first and second draft statutes were rejected but, eventually, an approved version was passed by Convocation on 17 June 1807. For the first time, graduands would be listed by merit in either or both Literae Humaniores and Mathematics.[90] Nothing is recorded in the Chapter minutes about the new statute, but then Christ Church's academic standards throughout the latter half of the eighteenth century had been high. Other colleges, though, began to follow its example with compulsory collections, and a new sense of competition was engendered.

Christ Church was full to capacity by the end of the eighteenth century.[91] Its success, both academically and socially, had encouraged young men to its doors, and they were being squeezed in wherever a corner could be found. Colman, who came up in 1780, described being put into the rooms of another of his tutor's pupils until that pupil returned to college but, he said, even 'this precarious tenure was envied by several of my contemporaries; for the college was so completely cramm'd, that shelving garrets, and even unwholesome cellars, were inhabited by young gentlemen, in whose fathers' families the servants could not be less liberally accommodated'.[92] Things were no better in the opening years of the next century when Frederick Oakeley was, throughout his whole first term, 'bandied about from one set of rooms to another' and was eventually sent home when the college authorities could find no place for him.[93] But Christ Church was still the place to be. The deans of the later eighteenth century had established the college even more firmly as a place of good, liberal, wide-ranging education for young men who would make their way in the world.

7

'Reading as if my life depended on my diligence': 1809–55

In 1808, George Chinnery watched in awe as the future Prime Minister, Robert Peel, romped home with the first double first in Oxford. It was, he said, in a letter home to his mother, 'the most splendid thing they ever heard'.[1] Cyril Jackson had exhorted Peel to work 'like a tiger, or like a dragon, if dragons work more and harder than tigers', and Peel took this to heart. In the term running up to his examination, he was working eighteen hours a day, taking off only one day – the day before his viva – to relax with a game of tennis.[2] His success vindicated Jackson's cultivation of bright young men and the reform of the examination statutes.[3] However, there were still doubts about the new system. Few men were offering themselves for an honours degree so, although Peel's was a great personal achievement, there was as yet little with which to compare it. There were some, notably Edward Tatham, rector of Lincoln College, who argued that the new system would do more damage than good, fixing Oxford even more firmly into the old classical, Aristotelian mould, with science abandoned purely because Bacon and Newton had been Cambridge men. The new statute certainly underlined Tatham's fears by eliminating science as a required element for a degree.[4]

Dean Jackson chose to retire in 1809, just as the new system began.[5] However, while his influence was still strong, Christ Church men achieved a good number of first-class degrees. The tutors whom Jackson had inspired maintained the standards that could well have slipped under his successors

George Chinnery wrote to his mother at least once a week during his time as an undergraduate at Christ Church between 1808 and 1811. He described the viva examination of Robert Peel, who was to be the seventh Christ Church-educated Prime Minister, in tones of awe and admiration.

in the deanery, and Jackson's legacy rested, according to Reginald Heber of All Souls, 'on an oligarchy of tutors' such as Frederick Barnes, Thomas Vowler Short, John Bull, John Cramer and Charles Longley.[6] During Charles Henry Hall's deanery, which lasted until 1824, Christ Church men received 94 firsts in 29 honours examinations.[7] Christ Church was at its zenith. But success did not come easily. During Hall's early office, prizes were created for those who had done particularly well in Schools, men who had achieved firsts being given dispensation from the college's exercises for their degrees. The Chapter had acknowledged that the old disputations had been superseded. On 4 June 1810, Charles Bathurst was granted grace for his BA both for his diligence and exemplary performance of college exercises, and for having obtained first place in both classes of the university's public examinations, exams in which Christ Church men took two of the eight firsts in classics and three of the six in maths. A few years later, in 1821, one of

> ## John Bull
>
> Bull had come up to Christ Church in 1808, and remained for many years as tutor and as canon. He was said to have 'the liveliest perception of the beauties of classical literature, as well as a great power of communicating it to others'. Between 1832 and 1857 he was Treasurer, during which time he saved the college from ruin.
>
> Bull transacted all college business with one well-known bank. The company's reputation was high, but Bull, talking to the banker over dinner one evening, was struck by his 'very pious and orthodox remarks, and by the change in tone in his conversation, such as might suit a canon of Christ Church but not a luxurious banker from London'. His suspicions aroused, Bull went to London the next day, drew out all the college's money and removed his papers from the bank. The day after, the bank collapsed.
>
> Muller (1901), 247; Couch (1892), 310–45

Charles's distant cousins, William Hiley Bathurst, was given a copy of the fourth edition (stamped with the college crest) of Clarendon's *History of the Rebellion* and *The Life of Edward, Earl of Clarendon*, as a reward for his double first.[8] Even commoners were occasionally recognised in the official record for their successes: in 1813, Philip Barker Webb was given a special mention in the Chapter Book for his Latin composition and awarded a prize of books to the value of £10.[9] In 1825, a sum of £100 at 5 per cent interest was left by Francis Burton, once Student and counsel to the college, for the purchase of books as 'tokens of merit' to undergraduates.[10]

But the men earned their prizes. Chinnery's letters, written from Christ Church between 1808 and 1811, describe his studies. At his first interview with Jackson, only a day or so after he arrived in Oxford, he was quizzed on his previous education – which had been given at home – including his proficiency in Greek. This, Chinnery admitted, was not as good as it ought to be because he had concentrated on modern languages, although he had read some Sophocles, some Euripides and a little Aeschylus. Jackson was very disparaging and pronounced Chinnery's Greek tutor, Reverend Mullens of Exeter College, a fool. Mathematics was the next topic for discussion and Chinnery's knowledge was better received by the dean despite Jackson's unfamiliarity with the algebra book, by Butler, that the young man had used.[11] His basic knowledge of mathematics was extended considerably during his three years at Christ Church, but Chinnery himself felt that its chief value had been to strengthen his mind and give it 'powers of tenacity'. In his classical studies, Pindar became a firm favourite: 'It is impossible,' he wrote home to his mother, 'to read Pindar without enthusiasm ... The mind eagerly enters into the nobleness of sentiment and dignity of expression; and the man who has done this and has successfully rendered these beauties into equivalents borrowed from his own language, cannot help feeling that he soars something above the common level of mankind.' (This last comment was later echoed by that extraordinary classical scholar, Gaisford.) Chinnery's lack of grounding in the classics was seen as a real disadvantage, however, and neither of his tutors, William Corne or Charles Lloyd, expected him to achieve a first [12]

Schools was a wearying experience. For three entire days, Chinnery was examined for his degree. The first day covered logic and translations between English and Latin, and English and Greek. Day two was taken up with vivas in ethics, rhetoric, logic and the classics. In the first three, Chinnery declared himself perfect, but was content to take his chances with classics. Day three was devoted to mathematics, and he was told that 'Newton and the Fluxions never were done so well in the Schools before'. Lloyd and his pupil were 'both in high glee'. In the end, Chinnery took a first in mathematics, but, as Lloyd and Corne had predicted, he just missed out in classics.[13]

Many men were exceptionally diligent in their work to achieve high results. William Gladstone recorded that he read constantly, even before arriving at Christ Church, and Henry Liddell wrote home that he had finished all the books required of him fifteen months before his examination.[14] One or two evidently drove themselves to illness: Benjamin Harrison, aiming for a double first in 1830, succeeded easily in classics but only took a second in mathematics – a position given to him purely because the examiner knew his talents – but the effort threw him into a fever from which his friends were

> ## Samuel Smith (1765–1841)
>
> Smith was the son of a headmaster of Westminster School. He came up to Christ Church in 1782, and was tutored by John Randolph and Phineas Pett. He left in 1803 for the living of Daventry, marrying Anne Brady, the daughter of a Jamaican plantation owner, in the same year.
>
> But he was only away for four years. He returned in 1807 as canon, and was appointed dean in 1824. The death of Anne in 1826, after the birth of their thirteenth child, affected him greatly and almost persuaded him to resign even earlier.
>
> ODNB

afraid that he would not recover, and which James Gaskell considered to be 'prejudicial to the cause of first classes'.[15]

However high Christ Church's achievements may have been, the system was still not perfect. Hall was appointed to the deanery of Durham in 1824 and was succeeded by Samuel Smith. Smith was 60, had come to Christ Church in 1782, and had already been a canon for seventeen years; a safe and conservative pair of hands. He only stayed for seven years before he, too, departed for Durham, but, although his deanery is almost as unfavourably remembered as Hall's, there are indications that it was more successful, not least for the quality of the new undergraduates – men who would make an impact both at Christ Church and beyond, notably Smith's own nominee, William Gladstone, together with Charles Canning, Henry Liddell and Robert Scott.[16] Many more were still elected through connections. Each potential canoneer Student had to present a letter in Latin setting out the reasons why he thought he should be elected, and being a relative of the dean or one of the canons was definitely accepted as a qualification.

Thomas Vowler Short's influence as Censor for the ten years between 1819 and 1829 has been seen as one of the reasons why the tone of Christ Church improved under Smith.[17] Short had made suggestions for improvements to the examination system, but they were not implemented until after

Thomas Vowler Short held the positions of tutor, censor, librarian and catechist between 1809 and 1829. He kept a notebook with succinct and often candid comments about the undergraduates. This, concerning Henry Bingham Baring, later soldier, director of Barings Bank, and Peelite politician, is a good example.

he had left.[18] Had he remained at Christ Church through Gaisford's deanery, the dean's resistance to any reform might have been tempered, and the post-Jackson decline in results arrested. A second lecture room, adding to the one in the basement of the Old Library, was built at the top of the Hall stairs in 1829 and a new entrance examination for commoners was introduced with tests in divinity, classics, and mathematics and arithmetic, designed to determine whether a pupil would be a credit to the college.[19] A secondary reason for the examination was to try to raise standards in the feeder schools. Westminster School had declined in its academic achievements, and the poorer quality of boys did not help to maintain good results in finals. The censors were conscious that mathematics and arithmetic particularly were 'apt to be grossly neglected' at school. Even those with particular skill in the subject, such as George Chinnery, needed further tutoring. Students may still have been able to secure a place through personal connections, but increasingly commoners were admitted purely on merit.[20]

Henry Liddell, as we have seen, finished his prescribed reading long before his exams, and wished to study further around his subjects. He asked to stay up over the summer but Dean Gaisford refused. Instead, Liddell stayed in Cuddesdon with A. P. Saunders, the recently departed maths tutor and curate of the parish.[21] Other men, too, wanted to expand their horizons, and the teaching of science, in spite of its neglect in the honours course, remained strong at Christ Church.

Pegge, for all his alleged lack of honesty, had been a prominent teacher and, when he resigned in July 1816, finding a replacement was problematic. James Tattersall, a Westminster Student and a doctor of medicine, was the only man qualified to take over under Lee's bequest, but he refused the post. The Dean and Chapter turned to John Kidd, another Westminster Student who had left Christ Church to study at Guy's Hospital, and then returned to sit his BM and take the Aldrichian professorship of chemistry. He was a staunch supporter of the teaching of science, but believed that it should be ancillary and complementary to the more traditional studies of the university. He had created his own lecture series, giving a firm grounding to scientists who were to shine in later years such as William Buckland and Charles Daubeny.[22] He was popular in Oxford, but his methods and beliefs were not always appreciated: Carus, physician to the King of Saxony, was disparaging of the anatomy school which, he said,

> brought back the times of Vesal to my mind ... All around the theatre, behind the amphitheatrical seats of the audience, were skulls and anatomical preparations, everything quite in the antique style. Prof. Kidd, a good-natured old gentleman, quite corresponded with these ancient treasures. He may, probably, formerly have had some talents, or at least some liking for personal activity and inquiry; or, at a later period, without any excitement from without, in a university devoted almost entirely to philology and theology (which is indeed no universitas), and without sufficient inward power and excitement, the

stagnation of all philosophical study, of natural history, soon put a stop to his activity.[23]

Kidd retired in 1845, and Henry Wentworth Acland, still unqualified in the medical profession for which he was aiming, was appointed in his place. During Acland's period in office, the Anatomy School would change its function completely.[24]

With Charles Daubeny at Magdalen and Robert Walker at Wadham, Acland worked to promote a new honours school in natural science, to put the subject firmly back on to an official footing, and for the building of a new museum.[25] He was keen that there should be a central facility, available to everyone, and wrote in 1844: 'it is quite clear that we have no right to assume ... that they [the natural history collections] cannot be moved into other buildings than those they severally occupy. At the same time it seems to be necessary that the University should have proper places for study and for instruction in those branches of the natural sciences in which she has determined to provide examinations.'[26] The Lee Trust continued to acquire new specimens from all over the world throughout the 1840s. Gifts were sent from Ireland, Australia and New Zealand, and £100 provided for the purchase of an elephant's skeleton.[27] In 1851, Acland reported to the Dean and Chapter that a new osteological case had been built, and room made for zoological and pathological specimens. The stock of skeletons was being improved and prepared for use, including that of a giraffe given by a Mr Hoare.[28] By 1857, the museum at Christ Church contained 'not only an admirably arranged collection for the study of physiology and anatomy, but also the nucleus of a pathological series for the use of medical students'. Acland himself had added about 2,000 specimens, many purchased from his own pocket.[29]

The Trustees were not keen on the transfer of the collection from Christ Church; the Trust had paid for the Anatomy School to be built to house the specimens, and there they should stay. In 1854, four years after the new school of natural science was introduced, a reading room and gallery were added to better display the collection, and there were proposals for a new dissection room should practical human anatomy lectures be permitted again.

Cardinal Thomas Wolsey by Sampson Strong, c.1610. No contemporary portraits of Wolsey survive, and all known portraits are based on a drawing by Jacques le Boucq dated c.1565.

St Frideswide with the ox of Oxford, and her priory in the background, from Christ Church Library's MS 101.

The first buildings of Cardinal College to be completed were the dining hall and the kitchen, ready to feed the college at Christmas 1526. Rudolph Ackermann's painting is early nineteenth century, but shows the kitchen much as it would have looked four centuries before.

This vignette in the corner of Strong's portrait of Cardinal Wolsey dates from the same period as Bereblock's rather crude illustration of the Great Quadrangle (see p. 78). It shows clearly the priory church, the dining hall, the kitchen with its enormous louvre, and auxiliary buildings.

Design of 1803 by G. Smith for a triumphal arch into the Meadow from Rose Lane.

John Riley's The Scullion, *painted in the 1680s, shows one of the college servants. There is much debate over who he may be, but it seems likely to depict John Shreve. It has been suggested that Shreve was a loyal supporter of the Protestant faith who came to represent the faithful servant and common man against the Catholic regime of James II and the Catholic dean of Christ Church, John Massey.*

The first Library at Christ Church seems to have been set up around 1561 in the old monastic refectory. Its painted ceiling, similar to the one in Duke Humfrey's Library at the Bodleian, was rediscovered and restored in the late 1950s.

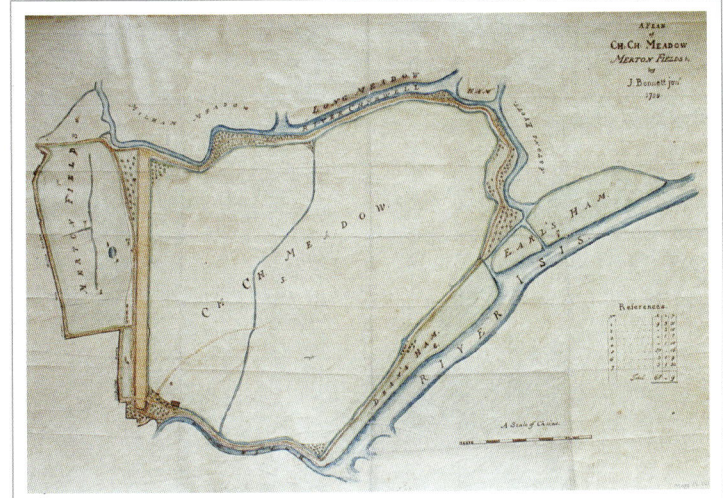

Bennett's plan of the Meadow, 1799, shows the walks already established around its edge, and the Shire Lake, which marked the boundary between Oxfordshire and Berkshire. Earl's Ham is the site of the college boathouses. North is to the left.

Coloured lithograph of the cathedral, probably from the 1830s, showing a service in progress, before George Gilbert Scott's restoration. Drawn by Russ, etched by Picken, and published by Day and Haghe.

Unattributed watercolour showing Edward Bouverie Pusey preaching in the cathedral on Advent Sunday, 1875.

The row over attendance at a ball at Blenheim Palace in 1893 prompted furious discussion in the press about the behaviour of young gentleman and aristocrats. A series of paintings recorded the events of the night of the ball, when angry students painted the doors in the Tom Quad red and daubed slogans damning Dean Paget and Censor Sampson.

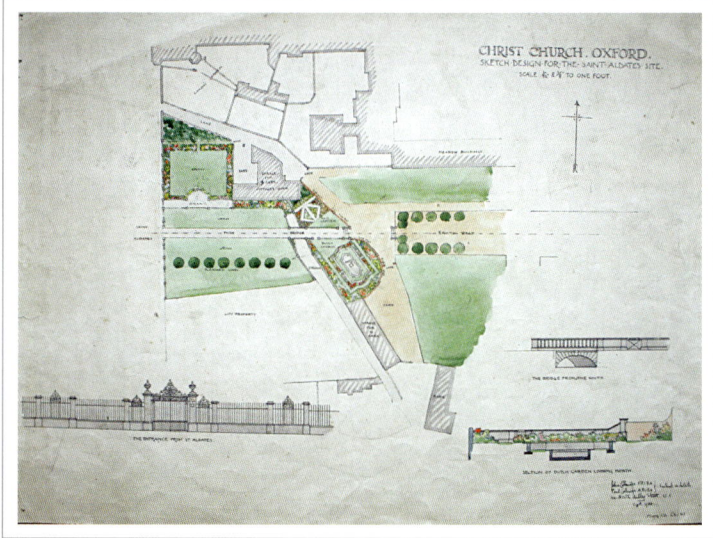

Design for the Memorial Garden by John and Paul Coleridge, dated 1926. The garden was paid for by subscription in memory of the Christ Church men who fell in the First World War.

In 1978, the momentous decision was taken by the Governing Body to admit women to Christ Church. The first female undergraduates arrived in Michaelmas term 1980, along with a Junior Research Fellow and the first Official Student.

FRESHMEN: OCTOBER 1980

Back row (l. to r.): BAER, G.C./ MASLEN, R.W./ YALLAPPA, S./ JUDD, R.F.

6th row: WILSON, H.N./ PAUL, K.D./ ARMOND, M.R./ FOSS, A.J.E./ SPRAGG, D.A./ GOWER, P.J. de P./ FOXALL, S./ INFIELD, A.P.A./ BURKILL, R.P./ WARD-THOMPSON, D./ MACLEAN, R.G.S./ BRISBY, T.A.T./ HARRIS, O.C.G./ WAN, M.W-Y./ TOTAH, M.F./ JONES, D.G./ CROW, M.A./ MATTHEWS, M.J./ MORLEY, C.J./ SUTTON, S.E./ JONES, P.F./ BRACE, H.M.

5th row: WRIGHT, M.W.F./ CONNORS, J.K./ WILLIAMS, G.E./ SHORROCK, M.H./ STEVENSON, N.A./ WASHINGTON, B.R./ WILLIAMS, D.E./ NORTH, J.R.J./ BICKET, H.A.C./ WHITE, D.J./ CHADWICK, L./ BUTCHER, J.A./ FINLAYSON, S.E./ TAYLOR, J.M./ BECK, S.L./ JACKSON, D.C./ MITICHSON, M.A./ WILKINSON, T.H./ SMYTH-OSBOURNE, R.R./ LUMSDEN, A.M./ HAZEL, R.M./ WALDER, I.H.M.

4th row: SOBOSLAY, A.P./ CROZIER, J.P.B./ MATHIAS, C.B./ SAUNDERS-DAVIES, N.O.S./ CURTIS, J.B./ BICKERSTETH, J.S./ McCABE, T.P./ HOLMES, R./ PEDLEY, M./ ROBINSON, H./ BROOKS, R.J./ HALL, A.M./ BROWN, A.S./ PILBEAM, C.J./ FERRARIO, C.V.J./ SCHNEIDER, H.J./ DAVIE, M.E./ BRAMSON, M./ HUGHES, A.R./ WARD, A.C./ KAVANAGH, S.J./ KIDNER, J.H./ LUFF, S.H.

3rd row: DUPREE, Rev. H.D./ MARSTON, G./ HOWARD, P.N./ STEWART, I.A./ LIGHTFOOT, P./ BROWNE, K.J./ GORDON, A.G./ BARKER, N./ ANSBRO, N./ ROWBOTTOM, M.G./ GREEN, T.C./ MASON, S.C./ RICE, F.C.M./ RIGBY, D.K./ KING, R.A.H./ ANDERSON, J.R./ ARTESANI, N./ CORDEN, R.M./ DESTRO, M.L./ ATTEW, M./ WILLIAMS, J.H./ KNIGHT, P.G.

2nd row: SCHLOSSER, W.S./ BURNEY, P.J.G./ LOWE, P.E./ CARPENTER, T.H./ HINCHLIFF, S.P./ LIDDLE, G.D./ LINFORD, M.R./ WEST, C.P.N./ LAWLESS, C.G./ ATTRIDGE, G./ JONES, R.W.L./ GODSON, L.B./ PODD, H.R./ DODGSON, S.J./ McALEER, A.A./ ANDREWS, S.D./ EVANS, M.J./ FREYBERG, A.P./ van ROOIJ, J./ HEYES, P./ MOORE, J.P./ STEPHEN, J.R./ TASKER, M.N.

1st row: CLOKE, J.M.P./ JACKSON, R.C./ PETCHEY, M.D./ KUNZ, C./ LUECK, M.A./ SEFTON, I.R./ STURDY, J.L./ PAGE, T.D./ OWEN-LLOYD, M.R./ GILCHRIST-FISHER, A.C.R./ WALL, K.M.F./ CROMPTON, M.R./ TROUGHTON, N.A./ EDDERSHAW, R.W./ DAVIES, J.M./ WRIGHT, D.A./ MACMILLAN, A.G./ FRANKS, H.J./ LEVINSON, C.M./ SCHOFIELD, N.B./ CARLEY, J.D./ HOPWOOD, P.J.

Fell Tower was constructed by Henry Liddell as part of his 1862–5 renovation of the Great Quadrangle. John Fell had apparently intended constructing an observatory over this archway, hence the name. The passageway to the arch is named 'Killcanon', as the winds that whistle through it are said to be biting enough to kill the canons!

The stairs to the Hall have been re-aligned at least once since Wolsey's time. The beautiful fan vaulting was commissioned by Samuel Fell in the 1640s and installed by a Mr Smith.

The north prospect of Peckwater Quad. Peckwater derives its name from the medieval inn which used to stand on the site. It was rebuilt in the early seventeenth century and then again in the first decade of the eighteenth. The floor plan of the building that was to become the New Library is in the foreground, with its front elevation depicted on the drawing held by the boy in the bottom left-hand corner.

The New Library was begun in 1716 to complete Peckwater Quadrangle. Dean Aldrich's original design was not for a library but probably for a particularly grand residential block. However, the need for more shelf space prompted a re-think, and plans were made to build the 'finest library of any society in Europe'. Its construction and fitting-out took nearly sixty years, partly as money was slow to come in for yet another project, and partly because the designs had to change to accommodate new gifts of books, artefacts and paintings.

The upper Library, painted by David Gentleman for the 1967 Oxford University almanack. The plasterwork decoration (detail below) was executed by Thomas Roberts in 1752–3, possibly with the assistance of the Swiss stuccoist, Giuseppe Artari. The shelves and gallery are of Norwegian oak. The paint scheme, of two shades of pink, white and judicious gilding, was devised in 1960.

The late eighteenth-century entrance to Canterbury Quadrangle. This gateway replaced the medieval structure shown in John Malchair's drawing (see p. 20).

The Great, or Tom, Quadrangle was largely constructed between 1525 and 1529. By the time Wolsey died, the south side was complete, and the east and west almost finished. Mercury was dug in 1670 as a reservoir and decorated first with a globe in the centre. The north side of the Quad was completed by John Fell in 1665, and Tom Tower erected in 1683.

Tom Tower, on the north side of the Quad, was erected in 1683.

When Kidd had stepped into Pegge's shoes as Dr Lee's Reader, the young William Buckland, still a fellow at Corpus Christi College, had taken over Kidd's readership in mineralogy in 1813. Buckland extended his lectures to include geology as well as mineralogy, and spent much time rearranging the mineral collections at the Ashmolean by type, and drawing maps, pictures and diagrams. Increasingly, he found that the study of geology and the then unnamed science of palaeontology came into conflict with orthodox religious belief.[30]

After his researches at Kirkland, Paviland and Wirksworth, Buckland's next series of lectures was on the '... composition and structure of the earth, the physical revolutions that have affected its surface, and the changes in animal and vegetable nature that have attended them ...' Fifty-two men, including Kidd and a significant number of senior members of the university, signed up for the series, which was published as *Reliquiae Diluvianae* in 1823. Although these new sciences were still not on the regular curriculum, it was felt to be essential for senior men, both those of scientific bent, such as Daubeny and Stephen Rigaud, and those with most definite theological leanings, such as Charles Lloyd and Frederick Barnes, to keep up-to-date with modern thinking.[31]

For Gaisford, however, these revolutionary ideas were unwelcome. He resisted the march of the university honours system, giving preference to the old college examinations. In spite of Gaisford's reputation for terrifying students taking up collections, this policy did not encourage hard work.[32] His reluctance to enter students for honours allowed other colleges to challenge Christ Church's academic pre-eminence. As Christ Church stuck rigidly to its policy of patronage, other colleges were appointing their scholars and their fellows on merit.[33] First-class degrees, numerous under Hall and Smith, even if not entirely the result of the endeavours of those two deans, almost dried up during Gaisford's time. Between 1831 and 1835, Christ Church men were awarded 28 first classes; between 1841 and 1845, the number was down to six.[34] Henry Acland was frustrated by the failure of the Governing Body to recognise anything but classics and a smattering of mathematics.[35] The quality of Students, and therefore of tutors, declined.

While other colleges were beginning to open scholarships and fellowships to competition, elections to Studentships continued to be in the hands of a Dean and Chapter perceived to be unduly influenced by position and birth. The patronage of the dean and canons was not universally abused, but there were accusations of nepotism, and no doubt some examples of it.[36]

Tradition and Gaisford's policies worked together to limit the number of good tutors available; in 1857, C.W. Sandford, speaking to the University Commission, laid the blame firmly at Gaisford's feet.[37] But, throughout the university, the opening of fellowships became the topic for discussion amidst growing dissatisfaction with the existing system.

* * * * *

It was not just academically that Christ Church began to slip after the retirement of Dean Jackson. Jackson's influence, and that of many of his predecessors, had extended way beyond the walls and out into wider society where a Christ Church nomination could easily forestall any contest for a prime position. Christ Church men were so liberally scattered throughout society that it was relatively easy for men still in college to obtain nominations to professorships, parliament and the church. The dean's choice would have been accepted by the Chapter almost without question. But Dean Hall did not share this wider influence. When, in 1817, the Speaker of the Commons and once Christ Church man, Charles Abbot, resigned his seat as the University's parliamentary representative, it was expected that the dean would immediately set about finding a successor. Hall did just that, but made a diplomatic and discourteous mistake in calling an extraordinary meeting of the college officers on an evening when Barnes, the sub-dean, was elsewhere, hosting dinner for the vice-chancellor and several college heads. He then found that his choice of George Canning to take Abbot's place was not universally supported in Chapter. Canning's leaning towards the Catholic cause divided the others, and Corne threatened to resign if Canning's nomination was approved. Hall saw the danger signs, and sensibly withdrew his suggestion. Vansittart was the sub-dean's choice, but Robert Peel was the ultimate and eventually unanimous proposal. While Lloyd, Peel's old tutor, was dispatched to London to tell his pupil the good news, the Chapter and resident Students were canvassed, along with the senior members of other colleges, to ensure their support. Peel was duly elected, the power of Christ Church as a body was confirmed, but Dean Hall had been seen not to carry the respect that his predecessors had enjoyed.[38]

The 'Catholic question' prompted another battle within Christ Church in 1829 when, on 31 January, Robert Peel wrote to the dean explaining that his position on the 'Catholic question' had changed. Having once stood firmly against any form of Catholic emancipation, he had come to realise that the political situation needed some flexibility. Peel offered to resign his position as MP for the University, a University which had just voted overwhelmingly in Convocation to stand against emancipation. Although his resignation was accepted, he was renominated immediately to stand in the by-election. Oxford was in a state of excitement; the 'fury of the No-Popery party ... knew no bounds,' stated Joseph Blanco White, and the still-clerical nature of the University assured a strong vote against Peel. The Senior Common Room had, at first, been strongly pro-Peel, but Lloyd advised against any obvious activity on his behalf. The prospect of opposition that might divide the University and the college did not sit easily with Lloyd. The Common Room's position was made even harder when the opposition candidate was revealed to be Robert Inglis, another Christ Church man just two years senior to Peel, who had remained firmly against Catholic emancipation. At some point during the short but factious campaign, in spite of Peel's double-first achievement 20 years earlier, the Christ Church protesters made their feelings graphically known. Hammered into the door of the Treasury, at the foot of the Hall stairs where it could be seen by anyone, the words 'No Peel' were spelt out in iron studs. In a similar vein was a mock concert programme lampooning Peel and his vacillating supporters, including the dean, who is listed in the running order to sing a ballad entitled 'How happy could I be with either' from *The Beggars' Opera*.[39] Electioneering was vigorous; men, particularly country clergymen, came into Oxford from all over England to place their vote. Peel was defeated by 755 votes to 609, in spite of having the support of academics and nobles, and Inglis was to stand as

> ## The Christ Church Choral Society
>
> The Choral Society was instituted in 1827, with its first meeting on 3 February. It seems to have been relatively short-lived. Meeting in a different private room each week, the resident was responsible for ensuring that the piano, hired for a full term, was installed in time for the meeting and that a pianist was engaged. The first 'director' was Philip Egerton, later politician and palaeontologist. New pieces of music were to be presented to the society each week, and any kind of vocal music was admissible. Membership of the society was by ballot, and men from other colleges could be admitted as Honorary members.
>
> It was a well-to-do society, most of the men being titled. The choice of music was eclectic. At the first meeting, there were songs by Henry Bishop from Colman's play *Law of Java*, first staged at Covent Garden in 1822, pieces from *Don Giovanni*, songs from Rossini's *Il Tancredi*, ballads such as the *Red Cross Knight* and glees such as Dr Hayes's harmonisation of *Gently Touch the Warbling Lyre*, for four voices.
>
> CCL MS 485

an MP for the University for the rest of his life. The incident of vandalism is ignored in the Chapter records, suggesting perhaps a tacit agreement with the wielder of the hammer, but the campaign had divided Oxford, even as it had assured Christ Church's political supremacy.[40]

Politicking may have been important to the senior members of colleges and to the colleges' and University's relationship with the state. To many undergraduates it was a diversion from studies and chapel.[41] But there were other distractions. Intellectual interests were met by clubs such as the Essay Club founded by William Ewart Gladstone in October 1829. With eleven friends, several of whom had been his contemporaries at Eton, the society was based on the Cambridge Apostles.[42] They met in Gladstone's rooms on staircase 2 in the fashionable Canterbury Quad, and the club, which aimed to be both intellectual and élitist, soon became known by his initials, the WEG.[43] In December 1829, Gladstone wrote home that 'the Essay concern

> ## William Buckland (1784–1856)
>
> Buckland was appointed a canon of Christ Church in 1825, having been a fellow of Corpus Christi College from 1809, and professor of geology from 1819. He was renowned for his lectures in which he expounded his theories about 'catastrophes' or great events in the history of the earth.
>
> He was an eccentric who harboured a desire to taste every living creature and to accommodate many of them within his lodgings in the north-west corner of the Great Quadrangle. Buckland's son, Frank, also had his father's fascination in exotic animals.
>
> ODNB; Bompas, *Life of Frank Buckland* (1885), 47–8

prospers – we had a capital Essay last Saturday from old Acland, as he is called by way of distinction from his brother – Gaskell talks of taking Phrenology for his subject'.[44] Gladstone's diligence, along with his religious fervour, met with little approval from the less academic men in college, some of whom actually broke into his room and gave him a sound beating.[45]

There was a great contrast between the academic men and the sporting men, but there were many shades in between. Gladstone's diaries and letters record his labours, but other diaries, such as that of John Buxton, an undergraduate from 1807 to 1809, show a life which consisted of little but breakfasts, dinners, riding out, visits to exhibitions and other fashionable pastimes such as taking the waters at Cheltenham.[46] Others seem to have managed to tread a middle path. Gaskell certainly relished good wine and good society, but was terrified of appearing ignorant in his examination on Euclid, and sat up all night 'reading as if my life depended on my diligence ... triangles, parallelograms, and angles I understand pretty well, but these diabolical circles in the third book are so like one another that I hope on my accounts as well as on theirs, we shall not come into close contact tomorrow'. His day, as he described in a letter home to his mother, was spent with chapel at 7 am, reading until 9 am, then breakfast and more reading until 11 am. Then there were lectures until midday, more reading until 2 pm,

> James Gaskell's account of his 'Little-Go' examination in 1830 suggests that it was not always so easy. In his letter home, he describes both written and viva examinations, lasting from 10 am until 4.30 pm, translating texts from Latin to English, and then translating a piece from the *Spectator* 'upon the subject of young ladies' into Latin. He answered questions on logic, too, and commented that the examiners were good-humoured and 'seemed unwilling to hear' his few mistakes. When his friend, Doyle, passed his little-go, Gaskell described him 'as much pleased about it as if he had been made Poet Laureate to his Majesty...'
>
> Gaskell (ed.), (1939)

followed by an hour of paying calls, writing letters or just thinking. He went out until 4.20 pm, had dinner at 5 pm, attended a wine party until 7 or 8 pm, and then enjoyed the company of friends until around 10 pm.[47]

Henry Acland, who came up in 1834, was a member of the Loder's Club and enjoyed riding, but he also attended lectures given by William Buckland and studied hard both for his BA and to improve his chances of a career in medicine for which he had been destined from childhood.[48] Francis Cowper, a few years later, described the life of a nobleman at Christ Church: his first concern was to get his rooms in Canterbury Quadrangle sorted out, throwing out the rather uncomfortable furniture that was there on his arrival, and filling it with his personal choices including a large hip-bath. There were amusements to be had; a heavy fall of snow saw men blocking the archway between Peckwater and the Great Quad during the night, and a decree by the dean against dogs in college caused the men to hide their pets under sofas and in cupboards so that scouts would not report them. But Cowper went to lectures, too – around thirteen each week for which preparation was necessary – and passed 'Little-Go'.[49]

Discipline, as always, took up much of the Chapter's time. During Hall's deanery, manners and behaviour were said to decline. The evidence from college records that behaviour was any worse under Hall than any of his predecessors is not, however, forthcoming. There was indiscipline, but

> ## Thomas Gaisford (1779–1855)
>
> Gaisford's appointment to the regius professorship, over the more eminent but Whig Peter Elmsley, was largely through the influence of the retired Cyril Jackson.
>
> On 12 May 1815, Gaisford was presented to the rectory of Westwell, a Christ Church living in Gloucestershire, the day after he married Helen Douglas. He leapt up the church hierarchy, serving on the Royal Commission on ecclesiastical revenues and patronage, and holding canonries at Llandaff, St Paul's, and at Worcester. Turning down the bishopric of Oxford in 1829, he was instead appointed to the golden stall at Durham, the position he was to exchange for the deanery at Christ Church in 1831.
>
> Gaisford's scholarship was legendary, and far more notable than his deanery which, in spite of his efforts to restore Christ Church to its position under Jackson, was not entirely successful.
>
> ODNB

nothing out of the ordinary. Edward Law, for example, was reprimanded for improper conduct, rudeness to the Censor and for keeping a dog in his rooms.[50] And it was in 1819 that Edward Stanley, soon to be prime minister, pulled the statue of Mercury from his plinth, an act which, according to W. F. Hook, made 'a very great improvement to the quadrangle'. These actions were considered to be those of intelligent and lively young men, not severe infractions of college rules and expectations.[51]

It was, perhaps, the unpopular Hall himself who gave the wrong impression of Christ Church at this time. The dean was perpetually in debt, and bailiffs were, allegedly, constant visitors to Christ Church.[52] Hall's son was sent down without graduating; it must have been most humiliating for the dean to have to request the acceptance by the Chapter of his own son's resignation from his Studentship.[53]

Dean Smith set out his stall early when it came to undergraduate behaviour. Almost immediately, he had to deal with two cases; the first more of an embarrassment, when he was obliged to rusticate Charles, the second son of the Duke of Wellington, for breaking open the back gates of the college.[54] The other, though, was a rare incidence of severe indiscipline when Cyril Page, a Student, along with a number of commoners and gentlemen commoners, attacked the keeper of the turnpike gate on the Abingdon Road. He was confined to college, and punished accordingly.[55] Nothing changed in his behaviour, however, and he was soon involved in yet more disruption. On 13 June 1825, Page was a willing participant in a riot in Hall at the celebratory dinner to commemorate the founder. The Chapter minute records that he and seventeen others had 'joined with those of other tables in the Hall during the time of dinner in most gross, unmannerly and ungentlemanlike conduct in the very presence of the Dean and Chapter'. The whole sorry group, all undergraduate Students – five of whom had only been formally elected the previous Christmas – were duly reprimanded. John Dowdeswell, who had been up before the dean only the week before for a violent disturbance in his chambers in Peckwater Quad and for abusing the Porter, was reprimanded for a second time, together with Page.[56] Richard Gresley, as the most senior of the Westminster party present, was required to write a remorseful Latin epistle to the dean.[57]

Inevitably, though, high spirits and rule-breaking were as common in the early years of the nineteenth century as they had always been. Gambling remained popular, and one Christ Church man, Thomas Hooker, was found guilty, in February 1811, of gaming to a 'very great and alarming degree'. To try to discourage others, Hooker and his friend Salter were rusticated.[58] Edward Borough, an undergraduate Student who appears to have been perpetually in trouble, was reported, in February 1821, for gaming in his rooms; and rusticated for a full year.[59]

Extravagance was common, with undergraduates – Christ Church men amongst the worst – running up colossal bills with local tradesmen.[60] It was not always the fault of the students, however. A town full of young men was bound to attract all sorts of scoundrels to prey on the rich and relatively innocent. Walter Hook was caught out almost immediately. His father had taken advice from Dr Goodenough, William's tutor, who suggested that £200 per annum plus his Student's stipend of around £50 would be more

> ## Charles Henry Hall (1763–1827)
>
> Hall was a Westminster Student. He came up to Christ Church in 1779 under Lewis Bagot, and found favour with Cyril Jackson. He was tutor, praelector graecae, praelector rhetoricae and Junior Censor before resigning his Studentship in 1795 on his marriage to Anna Byng, a daughter of Viscount Torrington. In 1799, Hall returned to Christ Church as a canon, and was, through the influence of Lord Liverpool, a former pupil, appointed regius professor of divinity in 1807. Liverpool's part seems to have turned Jackson against Hall, so much so that Hall complained to Liverpool about Jackson's hostility. It was Liverpool who ensured Hall's succession to the deanery in 1809.
>
> ODNB

than sufficient. Dr Hook paid all initial expenses – 'Every thing depends upon the start. Every thing should be arranged like clock work, and no dependence upon any aid beyond his allowance should be held out to him.' That was in December 1817. Within a month, Hook junior was apologising to his father for the costs involved in setting himself up in his rooms (his knives and forks alone had cost £4), but he did not think that any of the crockery he had ordered was unnecessary. However, he said, somewhat naively, that things had arrived which he was sure he had not ordered, in spite of assurances to the contrary from the shopkeeper.[61] James Gaskell, a gentleman commoner from Eton, reckoned that he could maintain his lifestyle with £500 a year and a servant. Writing to his mother, he said that no gentleman commoner had less, and few of the commoners had only £300.[62] Jacob Astley spent twelve months at Christ Church in 1846/7, and reckoned that his allowance of £400 per year had given him the opportunity to enjoy a year of hunting and other pleasures, and Robert Anstice managed on £150 including his Westminster Student's stipend.[63] Debt was a real problem. In 1848 the college butler, Thomas Dry, had to go to the Dean and Chapter to report that large numbers of men had not settled their debts with him after he had advanced them their college and university dues. The dean decided to remove the names of the offenders from the books, and to give their caution money to the butler once the men's college dues were met. How much this helped Dry is uncertain; he had already remarked that many of the debts already exceeded the reserved caution money.[64] Battels bills, although theoretically payable every term, often built up alarmingly. Local tradesmen naturally took advantage of the young men who were enjoying their first experience of independence and who wished to match hospitality with hospitality. Gaskell, almost immediately after his arrival at Christ Church, asked his mother for the name of his father's wine merchant in London – 'I shall be under the necessity of ordering a small hamper from London, unless I wish to be poisoned and cheated at Oxford.'[65] But Gaskell had no shortage of money. Less well-off men could find themselves in real trouble; the fictional Dudley, in *Christ Church Days*, received bills from 'grocers, wine merchants, print-sellers, tailors, *et hoc genus omne* [etc]', and was forced into the hands of a disreputable money-lender.[66]

There were other ways to spend money. In a city with a high proportion of men, prostitution was rife. The presence of women of the town in chambers was dealt with summarily; in 1816, Henry Cleaver was discovered by the censors to be entertaining a lady in his rooms, and was rusticated for a couple of months, during which time he had to prepare for an examination on the last four books of Thucydides, the two first decades of Livy and the plays of Sophocles.[67] William Carey was a little more devious: he and a friend took their ladies back to rooms in Lincoln College, but they were still discovered and received an appropriate reprimand.[68] Every now and again, cases developed into something more serious. In May 1853, John Hampden was charged with gross misconduct but failed to appear before the Chapter to give his case. Chapter rusticated him until the beginning of Easter term 1854.[69] Hampden's father, then Bishop of Hereford, appealed for some remission, and the canons conceded that the boy could come up during Michaelmas term in order to fulfil his residency requirement.[70] But Hampden did not take advantage of the benevolence: in October he was discovered to have absented himself without leave for an entire weekend to continue his 'divers low and irregular habits'. He was rusticated for a full year, his degree put back by a year, and he was demoted twelve places on the Student roll.[71] The Hampdens took legal advice, and the Chapter was advised to do the same; the last thing Christ Church wanted, and the very thing the Hampdens were after, was a repeat of the Shipley case when the Lord Chancellor as the Visitor's representative was brought in. Lavie, the Chapter Clerk, proposed that Lord Bethell, the Solicitor General, be retained as counsel. Three questions needed to be answered: did the Dean and Chapter have authority to degrade a Student; was the sentence disproportionate to the offence; and was the sentence open to such legal objections as would make it invalid? Everyone at Christ Church was agreed that the Chapter had authority to give such a punishment and felt that it was more than justified – there was apparently much evidence of 'the youth's depravity'. But John Meadows White, Hampden's lawyer, wrote to Lavie, 'My own knowledge of college life ... tells me that the ordinary habits of not merely its younger Members, but even of the Senior Common Room, would not tell to great advantage if raked up, and brought to light, for the purpose of punishing one whose folly rather than vice may have betrayed him beyond the ordinary reserve of a prudent man.' It was men of the world against men of the cloistered environment of the college. Hampden senior and the Chapter seem to have come to a compromise. After an apology from the guilty party, the rustication stood, but the remainder of the penalty was dropped. Hampden senior seemed less inclined to continue the fight; perhaps the last thing the bishop wanted was to revisit his own controversial time in Oxford.[72]

* * * * *

The arrival of the railway was seen by many senior men as a danger to the morals of young men. London, the races, and other distractions from academic life were suddenly within much easier reach. Robert Hussey, the Censor in 1844, was particularly concerned, and advocated that University officers be given the right to search and enquire on trains and stations.[73]

Less alarming to college authorities, unless they distracted too much from academic obligations, were sports. In the earlier years of the nineteenth century, these were organised privately, often with the involvement of local tradesmen and entrepreneurs, rather than being provided by the college. Hunting was popular with those who owned horses, a club being formed in the 1830s, and some local hunts allowed undergraduates who could afford it to join in. The first Oxford *v.* Cambridge cricket match was played in 1827 at the instigation of Charles Wordsworth, who had come up in 1825, but the sport remained a minority pastime for boys who had come from schools where it was popular, albeit an expensive one involving, as it did, much eating and drinking.[74]

The records of the Boat Club at Christ Church do not begin until 1860, but it was a Christ Church man who may have introduced rowing to Oxford, or at least promoted its development. William Lennox Lascelles Fitzgerald de Ros, an Irishman, brought over his own four-oared wherry in 1817, and had probably established a four-oar at Christ Church as soon as he was elected in 1815. Eight-oared races began that year, although the competition was between only Brasenose and Jesus colleges.[75] Christ Church entered in 1817 and won. The House retained the Headship of the river until 1827, except in 1823 when Christ Church refused to take part because Brasenose and Jesus had professional boatmen in their crews, and in 1824 when Exeter College won. William Gresley, the elder brother of the severely admonished Richard, recorded in his memoir how a race continued from Iffley lock in the early 1820s: 'They entered the lock together, and, for a short time, all was hushed in silence. Soon the creaking of the opening gate was heard and the boats sprang forth one by one ...'[76] The first University Boat Race took place in 1829 when Cambridge sent a challenge to Thomas Staniforth, captain of the Christ Church crew. The eight rowing for Oxford at Henley included Staniforth as stroke, three more Christ Church oarsmen, and a House cox.[77] For the first half of the nineteenth century, Christ Church dominated university rowing. The Henley regatta was popular with undergraduate rowers but less so with college authorities as it took place in term time. Under Gaisford, that strict disciplinarian, it became necessary to indulge in some trickery; in 1851, colleges entered their crews under false names, Christ Church's being the *Westminster and Eton Club, Oxford*. But they were caught out when a newspaper gave the correct name of the crew, and duly punished by Gaisford by being put back a term.[78]

Rowing as a regular pastime probably coincided with the increasing numbers of boys arriving from Eton.[79] The only school to which Christ Church was formally attached was Westminster, which sent its annual four or five boys as Students, with occasional canoneers and commoners. Other boys came from other schools or had been privately educated. Gradually, however, Eton began to send more boys – particularly those coming up as gentlemen commoners – to the college which had the strongest links with government. Gaskell told his mother in 1829 that there were 40 gentlemen commoners at Christ Church, of whom half were Etonians.[80] More than half the English landowners who sent their children to school sent them to Eton, and of all those who went to university, 35 per cent came to Christ Church (60 per cent of all those who came to Oxford). Trinity College, Christ Church's sister college in Cambridge, took 68 per cent of those attending that university.[81]

It was not all discipline and study, however. In 1810, during Hall's time as dean, there was a banquet to celebrate the installation of the new Chancellor, Grenville, but the most exciting event, in 1814, after the Peace of Paris, must have been the visit of the allied sovereigns to Oxford to receive honorary degrees. The evening before the ceremony there was sumptuous entertainment in the Radcliffe Camera for all the guests, and the next morning the honorands gathered in the deanery: the Prince Regent and the Duke of York, who were staying with Dean Hall, were met by the Prince of Mecklenburg, who had spent the night at Nuneham, and the Prussian princes left their accommodation in Dr Burton's lodgings in Peckwater Quad to meet their father at Corpus Christi College. The whole party processed to the Sheldonian Theatre in grand style. The journalist who recorded the event for *The Times* struggled to find words: 'To give a faint description of its splendour would be no mean task for the ablest pen.'

The Tsar and the Prussian emperor departed for Blenheim, but the Prince Regent stayed on at Christ Church with the Duke of York, Metternich, Blücher and the chancellor for a grand dinner on 15 June.[82] Blücher's short residence in Frederick Barnes's canonry in Peckwater Quad was most memorable. Thomas Vowler Short, then just a young BA, was given the task of escorting the hero marshal when he went out into town in an attempt to control his behaviour, a task evidently fraught with difficulty.[83] Rumour had it that Blücher slept with his boots on and with a bottle of brandy under his pillow. *The Times* writer recorded that he 'was perfectly visible, sitting on the end of his bed, the window being quite up, smoking his long pipe, in a white vest with a ribband over it, with a sedate military sang-froid. He advanced frequently to the window and bowed, whenever a tolerable number assembled without.'[84] But his unconventional manners did not mar his popularity or the acknowledgement of the nation for his achievements; a year later, the Dean and Chapter granted £100 for the relief of sufferers from Waterloo.[85]

* * * * *

Amidst all the discussions about cathedral and university reform, the control of student excesses and all the normal everyday work of the college, the Dean and Chapter had to deal with a major theft from the Treasury. All the indications were that it had been carried out by a member of the college. Opening the Treasury strong room to take out the money needed for the day's business soon after 10 am on Monday, 17 February 1828, Edward Goodwin, the deputy treasurer, was greeted by a grim sight. Open in front of him was a chest belonging to one of the canons, broken and empty; the baptismal plate had gone together with armfuls of banknotes. Goodwin was bemused. The Treasury was a secure place, with a stone vault, three locks on the outer doors and a further lock on the door to the strong room. Only three men had keys: Dean Smith, the Treasurer Dr Phineas Pett, and Goodwin himself; and only Goodwin's set was a full one.

Goodwin faced interrogation by the vice-chancellor; at 7.30 pm on Saturday he went to the Treasury, locked the strong room, every padlock and all the doors, and then put the keys in his desk which was locked separately.[86] On Sunday he had been into the Treasury twice, once in the morning and once in the early evening, but only into the outer office; then on Monday he had called in again, early, before his regular visit to the deanery. It was on his return to his office later than morning that things were found to be wrong. The first thing he noticed, said Goodwin, was the damage to Dr Woodcock's chest which had contained his plate and had been forced open. But the strong

'Reading as if my life depended on my diligence': 1809–55

During the late eighteenth and nineteenth centuries Christ Church educated eleven future Prime Ministers, of whom the first was George Grenville, who came up in 1730. William Gladstone, who matriculated in 1828, served as Prime Minister four times between 1868 and 1894, and Archibald Primrose, Lord Rosebery, held the post from 1894 to 1895.

box had apparently been opened with a key. The outer doors showed no signs of violence. The corridor to the strong room was constantly watched, and the lock of that door showed no signs of force either. Even the desk where the keys were kept was undamaged. Lying on the floor beside the chest which had held the cathedral's plate were a chisel and a fine long screwdriver.

The Treasurer, Dr Pett, explained that he kept his keys wrapped in newspaper in a small red box on his desk in his study. The box wasn't locked but, if he went away, he locked the box in a drawer. However, he had only used the keys once himself, and had never sent anyone else to fetch anything from the box. No one would have known that his keys were there. College servants were interrogated, and one stated that he had seen James Rose, apparently one of the college carpenters, with the screwdriver. Dr Pett's and Goodwin's personal staff said that they didn't know where any keys were kept.

In the meantime, searches were made, both for the silver and for the burglars. Christ Church turned to one of its old members, Frederick Adair Roe, who was police magistrate at the Marlborough Street station.[87] Roe's chief assistant, Plank, was dispatched from London to help solve the crime, and a reward of £200 was offered for information leading to the arrest of the culprits and the recovery of the silver. Unsurprisingly, information immediately began to come in. At the same time as some much-damaged silver was traced to a traveller in Hereford, an anonymous letter arrived accusing Rose and another man called Maddox of the crime, and announcing that they had fled north. Thomas Wheeler, Rose's apprentice, stood up for his master, swearing that the chisel and screwdriver did not belong to him. Much more dramatic was a confession from two men held in Warwick gaol, Sumervil and Beats. The men said that they had broken into Christ Church on Sunday morning, with Mr Sollomans, the fence, and three others from Birmingham and Lichfield. Rose, the insider, was named as the 'putter-up'. Some of the silver had been passed to the fence, the notes already cashed and the remaining silver melted down in a crucible to be found at the thieves' house. Rose was arrested, and thrown into the Castle prison, but none of the silver or the cash was ever recovered.[88]

* * * * *

The road to reform had been much travelled under Dean Jackson, and while traffic had slowed down under Hall and Smith, it was in danger of going into reverse under Thomas Gaisford. He was an extraordinary scholar. Although he had come up as a commoner in 1797, on account of his 'great diligence and proficiency in learning, and of the uniform regularity of his behaviour, strongly testified to the chapter by the officers of college', he was elected to a Studentship in 1800.[89] By the time he was 28, he had published an edition of *Hephaestion*, establishing his reputation among his colleagues, and assuring his appointment as regius professor of Greek in 1812. He left Christ Church in 1815, retaining the professorship, and did not return until 1831.

Oakeley described Gaisford as an amiable and kind-hearted man, but neither a man of the world nor equipped to deal with young men en masse. A scholar, without doubt, but one whose learning was for like-minded academics, rather than for undergraduates.[90]

The tercentenary celebrations, on 4 November 1846, must have been a joy to the dean – a chance to look backwards at the Christ Church he knew, loved and wished to preserve. Two cathedral services were held at 10 am and at 4 pm, one with a special anthem performed by the choir. At noon everyone assembled in Hall to hear Latin orations, including a commemorative speech by one of the Student Bachelors, for which he was paid £20.[91] In the evening there was a celebratory gaudy dinner 'served up in that style of elegance and excellence for which the cook of this college, Mr J. Faulkner, has become proverbial'. The seating plan reflected the Christ Church that was about to disappear: on High Table were the dean, the canons, special guests and the noblemen. The Masters came next with the chaplains and then Bachelors. The Students were halfway down the Hall. While the High Table, Masters and Bachelors dined on turbot, the Students had cod.[92]

Gaisford wanted to restore Christ Church's pre-eminence without the newly introduced University examinations and honours. Described by Thompson as a strong man who knew his own mind, his government of Christ Church was somewhat old-fashioned and reactionary.[93] A disciplinarian, Gaisford strictly maintained the distinction between the poorer and richer members of college; servitors, however talented, were not permitted to take

Studentships, a rather harsh ruling which, although traditional, suggests that Gaisford had forgotten his own mercantile, unaristocratic background. More importantly, it meant that Christ Church lost significant scholars to other colleges where fellowships were more open: men like William Stubbs, later regius professor and Bishop of Oxford, who had been given rare permission to use the Library to expand his knowledge of medieval history but had to take a fellowship at Trinity College in order to progress his career; and T. E. Brown, the Manx poet who, having received a double first, accepted a fellowship at Oriel when none was offered at Christ Church.[94] Academically, it was really only men who would come up as commoners who were tested for their abilities before being admitted; noblemen and gentlemen commoners were still often granted places purely on their background.

However, while Gaisford was refusing outright to have anything to do with reform of any sort, particularly within his own college, progress was all around him. With the advent of the Russell government in 1847, liberal reformers saw their chance. A Royal Commission was established in 1850 to inquire into the 'state, discipline, studies, and revenues' of both university and colleges, but Gaisford refused to answer any questions at all. He argued that the Commission was potentially dangerous to Oxford and Cambridge universities as independent bodies.[95] The principal aims of the Commission were to reform the governance of the University, and to re-establish some control over the largely autonomous colleges. When the report of the Commission was published – the 'Blue Book' – its recommendations included the revival and reform of Congregation from its old medieval and Laudian forms and its establishment as the electoral body for a wider and more representative Hebdomadal Board, the adoption of the 1850 University statute widening the examination system, and the opening up of fellowships, from the old methods of patronage and ancient tradition to elections on merit.

In addition, access to studies was to be improved, and the professors more closely involved in tutoring. The first was a University matter, but the second had a significant effect on all the colleges. The tutorial system had already been stretched by the 1800 changes to the examination system which had introduced mathematics as an honours subject. The 1849 proposals of the heads of houses to include natural science, jurisprudence and modern history as options made things still harder. Tutors suddenly had to be specialists in these additional fields. Henry Thompson, who matriculated from Christ Church in 1858, recalled that there were only seven tutorial staff – six classical tutors (Gordon, Prout, Sandford, Joyce, Bayne and Pickard) and Dodgson, who lectured in mathematics – who were expected to divide the 180 undergraduates between them.[96] There was still no single-subject specialisation; the honours degree remained predominantly classics with some mathematics, but, from 1850, undergraduates could choose whether to take, along with classics, any one of the other four options.[97] The expansion of a system of which he did not approve can hardly have been welcome to Dean Gaisford.

The use of college revenues to fund large fellowships was something that the Commission found unacceptable. According to the report, only 22 out of 542 available fellowships were truly open. Around 35 fell vacant every year, but with an average of only 13 first-class men each year, most were sinecures and totally untenable when, according to the Commission, the university should be reaching out to poorer students and to a wider community. At Christ Church, of course, without the conventional fellowship of other colleges, Gaisford could justify his lack of response. When the Commission argued that colleges no longer performed their original eleemosynary function, did not maintain a common life, that fellows no longer resided for study, and that college statutes should be renewed for a modern age, Gaisford effectively stated that, as Christ Church had no statutes, there was nothing to reform.[98] However, the Commission had revealed that the dean and canons divided the entire surplus income of the college – about £12,500 – between themselves (as they were permitted to do by convention), leaving the Student body with stipends of between £25 and £45 each depending on seniority.[99] Unacceptable as this was to the Royal Commission, to the Students of the House it was even more so.

The bill to bring into force many of the recommendations of the Royal Commission was largely put together by Gladstone, MP for the University and Chancellor of the Exchequer, who had conducted an immense correspondence with all interested parties, and the bill went through many alterations.[100] Christ Church requested the retention of servitorships to enable poor scholars to come to college, and even offered to increase the numbers of places for servitors.[101] Studentships, they said, were not restricted by birth, parentage or circumstances (although those servitors who had been passed over for election might have said differently).[102] Gladstone's labours prevented the imposition of direct Parliamentary intervention in the application of the reforms. Instead a series of broad principles were established to be interpreted and introduced by a Commission, all but two of whom were Christ Church men.[103] The commissioners were empowered to assist the colleges to draw up new statutes which had to be approved by two thirds of their Governing Bodies. Fellowships were to be awarded on merit, and undergraduate fellowships abolished, along with those possessed by individual schools.[104]

At Christ Church, the 1854 Oxford Act was considered rather unsatisfactory by all parties. The traditional system of nomination had been pre-emptively abandoned by the Chapter earlier in the year, to be replaced by one of restricted competition.[105] In agreeing to this, the canons had been quick to point out that they did not feel that

> in waiving the right of nomination which [we] have enjoyed from time immemorial [we] do not thereby admit that meritorious young men have failed to obtain as opportunities offered a place in the order of Students but [we] are of the opinion that the time has arrived for affording additional inducements to exertion amongst the younger members of the society and [we] hope that the step which [we] have now taken will prove not only beneficial to individuals but conducive to the welfare of the foundation generally.

But the Students, even the graduate ones, were still granted no say in the administration of the college, or even of the reforms and the creation of statutes which would directly affect them. The Dean and Chapter, that body of only nine men, who had governed the college and the cathedral since 1546, were left in sole charge, untouched by the Commission, and legislation to reform their powers was not possible while the Cathedrals Commission was still debating. Tradition was being pulled apart, but nothing new put in its place. An early draft of the bill suggested that at least some of the Students should have a say in the governance of the college, but the clause was ambiguous. Osborne Gordon, writing to Gladstone in 1854, before the bill was laid before the House, thought that it meant that the Students would be included in the decision-making processes, but would not be formally part of the constitution of Christ Church, a situation which, he said, was untenable both for the Dean and Chapter, who 'do not wish anyone to be associated with them in their position at all', and for the Students, who would 'not wish to be associated with them on unequal terms'. Under this scheme, the Students would be just 'stipendiaries called into Council' unlike fellows in other colleges who were truly in authority.[106]

Coincidental with the reform of the University and the colleges were the proposals to reform the cathedral bodies of England. These were aggravated by the bishops' negative response to the Reform Act of 1832, and the exposure of church wealth in John Wade's *Black Book*.[107] Combined with this criticism of its riches and its political stance, the church was under attack for its pluralism, nepotism and the general worldliness of its clergy.[108] Wade's attacks prompted an investigation into church endowments, and the Church Revenues Commission was established in 1832, followed by the Ecclesiastical Duties and Revenues Commission in March 1835. The first report was presented only six weeks after the commissioners were named. This did not touch on capitular bodies, just on episcopal boundaries and incomes, but it was inevitable that more was to come. There was a slight delay when Peel resigned, but Melbourne renewed the Commission immediately on taking office, and the second report came out in March 1836.[109]

This second report did deal with capitular establishments and their revenues, proposing that they be restructured in order to fund new churches in the growing industrial cities and to augment poorer livings. Non-residentiary canonries should be abolished, the numbers of residentiary canons and minor canons should be reduced, and the estates of the old foundation cathedrals (the medieval ones) appropriated.[110] Christ Church was found to have the second-highest income of all the cathedral foundations; Durham stood at the top of the table, with a gross income, in 1835, of over £32,000. Bristol, a deanery often held *in commendam* with that of Christ Church, was at the bottom, with an income of only £3,000.[111] Christ Church's response was, unsurprisingly, that it was a different type of institution altogether from other cathedrals. Its canons had traditionally been tutors as well as clerics and, to a certain extent, still retained their academic character. They accepted that tying new canons back into teaching by the annexation of more professorships to the canonries would be useful to both college and the University more generally. As for giving to poor livings, this was already being done, and any further donations laid down by law would be both detrimental and unfair.[112]

Three pieces of legislation came quickly out of the Commission's proposals, the last of which, the Ecclesiastical Duties and Revenues Act 1840 (usually known as the Cathedrals Act), prompted the greatest response from Dean and Chapter.[113] Christ Church once again used its extraordinary constitution to defend itself against the worst of the proposals. The Act limited the number of canons to four in most cathedrals, although Canterbury, Durham and Christ Church were allowed six, and Winchester five. The 'excess' canonries were to be suppressed as they became vacant, and their profits vested with the commissioners for the creation of new churches or transferred, in the case of some old foundation cathedrals, to form a corporate fund. One of the principal complaints against the unreformed cathedrals was absenteeism, which in some cases was so bad that vergers would not recognise canons when they did turn up. Under the Act, deans had to reside for eight months of each year, and canons for three, and their incomes were fixed. Non-residentiary canons were abolished, but honorary canons were permitted instead in new foundation cathedrals (those founded or refounded by Henry VIII). The number of minor canons or vicars choral was reduced to a maximum of six.[114]

Christ Church was under attack from all sides. Another problem, at least internally, which was to remain a constant irritation, was the administration of the capitular estates. If the Students ever achieved any power at all, would they be allowed any say over these? Gladstone's opinion was that the Students should be concerned principally with studies, discipline and economies of the college rather than the management of property. It was the first hint of a possible rift within Christ Church.[115]

These matters were to divide Christ Church for the next decade. Henry Thompson vividly described the place before things changed permanently.[116]

He came up from Westminster School in 1858, matriculating as a Student with his position guaranteed for life, provided he abided by the few conditions that had applied since 1546. It had been easy for Christ Church to become full of men who took life too easily, under no obligation or any pressure to achieve, and lacking any incentive 'for making the best of ourselves'. As a Westminster Student, Thompson was automatically granted leave of absence from his election in June until the beginning of Michaelmas term.[117] A tutor was allocated – Osborne Gordon, the Senior Censor – and a suggestion was made that he might read *De officiis*; but nothing more was said about preparation for study in October. There were, of course, additional lectures over and above tutorial sessions (which were held for several men at once) but the divinity lectures, given between chapel and breakfast, were unpopular and of little help, especially, as Thompson pointed out, as everyone was too hungry to concentrate! Attendance at chapel was compulsory, with Latin prayers every morning at 8 and every evening at 9.15.[118] Communion was on the first Sunday of the month and there were all the cathedral services as well, although attendance at these was not obligatory. Sunday services were not well attended, in spite of regulations, the day being seen as one for lazy breakfasts and wines, according to the author of *Christ Church Days*, although the first Sunday of term was different, when men gathered together with the townsfolk, and, on this occasion at least, the cathedral was packed.[119]

The first two terms were wasted, according to Thompson, preparing for Responsions at Easter.[120] There were lectures in arithmetic and Euclid, and in Greek and Latin taken with one's own tutor. But no one was unduly pushed, and private tuition evidently essential if one was to pass Honours. Men seeking to do well in logic apparently went to a fellow at New College to be crammed. One of the characters in *Christ Church Days* had three external tutors to help him in his frantic third attempt to pass Moderations. The thought of being sent down from Christ Church, and having to go to a hall rather than a college, horrified him.[121]

However, discipline was tight, and collections still caused an undergraduate to quake. Under Gaisford, who of course preferred the internal examination system, they were a 'grim reality' and they lost none of their terror under Liddell. But the men were divided into two groups, half being seen by the dean, and the other half by the sub-dean. The experience was evidently very different; the sub-dean was kindly and evidently not terribly well informed about the progress or otherwise of the undergraduates, and was consequently lax. Those who came up before Liddell, however, 'met with a very different treatment'.

In Hall, the manciple, butler and cook continued to enjoy their 'lucrative tyranny'. The noblemen dined on the dais in Hall, with everyone else, including the Students, arranged on separate tables below.[122] Everyone except the dean sat on benches. Servitors were no longer required to wait on table. The first half of the nineteenth century had seen the beginnings of reform, reluctantly acknowledged by a portion of Christ Church, and welcomed by many more. Thompson was an eye-witness to the changes that were to take place between 1858 and 1867.

'Water coming to the house of office': the plumbing

Bringing water into Christ Church, and taking away waste, was a preoccupation for the Dean and Chapter right from the start. There were proposals in the early seventeenth century to bring water from Oseney; the abbey had acquired the spring at North Hinksey in 1220, and had transported its water from there to the abbey by aqueduct, and the Dean and Chapter evidently intended to make use of Hinksey water. It was estimated to be 1,200 yards between Oseney and Christ Church, and the cost of boring, jointing and setting pipes over this distance was around £90, with an extra £30 for the water tower, wheel, cistern, forcer (the piston of a force pump) and other engineering.[1] But Otho Nicholson, benefactor to Christ Church library, financed the building of the Carfax conduit, and the modernisation of the Hinksey conduit, in about 1617. The Carfax facility housed two tanks, one for town and one for gown, and Christ Church suddenly had no need to pipe water all the way from Oseney.[2] Calculations were made of the relative levels at Carfax and at the Christ Church 'rails', and new plans made for a cistern at Christ Church. Herbert Westfaling wrote to Samuel Fell in 1637, describing examples of forcers in Worcester (which broke down frequently) and under the arches of London bridge – the most ancient in England.[3] At the same time, estimates were made for building a three-storey tower at Christ Church. Whether a floor of this tower was designed to hold the cistern is impossible to say, but the cost of over £2,098 was evidently prohibitive.[4]

In the early seventeenth century, the bringing of water into Christ Church occupied the minds of the Dean and Chapter. Wheels, pumps and pipework were discussed in some detail. The plan to lay pipes from Oseney Mill to Christ Church was expected to cost £120 (about £15,000 today, using the Retail Price Index).

The pipes beyond the college were often repaired at Christ Church expense: in 1663, for example, Mr Rawlins received £1 for his work over the year. Once inside the grounds, the Hinksey water supply appears to have been supplied directly to the deanery and the canons' houses, and to the kitchen. Mercury was added in 1670, and the Common Room and Canterbury Lodge at some time during the eighteenth century.[5] There were privies in most of the canons' lodgings, and communal ones in Peckwater, Canterbury and Chaplains' quads, and another over in the almshouse. William Pickhaver, one of the carpenters, was paid for four days' work making a grate for the 'water coming to the house of office', and men were paid every quarter for cleansing the privies or clearing the streams that flushed them out.

The conduit was in a central position right at the centre of the busiest crossroads in the town, and had evidently always been considered a nuisance. In 1787, it was moved to the northern edge of Carfax; just a few years later, a plan of the pipes in and out of the conduit was drawn up by Hickman. It showed the cistern, the main pipe bringing the water down from Hinksey Hill, the main pipe down the High Street, a branch pipe between these two and the pipe which carried the supply from the conduit to Christ Church.[6]

When Folly Bridge was reconstructed in 1825, and the pumping station for the city moved to the river at that point, Christ Church was granted permission to deepen the culvert which passed down St Aldates. This evidently caused problems for those who lived further down St Aldates from college, as springs had been diverted, thus depriving them of water. An agreement was reached between the Dean and Chapter and the city to rectify the problem by building a fresh culvert all the way down the street from Carfax to Folly Bridge, and to share costs.[7] Just four years later, negotiations began for a new contract for the supply of water to the whole of college.[8] The ten guinea rate to the University for water from Carfax was paid for the last time on 30 November 1868 when the supply from Hinksey was discontinued, and 'City water' was laid on throughout the college.[9] Before 1880, the City Water Works engineer, Mr Downing, investigated the water supply into Christ Church and found all sorts of problems. An agreement was drawn up the following year for Christ Church to instal 21 hydrants, supplied from the city mains. The cost was ten shillings per quarter per hydrant. The main bypass and stop-valve was situated right under Tom Gate.[10]

Piped water to rooms other than the kitchen, the deanery and the canonries took time to arrive. The Library was given a tap in 1908 to make the cleaner's life easier, but it was not until the late 1950s that student rooms began to be fitted with 'hot and cold'.[11] Meadows Building was added in 1959, leaving only rooms in Tom Quad and the Old Library to be plumbed in.[12]

Waste, as well as the supply of clean water, was something that occupied the Victorians mightily, not least for the avoidance of cholera. Oxford had three outbreaks – in 1832, 1849 and 1854 – and the city's water supply and sewers met with an increasing number of complaints until the 1860s, when the newly formed Board of Health commissioned reports from several engineers including Joseph Bazalgette. Christ Church was more obsessed than most, not least because the drains from all the nearby colleges – University, St Mary Hall, Oriel and Corpus Christi – ran across Merton Field. Only the cesspit for the lodgings of the president of Corpus Christi seems to have been dealt with properly, otherwise all drains and every other cesspit appear to have been emptied into the Meadow, and nature left to take its course.[13] In 1848, it was decided that something needed to be done to improve the situation. Egg-shaped pipes fifteen feet long were chosen as they were cheaper, and would reduce each college's contribution to £230, but Hoggar, the engineer, suggested that the costs be graduated. Merton and Corpus, it was felt, should contribute more, as they received the most benefit. Who paid for what, and when, is unrecorded, but no work seems to have taken place until 1854, when the City's street commissioners decided to go ahead with Sir William Cubitt's plans for Oxford's sewers. All the drains were to pass through the Meadow, which was 'the key to the whole system of drainage', and then on to an outfall below Sandford Lock.[14] The culverting and connection of the Trill Mill stream to the main sewer was part of Cubitt's scheme, but this was not completed until 1863, and much of the work on the city's drains was put off until the 1880s.[15]

Inside college, modernisation continued apace. New lavatories were installed in 1867 between the kitchen and the Hall, and by 1870, some of the Students, including Charles Dodgson, Robert Brodie and Thomas Vere Bayne, actually had their own, funded by the Governing Body.[16] The Common Room staircase, Great Quadrangle 1, was given its own lavatory in 1880, paid for by a 15s per term donation from any member occupying rooms on the staircase. The payments were to continue for fifteen years.[17] A new toilet block was built below the Common Room garden in 1881, replacing old privies in Tom 6.[18]

The year 1881 was significant for Christ Church, at least in terms of its sanitary arrangements. E. R. Griffiths, sanitary engineers, were called in to redesign everything from one side of college to the other. The college's drains were unsatisfactory, according to Griffiths, particularly those discharging into the Trill Mill stream. He warned that, sooner or later, the Thames Conservancy would complain about the pollution of the stream and demand that Christ Church's sewers be connected to those of the local board. Griffiths proposed that new stone drains should be built connected to the city's system, and the old ones filled or removed. While this work was being done, it would make sense to ventilate all the soil pipes in all the water closets.[19] An extraordinary 'guide' was produced, not only detailing all the fixtures and fittings – down to the make and design of every single toilet bowl and drain cover – but also explaining the arrangement of the pipework, and the maintenance of the whole on a daily, monthly and annual basis. Essential to Griffiths's plans was the connection of Christ Church to the mains sewer system, but by June 1881 the local board had still not undertaken the necessary works. The Governing Body proposed that Griffiths should take over, at the council's expense.[20] Some work was evidently carried out the following year, as Symm's submitted a bill for £109 4s in June 1882. But it was not until 1892 that a contractor, Best and Sons, was chosen, who agreed with Griffiths that much needed to be done, particularly on the north side of college where the whole drainage and sanitary system needed to be remodelled. It was proposed that the work would begin in the Christmas vacation, beginning with the whole of Meadows Building and the west and north sides of Peckwater Quad.[21] Symm's estimates show just how extensive the work was to be.[22] By November 1892, the Governing Body was beginning to panic about the costs and a committee was set up who decided that the work should be restricted just to the essentials to make the drains safe.[23] Best and Sons were employed as the sanitary engineers for the scheme, but it was no longer assumed that Symm's would do the work – even though this had been agreed by the dean, censors, Steward and Treasurer only a few days before. The job was put out to tender, and estimates came in from four different companies varying from £977 to £1,925. Symm's, whose tender was the lowest, was awarded the contract, and the work was completed by Christmas 1893.[24]

In 1972, the decennial survey noted that the provision and condition of toilets at Christ Church was well below late twentieth-century expectations, and should be dealt with as a matter of some urgency.[25] But it was not until the arrival of women in 1980 and the huge increase in the number of tourists during the 1980s that the matter was really considered by the Governing Body. Now, the provision of bathroom facilities seems as high on the agenda as the condition of the drains was in the 1860s.

8

'To conduce the welfare and usefulness of Christ Church': 1855–98

The second half of the nineteenth century saw Christ Church change completely. Its constitution was set down in writing for the first time, and its governance altered dramatically. Undergraduate life became more varied and less restricted than ever before. But the effort that resulted in these changes caused rifts and many arguments before settlement was finally reached.

When Gaisford died on 2 June 1855, the commissioners responsible for putting the Oxford Act into practice at Christ Church had only just been appointed. His death was probably opportune; the reformers would certainly have had a hard time of it with Gaisford as dean – but who to appoint in his place? The debate was not lengthy; what was needed was a new Jackson – scholar, gentleman, tutor, businessman, administrator and a man of integrity. Within four days, Henry George Liddell, member of the Royal Commission, was named as dean of Christ Church. Liddell was given a warm welcome, although many at Christ Church were uncertain about the appointment. Charles Sandford, much later in life when Bishop of Gibraltar, commented that Christ Church 'little wished to have one who was a liberal, and had been an influential member of the University Commission, to be [its] leader'. In the light of what was to come over the next few years, this is, perhaps, a surprising comment from Sandford. Liddell had indeed been an active member of the University Commission, attending all but one of

Henry George Liddell came to Christ Church in 1829, and was elected to a Studentship the following year. Apart from a few years away as Headmaster of Westminster School (1846–1855), Liddell's life was devoted to Christ Church, the University, and the publication of the Greek lexicon with his colleague Robert Scott. He oversaw the renovation of the cathedral and the construction of Fell Tower, Wolsey Tower and Meadows Building, as well as the constitutional remodelling of Christ Church in the 1860s.

its 87 meetings.[1] It would seem, however, that he was not anxious for total change; there were aspects of the old Christ Church that he felt were worth keeping. He was certainly unsympathetic to the demands of the Students, and later isolated himself from the process of reform, concentrating on the college buildings. But he was keen on relaxing the obligation to take holy orders (one of the few requirements for the tenure of a Studentship), and the extension of the professoriate.

The dean and canons were supposed to have presented their own scheme for reform by the first day of Michaelmas term 1855 but had failed to do so.² Gaisford's death may have been put forward as a mitigating circumstance; even if there had been any desire on his part to contemplate change, the deadline for submission fell at just the wrong time. Except for William Jacobson, and he only reluctantly and cautiously, the canons were unwilling to participate in any discussion.³ Jacobson and Liddell, however, acknowledged that there was little they could do against the advancing tide of reform, and stood against the rest of the Chapter: Frederick Barnes, Charles Ogilvie, Edward Pusey, Charles Clerke (the sub-dean), Charles Heurtley, John Bull and Richard Jelf.

As the Act demanded, therefore, two years after the passing of the Oxford Act, it fell to the commissioners to deal with the particular difficulties that Christ Church presented. It was no easy task; the Chapter, unsurprisingly, did not want to give up any of its emoluments to the Students, and the commissioners had no power to interfere with revenues. If Studentships were to be raised to the level of fellowships, then extra revenue had to be found. But where was the money to come from, and how many Students-cum-Fellows were there to be in the new Christ Church?

The sum of £5,480 had been paid to Students in 1856, and the Commission decided that the first place to look for extra money was in the suppression of two of the canonries – a term of the 1840 Cathedrals Act. One other thought was that the Students could be paid by an annual grant from the Dean and Chapter. This could have been purely by custom, but such a grant could equally easily be taken away by custom. Another possibility proposed by Osborne Gordon was the use of the Senior Masters' Estate. Gordon claimed that £3,916 8s could be raised annually from this and from an increase in room rents and fees.⁴ To increase fees and rents, however, would increase the cost of a university education for ordinary commoners, especially if, as was widely discussed, the ranks of noblemen and gentlemen commoners were abolished. This was immediately unacceptable to the commissioners, who wanted Studentships to be funded entirely from the foundation. It almost goes without saying that the Students themselves were not officially involved in any of the discussions, in spite of being the body principally concerned.

The suppression of the canonries seemed to be the only way forward. An Amending Act was introduced in June 1856 which allowed for the two canonries unattached to professorships to be abolished and for their revenues to be redirected to the Students. To Liddell, who advocated a bigger role for the professors, this was a move that would make Christ Church most definitely a college; even though these professors were still canons, the governance would be entirely in the hands of professors. Liddell's principal aims were first, to increase the stipends of the undergraduate Studentships to the level that would attract good candidates as commoners and potential Students, and second, to improve enough graduate Studentships to encourage good men to stay on as tutors. There were several ways to achieve this: to divert exhibitions previously reserved for commoners to the undergraduate Students – which was surely an act of dubious legality – and to either reduce the number of graduate Students or make additional funds available from Chapter. Liddell made the radical suggestion that four rather than two canonries should be suppressed – the two unattached and those attached to the professorship of pastoral theology and to the Lady Margaret professorship. Liddell was evidently not enamoured of the pastoral theology chair, and felt that its role could easily be added to one of the other theological professorships. As for the Lady Margaret professorship, this could be detached from any particular college, and funded partly by Christ Church and partly by Magdalen College, who were obliged to maintain a theological professor.

This proposal would have reduced the Governing Body still further to four canons and the dean. The revenue from four suppressed canonries was more than was needed just to increase the stipends of some of the graduate Studentships. The recipient was probably intended to be the regius professor of Greek, whose stipend was still the tiny £40 per annum that had been stipulated back in 1546.

Gladstone advised against Liddell's proposal; the inevitable objections to the suppression of four canonries might well jeopardise the chance to suppress just two. The Chapter was, after all, still the Governing Body of a cathedral as well as a college. The two canonries suppressed under the 1856 Amending Act freed enough revenue to allow some practical reform. On this particular piece of reform, however, neither the canons nor the Students were consulted, raising the already high irritation levels on both sides of the reform debate.

Three matters occupied the commissioners when drawing up the Ordinance for Christ Church: first, the principles for reform laid down in the Oxford Act; second, the less important reforms that were of particular significance to the colleges; and third, the peculiar needs of Christ Church. The crucial matters for consideration were the award of Fellowships and Studentships by merit, and for undergraduate Studentships to be converted into scholarships. The Studentship would then become a purely graduate body. Other matters for consideration were whether it should still be essential for Fellows and Students to be ordained, whether Fellowships and Studentships should be of a limited tenure, and how the study of science and mathematics would be introduced into the colleges.

The Chapter's reluctance to enter into any discussion with the commissioners meant that the draft Ordinance was prepared without any reference to the canons, let alone the Students. Communicating almost solely with Liddell, therefore, the Commission drew up a list of Fourteen Points which were presented to the dean on 10 December 1856:

1. Instead of 101 Students, there would only be 16 Senior and 61 Junior Studentships;
2. Senior Students were to be the teaching staff of the college and were to be elected from the University at large;
3. Senior Studentships should be worth at least £200 per annum. With the tuition fee added to a Studentship, eight tutors could have an income of between £450 and £800;
4. Senior Students should be required to reside for ten years from their election;
5. Of the 61 Junior Students, 40 (including the Vernon Studentship) should be open to general competition, and the remainder appropriated to Westminster School;
6. Junior Studentships should be worth £80 per annum and tenable for five years, similar to Scholarships in other colleges;
7. Westminster Students to receive £46 per annum from House funds.

The Lee Fund should afford 21 Studentships of £74 per annum, to be added to the Westminsters' stipend. These Studentships were to be valid for seven years on account of Dr Carey's benefaction;

8. Of the eight open Studentships vacant each year, three should be for mathematics and science, but only for 20 years;
9. Both Senior and Junior Students were to be elected by the dean, canons and Senior Students;
10. The direction of instruction and discipline should be vested in the dean, canons and Senior Students;
11. The power to deprive a Student of his place should remain with the dean and canons;
12. Two canonries should be suppressed if necessary. Half the income from one should be allocated to Domus (college funds), and the remaining revenue, with the revenues of the current Studentships and the Bostock exhibitions, should be allocated to the new scheme;
13. Fell, Boulter, Pauncefort, Gardiner, Frampton, Cotton and Paul exhibitions should form a fund to be applied partly to prizes and exhibitions open to competition among members and partly towards exhibitions for poor Students, without competition;
14. The number of chaplains should be reduced to increase the unsatisfactory income of the remainder.[5]

The Commission were particularly anxious to ensure that tutors had more influence in the administration of the educational side of Christ Church, and to ensure that a proportion of the Senior Studentships should be laymen. But the proposals were met with some caution on both sides. The Students were naturally dismayed that only a tiny proportion of their number were to be on the new Governing Body, and that the dean and canons would still retain overall power. Neither were the canons convinced. The sub-dean, Charles Clerke, wrote to Liddell giving Chapter's opinion of the Fourteen Points. They argued that there had never been a shortage of good tutors in the past, and that security of tenure was as important to a Student as the size of the stipend. It was not necessary to raise the incomes of those not teaching. Those in orders would receive college livings, which would adequately compensate for a small stipend during their college years, and those remaining could expect to become tutors, and therefore well paid, within a reasonable period. There was no need, therefore, to reduce the number of Students, limit their tenure, or to suppress canonries.

In fact, almost nothing was right with the Commission's suggestions. The canons complained that the commissioners had completely failed to take account of the fact that Christ Church was extraordinarily clerical in its make-up. To share power and emoluments with Students, particularly those from outside Christ Church, was unthinkable. They were concerned that Christ Church would not be able to maintain a House of alumni; Junior Students, funded for only five years, would 'betake themselves elsewhere and to other employments ... the college can hope for no recruits from among its own alumni, from those who have been brought up in its bosom, and have been bound together by all the ties of undergraduate friendship and the still more beneficial relations of tutor and pupil'.[6]

Liddell replied to Clerke from Madeira, where he was recovering from a chest infection, his exasperation with the Chapter evident in the tone of his letter. He was a practical man, and tackled each of the canons' points, without mincing his words. Increasing the value of Studentships, he said, was essential. It was position that men wanted first; tutoring with its associated revenue came later. Keeping stipends low was hardly likely to attract young men to compete for Studentships when there were more lucrative Fellowships elsewhere.

The suppression of the two canonries was necessary to provide the necessary funds. Liddell warned the canons not to be belligerent; if the canonries were suppressed by the University Commission then the proceeds would be given for Christ Church use. If, however, the decision was left to the current Commission on Capitular Bodies, the canonries would still be suppressed but the revenues lost. As for Christ Church losing its gremial nature, it would not be difficult to elect home-grown Students over those from other colleges. Besides, he ruthlessly pointed out, half the canons themselves were not Housemen! As for Students not being in orders, there were already the faculty Students, so this would be no more than the extension of a scheme that had operated by custom for centuries. There had long been complaints

> ## Osborne Gordon (1813–83)
>
> Osborne Gordon had come up to Christ Church in 1833 as a Careswell exhibitioner. Gaisford nominated him to a Studentship, and he was elected Censor in 1846. He was Senior Censor from 1849 to 1861.
>
> Gordon proposed further improvement to the University examination system, and served as a member of the Oxford Tutors' Association. He encouraged discussion on the 1858 Ordinances, and later on the 1867 Act, even though by then he had left Oxford for the college living of Easthampstead.
>
> Ruskin described him as 'a practical Englishman, of the shrewdest, yet gentlest type; keenly perceptive of folly ...'
>
> ODNB

that the Governing Body of Christ Church was far too separate and aloof from the governed, and Liddell advocated the acceptance of the proposed changes that he knew the commissioners would insist upon.[7] For all the tone of his letter, Liddell actually held firmly to the old Christ Church, failing to see, or choosing to ignore, the comparison between the position of Students at Christ Church and that of Fellows in other colleges.

Meanwhile, the one group affected the most – the Students – had barely been consulted. Although there must have been much debate over dinners, in rooms over a drink or two, and in the corners of quads, only Osborne Gordon was given the opportunity to say anything official, in his capacity as a member of the Tutors' Association. He had written to Gladstone back in 1854, stating that unless the college was to be reconstructed so as to give the Students the standing of Fellows, then it were best left alone. In February 1857, Gordon and the rest of the Students were given a copy of the Fourteen Points. Their proposals were entirely different:

- The educational side of Christ Church should be kept entirely separate from its cathedral function.

- The number of Students should remain 101, but there should be twelve college officers, tutors and lecturers financially independent of the Chapter through an endowment of £1,500 and the proceeds of the Lee Trust.

- Two science lecturers should be appointed and funded from Lee, and sufficient Bachelor Students should have increased stipends and assist with teaching.

- The dean's second-in-command should be a Student or ex-Student, appointed by the dean.

- Studentships should be filled from members of the House, except those from Westminster, not from the University as a whole, and elections should be in the hands of the dean, sub-dean and six of the college officers.

- The responsibility for education and discipline was to lie with the dean, the sub-dean, the officers, the tutors and the lecturers.

- Finances were to be the preserve of the dean, sub-dean and officers.

- Exhibitions were to be open to competition to all members of the House with some made available for poor students.

- Lecturers were to be relieved of the obligation to take orders, unless they were in the most senior group of Students, the theologi.

The Students' proposals were at once conservative and radical. Much of the old Christ Church was retained, but the intention that the Chapter be excluded from the governance of the educational establishment was clear. The Chapter was an alien body, as even Liddell had acknowledged. When Robert Hussey, long-standing Student and first regius professor of ecclesiastical history, died in December 1856 before he could take his place on Chapter, he was succeeded by A. P. Stanley, a Balliol man and secretary of the 1850 Commission. Now, four canons were men from other colleges. Hussey had also been the next in line to be sub-dean, a position (with the Treasurership) traditionally held by one of the non-professorial canons. With these two canonries on the verge of suppression, the sub-deanery would almost certainly be filled by a non-Christ Church man. 'All prescriptive right is abolished and indefinite authority given to the Dean and canons, the majority of whom in all probability will never have been practically acquainted with the education or discipline of the House', wrote Thomas Vere Bayne in July 1857. The Students tacitly acknowledged that the Chapter would still form the Governing Body of the House but, in their proposals for the educational establishment, attempted to ensure that there were men on the Chapter who understood how Christ Church operated.

Liddell failed to persuade the canons – his continued absence not helping matters at all – and the Chapter replied to the commissioners outlining their feelings.[8] But no notice was taken. Their intransigence had resulted in the preparation of the Ordinance without them, the only concession being the withdrawal of any proposal that the educational side of the college be made separate. As for the Students' suggestions, these stood no chance of acceptance. In some ways, they were ahead of their time. The ultimate extension of their proposals – that college and cathedral should be completely separated – was so far ahead that, despite later attempts to tackle the issue, Christ Church still remains a joint institution.

The first draft of the Ordinance was submitted to Liddell in June 1857, varying from the Fourteen Points in only minor details. But it was a recipe for friction, creating, in effect, three governing bodies. An electoral board (dean, canons and tutors) would elect Students and control the teaching and discipline of the Junior Students; another body (dean, canons and Senior Students) was to govern the Students; and a third group (the Dean and Chapter) would hold the power to deprive a Student of his position for misconduct and to make the rules governing residence.

When, on 9 January 1858, the final Ordinance was passed, taking note of some of the objections, there were 32 clauses which established the form of the new Christ Church. Undoubtedly, it was better than the original Fourteen Points or any draft. The Students were at least recognised, if not included on the Governing Body; mathematics and science were incorporated formally; and a number of lay Studentships were accepted. The potential for three conflicting governing bodies was averted, although the old and new systems were expected to work alongside each other. However, it did not rest well with anyone. Liddell tolerated the Ordinance, but the canons were less than pleased. Pusey wrote that he did not have much hope for the new Christ Church, and Dr Ogilvie felt that it was rather arbitrary in its principles and unsuccessful in its detail. And it still failed to raise Studentships to the level of Fellows in other colleges. In fact, the Students were actually in a worse position than before. Compulsory residence, for example, meant that some of the curacies, which could traditionally be held concurrently with Studentships, were no longer available to them. More fundamentally, centuries of custom and tradition, which had given the Students at least some standing, had been stripped away.[9] Osborne Gordon took the college living of Easthampstead in 1861, and shook the dirt of the Great Quadrangle from his feet, stating that 'Our new Ordinance has cut off any prospect of permanent settlement here'. Nor did the Censor, Thomas Prout, agree with the scheme: 'nor can I think that it yet meets the requirements of the case'. That 'yet' was to prove significant.[10]

Things did not begin well. Dr Bull, an inveterate Houseman, passed away in February 1858. He had been Treasurer for 25 years and William Jacobson, a non-gremial, was appointed as his replacement. For the first time, a senior officer was not a Houseman.[11] Just a year after Bull, Dr Barnes also died. A canon since 1810, Barnes had only been away from Christ Church for five years since his matriculation in 1790. His canonry, unattached as it was to a professorship, was immediately suppressed, leaving only three gremial members in the Chapter.[12] These, on the whole, were elderly men and by 1865, only Clerke had been a Student. The balance had shifted in favour of non-Christ Church men.

It was a recipe for dissatisfaction at the very least, compounded by the fact that the Senior Students were soon to include many non-Christ Church men, too. Under the Ordinance, the then censors, readers, tutors and lecturers were to become Senior Students without further election. All of them, even the two youngest, had experience of the way in which the 'old' Christ Church operated. But the predominance of Christ Church men among the Senior Studentship soon changed. Augustus Vernon Harcourt and George Luke were the first two newly elected Senior Students (in December 1859).

> The Chapter in 1830 consisted of Edward Dowdeswell, Frederick Barnes, Henry Woodcock, William Buckland, Edward Pusey, Edward Burton, Richard Jelf and John Bull. All but Buckland were gremial members of Christ Church.
>
> But, in 1836, Renn Dickson Hampden (Oriel and St Mary Hall) replaced Burton. Godfrey Faussett (Corpus and Magdalen) replaced Woodcock in 1840, Charles Clerke (Christ Church) replaced Buckland in 1846, William Jacobson (St Edmund Hall, Lincoln, Exeter and Magdalen Hall) replaced Hampden in 1848, Charles Ogilvie (Balliol) replaced Dowdeswell in 1849, and, in 1853, Charles Heurtley (Corpus Christi) replaced Faussett.
>
> So, when the Ordinance was sealed, the three most recent appointments were not Christ Church men.

Harcourt was appointed Dr Lee's reader in chemistry, Luke was a scholarly classicist, and both were Balliol men.[13] The following year, William Church, from University College, was elected Dr Lee's reader in anatomy. It was 1861 before George Blore became the first member of Christ Church to be elected to a Senior Studentship by examination.[14] The balance continued to shift; in 1862 there were six Senior Students from the old foundation, and six who were not. By the beginning of 1865, thirteen Senior Students had been elected, of whom seven came from other colleges.

Only the college officers remained men who had been elected to their Studentships before the Ordinance. After 1861, when Gordon left Christ Church for Easthampstead, Prout became Senior Censor and Charles Sandford was elected Junior Censor. For a while, the occupants of the two positions changed frequently, but settled down in 1863 with Sandford as Senior Censor and Thomas Vere Bayne as Junior Censor for the following seven years, two men who were to have a significant, and unsung, impact on the form and fabric of Christ Church.

The Electoral Board, set up under the Ordinance, consisted of the dean, the canons, the two censors and the four senior tutors. Eligibility for this Board was a potential minefield: the Lee's Readers did not count as tutors,

Meadows Building, designed by the Irish architect Thomas Deane, was constructed in 1863 by Joshua Symm. Alfred Axtell, in whose cart three members of Christ Church (Vernon Harcourt, Basil Prance and Teulon Sonnenschein) are relaxing, was first Symm's foreman mason and then his partner.

and so were ineligible; censors could sit on the Board even if they were not tutors, but once they had resigned their censorship, they could not remain unless they were tutors. As only four tutors could sit on the Board, Students had to wait, in effect, for a Board member to die in order to participate even in a small way in the governance of the college. There were many meetings of the Board, and it apparently functioned well, but the very limited role that it gave the Students did not really help to calm increasingly troubled waters.[15] It would not be long before agitation began again.

In the meantime, however, while the constitutional debates raged, Christ Church's natural position as the home of the aristocrat was acknowledged, almost for the last time, by the admission of the Prince of Wales to the roll. There had been many debates about whether it was better for him to live in college or to have a separate residence, whether he should even have an affiliation to any one college, or whether he should reside as an MA of the University or as a Visitor with access to libraries and lectures. In the end, however, it was accepted that, if the prince was to be formally matriculated as an undergraduate, then attachment to just one place was a necessary requirement.[16] In October 1858, the royal family were still undecided on whether the prince should go to Oxford or Cambridge, and to which college, but, by December, the matter was settled and discussion began about tutoring and accommodation. Dean Liddell had written to Sir Charles Phipps, equerry and secretary to Queen Victoria, expressing his opinion that it would be better if the prince lived in, giving him the opportunity to meet men of his own age, while still retaining a separate household in Dr Jelf's lodgings (which were used by the canon only during the vacations).[17] The Prince Consort preferred his son to live out, thus remaining 'entirely Master ... of the choice of society which he might encounter'.[18] Herbert Fisher agreed to act as tutor, and the figure of £600 per annum was proposed to teach modern history and law, specialising in narrative, constitutional and philosophical history, with common, statute and international law. The prince was taught Italian rather than Latin as his grammar was weak.[19] He would attend some lectures on chemistry and physics, but otherwise tutors would go to the prince and teach him on a one-to-one basis.[20] Academic dress, in this case a nobleman's gown, was expected and Liddell hoped that the prince would attend morning prayers. By the end of November, the prince, settled in Frewin Hall on New Inn Hall Street, had lunched or dined with the vice-chancellor, Dean Liddell, A. P. Stanley, William Gladstone and Vernon Harcourt, to name but a few.[21] By the end of 1860, Liddell was reporting favourably on His Highness's progress in history.[22]

Fifteen years later, the Prince of Wales's younger brother, Leopold, also came to Christ Church. He was not a particularly diligent student, lacking aptitude and suffering periods of sickness, but he evidently had a taste for art and architecture, fostered no doubt by attendance at Ruskin's lectures.[23]

During his time at Christ Church, Leopold appears to have developed a fondness for Alice Liddell, daughter of the dean and Charles Dodgson's inspiration. The relationship was not encouraged.[24]

But these events were merely an interlude in the main performance of constitutional reform. In 1864, barely a year after the settlement laid down in the Ordinance, disagreements began again. The debate was essentially the same, the canons on one side defending their position and their emoluments; the Students on the other fighting for equal recognition with Fellows in other colleges. But, as in so many disputes, other issues crowded in to complicate and colour the arguments.

Unconnected though it appeared to be, the matter of the stipend of the regius professor of Greek was fuel to the flame. The canons of Christ Church now received around £1,500 a year, and nearly all of them had some supplementary income from livings or other positions. A letter in *The Times*, from 'Oxoniensis', dated 29 November 1864, suggested that the dean and canons' incomes should be reduced to £2,000 and £1,000 respectively, and that the surplus so recovered be redistributed among the lay professors of Greek, law, medicine and modern history, none of whom had the benefit of free accommodation or income from livings.[25] The low income of the Greek chair had been a bone of contention for several years, with the Chapter refusing to consider any increase to the stipend, which was still at the £40 per annum set at its creation. Osborne Gordon, writing to Thomas Prout – soon to become agitator on behalf of the Students – on the very day that the anonymous letter appeared in *The Times*, advised him to stress the plight of the Greek professor. If Prout was about to start a fresh campaign on behalf of the Students, then to support an increase in the Greek professor's income could only work to his advantage. Gordon encouraged Prout to write to *The Times*, and hinted that he would be prepared to come out in support. 'The Ordinance', he wrote, 'is a snare and a delusion. If the Commissioners intended the Students of Ch.Ch. to be as good as other Fellows and thought they would be so, why did they not put them in the same position?'[26]

Two days later, on 1 December, a further letter appeared in the paper. The redistribution of the canons' income should not be directed towards professors, but to the college and the teaching of Christ Church men, for which the place was founded. The writer is unknown, but probably prompted by Prout, who followed up with one of his own, published on 7 December. He did not mince his words: the Students had not been consulted on the Ordinance; Christ Church had never been properly investigated, as the Ecclesiastical Commissioners saw it as a college and the University Commissioners as a cathedral; partial reform had only served to confuse the situation still further; canon-professors forming the Chapter meant that the college was governed by men who did not teach in the college, or in many cases did not even come from the college; and the Students had no real power in the administration of revenue or domestic arrangements. It was here that Prout commented on the position of the Greek professor; the dean and canons, entirely responsible for the finances of the House, had 'allowed their own incomes to grow enormously, while all other interests have been starved; for instance, payments to College Officers and others (and I may add now the Regius Professor of Greek) had remained at their 16th century level. The result was that the proportion of revenue reserved for educational or other college purposes is very scanty indeed.' But Prout had by no means finished. Students were inferior to Fellows in other colleges, both in pay and in position. Students elected from other colleges were dismayed at their new low status, and it would not be long, asserted Prout, before few competed for election. Three things were demanded: that Students be made equal to Fellows, that the Dean and Chapter receive fixed stipends or a set allotment from estate revenue, and that all accounts should be properly inspected.

The public debate died down for a while, during which time there was much lobbying and meeting between Students. On 11 February 1865, a group of eighteen met in Prout's room and agreed to take their demands to the Dean and Chapter. The Chapter, backed into a corner, voted through an increase in the stipend of the regius professor to be met from the incomes of the dean and canons. But the concession backfired: if it was possible to raise one stipend, then why not others? The Chapter agreed that a committee should be established to consult the Students and to discover what their grievances were – as if they did not already know.

The Students began to prepare their case, beginning with a meeting on 18 February 1865 attended by eleven Senior Students and four resident Students of the old foundation.[27] Delegates were chosen – Thomas Prout, Charles Sandford and Augustus Vernon Harcourt – to attend the Chapter committee. The first proposal, that the Students should be equal to Fellows, received fourteen of the fifteen votes. Only Liddon stood against, objecting not so much to the proposals, although he thought they were rather too radical, but to the presentation of a divided college to the outside world. He was wary, too, of going to Parliament again. It was government interference which had prompted the Commission and the Ordinance in the first place; to go to Parliament now would, in a way, endorse what had been done. That he disliked Prout did nothing to help.[28] The second demand, that Students should have the right to vote in the election of Students, was carried by ten to five. Three more propositions, not forming part of the major case, were framed for presentation: that college offices and lectureships should be endowed so that part of the Tutorial Fund could be released to create additional tutorships in order to maintain a balance between teachers and pupils; that college servants should be salaried rather than paid from profits – a debate that was already rumbling, and would have great consequences; and that cathedral services attended by junior members should be regulated by the dean, canons and college officers who were in orders, a necessary concession to ensure that the canons would still take part in discussions.

Osborne Gordon, still in regular contact with Prout, pointed him in the direction he thought might stand a chance. The Chapter, with fixed incomes, should manage the cathedral, he said, but the college should be run by the dean, a sub-dean, the Treasurer and six Senior Students. This was a far smaller Governing Body than Prout envisaged but one that excluded the canons from the day-to-day administration of the educational establishment, and put the Students in the majority.

The two parties came together on 25 February, but it was not a happy occasion. The Students' proposals were rejected wholesale, with the minor concession that the committee would consider the appointment of a Student bursar to manage the revenues set aside for domestic administration. In the face of this refusal, the Students met again, and agreed to appeal to a higher authority. A good-mannered holding reply was sent to the Dean and Chapter expressing disappointment, and Prout started work, first approaching the MP George Ward Hunt, an alumnus and ex-pupil of Osborne Gordon. Hunt did not hold out much hope for a reopening of the matter so soon. Others, though, thought differently. Archbishop Longley felt that the Ordinance had not considered the Students sufficiently and warranted reconsideration, and Lord Harrowby recommended sending a statement of the changes required to the Commission. Prout took the advice to the Students on 13 March, and the committee agreed to sketch out a constitution for Christ Church that would satisfy them.

A statement was duly prepared which set out the reasons the Students felt that the Ordinance had failed, and why the present constitution in which the college was governed by professors, in which the censors found themselves in a difficult position of being both governors and governed, in which the college servants could take advantage of their monopolies, and in which the Students suffered an inferior status to that of their colleagues elsewhere, was flawed. The Students proposed two possible schemes: the first, a Governing Body of dean, canons and Students which would administer revenues and elect all Students; and the second comprising the dean and an equal number of canons and Students with a separate electoral board. There would be a deputy for the dean in the educational establishment who would carry the old title of Censor Theologiae, and a Student bursar to manage the general economy. The college officers would be appointed by the Governing Body, and the incomes of all Governing Body members would be fixed within certain limits. The Dean and Chapter would, of course, continue to handle all cathedral business.

The document was sent to the old Commission, and to Hunt. The trickiest Commissioner was likely to be the conservative John Awdry. Convince him, thought Gordon, and Prout would be well on the way to achieving his ends. Consequently, Prout framed his covering letter to Awdry carefully, expressing his concern at asking the Commissioners to reconsider so soon, but hoping that the Students' case would be clear. Awdry's reply suggested that the Ordinance was not perfect, but he found it hard to see how a middle course could be steered between the present situation and a complete severance of cathedral from college, a move he felt was completely undesirable.

Prout, unsurprisingly, felt that Awdry was wrong. With 20 years' experience of Christ Church, he was sure that joint governance was possible and practicable. He approached another heavyweight, Lord Derby, a Christ Church man, Chancellor of the University, and once prime minister. Derby acknowledged the Students' case but did not feel that further interference by Parliament was a good thing, possibly jeopardising the independence of the University. But interference was just what Prout and the Students wanted.

Everything stopped for the summer, during which there was a new parliamentary election, Charles Dodgson was diverted by the publication of *Alice in Wonderland*, and Dean Liddell set out to holiday in Switzerland. Over the vacation, however, a new gremial member, Herbert Salwey, was elected to a Senior Studentship, and Jacobson left the Chapter for the bishopric of Chester. Payne Smith was appointed in Jacobson's place as regius professor, and Walter Shirley, the regius professor of ecclesiastical history, was made Treasurer after only eighteen months as a member of Christ Church. He was confronted with problems almost at once when, within only two months, the 'Bread and Butter Row' erupted.

Throughout their discussions, the Students had been fighting for better administration of the domestic economy of Christ Church, constantly demanding the appointment of a bursar and the ending of the monopoly system enjoyed by the senior servants. In March 1865, 108 commoners of the House had presented a petition to the Dean and Chapter complaining about the charges made by the butler on basic items such as bread and butter. The butler purchased these wholesale, and then sold them on to the students at a profit of around 60 per cent.[29] Professional auditors were called in to examine all the accounts, but, before a report was made, the butler's alleged abuses – along with those of the manciple and the cook – were made public, and an acrimonious exchange of views was published in *The Times*, the proprietor of which was John Walter, an alumnus and father of an undergraduate.[30] The purchase of goods and their forward sale to students had been commonplace across Oxford from medieval times, but other colleges were reviewing, or had already changed, the way that their domestic economy was managed. The 'Bread and Butter Row' just highlighted the exclusive and conservative control of the Dean and Chapter over appointments and revenues, and became a flashpoint in the debates over reorganisation of the whole constitution. Shirley, the new and inexperienced Treasurer, allowed himself to be drawn into the public debate, foolishly making the arguments personal by laying the blame for the present tariffs at the feet of Osborne Gordon. He was firmly put down by both the censors and Gordon himself, who wrote that, because the dean and canons controlled the finances, it was they who had to appoint the salaried bursar, the only sensible solution to the difficulties. It was the system that was at fault and not the man.

The publicity affected the Chapter deeply; only a fortnight after the last letter appeared in *The Times*, the Treasurer and the two censors met to draw up a paper on the management of Christ Church's domestic economy. A Steward was to be appointed, elected by the Senior Students and resident Students; the manciple's position would be abolished, and the cook and butler put on fixed salaries plus half the net profit of their departments; and dinner would be provided at a fixed price.[31] The proposals were accepted by the Chapter on 9 December and, only two days after that, Robert Godfrey Faussett was elected Steward at a meeting in the Common Room.[32]

Meanwhile, as the Bread and Butter Row raged in the press, the Students continued their more formal battles towards a change in the constitution. A sub-committee was established – Prout, Sandford and Harcourt, with Bayne joining in later – to draw up proposals which the government might take seriously. On the advice of Chichester Parkinson-Fortescue, MP and Secretary for Ireland, once a Westminster first-class classicist and pupil of Osborne Gordon, the committee prepared a memorial for presentation to the Prime Minister asking for specific reforms or for a Commission of Inquiry with a view to reform. It was printed ready for signature by 9 December. But the canons, having just made their concession over the appointment of a steward, made a fresh proposal. They did not want a Commission appointed to discuss matters defined by the government, but suggested that the cases of both sides be submitted for arbitration to the equivalent of a Commission that would sit in private. The publicity of the Bread and Butter Row evidently rankled.

The Students were taken aback, and a difference of opinion divided them. Some felt that the canons' suggestion had come just too late, and that the memorial should go forward as agreed. But others, notably Sandford and Bayne, thought that the Students' case could be damaged if they refused an offer of arbitration, which, suggested Sandford, would also take less time, as they would be less likely to get caught up in another change of government.[33] Conditional acceptance of the offer of arbitration was voted, and over the course of a rapid series of meetings, replies to the canons were drafted.

The questions over which the canons wanted arbitration included their share, or otherwise, in the election of Junior and Senior Students, in the government of Christ Church as a college, and whether or not there should be any change in the management and application of revenues. As far as the canons were concerned, the status of the Senior Students was not an issue. However, Prout wanted discussion about the whole of the administration of Christ Church and put forward his own topics for arbitration. Seven men voted in favour of Prout's proposal, but five abstained, including both censors. The canons then decided that the arbitrators should be left entirely free to make their own investigations, and the dean agreed. The Students were not happy, and summoned a meeting for 18 January of the Students of both foundations, both resident and non-resident.

Before the meeting, Prout took further advice, this time from three ex-Student barristers – Arthur Milman, also dean of St Paul's, Alfred Bailey and Arthur Whateley – and all three men felt that Prout's proposal should definitely be a condition of arbitration. Milman suggested, too, that there should be five arbitrators, rather than the three that the canons and Students had agreed.[34]

The meeting on 18 January was attended by 26 Students, 11 Senior Students and 15 out of around 40 of the old foundation. As in so many committee meetings, much of the discussion focused on the actual meaning of terms; eventually, however, Prout managed to secure an agreement that arbitration without the Students' basic principle could be no arbitration at all. There was much disagreement, and a wide variation in views, so Prout came up with a compromise. If the canons would not agree to the principle of the Students' admittance to full Governing Body powers, then they would make the terms of reference of the inquiry as wide as possible. The new motion proposed 'to refer the whole question of the Elections to Studentships, the Finance, and the Government of the College to Private Commissioners, who shall be nominated by the Dean, the Canons, and the Students ... [to] frame such a scheme for the future Government of the House, and the management and application of its revenues, as they may deem most likely to conduce the welfare and usefulness of Christ Church'. It was passed unanimously. Milman's suggestion that there should be five commissioners, two named by the Dean and Chapter, two by the Students, and one by the Dean alone, was also put forward. The non-resident Students accepted that full power to handle the matter should be left with the resident Students, and it was agreed that, should the Dean and Chapter refuse the resolution, then they would proceed with their memorial to the Crown.

The resolutions were accepted, after a little more manoeuvring on both sides, and an objection by the canons to one of the Students' choices of referee (as the arbitrators were to be called). From a list of ten possible candidates, the Students had chosen Sir William Page Wood and George Ward Hunt as their referees. The canons felt Hunt to be less than unbiased, so the Students reconsidered. In the end, the five chosen referees were Sir Roundell Palmer (picked by the dean), Archbishop Longley and John Taylor Coleridge (picked by the canons), and William Page Wood and Edward Twistleton (picked by the Students). Longley was to chair proceedings, and Twistleton was to be secretary. They were a distinguished group of men, including four barristers. Only Longley was a Houseman but Coleridge, Palmer and Twistleton had all been at Oxford colleges, and Wood had been a member of Trinity College, Cambridge.

In March 1866, the referees were given a statement, prepared by the dean, which set out the history of the constitution of Christ Church. In June they began to collect their evidence. Although little record survives of the referees' methods and deliberations, it seems that the dean and the Treasurer were seen at Lambeth Palace on 13 June; Pusey, and any other canons who wished to give evidence, on the following day; and the Senior Students on the days after that. The Students had chosen Sandford, Prout, Harcourt and Giffard to give evidence, with possibly Faussett as Steward, and Henry Thompson. The referees seemed to be placing an emphasis on finance and electoral power. Control of the cathedral was a central point for the canons. Pusey, in particular, was concerned that the cathedral could easily become merely a college chapel, with the loss of the Chapter's control over who preached, the times of services, and the nature of those services.

The Referees' Award, with seventeen recommendations, was signed just before Christmas 1866, and formed a complete acceptance of the Students' case. The Governing Body was to consist of the dean, canons and Senior Students (including those resident Students still on the old foundation), and all powers, possessions and revenues were to be vested in the Governing Body: the Dean and Chapter were to retain power over the cathedral, the deanery and the canonical lodgings, although Pusey felt that his fears were in part justified as the cathedral was to become a college chapel, under the regulation of the Governing Body, between the hours of 9 am and 1 pm on Sundays and saints' days; funds were to be set aside for the management and maintenance of the cathedral and Chapter House; £500 per annum was to be given to the Greek professor; the emoluments of the Senior and Junior Students were to be increased to a set level; the powers given to the governing bodies of other colleges in the ordinances of the last Commission were also to apply to Christ Church; and there were to be no differences in class or status between any commoner members of the House.[35]

Although the debate continued, the referees' proposals formed the basis of the bill presented to Parliament. Long meetings – nearly seven hours in total – were held in the Senior Common Room on 5 February 1867, continuing into the next day, thrashing out the finer points about the use of the cathedral, the Dean's power to remove college officers, and the administration of trust funds.[36] Soon, all that was left to be discussed was the election of Students. The canons had never been happy about the inclusion of non-resident Students on the electoral board, and Prout proposed that the electors should consist of the dean, resident canons, resident Students, and only non-resident Students if they were asked specifically to participate in an election. The canons turned this suggestion down, and stuck firm to their original demands, all but Henry Mansel signing a letter delivered to the next meeting.[37]

Roundell Palmer, the dean's referee, was asked if he would take the necessary bill to the House of Commons, but he agreed only on condition that the canons be persuaded to consent to all the points in the Award. He doubted that Crown consent would be given if there were any dissent. Liddell took the canons aside. Whatever he said, it worked; the canons withdrew their request to reserve the right to oppose the one clause, acknowledged that they had perhaps misinterpreted the referees' original meaning, and accepted that it was necessary for Christ Church to present a united front. The bill was laid before Parliament, with Royal Assent being given on 12 August, and the effective date of the new Statutes being 11 October 1867.[38]

The first meeting of the new Governing Body took place on 16 October, with business seemingly as usual.[39] Present at that meeting were the dean, Canon Charles Clerke (sub-dean), Canon Robert Payne Smith (now Treasurer after the death of Shirley in November 1866), Canon Henry Mansel, Thomas Chamberlain, Thomas Prout, Robert Faussett (the Steward), Richard Benson, Charles Sandford and Thomas Vere Bayne (the censors), Charles Dodgson, Henry Thompson, Augustus Harcourt and William Church (the Dr Lee's readers), George Blore (Greek reader), Charles Hoole, Charles Martin, Robert Brodie, Herbert Salwey and John Shadwell. Having won their victory, the Students were hardly breaking down the door to attend.

The new statutes consisted of 29 clauses. The first laid down the membership of the foundation: the dean, 6 canons, 28 Senior Students, 52 Junior Students, the chaplains, ministers, and servants. The canonries were to be annexed to the regius professorships of divinity, Hebrew, ecclesiastical history and pastoral theology, to the Lady Margaret professorship of divinity, and the archdeaconry of Oxford. The Governing Body was given leeway to increase the number of Studentships, both Senior and Junior, as money permitted.

The Governing Body was to have power over the disposal and management of all the foundation's revenues. Resident Students of the old foundation were to be considered members of the Governing Body. The powers of the Chapter over the cathedral were laid down and reserved to them, and funds were to be set aside for the cathedral fabric and the administration of the cathedral. The college seals were moved from the Chapter House to the Treasury – a significant move which, for all its matter-of-factness in the Governing Body minutes, must have struck hard at the canons.[40]

The longest clause by far was clause XV, which laid down procedures for the election of Senior Students. That they should be Anglican was still a requirement. Senior Students in all academic fields of study should be selected. Nine of the 28 were to be laymen. A year's probation was introduced, during which time a Senior Student would receive the emoluments of a Senior Studentship (then £200 per annum before benefits) but would not be entitled to vote until formally elected after the probationary period. Married Senior Students were still not permitted. Taking a canonry required a Student to vacate his position. Discipline of Senior Students lay in the hands of the whole Governing Body.

Did much change? The canons lost their exclusive power over the administration of college and cathedral, but retained control over the cathedral, and a place in the government of the college. For the Senior Students, their ultimate aim of parity with their colleagues in other colleges was achieved, vindicating Prout, without the destruction of Christ Church as a unique joint foundation.

In other ways, things continued much as before. However, with a much bigger Governing Body, committees became an essential means of conducting business. At the first meeting on 16 October 1867, a Standing Orders and Bye-laws Committee was established, along with a Treasury Committee to look at the management of funds. By the end of the academic year another nine committees had been established.[41] To the canons, who were used to sitting round the table in the Chapter House to thrash out business and discipline, it must have seemed a far more cumbersome system.

Even so, not everything had been completely settled. A new University Commission, set up in 1877 to amend the conditions under which fellowships were held, would fundamentally alter Christ Church's constitution. Initially, the canons were unafraid. Salisbury, an old Christ Church man, was in charge and the Conservatives were in power. By 1880, however, things had changed; there had been a general election, the Liberals were in power, and any notion that there should be any denominational privilege was unacceptable. Amendments were made to Christ Church's statutes whereby only three Students were required to be in orders. The Tests Act, passed in 1871, had already ensured that men from religions and denominations other than Anglicanism could enter the University.[42] Now it was possible for the canons to be the minority in a secular or non-conformist Governing Body. It was not until 1882, with the next revision of statutes, that Christ Church permitted its Students to marry, a delay in reform which had caused the loss of good tutors to other colleges who were more modern in their thinking.[43]

No sooner had the statutes been settled, more or less to everyone's approval, than there came another crisis. Liddell's building and maintenance projects, the appalling harvests of the 1870s and the time it was taking for old-fashioned beneficial leases to run out, had put Christ Church in dire financial straits. This was not entirely unexpected: as long ago as 1877, the Copyhold Commissioners had been informed that 'the finances of Christ Church will be seriously affected during the next seven years by the operation of running out leases and raising loans in lieu of fines'. Then an annual falling-off of income was anticipated until 1885, when things were expected to improve.[44] But on 2 March 1886, the Finance Committee reported to Governing Body that 'the indebtedness of the House is very greatly in excess of that of any other College, in proportion to its available external income'. Further borrowing had to cease immediately, except for emergencies, and the sum which was to be paid into the pension fund should be held back. Seven recommendations were made, that:

- separate bank accounts should be kept for corporate and trust funds;

- the steward should keep a separate account for the Tuition Fund into which fees and the Governing Body's capitation grant should be paid;
- the capitation grant should be restricted to £1 per head, and for 1885, the sum of £50 should be paid into the existing pension fund which then stood at £581 16s 9d;
- 5 per cent of the quarter's dividend should be kept back from all Studentships;
- an application was to be made for permission not to elect to empty Studentships for one year;
- the dinner allowance and Governing Body lunches should be suspended until further notice;
- there should be no gaudy.[45]

The Treasurer, Godfrey Faussett, warned that these solutions were probably only the beginning. If income continued to fall, then salaries would have to drop. He discussed which estates were likely to bring in increased rents, or were ripe for development. Income would be steady, but expenditure was excessive. Much of this was 'one-off' capital expenditure which would, eventually, be offset by income. In the short term, Faussett proposed two ways in which the excess of expenditure over income could be met: £4,000 could be borrowed, and the regular vote of monies to the Pension Fund – this time £1,300 – could be rescinded. He also suggested that the Land Commissioners be approached for an extension to the period of loan repayment from 28 to 30 years.[46]

Some years earlier, in 1872, the Cleveland Commission had slated Christ Church, particularly for the alleged misapplication of its income. The figures revealed that Christ Church had the same number of undergraduates as Balliol College but an income over six times greater (£49,000 as opposed to £8,000), and yet still managed to be in dire financial straits. Treasurer Faussett responded that Christ Church had responsibilities that were unique, not least the maintenance of the Chapter and the cathedral. The agricultural depression had also been disastrous for an institution whose income was founded so solidly on agricultural land. Between 30 and 35 per cent had been wiped off the rental value of the estates.

The debate about finance which raged in the 1880s was a thinly veiled attack on Faussett who, in spite of a spirited defence by Charles Dodgson, was evidently to be made the scapegoat. At the start of Michaelmas term 1886, Bartholomew Price (Master of Pembroke College, professor of natural philosophy, and member of the Cleveland Commission) presented a report on the state of Christ Church's finances: the place was massively in debt, owing £203,556 10s 6d in Fine Loans alone. Price suggested, as Faussett had done before, that the Governing Body ask the Land Commission for an extension to the loan periods during which time, Price insisted, income would increase. By 1889, however, the debt was still around £180,000, and fresh agreements had to be drawn up with the Board of Agriculture extending loan periods still further.[47]

All the while, undergraduate life continued. There was, in theory, no difference any longer between the wealthy, aristocratic members of college and those at the other end of the social scale. A motion was passed in December 1868 that 'there shall be no distinction in respect of Academical dress, designation, college charges, or college payments among undergraduate members of the House, not being Junior Students nor Exhibitioners within the House'. It was ratified on 27 January.[48] However, there would always be differences. Christ Church drew the majority of its undergraduates from the top public schools of the time. In the mid-nineteenth century, when the Clarendon and Taunton Commissions reported, about a third of all Oxford men came from just nine schools.[49] A third of all the Etonians were at Christ Church. By the mid-1890s, Christ Church – along with Balliol, Magdalen, New, Oriel, Trinity and University Colleges – drew around 70 per cent of its men from a group of 50 schools headed by Eton, Winchester, Rugby, Charterhouse, Harrow and Marlborough.[50]

On the night of 10/11 May 1870, members of the Loder's Club (the Christ Church Society) stole all the statues from the Library, allegedly to avenge the dismissal of Timms, a friendly porter with a knack of turning a blind eye to undergraduate excesses. Lighting bonfires between the statues,

> ## Charles Lutwidge Dodgson (1832–98)
>
> Charles Dodgson, better known as Lewis Carroll, wrote *Alice in Wonderland* and *Through the Looking Glass*, works both immensely popular and innovative in the realm of children's literature.
>
> At Christ Church, Dodgson was Curator of Common Room, a role which he filled with an enthusiasm bordering on obsession. He was also active in the great changes that took place in the 1860s, having been elected to a Studentship in 1852 and then to the mathematical lectureship in 1855. He was a hard-pressed tutor, at one time having 70 pupils, most working towards Responsions, and delivering up to seven hours of lectures each day.
>
> A man never afraid to give his opinion, he also appears to have been a loyal friend to colleagues such as H. P. Liddon, with whom he travelled widely, the much-put-upon Vere Bayne, and the financially battered Faussett.

the perpetrators just intended to leave a mark, but damage was done to the busts of Gaisford, Frewin and Guise, as well as the bronze of Marcus Modius and the early statue of Aphrodite and Eros.[51] The guilty parties refused to confess, and their peers vowed to screen them. The dean was shocked and, in a statement to the Governing Body, expressed his opinion that if this act of vandalism had been committed by the men of the town, everyone would call for the severest punishment that the law could inflict. The Governing Body agreed that a solicitor should be instructed. On 18 May, *The Times* leader announced that the act was 'the most brutal and senseless act of vandalism that has disgraced our time'. He suggested that even the most imaginative of authors could not have dreamt up something 'too monstrous to be accepted by a gallery of cockneys'.[52] But the act had been dreamt up, and it was only the threat of legal action, and much publicity in the press, that prompted the perpetrators to give in their names and apologise to the dean. Proceedings were forgone, but three men, including Edward Marjoribanks, who had been the first to break into the Library, were expelled, two rusticated, and two more gated until they had taken Responsions when they, too, would be rusticated.[53] Dean Liddell, of whom there had been high hopes that he

'To conduce the welfare and usefulness of Christ Church': 1855–98

Francis Needham, Lord Newry, came up to Christ Church in 1860. This photograph (at left) of his living room in Tom Quad, now used as the Graduate Common Room, shows the spaciousness and comfort afforded to gentlemen and aristocrats. In stark contrast is the attic room which would have been used by one of the less well-off undergraduates.

would turn out 'gentlemen and useful members of society', commented in a speech to the Governing Body on the difficulty of controlling 'the class of young men who have long been in the habit of resorting to this place ... Young men of large fortune have little to fear from such penalties as we can impose. Their parents often look without severity, or even with a half sympathy, on acts similar to those in which they formerly took part themselves, and by long traditional habit take a sort of pleasure in hearing of practical jokes played within the precincts of a College.' Liddell was firmly of the opinion that there was nothing malicious in the disturbance, and that all that was needed to deal with such matters was to create a better, more enlightened feeling between the undergraduates and the senior membership.[54]

But it is the 'Blenheim Row' which erupted in November 1893, which is probably the most famous example of the disruption that could be caused by the better-off members when their pleasure was restricted and attempts made to curb their aristocratic privileges. A number of Christ Church undergraduates were invited to attend a ball at Blenheim Palace to celebrate the coming of age of the duke. Although permission was granted by Dean Paget and Sampson, the senior censor, there were qualifications which the undergraduates refused to accept. Angry at the curtailment of their amusements, the offended students painted slogans, such as 'Damn the Dean' and 'Damn Sampson', in various colours on the doors and walls of the Great Quadrangle. The bell-rope of Great Tom was cut, underlining the irritation of the young men at the continuing imposition of a curfew. According to the report in the papers, the undergraduates circulated a skit likening Christ Church to a college which 'unites all the advantages of a preparatory school with the affectionate superintendence of home life. Puritan principles! Venial porters!! Indifferent dons!!! No encouragement is extended to the meretricious pleasures of dancing ... By a strict prohibition of life and absolute disregard of the more flagrantly immoral state of the inhabitants, the House system is admirably suited to repress the former and to increase the latter ...'[55]

Francis Paget, appointed to the deanery in 1892 after Liddell's resignation, was a quiet and thoughtful man, but had a hard act to follow. His intention, no doubt, was to deal with rowdiness firmly, but the behaviour of junior members, and the reaction of those who supported it, had evidently not changed since 1870. High spirits were normal for young men, and particularly among those who had cash to burn. The undergraduate who had supplied the paint was sent down, but the remainder, on the advice of a parent, kept silence. After a second incident in the summer of the following year, when all the windows in Peckwater Quad were broken after a Bullingdon Club dinner, Sampson stood down as Senior Censor, after sixteen years in the post, probably feeling that he had lost touch with the younger members of college, and that it was no longer possible for him to foster that 'better feeling' that Liddell had been so keen to develop more than 20 years before.[56] After this, no one held the censorship for more than six years.[57]

In spite of the relative benevolence towards undergraduate antics, the Blenheim and Bullingdon rows damaged Christ Church's reputation, and numbers dropped for a brief period in the mid-1890s. Up to 50 sets of rooms stood empty, a far cry from the overcrowded state at the end of the previous century.[58]

With the new constitution, teaching began to change. Previously, a

> ## Francis Paget (1851–1911)
>
> Paget, the son of a distinguished surgeon, was educated at Shrewsbury School, and came up to Christ Church as a Junior Student, or scholar, in 1869. He took a first in classics in 1873 when he was elected to a Senior Studentship. A reserved man he was, nonetheless, an effective tutor. He voted with Pusey against Reginald Macan (see p. 271), and then took a living in Bromsgrove for three years before coming back to Christ Church as a canon and regius professor of pastoral theology.
>
> Paget held the deanery for eight years. He was interested in education beyond Christ Church, and supported Lady Margaret Hall and the foundation of Reading University College.
>
> The dean was promoted to the bishopric of Oxford after the death of Stubbs.
>
> ODNB

mere seven tutorial staff were expected to teach the full curriculum. At the beginning of Michaelmas term 1837, for example, William Hussey, who had only just taken his own MA, was tutor to 9 Students, 4 noblemen, 4 gentlemen commoners, 27 commoners and 3 servitors.[59] But after 1867 came an increase in the number of teaching fellows, several appointed to teach specific subjects that were either being introduced or formalised.[60] Natural science, law, and modern history had all been added as degree subjects in the 1850s, with more following. Men were first examined for honours in theology in 1869, and oriental languages appeared in the class lists in 1887. The school of English was the last to be introduced before the turn of the century.

Christ Church had always led the way in the teaching of science and, under Acland and A. G. Vernon Harcourt (the first Lee's reader in chemistry), this developed further. When the specimens from the Anatomy School were finally transferred to the new University museum in Parks Road, Harcourt set about converting the old school into a chemistry laboratory where he worked particularly on gas analysis with William Esson and H. B. Dixon, and on the development of anaesthetic apparatus.[61] In 1869, the first Lee's reader in physics, A. W. Reinhold, was appointed, followed shortly by R. E. Baynes, a practical man who wrote textbooks on heat and thermodynamics.[62] The physics reader was expected to teach undergraduates studying for degrees in both natural science and in mathematics, in mechanics, hydro-mechanics, pneumatics, sound, light, heat, electricity and magnetism by mathematical reasoning or experimental demonstration. Pure mathematics, theoretical mechanics, astronomy and Newton's *Principia* were not, however, on his list of duties.[63] Physics was taken up more slowly than chemistry but, across the University, the number taking the subject as final honours doubled from 12 to 24 in the last 15 years of the nineteenth century.[64] Physiology, many of the specimens for which had been collected by Acland, became increasingly popular throughout the period, too. At the end of the nineteenth century, Christ Church was one of only five colleges which employed more than one tutor or lecturer in science subjects.[65] With its own well-funded laboratory, Christ Church could develop its science teaching in a way that other, perhaps poorer, colleges were unable to do.

Modern history was originally a joint degree with jurisprudence but, in 1872, both subjects were offered separately. In 1866, William Stubbs was appointed the second regius professor after the establishment of the honour school. Stubbs had come up to Christ Church as a servitor in 1844, but had run up against Gaisford's reluctance to advance any man of such lowly status. No sooner had he taken his BA than he was elected to a fellowship at Trinity College, and then to Oriel, the college to which the regius professorship was attached.[66] It was Stubbs who created the modern history curriculum, concentrating on a narrative constitutional history to prepare men for public service.[67] Arthur Hassall's election in 1883 saw the beginning of the great flourishing of the subject, but it was some time before results showed in the class lists.

Academic results were not particularly brilliant during Liddell's deanery. He was singularly unimpressed with the achievements of the more aristocratic members of college, and made a symbolic gesture in 1862 by altering the seating arrangements in Hall; for the first time, noblemen were ejected from High Table, no longer sitting above their tutors.[68] Coming right in the middle of the debates over constitutional changes to Christ Church, this simple decision caused considerable acrimony. The Student MAs evidently asked the dean for permission to sit at High Table in place of the noblemen. The canons took offence, and felt that they were to be ousted from their rightful place. Jelf suggested that it was 'the crowning act of a system tending, if not intended, to ignore and degrade the canons'. It was, of course, eventually resolved, less to the satisfaction of the canons than to the Students', who retained the right to dine on High Table as guests.

The canons' reaction to one small Christ Church incident can be seen as part of a wider fear that clerical Oxford, particularly of the High Church in the University, was in terminal decline. The case of Reginald Macan highlighted the concerns of the High Church men. In 1877, Macan had spoken against theologians as theoretical teachers, and in the same year gave a Hibbert Trust lecture which revealed views on the resurrection that were less than conventional. In 1882, when Macan's Studentship came up for re-election after his marriage, 'discussion and strife of tongues broke out' over his eligibility. The meeting was held on 15 June and it seemed that everyone in attendance had an opinion. Voting was meant to be secret, but Macan himself said that there was no doubt at all about who had voted which way. Marriage was no longer a disqualification for election to a Studentship, so it can only have been Macan's unorthodox theological views that concerned the Electoral Board. Harcourt argued that this was equally unimportant in determining whether Macan should be re-elected, but he failed. The meeting voted 16 to 11 against, the dean using his 2 votes for Macan. Macan's own analysis of the voting revealed that those voting for him were 5 clerics and 5 laymen. The 16 dissenters included all 6 canons, mustered by Pusey, but also 3 men who fought tooth and nail for the rights of Students only 15 years before: Prout, Bayne, and Dodgson.[69] John Stewart, the philosopher, who was re-elected at the same meeting, felt some embarrassment, but Macan was remarkably stoical in the face of a considerably reduced salary and an uncertain future.[70]

Wherever one sat in Hall, and whatever one's status, the importance of dining at Christ Church could not be diminished. In the years immediately after the reform, gaudy dinners in their modern form were established. In 1871, the June gaudy, at which Nash's commemorative speech was given, was set as a Founder's Day celebration. There was to be evening prayer at 5 o'clock, followed by the Commemoration Speech in Hall at 6.30, a copy of which was still to be deposited in the archive, and then dinner. Now, invitations to dinner and to spend the night in college were sent out by the dean, the sub-dean and the censors, rather than the canons. On the list of guests were Students on the Old Foundation who were not on the Governing Body, former canons whose names remained on the books, former Students of MA status and above, the Honorary Students and the chaplains. The Steward was instructed to prepare for 100 guests, and Vere Bayne, administrator extraordinary, was put in charge of the receipt and collation of the replies.[71] The first college ball was requested by 99 undergraduates in 1881. It was to be held on the Monday of Commem week, that period of great celebration at the end of every academic year.[72] At the same time, although not universally approved by the Governing Body, a grant was given towards a Christmas entertainment for college servants.[73]

The appointment of a salaried steward in 1865 also allowed the Hall to be used by outside groups on a much more commercial basis: the first recorded function was a luncheon for the delegates of the Co-operative Congress in 1882, followed shortly by a concert by Oxford University Musical Club (permission for the last being granted strictly on the condition that the concert was over in time for dinner preparations).[74] In 1890, the Headmasters' Conference took over the Hall for its annual meeting.[75]

The appointment of the steward was not just a response to the Bread and Butter Row, either, but part of a far wider criticism of college catering in general. At around the same time, Trinity, Pembroke and Merton Colleges had all wrested control of the kitchen from the manciples and cooks and put it into the hands of their bursars.[76] At Christ Church, rules for the administration of the Steward's Office were set down for Lent term 1866, and once again regulations for the payment of battels bills – which included not only the actual cost of a man's meals, but an additional sum to pay for the 'Establishment' – were reiterated.⁷⁷ Prices of all goods available from the buttery and the kitchen were set by the Steward, rather than by the butler and his colleagues. A commons of bread was 1d, eggs were a penny-half-penny each, a quart bottle of beer, stout or cider cost 7d. Cases of drinks could be taken to rooms: pale ale cost 8 shillings per dozen quarts. Bottles could be returned in exchange for 2 shillings per dozen. The kitchen operated like that in a hotel. Breakfast was served in Hall between 8 and 9 am, and lunch between 1 and 2 pm. Dinner was promptly at 6 pm at a price of 1s 9d. Guests were permitted at a special table, provided that they were booked in by 10 am. Breakfast and luncheon could be ordered to eat in one's rooms, if one preferred. Supper, too, could be provided up until 10 pm. Dinner was the only meal that students were expected to attend, although it could be supplied directly to rooms if a man was ill. Just so that the privilege was not abused, the allowance for dinner under these circumstances was a mere half a crown (2s 6d). Half a cold duck would set a student back 1s 6d, or he could have a mutton chop for sixpence. A sole with sauce cost a shilling. Scouts, waiters and other college servants were on fixed wages, and gratuities were forbidden.

In the 1870s, however, domestic management was again called into question. When Henry Grant, the long-standing and highly efficient butler, died in 1876, a committee had to be established to make arrangements in his absence.⁷⁸ A further committee was set up just three years later to investigate the management of the kitchen and the buttery, and was granted £100 to obtain skilled help and advice.⁷⁹ After four months, the committee reported, and the Governing Body agreed to employ a 'gentleman' to take charge of the Hall on a salary of £200 per annum. He was to be responsible for all the purchase and sale of food, and would have authority over all but the most senior kitchen and Hall staff, including their appointment and dismissal.⁸⁰ Arthur Acland, soon to be appointed senior bursar at Balliol College, was made the new Junior Steward.⁸¹ Perhaps unsurprisingly, Faulkner, the head chef, tendered his resignation immediately.⁸² When the Steward was first appointed in 1865, Faulkner had already been chef for 27 years, and the considerable lightening of his wallet then was undoubtedly not to his liking. This further imposition of a new man over him, especially when the Steward assured the Governing Body that Faulkner was a reliable and trusted member of staff, must have been the final straw. In 1881, Acland took over from Faussett as Steward, and the division of labour between the Treasury and the Steward's department began.[83]

Whilst the Governing Body and the Chapter were still thrashing out the complex management of college and cathedral after the 1867 Act, undergraduate life was changing beyond all recognition. Not just the terminology – undergraduate Students were first Junior Students and then Exhibitioners or Scholars – but teaching expanded, the tutorial began to appear, and the opportunities for students of all ranks to enjoy a social life widened as never before.

* * * * *

Christ Church had been Head of the River sixteen times between 1817 and 1849, but its pre-eminence waned, and the college was not to be Head again for nearly 60 years.[84] Individual rowers still made their mark, however; W. A. L. (Flea) Fletcher, an Etonian who came up to Christ Church in 1888, rowed for the University crew from 1890 until 1893. Oxford won all four races.[85] At the same time as the college was failing on the river, it was the dominant college, followed closely by Balliol, in real tennis. An annual singles tournament was inaugurated in 1850 – Christ Church had nineteen winners between 1850 and 1914 – and there were Varsity matches from 1859, the earliest of which were played in London.[86] Lawn tennis became fashionable in the 1880s, and a club was definitely in existence at Christ Church from 1883, encouraging men like John Pius Boland, who won gold medals for both the doubles and the singles – on the same day – at the first modern Olympic Games in 1896, playing with a racket purchased from an Athens market and in a pair of borrowed plimsolls.

Some colleges, particularly Balliol, were strong in team sports, but for a while Christ Church clung to its individual and gentlemanly activities such as hunting and beagling; the college maintained its own pack of beagles throughout the latter part of the nineteenth century and into the twentieth.[87] However, organised college sport was definitely on the rise.[88] An athletics club had been founded by 1870, and cricket even earlier, by 1859, having been introduced much earlier as an adjunct to the Bullingdon Club with the social side then far more crucial than the game itself. Varsity matches began in 1827, and later became a hugely popular fixture in the country's summer calendar.[89] At Christ Church, the rise of cricket meant the building of a new pavilion in 1861, and the preparation of the ground, which was leased to the University cricket club from 1885.[90] The groundsman, John Ambler, was also employed as umpire and bowler. Rules for the club were printed in 1864.[91] The college cricket club spawned other teams such as the Warrigals and the Nondescripts, which played local school or town teams.

Sport was a means whereby men from less exalted social backgrounds could be accepted at a college which was perceived to be aristocratic. William Edwards, the son of a Sussex clergyman, came up to Christ Church in 1864 as a servitor; he wanted to row, and asked, probably with some trepidation, if he could join the Boat Club. It must have been almost unheard of, but Humphrey Senhouse, old Etonian and President of the club, was rather more enlightened than Edwards might have expected. He was accepted, and proved his worth, stroking in both the Torpids and the VIIIs, with two fellow servitors in the boat with him. The following year Senhouse asked Edwards to row with him in the Varsity Pairs.[92]

In 1889, subscriptions to several different clubs were brought together by the creation of the Consolidated (or Amalgamated) Clubs, and undergraduates could pay this at the start of term with their battels bills. An easy and centralised method of subscription helped to break down social barriers, and was designed to 'promote economy, to diminish the general total subscription, and to strengthen the Clubs'. Included at first were the subs to the Athletics, Beagles, Boat, Cricket, Football and Philharmonic Clubs, along with the newly founded Junior Common Room.[93] The entrance fee was set at £3 with a termly subscription of £1 16s. Christ Church's Junior Common Room was set up in 1886, with official sanction from the Governing Body, and rooms allocated in Tom 6 for relaxation with newspapers and magazines, and refreshments.[94]

There were, of course, social activities besides sports. Clubs of the period, other than Loder's, included the Anonym, a debating society focusing on topical issues of the day as long as they were not theological; the Twenty, a dining and light-hearted debating society; the Wolsey, another debating society for which any doctrinal issue was a no-go area; the Mermaid, founded in 1895 to read plays; and the Philharmonic Society, which practised regularly, and in 1885 performed Brahms's cantata *Rinaldo* in Hall. A Reading Society was proposed in 1885, but there is no evidence that it ever made it past the drawing board. And theatricals, which had died a death at Christ Church in the seventeenth century, were revived in the 1860s. In 1863, plays were put on in the Upper Library, with more at the end of Michaelmas term 1864. The choice of production that Christmas was lightweight: *My Dress Boots*, a new farce in one act by Thomas J. Williams; *The Maid and the Magpie*, by H. J. Byron; and *A Thumping Legacy*, another farce, by John Maddison Morton, published in 1843. The following summer, four more plays were presented, probably by the Cardinal Club, which was definitely running by 1866. Serious works were still not on the agenda; *A Most Unwarrantable Intrusion* and *Ticklish Times* were both one-act comic interludes by Morton, performed with *La! Somnambula!*, a burlesque by Byron. The vice-chancellor, Francis Leighton, frowned on such comic productions and decreed, in 1869, that all theatricals within his jurisdiction were banned. It was a Christ Church man, James Adderley, who ensured that popular dramatics continued, conducted out of the sight and control of the vice-chancellor. His society, the Philothespians, was evidently unpopular with the University, but it survived through the support of Christ Church senior members and even of Mrs Liddell.[95] The Liddell family was certainly not averse to play-acting, with productions taking place privately in the deanery. The dean even tolerated a farce about his daughters, called *Cakeless*, performed by undergraduates in around 1870. In spite of Leighton's disapproval, the Philothespians became a University club, and in 1883 was properly recognised. There were two conditions: plays should either be Shakespeare's or Greek, and no man should play a female role without the permission of the vice-chancellor. But the farces and popular entertainments continued in Commem week, right at the end of the summer term, when central jurisdiction was hardly effective. In 1898, the Cardinal Club performed scenes from Elizabeth Gaskell's *Cranford*.[96]

More serious activities included the Oxford University Volunteer Corps, the forerunner of the Officer Training Corps. Between 1859 and 1873, nearly 300 Christ Church men, both senior and junior, were members.[97] Activities like the OTC were part of a wider involvement in empire and social welfare.[98] The Oxford Mission in Calcutta was founded from Christ Church to work as a missionary body towards the conversion of India. Its hostel was called 'The House' and the yard, 'The Meadow'. In 1850, a Christ Church contingent had set sail for New Zealand to establish a new colony there on Tractarian principles. Of the 50 men who subscribed to the Canterbury Association, the aims of which were to create another Oxford, 30 were Oxford graduates and were led by John Robert Godley, who had matriculated from Christ Church in 1832.[99] Closer to home there was the Christ Church (Oxford) Mission in Poplar in the east end of London. Founded in 1882, the mission aimed to help boys from the poorest families.[100] Academic 'mission', too, was important to Christ Church men. Michael Sadler, the Steward from 1886, was secretary of the extension lectures sub-committee of the Oxford Local Examinations Delegacy. Halford Mackinder, the geographer, was one of the same group, and gave lectures at extension centres. No doubt through Sadler's influence, Mackinder was appointed to a Studentship in 1892 in order to enable him to develop an extension college in Reading.[101] Dean Paget was an enthusiastic supporter of the Workers' Educational Association, founded in Reading in 1904.

Even closer still to home was the decision in 1869 to set up a reading room for college servants. In June of that year, £300 was set aside for a room for servants to use during the vacations for general reading, night classes and occasional lectures. It was to be built at the north-west end of Dr Payne Smith's lower garden.[102]

While the college was looking outwards, despite the ever-growing number of subjects available, facilities for its own undergraduates to study were less than adequate. Insufficient library provision was a problem across

Between 1859 and 1873, nearly three hundred Christ Church men were members of the Oxford University Volunteer Corps. Cecil Mills came up in 1857. He was vicar of Barford in Warwickshire from 1865.

the University; men like Falconer Madan at Brasenose were rare in wanting to open up libraries for undergraduate use. Colleges were generally far from generous in their provision of texts for the curriculum, with many tutors believing that men should bring their own books.[103] The Library at Christ Church was for the use of senior members, and occasionally other academics. After the constitutional changes, a committee took over its management, now funded directly from the Treasury with an annual grant of £150 rather than a share of fees paid for degrees as in the past. Every member of Governing Body was entitled to have a key, which he paid for, and was permitted to take home up to ten books during the vacations. For a salary of £60 per annum, the Librarian's job was to reside during full term, to take note of *libri desiderati*, check the bills, and have authority over the 'minister' who was in attendance in the Library during opening hours. A new catalogue was commissioned in 1882, and a grant of £250 made for its compilation. But none of this helped the undergraduates. It was not until June 1884 that a proposal was approved to set aside the lecture room in Tom 4 as a reading room for honours undergraduates. Books considered appropriate were transferred from the main Library, and a grant of £35 per annum made for the purchase of new books and their binding. An additional grant of £100 allowed the purchase of a complete set of Teubner classical texts and other 'standard and inexpensive editions of standard authors, English and foreign, prose and poetry, as may be judged useful'. A board was set up to run the reading room, consisting of the dean, the Librarian and three more members of Governing Body. Two undergraduates were co-opted in the first instance, but they showed a distinct lack of interest in meetings, and their attendance ceased to be requested from 1897. The reading room, largely unsupervised, was not a great success.[104] Some of the comments in the widely used suggestion book are much as one would expect. Missing books were a regular problem, leading one undergraduate to suggest that all the books, not just a few reference works, should be confined to the reading room. It was an unpopular idea, partly because the room was not particularly pleasant to work in – it was too hot, then too cold, then smelt horrible. One entry suggested the purchase of an anemometer to measure the strength of the draughts.[105]

Undergraduate bad behaviour and the resulting disciplinary cases recorded in the later nineteenth century are much the same as any in the previous three centuries. Courtenay Boyle, for example, was summoned and charged with idleness and extravagance, and George Pruern was accused of cheating in his examinations.[106] And, although the status of the perpetrator is unknown, the Governing Body offered a reward of £50, through the discreet hands of police Superintendent Head, for information leading to the discovery of the person who put oxalic acid in the chef's tea on 21 February 1880.[107]

After 1867, as disciplinary cases concerning undergraduates became the responsibility almost exclusively of the Junior Censor, these appear infrequently in the Governing Body minutes. A curious little volume called

In June 1884 the lecture room on staircase 4 on Tom Quad was set up as a reading room for undergraduates reading for honours. Books considered appropriate were transferred from the main library, and grants given for the purchase of new books. It survived until 1932.

'Animadversiones' records, at one end, lists of pupils from 1866 to 1891, possibly in the hand of Dodgson, with their success or otherwise in collections in Latin prose, grammar, arithmetic, Euclid and algebra, and, more generally, 'books'. But the other end of the book, beginning in the summer of 1835, lists punishments doled out to young men for irregularity or inattention and all those other undergraduate misdemeanours which had littered the records for the previous 300 years – bonfires, breaking curfew, damage to property, even rioting after football matches. Most punishments involved making abstracts or translations of various texts or lecture series. Mr Astley, for example, was required to bring a complete abstract of his logic lectures after the Christmas vacation of 1836, and in 1841, Hardinge was expected to 'make himself perfect in vulgar and decimal fractions during the vacation and to proceed with the maths lecture next term'. At the beginning of the following term, Hardinge would be subject to examination by the lecturer. Termly collections were a regular feature of undergraduate life. On 8 December 1892 men who had not performed as well as they should have done were given their judgements: Richard Bennett, Kenelm Pepys (Lord Cottenham), Robert Robertson and Clarence Wilson were all told that they would be rusticated for a term. Subsequently, their work and behaviour would be reported on every fortnight. On the first unsatisfactory report they would be sent down. Three more men – Ralph Adderley, William Ferrand and Alexander Mackenzie – although not in the same category as Bennet and his colleagues, were still subject to a fortnightly report. Should they fail, they too would be sent down. Still more men – Hugh Blackett, Amyas Champernowne, George Gibbs, George Morris, James Oxley, Arthur Still and Giles Fox-Strangways (Baron Stavordale) – were to be monitored for their progress and their regularity at their lectures and classes. Censorial displeasure was evidently as successful as ever, and all the men, with the exceptions of Lord Cottenham and Mr Oxley, showed great improvements.[108]

Paget resigned the deanery in 1901 when he was appointed Bishop of Oxford. The college he left had changed almost out of recognition from the one from which Cyril Jackson had departed a century before. In 1801, a bachelor's degree was much the same as it had been for centuries, with its concentration on classical and theological texts; but by 1901, there was a range of disciplines; examinations were increasingly written rather than viva voce; clubs and societies, sporting or otherwise, were organised within both colleges and university; and the student base was broader than ever, with a more cosmopolitan intake and a wider range of careers available on completion.

'More like some fine castle, or great palace, than a college ...': the buildings

It is impossible in one chapter to give more than the briefest outline of the story of Christ Church's buildings and architecture, a topic that could fill a book in itself, for there is barely a moment in its history when one corner or another has not been under scaffolding.[1]

There were three great builder-deans: John Fell and Henry Aldrich in the later seventeenth and early eighteenth centuries, and Henry Liddell in the nineteenth. These men had the inspiration to create imposing new buildings, or to refurbish and restyle the older ones – which is not to say that the men before and after have not had their part to play in making Christ Church the place it is today.

Little had been done after Wolsey's fall, when the college was left with no more than a partially demolished abbey church, its associated monastic buildings, three-quarters of a quadrangle, and the most imposing dining hall and kitchen in Oxford. The canons of King Henry VIII's College merely made the place habitable. In 1546, the Great Quadrangle was a public thoroughfare, so unseemly that the college porter was permitted to keep a dog just to keep the townspeople's cattle and pigs away.[2] And so it fell to the new dean and his Chapter to begin to turn the abandoned construction site into a functioning college and cathedral. From as early as 1550, deans had occupied the north-east corner of the quadrangle, and the canons were scattered about the site, the most senior occupying the newest buildings, the most

'More like some fine castle, or great palace, than a college ...': the buildings

junior the lodgings in the medieval Peckwater Inn and Canterbury College.[3]

The first task was to fulfil the bequest of Thomas Palmer, the auditor. In 1559, he had left £20 towards the completion of a tower over either the Hall stairs or the Great Gate. The Chapter plumped for the Hall stairs – perhaps to ensure that they did not get wet on their way to dinner – and the tower was certainly in place by 1566 when Elizabeth I came to visit.[4] A more vital job was to seal the west end of the cathedral, replacing the temporary wooden shuttering put in place in the 1530s with stone salvaged from Oseney abbey, and to install a new window.[5]

The sixteenth century saw consolidation and tidying-up, but at the beginning of the seventeenth, thoughts were turning towards more ambitious schemes. The matriculation statute of 1581 brought many more students into the colleges and new accommodation was sorely needed, especially as the student population was becoming ever more gentrified. Dean Thomas Ravis, a born administrator and committee man, looked to Peckwater Inn.[6] A huge medieval inn, Peckwater had been acquired by Wolsey initially as lodgings for his workforce.[7] In 1600, the builders moved in, first adding cocklofts and chambers, and then in 1616 adding a completely new east wing.[8]

As the social standing of the undergraduates rose, facilities were reviewed. The full and old-fashioned library, housed in the monastery's refectory, underwent a major renovation. Otho Nicholson, the benefactor who had given the city its fresh water conduits, paid for its refurbishment with new presses to replace the lecterns, and a beautiful painted ceiling.[9] No doubt the Chapter looked at the cloister more generally as this work was going on, and it may have been at this time that the rooms over the south and east cloisters were built, providing space for the cathedral's archive and a room that would shortly become the Allestree Library. One irritation that came up for long discussion was the inconvenient and sole access to the cathedral through the small south door. It was hardly fitting for a cathedral or for grand University occasions. A proposal was put forward to cut through the canons' lodgings and make a proper west door. The two canons whose residences would be affected were less than certain about this; although one

The refectory of St Frideswide's priory was adapted into a library for Christ Church, probably in the 1560s. Soon, the collections were too big for the old-fashioned presses, and the library too quaint for a grand college with aspirations to be even grander. When the New Library opened in the 1770s, this building was reconfigured for undergraduate rooms. The drawing was made by Thomas Gooch before the conversion, but not published until 1817.

was convinced, the other was evidently against the proposal, and the south door remained the only entrance for another 250 years.[10]

Changes in religious practice and fashion meant that no sooner had the carpenters left the Library than they were moved into the cathedral. Brian Duppa, friend of Archbishop Laud and tutor to the future Charles II, swept through the church removing old memorials and stalls, installing the pulpit and new screens to make worship more seemly, and commissioning painted windows by the van Linge brothers. New marble steps up to the sanctuary were put in place, and a pavement laid in the nave.[11]

Samuel Fell, Duppa's successor as dean, just had time to install the

'More like some fine castle, or great palace, than a college ...': the buildings

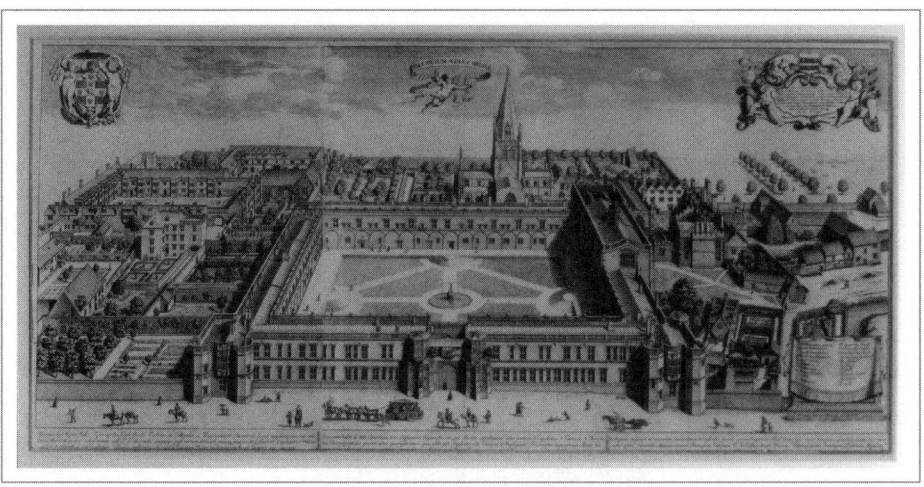

David Loggan's engraving of Christ Church from his Oxonia illustrata *(1675), a set of bird's-eye views of all the colleges, academic halls, and university buildings, together with a map. It was intended to accompany Wood's* The History and Antiquities of the University of Oxford *(1674).*

fan-vaulting over the Hall stairs before the chaos of the Civil War; and the vast expense of having king and court resident at Christ Church meant that building work came to a halt.[12] But in 1660, John Fell was appointed, the first of the builder-deans, and oversaw the beginning of the great rebuilding of Christ Church that was to last for over a century. After the reinstallation of the organ and basic repair works to the cathedral fabric, Fell looked to the confusion that was the north side of the Great Quadrangle and vowed to build rapidly.[13] Richard Allestree was promised that he could have one of the two new canonries that would occupy the site, and Fell honoured his word by 1665. The completed quad, finished in the same style with which Wolsey had begun, drew admiration; it was 'more like some fine castle, or great palace, than a College...' [14]

The unfinished front gate next needed attention, but before Fell could concentrate his mind on creating something fitting, there was a disastrous fire in Chaplain's Quad. Canon Gardiner's house was destroyed and another had to be blown up to create a fire-break and protect the Library. Killcanon was built for the homeless Gardiner, Mercury was dug to provide a reservoir

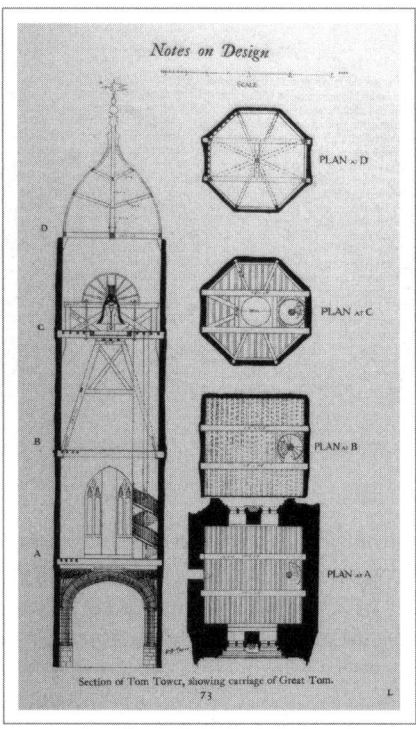

W. D. Caröe's twentieth-century drawing of Tom Tower shows Wren's design clearly.

to protect against future fires, Chaplain's Quad was rebuilt, and the opportunity taken to provide more accommodation with the new Fell's Buildings.[15] Work began in 1669 and continued for ten years, after which the indefatigable dean returned to the problem of the gate. Wolsey had left this unfinished, presumably intending to add a tower to contain the archives or perhaps as a residence for the dean, but he died before it could be completed. Fell called on Christopher Wren to design something fitting for the grandest college in Oxford. Plans were approved in late spring 1681, the builder Christopher Kempster, who had worked with Wren on St Paul's, was appointed, and work was completed by Michaelmas 1682.[16] Great Tom rang from the new tower for the first time on Restoration Day, 29 May 1684.

For the last years of his deanery, Fell could sit back and admire the completed Great Quadrangle.[17] Following in his footsteps, after the very brief

'More like some fine castle, or great palace, than a college ...': the buildings

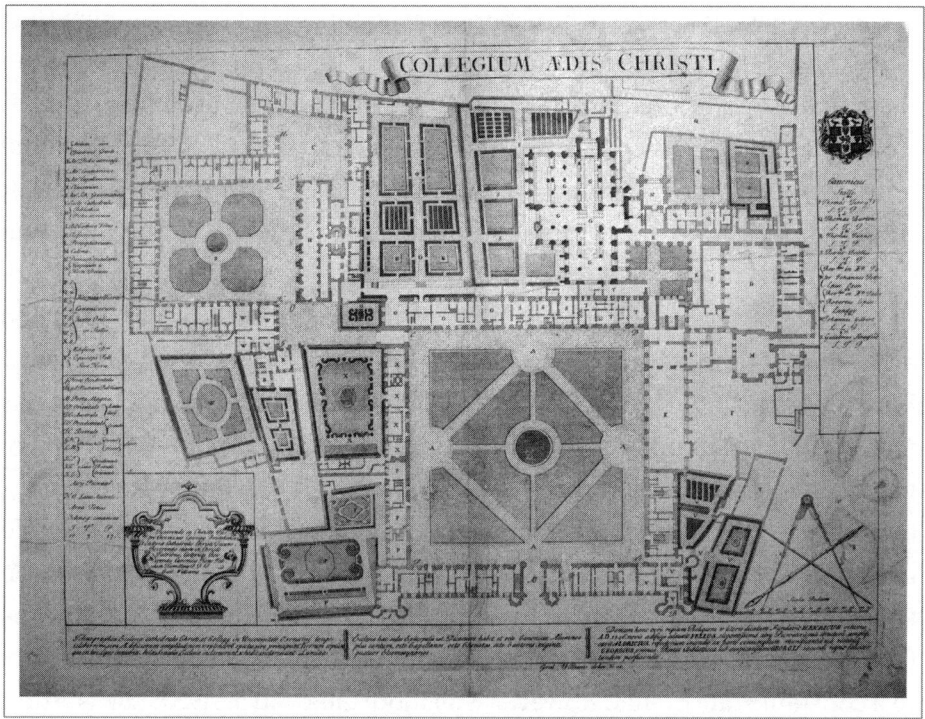

William Williams's 1730s ground-plan of Christ Church.

deanery of the Catholic Massey, came Henry Aldrich, a man whose talents could hardly be surpassed. At first, Aldrich concentrated on settling Christ Church on to its upward academic trajectory, but he then embarked on an ambitious project which would keep the builders busy for the best part of a century.

Peckwater Quad was beginning to look a little unkempt by 1700, the more so as Christ Church was increasingly seen as the college for the sons of noblemen and men of influence. Aldrich drew up his own designs for a complete rebuild in the Palladian style, consisting of a three-winged edifice to the north, east and west, and a separate building on the south side. Everyone seems to have been ready to start, once funds came in, for no sooner had Anthony Radcliffe's benefaction of £3,000 been received at the end of 1706, than the foundation stones were laid.[18] It was a huge project, supervised by William Townesend and watched over by Aldrich, and was built in stages, allowing two sides to be occupied at all times while construction took place on the third.[19] The dean died before the final touches were added to the interior, and before his plans for the south side could even be started. It would seem that his idea was for another residential block, its design based on Michelangelo's Capitoline palaces, but there were no finances in place. It was not until 1716, when Robert South made a bequest, that the Dean and Chapter could make a decision.

The old college library was full to capacity; a number of new gifts had arrived, including those of John Morris, the regius professor of Hebrew, of Robert Burton and of Aldrich himself, whose library included not just books and pamphlets but manuscript and printed music.[20] The plan was therefore to turn the south side of Peckwater Quad into the 'finest library that belongs to any society in Europe'.[21] Building was slow, dependent on the gifts of old members who had already contributed to the rest of the quad. The dean even tried a lottery ticket, but unsuccessfully.[22] By 1739, twenty years after the foundations were laid, the shell was complete.[23] Plans for the interior were in a constant state of flux, however. Still more gifts had arrived: Lewis Atterbury's pamphlets; 5,000 books from Canon Stratford; books and scientific instruments from the 4th Earl of Orrery; and the vast library of books and manuscripts that had belonged to William Wake, Archbishop of Canterbury. The shelving designs were changed at least twice, and it was not until the 1760s that all the finishing touches, decorative and practical, were made.[24] But just as the brick-dust and plaster were cleaned from the shelves ready to receive the books, Christ Church was given the vast and extraordinary collection of Old Master paintings and drawings accumulated by General John Guise.[25] It must have been a difficult decision, but the Chapter opted to close in the fashionable open loggia beneath the Library and turn it into a gallery. The workmen returned, and it was another five years before the books were moved and the Library open for business in the summer of 1771.[26]

Even before the accounts for the Library project were closed, Christ Church's pre-eminence in science and mathematics was enhanced by the gifts of John Freind and Matthew Lee which made possible the creation of a new Anatomy School and the readerships to go with it.[27] Henry Keene, who had managed the conversion of the ground floor of the Library, was given charge of the project to make a theatre suitable for teaching practical anatomy. Built alongside the kitchen, the School soon became known as 'Skeleton Corner'.[28]

These major projects were not enough, however. The 1770s and 1780s saw the conversion of the old Library into rooms for Westminster Students, the creation of a muniment room in the cloister and the complete rebuilding of Canterbury College.[29] The medieval buildings, already damaged during the construction of the Library, must have looked very miserable beside all the new grandeur. Richard Robinson, once a Student and then Archbishop of Armagh, gave munificently. His first gift was sufficient for the north and much of the south side, then he funded the triumphal arch, and finally the south-west corner, which matches Peckwater Quad in design, and was to be accommodation for only the highest-status undergraduates.[30] Alongside the great tasks continued maintenance, repairs and alterations.[31]

As the nineteenth century began, with Christ Church at its academic zenith, there was the briefest of lulls. No serious construction projects were begun after the completion of Canterbury Quad and the opportunity was taken to set up a new building fund to prepare for further work. But the peace would soon be disturbed. In March 1809, the south-west lodgings caught fire and were completely gutted. The rebuild included stone rather than wooden staircases, and iron balustrades. The dean paid personally for water to be brought from the city's water works so that Mercury, which had proved invaluable but still not sufficient to its task, could be supplemented. A new fire engine was urgently purchased and, very soon, the process of lighting Christ Church with gas was initiated.[32]

The second half of the nineteenth century saw a huge rise in matriculations after the abolition of religious tests (which had, in effect, restricted admissions to Anglicans), and as boys from the new grammar schools and from the new industrial and commercial aristocracies began to arrive. Christ Church had a waiting list for a while and it became evident that still more accommodation was needed: Chaplain's Quad and Fell's Buildings had outlived their useful lives and were demolished in 1862 to make way for Thomas

This early photograph shows the Great Quadrangle before Dean Liddell's major building and restoration projects. The 'tunnel' to the cathedral would be cut through in the 1870s, and Wolsey Tower built over the Hall stairs a decade later. Fell's balustrade was still to be replaced by the battlements and the elaborate pinnacles on the Hall roof, and Mercury remained empty of its fountain until the 1930s. The arches of Wolsey's proposed cloister are almost invisible.

Deane's 'Rhenish Gothic' edifice, Meadows Building; and 57 new sets (or student rooms) were provided in record time, with the first staircase ready by the beginning of October 1864.[33]

Meadows was the first major project of the third great builder-dean, Henry Liddell. For over 40 years, Christ Church had been relatively clear of scaffolding, but Liddell was not one to leave things unchanged.[34] Restoration of the cathedral, which had barely been touched since the seventeenth century, was high on his list of priorities. The heating had been overhauled in the 1850s, and Burne-Jones's Frideswide window installed in 1858, but a decade later George Gilbert Scott submitted his plans and estimate (over

£37,000) for a complete refurbishment. The interior, particularly the nave, was remodelled, turning the diocesan cathedral into even more of a college chapel, and the west end was given a more 'Romanesque' appearance with its rose and round-headed windows.[35] Last but not least, the 'tunnel' from the Great Quadrangle into the cathedral was created, finally fulfilling the plans made by the Chapter in 1617.

During the work, Scott mentioned to Liddell that the cathedral spire was in a poor state, and no longer able to carry the weight of the bells that had hung there since 1546. They were moved, after much agonised debate, to the new Wolsey Tower.[36] The dean's energy was undiminished, and he spent the next few years bringing the Quad into a more uniform condition: Fell's balustrade was replaced with decorative battlements; pinnacles were added to the Hall roof; the cloister shafts were restored; the terrace lowered to show off the springers; the windows in Hall were replaced; and the Fell Tower constructed.[37] When the anatomy collections had been transferred to the new University Museum, the School was converted into a chemistry laboratory. The Chapter House was restored, and the archive evicted from the cloister. This half-century of constant labour concluded with the installation of electricity throughout the college.[38]

Two world wars brought new projects almost to a halt, attention being increasingly focused on the protection of the site, its treasures and its residents. In 1935, the boathouse was erected to replace the dilapidated college barge, but it was not until the 1950s that changing undergraduate requirements prompted fresh consideration about college accommodation.[39] The coalyard alongside Blue Boar Lane was the obvious site for expansion, and provision for a lecture room, a picture gallery, residential rooms for senior and junior members, dedicated law and science libraries and an archive were all discussed. The architects, Powell and Moya, submitted their plans for a Modernist structure that would sit comfortably within the ancient wall and maintain the tradition of staircases, but this meant that the gallery, dedicated libraries and lecture theatre were all abandoned, the last for another half-century.[40] Building was delayed for financial reasons, and because of the dangerous state of the Library's decayed stonework. An urgent restoration project dealt first with the exterior of the Library, and then with the interior, which was redecorated according to schemes devised by John Fowler. The whole of the Library's ground floor was given over to books, and the pictures were moved out, thanks to a gift from Lord Forte which allowed the development of a proper picture gallery, again designed by Powell and Moya. Once the Library was safe, the new Blue Boar Quad finally went ahead, and both it and the gallery were opened formally by the Queen on 2 May 1968.[41]

Lecture rooms had always been needed, and although a seminar room had been provided in Blue Boar, there was still a shortage of teaching space. One possibility was the old Anatomy School but, amid some controversy, the Senior Common Room acquired the building for meetings and lunches. On 27 January 1971, a Governing Body meeting was held there for the first time. Another plan was to have a lecture theatre even further to the south, close to the Memorial Gardens, or the offices under the Hall might have been used when the Steward and Treasurer moved out in 1973. The first was not followed through, and the offices were converted into a Law Library.[42] It was not until Blue Boar Quad underwent a major refurbishment between 2007 and 2009 that a lecture theatre was provided, meeting the needs not only of students but also to provide a venue for conferences – an increasingly important business opportunity.

Construction has been a constant theme in Christ Church's history, sometimes prompted by the needs of students, sometimes by the state of the buildings. At times, money has flooded in, allowing projects to be carried forward apace; at others, finances have only come in gradually and schemes, such as the Library, have taken decades to complete. But from 1546 to the modern refurbishments and renovations of the twenty-first century, the college has respected and enhanced its architectural heritage.

9

'Half arsenal, half hotel': twentieth-century Christ Church

The Annual Report for 1899/1900 – a single-page affair reporting only the most essential of information – celebrated, in just a few short lines, Christ Church's past; but it also anticipated decades of unrest.[1] Charles Dodgson's portrait was placed in the Hall in that year, commemorating a man who had put Christ Church on the map in a way that no one could have expected 50 years previously. Dodgson had fought alongside Vere Bayne and Sandford for the great reform of the Christ Church constitution, but he liked the old ways, too. He had been a stickler for form, and for forms, bombarding his colleagues, particularly the long-suffering censors and Steward, with notes and comments, and documenting the management of the Senior Common Room in a way not seen before or since. In that same year, Henry Thompson published his history of Christ Church. In a compact but comprehensive account, he covered almost every aspect of Christ Church life, picking out of the archive, and from other sources, the most salient and enlightening aspects of the previous 350 years.

But it was the two other notices in that brief report that gave a foretaste of times to come. It explained that there had been no gaudy in June 1899 because of the war in South Africa, and announced that the colours of the Light Infantry had been placed with some ceremony in the cathedral.[2] War was to dominate the first half of the twentieth century, and Christ Church was not immune to the difficulties and changes that were to come.

> ## Thomas Banks Strong (1861–1944)
>
> Strong came up to Christ Church in 1879 as a Westminster Junior Student, and took a second in classics in 1883. He was appointed a lecturer and then to a Studentship in 1888. He held both the junior and senior censorships, and was a popular tutor.
>
> Strong was made dean in 1910 on Paget's recommendation. He proved an able administrator and leader, particularly during the difficulties of the First World War. A musical man, he worked tirelessly with the cathedral choir, even giving financial support to the future organist and composer William Walton. He also worked to widen access to higher education through the Workers' Educational Association.
>
> J. C. Masterman, who was interviewed for a Studentship in 1913, said that Strong 'ate and drank more quickly than anyone I have ever met; he probably regarded both eating and drinking as an interruption to thought and conversation'.
>
> He was a good intermediary between college and cathedral, minimising any friction between the two. Strong remained dean until 1920 when he was appointed to the bishopric of Ripon. He returned to Oxford as bishop in 1925.
>
> Masterman (1975); *ODNB*; *Christ Church, 1943–4*

At first, however, things carried on much as before. There were innovations, such as electricity, which was installed between 1901 and 1903 just in time for the arrival of the first six Rhodes Scholars, all from America, in 1904.[3] The St Aldates' frontage was under repair, and Caröe was involved with the modernisation of the kitchen, and the installation of the staircase between the Hall and the Common Room. Gifts continued to arrive, including the portrait of William Penn from Haverford College, and the original triple portrait of Fell, Dolben and Allestree to replace the copy which had always hung in the Hall. There was another year without a gaudy – in 1910 – following the death of Edward VII.

Educational standards were high: four out of seven firsts given in

'Half arsenal, half hotel': twentieth-century Christ Church

Thomas Banks Strong, dean from 1901 to 1925, presided over a cosmopolitan college. Before the First World War, Christ Church was full of aristocrats, gentlemen, scholars, and sons of successful entrepreneurs. During the war, he administered both college and university through difficult times, trying to maintain 'business as usual'. Then, in 1918, he managed to create an environment in which men returning from the war, whether ex-students or military men taking advantage of the specially designed short courses, and new boys could settle and study together.

theology in 1913 were to Christ Church men. At the end of the nineteenth century, 'Greats' still dominated the humanities curriculum as it had done for centuries, deemed to be all that was necessary to equip a man with the right mental attributes to tackle whatever he met in life. As the century turned, however, modern history was beginning to take over, and had become the largest school in the university. Already a good degree in history was reckoned almost as good as one in classics. The history faculty was created in 1913, and Christ Church began a dominance of the history

Sporting activities were very popular in Edwardian Christ Church. Beagling and hunting both had strong followings. In rowing, Christ Church was Head of the River in 1908, 1909, and 1910.

schools, outstripping its rivals – New and Balliol Colleges – under the guidance of Keith Feiling, which was to last from 1919 at least until the outbreak of the Second World War.[4]

The college, under Thomas Banks Strong, was in its Edwardian cosmopolitan prime, something of which he was proud. The sons of European nobility such as Prince Paul of Serbia and Prince Sergius Obolensky were members, joined by royalty from further afield, including the Crown Prince of Siam and the grandson of the Maharajah of Kapurthala. Ambassadors' sons were counted among its numbers, in addition to those of entrepreneurs and businessmen in all walks of life such as brewing, shipping, banking and manufacturing.[5] In 1911, the college was considered for the Prince of Wales, but its mix of students evidently bothered Lord Derby, whose advice had been sought by George V. To Derby, the place was full of the *nouveaux riches*.[6]

In sport, the college was holding its own. In 1908, the 1st Eight went Head of the river, its crew including Apsley Cherry-Garrard, soon to join Scott on his expedition to the Antarctic.[7] Christ Church remained Head in 1909 and 1910, and other sportsmen represented Oxford in Varsity matches in cricket, rugby, football, athletics and golf. Young men, as ever, indulged in favourite activities as well as discovering new ones. Eric Dodds, later regius professor of Greek, was a member of the 'hashish' club begun by a student at University College who returned from a holiday in north Africa with some cannabis resin. Experiments were carefully controlled; only one man was allowed to try the drug each evening, and then no more than twice, while the others watched and monitored the results.[8] Other, more academic, pursuits included the completion of Godfrey Arkwright's catalogue of Aldrich's music manuscripts and Aitkin's catalogue of the pre-1600 printed books which were not in the Bodleian (some 6,000 volumes), and Tancred Borenius had started work on listing the pictures in the Gallery.[9]

But these gentle activities and mixed friendships were brought to an abrupt end with the outbreak of war in August 1914. Although the Governing Body, bolstered by the commonly held optimism that all would be over by Christmas, rejected a proposal to insure the fabric, books and pictures against bomb damage, Oxford was affected directly by the war in a way unseen since the seventeenth century. As in 1642, when it was said that the University and college buildings became 'half arsenals and half hotels', town and gown united in a common effort.

Christ Church usually saw between 60 and 70 freshers each year, but in 1914 there were only 14 new arrivals, making a total undergraduate body of 30 including 5 Rhodes scholars from America and 4 from India. The names of 900 members, past and present, were already on the roll of service, including 6 from the Governing Body, many of them processed through the special committee set up by the vice-chancellor and the dean.[10] J. C. Masterman, when appointed to his lectureship in 1913, was advised by the dean to take a year in Germany as a change from Oxford and to prepare himself for teaching – advice that was to keep Masterman away until 1918; finding himself trapped in Germany as the borders closed in August 1914, he was soon interned.[11] Eric Dodds, who had slipped from Germany into Holland just in time to avoid a similar fate, said that the University consisted 'chiefly of young boys putting in time while they awaited their call-up, plus a few crocks, a few overseas students, and a number of women'.[12]

For those few who remained, Strong tried to maintain 'business as usual'. The choristers, who included William Walton, continued with their music, football and rowing, but there were, of course, few extra-curricular opportunities with so many men away. There was no rowing or team sport from the summer of 1914 until 1919, with other societies being held in abeyance.

* * * * *

Soon, however, in spite of the continuation of the daily business of education, the hostilities came to dominate decisions as undergraduates and the younger fellows disappeared from the darkened quadrangles. In place of students came the military, and refugees from Belgium and Serbia. The Oxfordshire and Buckinghamshire Light Infantry were, in part, billeted in Christ Church – the officers making use of the Common Room Smoking Room as their mess – until their more permanent barracks in Cowley were ready; and Christ Church, with Brasenose College, became home to the Royal Flying Corps from 1915. The chemistry lab was taken over by the Military School of Education. Canon Henry Scott Holland described the scene at the beginning of October 1916: 'Oxford begins next week, and we shall be more entirely a Camp than ever. Our 200 flying-men keep Ch.Ch. alive: and now and again Peck wakes to quite its historic noises'. When Holland died in March 1918, the cross placed in his hands was a gift from the Serbian students, a squadron of airmen stood to attention as the coffin was processed into the cathedral and an aeroplane passed low over Christ Church in salute.

At the beginning of the war, the senior members of Christ Church decided to follow the king's example and to give up alcohol for the duration, but the resident officers ensured that the stocks of wine were steadily depleted – to the Common Room's profit. No gaudies were held from 1916 to 1918 and, when rationing was introduced in 1918, high table meals were reduced with meat served only on Tuesdays and Thursdays, and with guests permitted just on 'meatless' days. The exigencies of war, however, did not stop complaints: J. G. C. Anderson wrote in July to the Steward's secretary: 'turnip soup ... had better be avoided in the future. It is food for cows and there is absolutely no need to serve such stuff. Haddock is a fish that needs

> Of the men of the 1st VIII of the summer of 1914, one was a 2nd lieutenant, 3 were lieutenants, 3 were captains, and one was a major; 2 were killed in action; 3 received the MC (one with bar), and 1 the Military OBE and was mentioned in despatches. Most served on the killing fields of France and Belgium, but one was in India and Mesopotamia, and another in Salonika as part of the RAMC.

far more skilful handling than the Christ Church staff is capable of, to be palatable at all. The spaghetti was solid food but very uninteresting ... I think the Ch. Ch. staff would do well to use a cookery book, as they appear not to have the slightest idea of what to serve.'[13] Part of the Meadow was temporarily taken from the Yeomanry, who had traditionally drilled there, and handed over to the Allotment Association.

But the real toll of the war was brought home in the weekly lists of casualties in the *Oxford Magazine* and in the obituary columns of the college's Annual Report. The reports are bald statements of fact, and yet there is a distinct feeling of melancholy mixed with real pride in the courage of the college's men. In the first year of the war, 63 men were recorded as dead or missing, several of whom had been mentioned in despatches. By the end of October 1915, six men had been awarded Distinguished Service Orders and five the Military Cross.[14] Of the Christ Church men who served, 16 per cent were killed, many of them junior officers who led their men 'over the top'. Across the University, nearly 29 per cent of those who had matriculated in 1913 died. Among Christ Church's losses were Andrea Angel, blown up developing explosives at Woolwich, and Charles Fisher, the Senior Censor, who died with almost the entire crew of HMS *Invincible* at Jutland. The first old member to die was Stephen Christy, a captain in the 20th Hussars, who was killed in action on 3 September 1914 at La Ferté. Second Lieutenant N. M. K. Bertie, at 18, was the youngest to be killed in that first year.[15]

Throughout the war, the cathedral was the focus for cultural activity, although with the conflict as a constant backdrop. The Yeomanry's colours were hung above the sub-dean's chair in August 1914 for the duration of

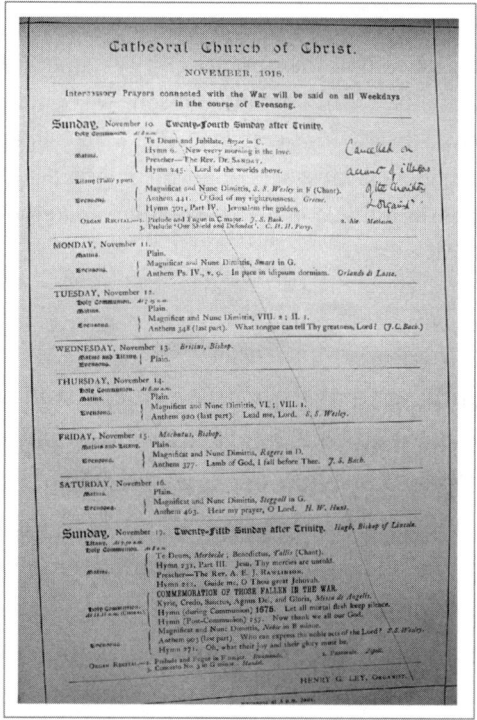

When the Armistice was declared in November 1918, plans for thanksgiving and memorial services had to be abandoned as the choristers and organist had been laid low with the influenza that was sweeping through Europe.

hostilities, and organ recitals were given on Saturday afternoons and Sunday evenings in the summer months to raise funds for the Red Cross. On the third Sunday of every month, commemorative communion services for the fallen were held; there were special services at Easter and Christmas for the troops in residence, and regular Parades. At first the military men occupied only the north side of the cathedral, but soon khaki began to appear among the choir as the lay clerks joined up. The precentor had already left as chaplain to the 2nd South Midland Mounted Brigade, and chaplains and singers were brought in from other colleges to join Walton and the other choristers in the choir stalls.

When the armistice was finally declared on 11 November 1918, Christ Church was in the grip of the Europe-wide influenza outbreak; with organist and choristers all laid low, celebrations had to be postponed. Instead, a commemoration service was held in the cathedral a week later.

Only 42 undergraduates were in residence during Michaelmas term 1918. But from January 1919 the floodgates opened. As the year progressed, 245 new faces appeared at Tom Gate in addition to those who had arrived at the end of 1918 and all those who returned to complete their interrupted studies. Most would have attended the first real service of remembrance held on All Saints Day 1919, close to the first anniversary of the Armistice. Many were returning students, but others were servicemen given the opportunity to study at university for the first time, and still more were fresh-faced 18-year-olds for whom the experience of war had been second-hand. The remembrance service and the memories it prompted were in stark contrast to the determined effort to return the college to normality. John Masterman remembered both the 'speed and determination with which Oxford resumed its peacetime life' and the 'wide and healthy tolerance of the returning warriors which enabled them to continue and coalesce easily and amicably with the younger men'. The influence of the older men was good, and they tolerated rules which must have seemed childish with remarkable patience and good humour.[16] The college had probably never been so mixed, so democratic or so full. The dean commented that 'the House was never before more conscious of its union and its corporate life' – a large and broad church and not a 'colony of cliques'.[17]

Although there were, as ever, men such as Robert Baynes, Dr Lee's reader in physics and now the oldest of the Students, who constantly reminded everyone of how things were done in the past, there was a real desire to look forward.[18] But first, a memorial to the fallen needed to be established. There were debates, not about the creation of a permanent roll of honour which went through without question, but about creating a useful memorial by extending the buildings to provide at least 30 extra rooms. A *Liber Vitae* was placed in the cathedral, and the memorial tablets – which recorded just names and honours, with no military ranks – were unveiled on Armistice Day 1921 by Thomas Strong, the man who had seen Christ Church through the turmoil of the war years. The book and the tablets were paid for by the Governing Body, but the final proposal was to be funded by appeal. However, funds did not pour in, and subscriptions were insufficient to allow any building scheme to get off the ground. By the end of 1926, the fund stood at £4,000 and a disappointed Dean White wrote again to old members proposing a different idea; a war memorial garden to the south of Christ Church. This proposal had a mixed reception: some men requested the return of their donations, but others approved wholeheartedly, including His Majesty the King of Siam who gave £500.[19]

The creation of the Memorial Garden had been mooted in 1924 when the council expressed a wish to widen St Aldates. The proposal included the demolition of the old buildings on the east side of the street, and the partial redevelopment of the site, with new shops and offices south of Trill Mill, and leaving open the northern part, closest to the gate to the Meadow. In the event, a resolution was passed to keep the whole area clear. The old stables would be demolished, the choir school classrooms moved to Brewer Street, and the garages rebuilt more discreetly. At a meeting with the council in January 1926, the memorial gates were first suggested, and the decision taken not to erect a building or even a wall within 150 feet south of the Meadow Gate. A wide pathway with lawns and flower beds was created from the street to the Broad Walk, and an inscription laid just inside the gates chosen from *Pilgrim's Progress*: 'My sword I give to him that shall succeed me in my pilgrimage.'[20]

Dean Strong had been appointed Bishop of Ripon in 1920, and there was some panic over the appointment of his successor. Lloyd George wanted William Temple, who had only just been appointed to the bishopric of Manchester, but he was not a popular choice among the Studentship. Many thought that Temple would just use Christ Church as a stepping-stone to greater things – correctly, as it turned out – and not stay long enough to make a good dean.[21] Another concern was that, politically, he leaned a little to the left.[22] Birkenhead, the Lord Chancellor, came up with an alternative, Henry Julian White, and went into battle with Lloyd George on Christ Church's behalf. The Prime Minister took some persuasion, but Birkenhead eventually won through.[23]

> ## Henry Julian White (1859–1934)
>
> White had come up to Christ Church in 1878, and took degrees in both classics and theology. After his ordination, he began work with John Wordsworth on the critical edition of the Vulgate New Testament. Progress was slow, and became slower once White was appointed to the deanery.
>
> He was said to be a snob and excessively deferential to the influential and famous. But he was equally deferential towards any scholar, however obscure, whom he respected. He was a man of great integrity and humility, and a scholar himself.
>
> On one occasion, White was required to discipline an undergraduate for being caught in bed with a girl. It was later revealed that the girl was, in fact, a boy. Dean White commented that 'one lesson which my long experience has taught me is that whenever a case looks black, on inspection it almost inevitably turns out to be blacker still.'
>
> Masterman (1975), 178; *ODNB*; Ayer (1977), 84

The new dean presided over years of relative calm. There were tragedies, such as the deaths of Rupert Buxton and Michael Llewelyn Davies, who drowned in Sandford Weir on 19 May 1921; but there were also triumphs.[24] In academic life, Frederick Soddy was offered a Nobel Prize for Chemistry, and Christ Church men were showing better results in schools.[25] Sporting achievements included Tom Longstaff and Edward Strutt's attempted ascent of Everest in 1922, and Herbert Percy Jacob's place in the England rugby team.[26] Closer to home, Christ Church went Head of the River in both Torpids and Eights in 1924 and held on to the position in the following year. Five Housemen were in the Oxford crew in 1925, echoing Christ Church's contribution to the first-ever Varsity race. Twenty-eight Housemen were returned to Parliament in the 1923 election including Anthony Eden, later prime minister. And the college statutes were revised again.[27] Building repairs and improvements rocketed ahead: the coats of arms under Tom Tower were repainted and gilded, Peckwater Quad was resurfaced, new wrought-iron gates were put up in addition to the wooden ones at Canterbury Gate, electric lighting was installed in the Library, and the lighting in the cathedral finally completed. A new Mercury was erected, the short-lived top floor of the Anatomy School was removed, squash courts were built, and two new gardens created.

The year 1925 saw the 400th anniversary of the foundation of Cardinal College. To commemorate Wolsey's foundation may have appeared an odd thing to do. His college had foundered after only five years but it was still his design that had shaped the Christ Church of Henry VIII. Frederick Arnold, writing about earlier celebrations, summed up: 'The Christ Church mind ... hardly venerates the memory of its royal founder, Henry VIII. It rejects the bad king, and faithfully clings to the tradition of the great cardinal. We know that if the king had left the cardinal alone, grand as our house is, we should have had something much grander. The king merely murdered the founder, confiscated the revenues, stole the conception, and did imperfectly what had been planned in a wonderful scale of wisdom and munificence.'[28] Perhaps a harsh judgment; Henry had, after all, died only a few short weeks after signing the foundation papers, and his plans may have been just as grand as those of his unfortunate prelate. Arthur Hassall, in the souvenir issue of *Cherwell*, commented that Henry VIII would have been enraged to discover that Christ Church was celebrating Wolsey's foundation.[29]

The celebrations were conducted during Commemoration Week, that last week of Trinity term which always staged the glamorous balls and other end-of-year excitements. On Saturday 20 June, the 'Christ Church floor-polisher' was held; on the Sunday there was more music on the Hall staircase; and on Monday, the Christ Church Ball at which, announced the editor of *Cherwell*, 'some thousand dancers will celebrate the munificence of Cardinal Wolsey in the largest tent in Europe'.[30] The 'ball-room' marquee was set up in Peckwater Quad, and the dancing was accompanied from 9.30 pm by Marius B. Winter's orchestra. At midnight, Vincent Lopez and his band took over at dance number eleven on the programme.[31] Awnings had been erected from Tom Gate around the south and east sides of the quadrangle and into Peckwater and Canterbury Quads, with a crush room created between the Library and Killcanon. A running buffet was laid on outside the

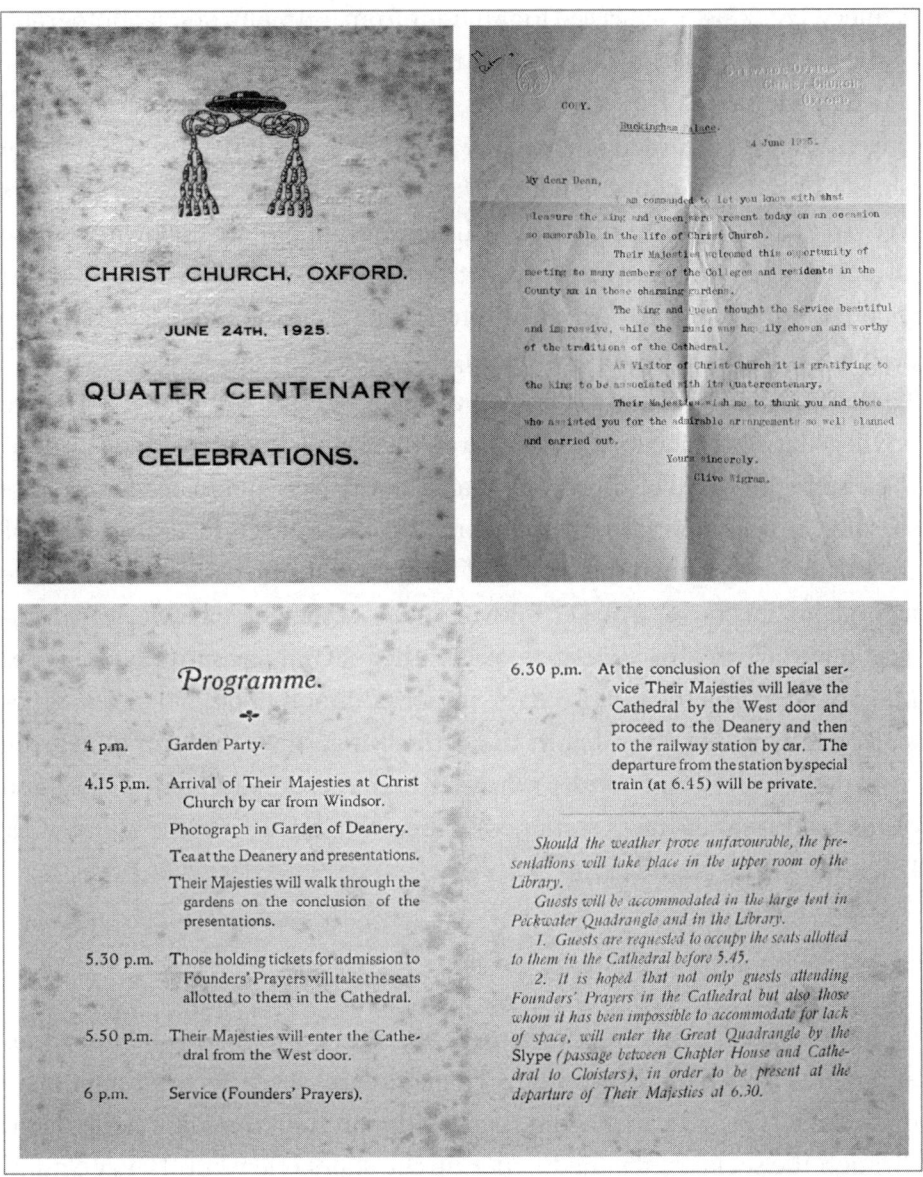

In 1925, George V and Queen Elizabeth visited Christ Church as part of the quatercentenary celebrations. In spite of Wolsey's fall from grace, his foundation has always been remembered as much as those of Henry VIII.

deanery, breakfast was served for an hour from 4.45 am, and a photograph of the gathering was taken in Tom Quad at 5.30.[32]

The climax of the celebrations was the visit of King George V and Queen Mary for a garden party at the Deanery on 24 June, the first event at Christ Church to be caught on film. *The Times* reported the occasion: readers were treated to a potted history of Christ Church, and the following day to an account of the garden party. Although flags were flown throughout Oxford for the occasion, Christ Church remained undecorated, 'considering, perhaps, the graciousness and dignity of its buildings its best adornment'. Three thousand guests were invited to the party although only 100 were privileged to enter the inner sanctum of the deanery garden. Two-thirds of these were men, and of those, only half a dozen were not in academic dress so, said *The Times* special correspondent, 'the blaze of scarlet and crimson of the Doctors' robes amid the setting of the greenery and old grey walls made a gorgeous spectacle'. The Queen wore blue, 'somewhere between hydrangea and hyacinth'. His Majesty 'looked rather old but pleasant', said Charles Murray, watching the visit from the Junior Common Room.[33] The less privileged guests were served tea in the cathedral garden, through which the royal party walked for Founder's Prayers, to the accompaniment of the band of the Coldstream Guards stationed in the south transept gallery, and of Dr Ley, improvising on the organ.[34]

* * * * *

Coming up to Christ Church in the 1920s and 1930s was as mixed an experience as it had always been. The staircases were, as ever, populated by a diverse group of men from the wealthy on the grand first floor, down through the social ranks the further up the stairs one went. Henry Smith, later a Civil Service economist, arrived as an extra-mural scholarship boy from industrial Portsmouth, and was given rooms in the attic of Peckwater Quad where he ate his breakfast and lunch, saving every spare penny of his scholarship money to send home to his mother. Lunch was according to one's pocket: either bread and cheese or a five-course meal with wine, served by one's scout.[35] Charles Murray, arriving as a graduate student from

Australia in 1924, found the place wonderful. Having a scout was extraordinary, but a delight. Murray assimilated rapidly, buying a bicycle, some loud ties and plus-fours. He found it amusing that the college baths did not open until a few days after term had begun, and that he had to descend to a 'subterranean region' and join a queue. His tutors tore his essays to pieces, which pleased him, as he felt he would have learnt something by the time he left Oxford. And he was conscious of the difference between the young men in Oxford and their contemporaries back in Melbourne:

> I am more and more impressed at the polish and easy manner and general savoir faire of these undergraduates. Often they become most amazingly childish but even then in a quite distinctive way. They are much more men of the world, with an air of assurance than our Melbourne people. Home and school training no doubt combine to produce it. They take the deference of servants etc. quite for granted. Yet in other ways they are most democratic. Youthful earls and lords are on exactly the same footing as others, except for the quite substantial advantages that larger purses bring, in the way of standard of living.[36]

Murray's Christ Church was apparently the same as Thomas Strong's.

Politics were ever to the fore between the wars, and the Union, the training-ground for many future public figures, was frequently presided over by men from Christ Church. Only Balliol had more Union officials between 1919 and 1939.[37] Nascent politicians were making their mark: Quintin Hogg had been President in 1929, and Philip Toynbee, in 1937, became Christ Church's fourth President in three years.[38] There were more Christ Church men in the House of Commons – 37 after the 1931 general election, which saw a Conservative landslide victory – equalling Trinity College, Cambridge, much to the satisfaction of the writer of the Annual Report. But the 1930s saw the growth of radical views across Europe and although within the walls of Christ Church things may have appeared to be much as they were in the 1920s, it was evident from early on that change was afoot.

When the General Strike broke out in 1926, many men went to help break it. Volunteers from the University were enrolled for emergency service in their own colleges, but it was expected that undergraduates should help out either at home or in other areas rather than work in Oxford. Examinations were postponed for a week, and 200 undergraduates from Christ Church, and senior members too, such as John Masterman, Gilbert Ryle and R. H. Dundas, worked in all trades, some as stevedores in the docks, others on the railways. The dean was overcome: 'I was proud of Christ Church last year, when all England came to honour us at our Quatercentenary Celebration; but I am still more proud of her now that she has proved herself not unworthy of the high honour shewn to her then.'[39] Although typically conservative, both with a lower-case and upper-case 'C', the college did have staunch Labour supporters within its ranks.[40] During the strike, men with left-wing leanings offered their aid to the TUC or picketed. Tom Driberg went to the Communist Party and was given the task of distributing leaflets. He was soon arrested, and found himself questioned first at Bow Street and then at Scotland Yard.[41] Henry Smith was a member of the University Labour Club and published a socialist magazine, *Plan*, from 1930 to 1932, during his time as an undergraduate, arguing that the fall of the Labour government in 1931 had been caused by lack of planning and that the party needed to be organised and prepared.[42] The Labour Club had a social arm nicknamed the Pink Lunch – Christ Church members included Frank Pakenham, Roy Harrod and Patrick Gordon Walker. Frugal lunches were taken in various Common Rooms or cheap restaurants while a member or a visiting politician spoke briefly before discussion and debate.[43] At almost the same time, Frank Hardie presided at the Union when the motion was proposed that 'This house will not fight for King and Country'. The debate, won handsomely by the pacifists, was widely reported, largely by critics who were horrified by the lack of patriotism shown by the country's young men. In some quarters the debate was said to have precipitated the Second World War.[44]

One of the first signs in Oxford that all was not well in Europe was the arrival of refugee scholars from the continent. In 1931, Albert Einstein, perhaps the most famous figure to enter the House, arrived as the first of a group of such academics, many of whom were helped by Frederick

Albert Einstein was offered a Research Studentship in 1931. He divided his time between Oxford and America until 1935, when he departed for the greater safety of Princeton. Einstein asked that the stipend he received from the Governing Body be used to help other scholars whose position in Germany had become perilous.

Lindemann. Lindemann, later Lord Cherwell, was concerned for the safety of prominent scholars, particularly those of Jewish extraction, and became famous for driving his Rolls around Europe to rescue these men and bring them to a relatively safe exile in England.[45] Einstein was given a research Studentship and stayed officially for just two years before leaving England for Princeton, still concerned about the Nazi threat. His appointment at Christ Church was not universally approved; in a time of economic crisis, some thought that giving emoluments to a non-British subject was wrong.[46] But the dean stood firm, expressing his opinion that securing for Christ Church one of the greatest scientists of the age was something of which to be proud.

When Einstein left for the States, he asked that his stipend of £400 be used to help other refugee scholars.[47] Lindemann worked to ensure that the funds were used to assist mainly German physicists, but also academics such as Eduard Fraenkel, the classicist, who came to Christ Church for a short time before his election to a professorship at Corpus Christi. Paul

Jacobstahl had been professor of archaeology at Marburg University until 1935, when he was dismissed as a consequence of Nazi policy against non-Aryans. Jacobstahl was granted leave of absence from Germany in 1937 to work in Oxford just for Trinity term 1937, but he never went home. The correspondence in his file shows frequent extensions to his contract, and on 2 January 1939 the Home Office lifted any limit on Jacobstahl's residence in the United Kingdom. When war broke out he was arrested and interned on the Isle of Man for a year until feelings mellowed against foreign exiles.[48] Jacobstahl's presence in Oxford promoted and inspired the study of European Celtic archaeology.[49] Felix Jacoby, whose specialism was ancient historiography, arrived in England just before the outbreak of war in 1939. In the opposite direction, men from Oxford, recognising the fascist threat, went to fight in Spain, that ghastly prelude to the Second World War. Lewis Clive, who had been a rowing blue and Olympic medallist in 1932, was killed in action in 1938.

Science at Christ Church between the wars was led by Lindemann, who gave twice-weekly lectures to undergraduates, and Collie, who gave lectures both in the university's Clarendon Laboratory and at Christ Church. But the laboratory assistant was in the RAMC Territorials, and went off to war in 1939, and the Christ Church laboratory closed its doors for the last time in 1940. The equipment was sold off or redistributed among the university laboratories, and Alexander Russell, Dr Lee's Reader, ceased to be involved in much practical work thereafter.[50]

There were other changes, not large, but changes which reflected the mood of the time. The appointment of deans was always difficult because of the dual nature of Christ Church. With the reform of Christ Church's constitution and the general move away from clericalism in the university, it became harder still. The dean had to be both a head of house, with all the necessary administrative skills, political acumen and academic credentials, and a clergyman in charge of a cathedral. When Dean White died in 1934, Stanley Baldwin avoided the arguments that had raged between Lloyd George and Birkenhead over White's appointment by writing to the Students, using T. B. Strong as his intermediary, asking them to meet immediately after

> ## Alwyn Terrell Petre Williams (1888–1968)
>
> A. T. P. Williams, a Lancashire man, was a graduate of Jesus College, and a fellow of All Souls between 1911 and 1918.
>
> He was appointed as second master at Winchester College in 1916, bringing a new status to history and modern languages as academic subjects. He had been headmaster of Winchester for ten years before Baldwin recommended him as the new dean of Christ Church. Masterman described him as a man of 'outstanding intellectual gifts, a fine voice, and a splendid and virile appearance'. He was accessible to everyone, and particularly supportive of the boat crews. Williams was said to be an authority on P. G. Wodehouse's character, Jeeves.
>
> Williams was only at Christ Church for five years, before he was appointed to the bishopric of Durham
>
> Masterman (1975), 180; *ODNB*; Hopkins (1975), 47

the funeral to discuss whom they would like as the new dean. Only three names were seriously discussed: Williams, the head of Winchester School, Cyril Alington, once head of Eton and recently appointed Dean of Durham, and Holmes Dudden, the master of Pembroke College. The Student body, in secret session, came down firmly in favour of Williams, and Baldwin accordingly put his name forward to the Crown.[51]

Just after Dean Williams was installed in 1934 – a man who was remembered later as 'flawlessly efficient' – a new House flag was flown for the first time, and a Royal Standard (not of the present monarch, but of Henry VIII) was acquired for state occasions and celebrations. A college register was begun, a means of keeping up with old members. Caution money, that age-old insurance against undergraduate indiscipline, was abolished, and a new college service was instigated on Sunday mornings. Whether or not because of the worsening political situation, there seemed to be a need to establish a sense of community. One real link with the past was severed in 1937 when William Francis, the dean's verger, died. He had begun work as Dean Liddell's footman in 1859, becoming a verger in 1867 until his

> ## John Lowe (1899 – 1960)
>
> John Lowe had come up to Christ Church as a Canadian Rhodes Scholar in 1922. He took firsts in Literae Humaniores and in Theology, and also rowed and ran for the college.
>
> Before his appointment as dean, which was suggested by Gilbert Ryle, the philosopher, Lowe was professor of New Testament studies at the University of Toronto. He took up his new post in 1939. He responded diligently to the immediate problem of war that coloured the first six years of his 20-year term in office.
>
> In 1948, Dean Lowe was appointed vice-chancellor of the University. Pressure of work possibly caused him to suffer a severe stroke whilst on a tour of universities in the Indian sub-continent.
>
> One of the most famous incidents of Lowe's deanery was his trip, in 1950, to Torquay from the Meadow, in that most novel of transports, a helicopter, prompting verse naming the dean a new Ganymede.
>
> Masterman (1975), 180; *Christ Church, 1938–9 and 1950*

retirement in 1934. But as Francis was buried, and a memorial plaque erected in the cloister to commemorate his long and faithful service, so the Steward was giving demonstrations on the handling of incendiary bombs with long-handled shovels.

Dean Williams resigned in 1938 when he was appointed to the bishopric of Durham. His successor, John Lowe, had a major challenge before him. According to the editor of the Annual Report, Lowe 'faced this sea of unwonted and unexpected tasks with notable sang-froid.'[52]

It was not just the prospect of war that occupied Lowe and the Governing Body: discussions were under way on the separation of college and cathedral, a topic that had been raised but soon discarded in the 1860s. Two months after Dean Williams's appointment to Durham was announced, but before he left Oxford, a committee was set up to consider whether, in the interests of Christ Church, particularly of its educational side, laymen should be eligible for the headship and, if so, what steps would be necessary to effect the change. The Committee on the Headship of Christ Church – the sub-dean, Henry Goudge, and Leonard Hodgson for the Chapter, and the Senior Censor (Michael Foster), Gilbert Ryle, Roy Harrod, J. N. L. Myres, Samuel Grant Bailey and Colin Dillwyn for the Students – issued a report in May 1939 to the Governing Body which outlined why some members felt the constitution as it then stood was unsatisfactory and gave the two main methods by which a change could be made.[53] The principal reason for suggesting that it might be wise to allow a layman to hold the deanery was the decline in the number of available and qualified clerical men. According to Ryle's statistics – which some members of the committee, particularly Canon Hodgson, felt were wrong or, at least gave the wrong impression – in 1939, only four heads of house (about a fifth of the total) were in holy orders, whereas over half had been clerics in 1900, and the number of clerics holding first-class degrees in non-theological subjects had plummeted.

Two possible means of effecting the change were explained. The first was the 'presidential scheme': this would retain the dean as titular head of house and actual head of Chapter but have a president as second-in-command who would run the educational establishment. The president, or whatever title was chosen, could be a layman. Issues such as the president's control over finances and general policy would still need to be resolved. If he were given these, then he would be made effective head of house. Further suggestions were made about the possible division of labour, and it was pointed out that the statutes as they then stood actually gave the Governing Body powers to create a presidential role should they choose to do so. The scheme would not require an Act of Parliament, and would be relatively quick to implement.

The second proposal was the 'clean cut' which would create two entirely separate bodies; a cathedral Chapter and a college. The dean would then be head of the Chapter only, with a master of the college who could be a layman. The cathedral would be granted a capital sum administered by the Ecclesiastical Commissioners, and the buildings could be reordered so that the canons' lodgings would be closest to the cathedral. There was no intention to push the cathedral out altogether and it was evidently anticipated that the church would continue to act as both diocesan cathedral and college chapel. This proposal would require the approval of Parliament, the Church Assembly and the University, and would probably require a Royal Commission to hammer out the details. As such, it would be a much longer and much more complex process. The report laid down the probable legal process that would be required to bring the 'clean cut' to fruition. Not least among the proposals was the renaming of the college; if the cathedral was to retain the name 'Christ Church' as seemed logical, then it was suggested that the college be renamed 'King's College'.

The report was given to the Governing Body, with a note that Foster, Myres and Grant Bailey had all requested that the recommendation 'that no action be taken' be added. There was a vote at which nine members voted for separation, but nineteen preferred to maintain the status quo.[54]

The outbreak of war brought the debate to a necessary close, however, and Lowe took on the task of preparing the college for yet more hostilities. The editor of the Annual Report noted that the dean had 'rallied and directed the staff with prompt alacrity'. Air-raid precautions were established, and Christ Church's sandbag barricades were said to be the 'most scientifically constructed in Oxford'. Ninety students from Brasenose College took over Meadows Building when their premises were requisitioned as a hospital, and 25 men from Pembroke College were lodged in the Old Library and in Tom Quad. During 1938, Tom continued to strike, although the 101 was stopped. The pictures from the Hall were stored in the Senior Common Room cellar and under Killcanon, and pictures, manuscripts, incunabula and particularly valuable early printed books from the Library were moved down to the basement of Peck 9.[55] Renaissance drawings, still in the Library at this time, were sent to the Ashmolean for safe-keeping, and the coin collections followed on permanent loan.[56] Photographs of the Library interior were taken 'just in case'. Black-out blinds were hung in the Hall, and fire-watching duties shared between junior and senior members. Iron railings from the front of college, Meadow Gate and around the Library were removed as part of the war effort.

Christ Church also acted as a halfway house for refugees from more

Many Christ Church men served during the wars in many different capacities. Hugh Trevor-Roper was one of several employed by the intelligence services. Others were on more traditional active duties.

dangerous areas of the country. The wives of Students received children from Kent on their way to billets, and refugees from the blitz in Bristol, making sure they were fed and thoroughly bathed.[57] The sub-dean tried to ensure their spiritual welfare, too, baptising them all before they carried on their journeys. Besides the refugees and students from other colleges were cadets from the Royal Air Force who were fully matriculated undergraduates but had their own classes – 22 were on the freshers' list in 1941, and there were summer schools for visiting soldiers. Ordinary undergraduates could defer their service provided that they joined the Officer Training Corps with all that entailed. There were staffing problems right from the start. Many men had been called up, and women were helping the remaining older scouts before the end of 1939.[58] Those staff who did remain were given allotments carved out of the old rugby pitch, with eggs and vegetables being supplied from the college's farm at Cassington.

Away from home, Christ Church men were serving in all manner of ways, not just in the regular forces. Of the squad that won the 1938/9 Intercollegiate football cup, two men were in the Royal Naval Volunteer Reserves, one began the war in the Coldstream Guards but ended up in the Ministry of Production, and another served as a member of the Admiralty Computing Service founded in 1943. One was killed on active service in Italy. Other members were involved in intelligence, particularly cryptography and radio interception, often recruited by Dick White, the only man to have been head of both MI5 and MI6; men such as Gilbert Ryle and Hugh Trevor-Roper (who worked in the Radio Security Service), later joined by Denys Page and Charles Stuart.[59] Trevor-Roper continued in service in the months immediately after the war, researching the truth behind the death of Hitler.[60] John Croft and Edward Boyle worked at Bletchley Park with Keith and Mavis Batey, and Maurice Wiles. Masterman was recruited as secretary of the Twenty Committee, running double-agents and the 'Double-Cross system'. Michael Howard was invited to join the RAF to play the oboe in its orchestra until his tutor, Keith Feiling, suggested that it would might not be an easy thing to confess to after the war.[61] Several Christ Church scientists – men such as A. H. Cooke, C. H. Collie and Martin Ryle – were researching in new fields such as radioactivity, radar, rockets and nuclear power. Michael Grace worked on acoustic underwater mines before following a career in nuclear physics.[62]

Another Christ Church man, George Bell, took an opposing stance to some of his House colleagues. Bell had come up to Christ Church in 1901 and went on to a career in the church. During the war he was Bishop of Chichester, and stood firm in his defence of the German church and against the blanket bombing of German cities. He tried hard to convince the nation that not all Germans were Nazis, a fact that was difficult for the ordinary people of Britain to accept when they suffered nightly bombing. Bell appealed in the House of Lords, facing other Housemen whose opinions were diametrically opposed to his – men such as Charles Portal, the Air Chief of Staff, Frederick Lindemann and Lord Cecil. Anthony Eden, then foreign secretary and also a Christ Church man, called Bell a 'pestilent priest' – a reference, no doubt, to another troublesome bishop about whom Bell had encouraged T. S. Eliot to write.[63]

As in 1919, many of the new arrivals in 1946 were servicemen on shortened courses, often several years older than the ordinary freshers, and sometimes married with children. The 'last war wanderer', Denys Page, whose service had been with the Foreign Office, returned in 1946 from south-east Asia. A commemoration service was held in March of that year, and the other side of the cathedral 'tunnel', opposite the memorial to those who died in the First War, was soon inscribed with the names of those Christ Church men who had died serving their country.

But generally, normality resumed quite quickly. The 'treasures' were returned from their safe-houses, and rumours that the Orrery scientific instruments had been buried were eventually proved to be unfounded when they were discovered, in 1948, in the basement of the Old Ashmolean museum.[64] The beagles returned in 1946, only to suffer a problem with distemper in the pack in 1949. The Nondescripts, Loder's (with Ludovic Kennedy as their president) and the Twenty Club began again within the year. In spite of rationing, celebrations for the quatercentenary of Christ Church offered an opportunity for rejoicing. There was a royal visit on 24 October, a dinner in Hall, and W. G. Hiscock published his *Christ Church Miscellany*.[65] On foundation day itself, a production of *Henry VIII* was staged in the Hall.[66]

Rationing, which seemed even more severe than in the previous six years, was no help in the freezing winter immediately following the war. In March, gales and flooding caused the loss of many trees on the Meadow. Coal was strictly limited, and men huddled together, keeping one room properly warm instead of several rooms poorly so. Everything froze, and layers of clothes were needed even in bed. A meagre diet was eked out with food parcels sent for the wealthier men whose families had large estates.[67] Not until 1954 was meat rationing lifted, prompting the roasting of a huge 230lb baron of Hereford beef before one of the great fireplaces in the kitchen.

* * * * *

It was not long before academic relations with Germany were restored. In 1948, Dr Wolfgang Schmidt, classicist and philologist, arrived as a visiting scholar from Cologne via the British Council, and the German Academic Exchange Service (DAAD) was re-established in 1952. Michael Foster, philosophy tutor, had worked hard on 'rehabilitating the young men of Germany' and, after his death, a scholarship scheme was devised to bring German undergraduates to Oxford for two years.[68]

New ideas were introduced, too: the status of Student Emeritus was introduced as a token of thanks for long service to Christ Church; the first Christ Church/Trinity College servants' lunch took place in 1948; the Boat Club opened an appeal for new boats; and the Christ Church United Clubs were relaunched, modernising the old Poplar Mission for a new generation. Some of the buildings were altered, although it was some years before a major project was proposed; in the three years following the end of hostilities, the undergraduate refectory was established in the basement of the old Anatomy School, the Law Library was refurbished, and the old laboratory altered to act as a Picture Gallery and exhibition and display area for the manuscripts, printed books and ephemera of the Evelyn Collection.[69] In 1950, the first old members' address list was printed alongside the first college history for half a century, written by Hugh Trevor-Roper, which was to be sold to visitors for 2s 6d.[70]

Sport was quickly revived after the war. Blues proliferated in athletics, rugby, cricket and rowing; less serious clubs such as the cricketing Nondescripts and Warrigals, and the rugger-playing Runcibles, played local teams from colleges and villages. Fashionable sports, such as skiing, found their way into the annual reports when Christ Church men took first and second places in the inter-college slalom at Sestrière in 1953. Prowess in fencing and golf were celebrated, even if results in the more traditional sports were more sought-after than achieved during the 1950s. The famous 'hole-in-one' from outside Peck 4 into Mercury over the top of the Library and the Fell Tower was made in 1951 by P. F. Gardiner-Hill, then captain of the University golf team, an achievement encouraged by the Senior Censor, Eric Gray, and 'Hooky' Hill, the steward. In the same year, two members of the Wagers Club – T. W. Beaumont and R. G. Cooke – walked to London in sixteen and a half hours, sustained by sandwiches, brandy and champagne. Members

'Half arsenal, half hotel': twentieth-century Christ Church

The Christ Church Private Fire Brigade, winners of the Herbert Morrell Cup in 1948. The Steward, D. V. 'Hooky' Hill is seated front left and Mr Borrett, the Head Porter, at the other end of the row.

of Christ Church represented the University in athletics, Eton fives, lacrosse, squash, boxing, chess, polo, judo and rifle-shooting. The Boat Club appeal was successful; by 1951, the club had acquired a new first VIII, a light IV and a clinker VIII.[71] More obscurely, the House Private Fire Brigade, set up to protect the college buildings during the war, won the Herbert Morrell Cup in the annual Oxford and District Fire Brigades Competition.

The Dramatic Society was at its height during the 1950s, going on tour in Germany for several years in succession, taking productions of *Murder in the Cathedral*, *The Firstborn*, and *A Midsummer Night's Dream* around several cities including Bonn, Heidelberg and Freiburg.[72] At home, plays were performed in the cloister, the Hall, and in other venues around Oxford.

Modernisation was the watchword during the 1950s. Numbers were high, around 500 in total, and new facilities – not least extra bathrooms – became essential. In 1957, fifteen rooms in the Castle Hotel needed to be taken for freshers, and plans for a new quadrangle began to take shape. By 1958, all rooms in Peckwater and Canterbury Quads had basins with both hot and cold water where 'hitherto, running water has come only through the roof', and Meadows Building was fitted out in the following year. Self-service lunch – soup, sausages and pies – was introduced in the Junior Common Room, and two original gifts made by W. H. Auden: a fridge for the Senior Common Room (not least so that his Martinis could be served at the correct temperature) and a sound system for the Hall. Restoration of the Library and cathedral was begun, and the Science Reading Room established in response to the introduction of new schools in engineering and biochemistry which were added to the established sciences of chemistry and physics.[73]

But that decade was probably the last of 'old' Christ Church. Dean Lowe retired in 1959 and died in 1960. He was followed by R. H. Dundas and F. A. Taylor, both stalwarts of the one-to-one tutorial style of teaching established in Oxford from the late nineteenth century, and which became a hallmark of the University and colleges. In the pre-First World War period, Apsley Cherry-Garrard found the experience less than stimulating; most Oxford dons, he said, were 'content to live like gentlemen, passing to the younger generation the knowledge that had been amassed by others'.[74] But others found it inspirational or terrifying. E. R. Dodds recalled that his tutor, A. B. Poynton, treated the tutorial as a form of intercollegiate competition and was determined that his 'stable should do the College the maximum of credit'. Weekly essays were supplemented with extra sessions in the evenings to polish unseen translation skills.[75] A. J. 'Freddy' Ayer likewise found the tutorial an encouragement to individual study. Obviously, tutors varied in their abilities, but most, he said, were conscientious. Ayer was taught by Michael Foster, Robert Dundas and Robert Longden, but the tutor whom he most respected was Gilbert Ryle.[76] In the 1930s, Henry Smith, who had come up as a mature student from a less than privileged background, also considered himself extremely fortunate in having Gilbert Ryle as his tutor, together with Roy Harrod. He felt that tutorials were designed to make one think for oneself, the tutor being there to 'rectify misconceptions, suggest alternative interpretations, select books within the reader's capacity as it becomes apparent ...'[77]

Dundas had seen the tutorial as the most crucial part of his activities at Christ Church, and tried to meet with every undergraduate, partly to teach them the facts of life – a habit which some found amusing, while to others it was extraordinarily embarrassing.[78] Unlike Cherry-Garrard's tutors, Dundas made every effort to keep up-to-date, and pass on the newest ideas to his pupils.[79] Keith Feiling, colleague of Dundas, was praised by Hugh Trevor-Roper for his use of the tutorial by which, 'thanks to that dialectical exercise, undergraduates are weaned from the dogmatism of received opinions and led forward to think for themselves'. It was through the tutorials of Feiling and Masterman that Christ Church obtained more first-class degrees in history than any other college.[80]

After the resignation of John Lowe in 1959, his place was taken by Canon Cuthbert Simpson, another Canadian and erstwhile Rhodes Scholar, who held the deanery for ten years, dying suddenly, aged 77, in June 1969. His was a building deanery, much in the mould of John Fell or Henry Liddell, overseeing the construction of Blue Boar Quad and picture gallery, the restoration of the Library, both inside and out, and of the cathedral. Masterman said that he was the 'best loved of all deans', and the first choice of the whole of college.[81] Renowned for the strength of his Martinis, he was a hospitable dean, his doors being open to both undergraduates and senior members. But in administration he was probably more of a cathedral than a college dean, keen to promote the cathedral in the diocese, concerned with the dignity and beauty of cathedral services, and with the improvement of the choir school.[82]

It was under Simpson that dramatic changes were to take place in the university and in the college. The decade saw University-wide changes. Of course, it was the era of student riot and rebellion, particularly in Paris in 1968, but that year passed without the mention of any significant disturbance at Christ Church, or in Oxford at large. Even the petition from the Junior Common Room against the alteration of the appearance of Tom

Quad, the only apparent rebellion against the Governing Body for a century, was reported in the *Evening Standard* on 6 June to highlight just how quaint the English could be when students elsewhere were engaged in political unrest and violence.[83] Consultation between junior and senior members of college was formalised with the creation in 1974 of a committee on which representatives of both sat, and the presidents of the Junior Common Room and the newly established Graduate Common Room have long been invited to meetings of Governing Body committees.[84]

But there were issues in the 1960s, following the Hardie and Harrison reports into various University matters, which caused much debate and discussion, notably admissions policy. The ever-increasing numbers of undergraduates meant that many members had to live out, in digs. This prompted a building programme in many colleges to bring students back within the walls and to revive community life; at Christ Church, the new Blue Boar Quadrangle was the result. Entrance to the university was to become, or be proven to be, by academic merit alone. Merely being the son of an old member or good at sport were insufficient qualifications.[85] Scholarship and entrance examinations became almost the same thing. But a pure meritocracy was not seen by everyone as a good idea: Steven Watson, a Christ Church Student since the war, felt that wider considerations should be taken into account, not least a candidate's future responsibilities, as well as the feelings of 'loyal old members'. Increasingly, it was subject tutors who selected their pupils. Oxford, with Cambridge, joined UCCA in 1964, while still retaining their own entrance examinations. But if academic achievement was the most important result of an undergraduate career, then Christ Church was slipping. From the 1940s to the 1960s, it plummeted in the league table. The colleges that were achieving the best results were those that drew from both public and grammar schools, and Christ Church was top-heavy with boys from independent schools.[86] Every year, in the Annual Report, the editor listed the schools that were represented most in the Tutors' Book. From 1949 to 1970, between 20 per cent and 30 per cent of all members *in statu pupillari* were from a very limited selection of schools, predominantly Eton, Westminster, Charterhouse, Ampleforth, Harrow, Winchester and Portsmouth Grammar School.[87]

The editor of the Annual Report declared that: 'We have been much too easily satisfied with what we were about to receive annually in the past, letting people who have heard of us come to us instead of seeking systematically, as some colleges in both universities have done, for new contacts in schools everywhere.'[88] Something needed to be done, particularly to foster links with schools that were less well represented in Christ Church's matriculation lists. Schoolmaster Studentships were established in 1964, with the first arriving in Michaelmas term 1965. The Studentships were designed to give schoolteachers a chance to spend a term in college, reading and researching topics of their own interest, and assisted Christ Church in developing closer contacts with their schools. The same year, a Tutor for Admissions was appointed, the first being Dr Paul Kent – whose efforts to reach out had already been demonstrated with the foundation of the Graduate Common Room – with the responsibility of 'making, maintaining and extending contacts with schools of every kind throughout the country'.[89]

It was soon after Simpson's arrival that the idea of a Graduate Common Room was put forward. Under the old constitution, graduate Students were part and parcel of the fabric of the House. Working towards a higher degree was expected, up to a point, especially if one wanted to gain the extra emoluments of a tutor. After 1867, however, when the stipendiary Students were all graduates and increasingly were all tutors, the postgraduate as we know them today almost disappeared. Between the wars only 10 per cent of students were postgraduate even though the DPhil had been introduced in 1917.[90] Some graduates took a second BA in a different subject from their first, and much postgraduate research was done by lecturers, but this last become increasingly difficult as lecturers began to be used to ease the cost of tutorial posts.[91] After the Second World War, numbers rose, so that postgraduates made up 23 per cent of the student body by the mid-1960s, but they were left very much to their own devices, almost abandoned by both university and their colleges.[92] Many of them lived out, so there was no contact even with scouts or with other students.[93] Even basic information, such as which railway station in London one had to use to get to Oxford, was not provided, partly through benign thoughtlessness but partly because it was thought that someone coming to Oxford to follow postgraduate study ought to be able to work this out for themselves. In 1960, however, a group of tutors got together to try to make things easier for graduate students, particularly those coming from abroad. Graduate students were seen as a different breed from undergraduates, needing contact not just with other students but with senior members, too. Christ Church was among the first colleges to establish, or re-establish, a Graduate Common Room and to appoint one of its senior members as Tutor for Graduates who would be responsible for graduate admissions, and serve as a contact point that had been lacking before.[94]

It was Simpson's successor, Henry Chadwick, however, who struggled with the biggest change in the constitution of Christ Church: the arrival of women. Christ Church had always had more women than any other college. In most, until the later part of the nineteenth century, only the head of house had been permitted to marry. At Christ Church, though, the canons, too, had families. As a consequence, from the earliest days there had been mothers and daughters in numbers unknown elsewhere. But women as students were still a relative novelty, the five women's colleges having only been founded in the late nineteenth century. Vernon Harcourt, Dr Lee's reader, was one of the first tutors to allow women undergraduates, well chaperoned, to attend his lectures. Contact between male and female undergraduates was strictly controlled until very recently, and most men, at least until the end of the Second World War, had little opportunity to meet women.

During the 1950s, there had been discussions about redressing the balance between the number of women and the number of men at Oxford. It was jested that 'Christ Church would have the easiest case. It would point out that it was a Cathedral as well as a College, a Chapter as well as a Governing Body. You couldn't, I imagine, even a hundred years hence, have a woman Dean of a cathedral?'[95] Talk of mixed colleges began in the 1960s. Christ Church's Junior Common Room had voted in June 1964 to ask the Senior Common Room to discuss the possibilities of going co-ed, and New College proposed it seriously in 1965.[96] The principal concern, University-wide, was the future of the women's colleges, both for their endowment and for academic standards, but pressure was increasing, not least because

> ## Henry Chadwick (1920–2008)
>
> Henry Chadwick was a Cambridge man, only the third such to become dean up to that date, and the first for 400 years. But he had been regius professor of divinity for a decade before his appointment to the deanery so he was well-known and a popular choice. According to Masterman, he was 'head and shoulders above all others who could have been appointed'. But, much loved as he was, Dean Chadwick found decision-making difficult, which made meetings hard for both him and the Governing Body.
>
> He resigned in 1979, coming out of retirement some years later to follow another Christ Church man, Hugh Trevor-Roper, to the mastership of Peterhouse.
>
> Masterman (1975), 181

schools were increasingly mixed as the comprehensive system took hold. The Annual Reports document the progress of the debate within these walls. In 1965, the editor commented that all the arguments in favour of mixed colleges had impressed few, and that there were better methods of levelling up the ratio of women to men. All sorts of arguments against the admission of women were put forward: the potential damage to the women's colleges, the worries that there would not be sufficient women of the right calibre, or that women would be shared too sparingly between the colleges. Even practicalities such as the provision of sufficient toilets and bathrooms was raised as a problem.

In 1972 it was agreed that five colleges would try a five-year experiment to admit women, of which, in spite of an announcement in *The Times*, Christ Church was not one. But, before the review period was over, the Sex Discrimination Act had been passed. All evidence suggested that the women's colleges would not be damaged significantly and several were already considering going mixed themselves. The vote to allow co-education was close in Congregation, but the men's colleges were quick to open their doors, in spite of requests for the changes to be made slowly across the University.[97] 'The

University decided not to regulate any such progression and then certain colleges refused to be bound by any ordered programme evolved by agreement.'

At the beginning of 1979 only three of the men's colleges remained single-sex: Merton, Oriel and Christ Church.[98] A vote was taken to amend the statute on 25 May 1977 to open senior membership to both men and women, but any further changes would require a two-thirds majority vote. A female research lecturer, Dr Penelope Challoner, was admitted in 1978 when the Governing Body voted to allow academic posts to be offered to women, but it was not until Michaelmas term 1980 that women were admitted as undergraduates, and the first female Student, Judith Pallot, was elected.[99] The motion to admit female junior members was passed, and 'the House thus resisted the temptation to remain untypical and gained a new lease of life, or lapsed into "modish idiocy", according to one's point of view'.[100] There are suggestions that the environment began to change immediately. One of the young men who were at Christ Church in 1980 recalled that 'overnight the sofas stopped falling, and the puking at least became more discreet ... Christ Church [was] belatedly made safe for Beauty, Culture, and Modernity'.[101]

Henry Chadwick resigned the deanery just before women arrived, and the practicalities of their admission were managed by Dean Eric Heaton, another Cambridge graduate. According to his contemporaries, Heaton was a good businessman, and an excellent chairman.[102] Senior clergymen throughout Christ Church's history have tended to be men of influence in the political world, often with landed estates of their own and experience of managing business, as well as being academics and churchmen.

The year 1969 also saw the revival of discussions over a split between college and cathedral. Hugh Trevor-Roper, in private correspondence, recalled the debates of three decades before, and thought that the 'cost (financial, administrative, and in social disruption) of an Act of Separation' should be avoided. But he did make suggestions; the only possible moment of secularisation, he felt, would be during a period of extended vacancy when there was no possible clerical candidate for the deanery. This would allow the appointment of a layman which, he maintained, was perfectly legal. The only other way would be to isolate an impossible dean to the point at which his position became untenable, which would be singularly unpleasant, at the very least.[103] Secularisation would require the radicals who wished for it to be more radical than they would probably wish. The status quo was likely to remain the most acceptable as long as there was any possible candidate for the deanery.

In the later twentieth century, this combination of clergyman, academic and administrator has become far less common, and the character and interests of the deans often reveal them to be either a 'college' dean or a 'cathedral' dean. Dean White was thought to be a 'cathedral' dean, leaving the administration of the collegiate side of Christ Church life to its officers. Henry Chadwick struggled with decision-making but was a scholar second to none and, it is said, after his departure, that links between the college and the cathedral were weakened. Deans Williams and Simpson, on the other hand, involved themselves zealously on both sides, whereas deans Lowe and Heaton were, perhaps, more 'college' men.[104] It was Heaton who pushed for the creation of an association for old members, and Lowe was an active supporter of college sporting teams.

Contact with old members has been important throughout Christ Church's history but it is only recently, with threats to the funding of universities and the need to ensure that the college is safely and independently financed, that it has become crucial. Now, the Christ Church, with the whole university, has become dependent on the generosity of its old boys and girls. From the maintenance of an address list by the Steward's Office, largely to ensure that no one was missed off the invitation list to gaudies, and then for appeals for the funding of Blue Boar Quad and St Aldates Quad, the Development Office has been one of the significant changes of the later twentieth century. At first, in 1994, this consisted of a part-time Development Officer and a database manager but has increased, within a decade, to its present size of around six or seven staff.

Other departments have been created or have grown significantly. No longer can the administration of Christ Church be managed by a college secretary and an accountant. Since the 1960s, office staff have grown to include tutorial and censorial administrators, a Steward's Office of around ten (including the conference administrators), and a Treasury staff of seven or eight. Only the Library, in spite of its ever-increasing significance for undergraduates from the 1960s, manages with fewer staff than it had in the eighteenth century.

Christ Church has changed in other ways, too. Tourism and the conference business, like the Development Office, are very modern developments which have become vital. Christ Church has always had to be open to the public as its chapel is the diocesan cathedral and, as such, a church to which anyone may come. But it has always been on the 'heritage trail' too. Guests visited the Library from its opening and their presence was resented, at least by Vere Bayne in the later nineteenth century, who reminded Governing Body that it was meant to be a place of study, not a showcase. The huge dining hall with its collection of portraits is frequently pictured with parties of visitors, and Tom Tower still has on its wall the instructions and costs for visitors wishing to toll Great Tom. In 1881, the Governing Body decreed that notices should be placed at the entrance to all three attractions with the admission charges. To visit the Hall cost 2d per person, and the same again to see Great Tom. Tolling the bell was only permitted between the hours of 2 and 5 in the afternoon, when the Library was open, and men could escape from the noise if they wished to study. To visit the Library cost 3d per person for groups of up to four people, and 2d per person for every additional visitor in a group. Special rates could be negotiated for large parties and school visits.[105] It was only in the later twentieth century, however, that the management of tourists became a problem. Between 1 April and 31 May 1976, 16,000 tourists paid to visit the Hall, all coming in through Tom Gate. Only groups of more than ten were expected to pay for admittance, and guides were getting clever, sending their parties in small groups to reassemble inside. The following year, the kiosk at Meadows Gate was installed, and all visitors came in that way, paying 30p each. Custodial staff were employed to make sure that a strict route was followed, their wages coming out of the revenue generated.[106] Now, around 250,000 paying visitors come each year.

The conference trade, during the vacations, has become an essential means of balancing the books. This, too, has historic precedent. Dinners were held in Hall for visiting groups of businessmen and academics from the late nineteenth century. The Headmasters' Conference, for example, was entertained there in 1899, but after the Second World War, business began to flourish.

Many of the changes have been prompted from outside Christ Church's walls. Government influence has increased considerably. University Commissions have always caused occasional hiccups in college life, at least since Laud's reforms in the seventeenth century. The nineteenth century prompted changes University-wide and within the colleges, changing their complexion permanently. At Christ Church, ecclesiastical commissions also had their impact. Another century on, the Harrison, Hardie and Franks Reports, although principally concerned with the administration of the university, had considerable knock-on effects for all the colleges, not least for Christ Church. A real attempt was made to widen admissions to include quality candidates from the grammar and technical schools that had been expanded and encouraged under the 1944 Education Act, and the attention given to postgraduate students was improved. Colleges with few or no endowments were assisted by contributions from relatively wealthy colleges, of which Christ Church was one.[107]

Governance within Christ Church changed, too. The Franks Report had recommended that all University posts should be attached to fellowships in a college, a policy which, when combined with the creation of new honours schools in a wide variety of subjects, led to much-enlarged Governing Bodies.[108] Meetings which could once have been conducted, board-room style, around a single table became potentially overpopulated and unmanageable. There was a risk that fewer members would attend, and smaller groups, particularly the 'old censor caucus', as it has been described by one emeritus Student, could hold far greater sway over decision-making. Trevor-Roper cautioned against this: some colleges, such as Trinity College in Cambridge, had a college council, rather like a Cabinet, and a similar idea had been advocated by Dean Lowe. But formal government by a smaller body was resisted.

The role of the censors has always been important, however. Not on the Governing Body until 1867, they were still a crucial link between the Students and the Chapter, and are now just as important a link between both the junior and senior members, and the Governing Body. The late twentieth century saw the culmination of centuries of student petitioning for a say in college affairs. The efforts of the Students in the sixteenth and seventeenth centuries to have a greater share in the governance, as well as the profits, of the foundation fell on deaf ears until the middle of the nineteenth century, when reform in both the University and the colleges forced a sea-change in the administration of Christ Church, turning its administration from a small Governing Body of just nine men – whose responsibilities, as well as their rewards, were great – to a much larger, and ever-growing, body of both academic fellows and professional administrators. The inclusion, from the 1970s, of junior members, if not in the decision-making process, then at least at a consultative level, would be seen by their early predecessors as a huge and welcome step forward.

10

'Through all the vicissitudes of English history': Conclusion

To sum up Christ Church and its history is more easily said than done. John Masterman, history tutor, Student, wartime intelligence officer and later Provost of Worcester College, described the essence of Christ Church as 'Freedom and Continuity' with diversity as its keynote. Its size has allowed men to feel part of a community without being pressed into conformity, but its history, perhaps especially its government by custom rather than by statute, has ensured a continuity and stability that has given it security to allow individuality.

The House has had to endure a reputation of being like cream – 'rich, thick, and full of clots' – populated by 'wealthy and prejudiced aristocrats'. When Thomas Strong resigned the deanery in 1920, he commented that, although much of the criticism directed against the university was false, 'we should be open to very damaging comments if we failed in point of learning, if our members wasted their time in frivolous and expensive pursuits'. The Brideshead connection has not helped, but, for all of its existence, Christ Church has catered for a huge diversity of men and women, and encouraged scholars, politicians, financiers, explorers, sportsmen and a whole host of other professionals. Strong's valedictory sermon finished positively: 'I think, however, that we shall be able to put ourselves beyond criticism most easily if that strong corporate feeling which we have happily regained and intensified should find expression in a really strong sense of responsibility for the well-being of the House in all its aspects.'[1] Strong was, of course, speaking to the post-war members of college – that extraordinarily wide-ranging and cosmopolitan body of men who occupied Christ Church in those years; but a list of all the Christ Church members who appear in the *Oxford Dictionary of National Biography* demonstrates the richly varied body of people that Christ Church has always comprised. Hugh Trevor-Roper points out that Christ Church had not produced a saint, but only by accident of history. More important, however, is that the pages of the archive – that corporate memory of the college and cathedral, and the memories of most members – reveal an establishment that is mixed, friendly and successful in all sorts of ways.

To pay for such an education, the governing bodies have had to manage an endowment the income from which only just manages to keep up with costs. Landed estates, which so often seem the property of the privileged, have been mixed blessings over the years, but generally have been a stable source of income. The glorious buildings which Wolsey and his successors built for the college and cathedral to inhabit provoke jealousy beyond the walls, but headaches within, for their maintenance is expensive, and has been shown to be so from the beginning, in spite of the generosity of members and charities. Their design is unsuited to modern educational needs, and adaptation difficult under regulations governing listed buildings. The archives are riddled with accounts of changes to buildings, battles with those who would rather there was no change or with those who want more, and the endless balancing act between income and expenditure.

As in any business or collegiate establishment there are disagreements, crises, conflicts of personalities, and even disasters, some of which appear at the time to be pulling the place apart. The reign of Mary caused alarm, the English Civil War raised deep concerns about the future of a royal foundation and the reign of James II evoked fears for the Anglican cathedral. The constitutional arguments and changes of the nineteenth century created rifts that might have become unbridgeable. More recently, there have been heated and serious debates over the possible separation of college and cathedral, and over the admission of women. But all of these have been weathered,

'Through all the vicissitudes of English history': Conclusion

usually through a spirit of compromise or with a metaphorical shrug of the shoulders. Sometimes changes have been forced upon the college, particularly by commissions such as the Oxford and Cambridge Commission, the Ecclesiastical Commission, and in more modern times, the Franks and North Commissions. But Christ Church and many of her neighbours have survived these; they will, no doubt, with compromise and possible deviousness, survive more. Christ Church's dual nature has allowed it to be a cathedral when it suited, and a college when that was more appropriate.

It is James Morris's note in the programme for the *Son et Lumière* held in 1968 which sums up Christ Church's history. Great personalities and talents have passed through the quadrangles, but if the above much-flawed account of this college and cathedral shows anything, it shows that 'in a way the very same people have been living and working in those buildings through all the vicissitudes of English history, from the indistinct sages of antiquity to the all too vivid undergraduates of today'.

Appendices

Deans

Richard Cox	1546
Richard Marshall	1553
George Carew	1559
Thomas Sampson	1561
Thomas Goodwin	1565
Thomas Cooper	1567
John Piers	1570
Toby Matthew	1576
William James	1584
Thomas Ravis	1596
John King	1605
William Goodwin	1611
Richard Corbett	1620 (also Bishop of Oxford, 1628–32)
Brian Duppa	1629
Samuel Fell	1638
Edward Reynolds	1648
John Owen	1651
Edward Reynolds	1659
George Morley	1660
John Fell	1660 (also Bishop of Oxford, 1675–86)
John Massey	1686
Henry Aldrich	1689
Francis Atterbury	1711
George Smalridge	1713
Hugh Boulter	1719
William Bradshaw	1724
John Conybeare	1733

David Gregory	1756
William Markham	1767
Lewis Bagot	1777
Cyril Jackson	1783
Charles Henry Hall	1809
Samuel Smith	1824
Thomas Gaisford	1831
Henry Liddell	1855
Francis Paget	1892 (also Bishop of Oxford, 1901–11)
Thomas Banks Strong	1901 (also Bishop of Oxford, 1925–37)
Henry White	1920
A. T. P. Williams	1934
John Lowe	1939
Cuthbert Simpson	1959
Henry Chadwick	1969
Eric Heaton	1979
John Drury	1991
Christopher Lewis	2003

Of the 44 deans, 6 were educated at Cambridge, including the most recent 4; 38 were at Oxford, most as undergraduates but a few as postgraduates, of which 26 were at Christ Church; 17 had been taught at Westminster School, 2 at Eton, and 2 at Magdalen College School.

Ten deans died in office – most in the middle years of the eighteenth century: William Goodwin (1620), John Fell (1686), Henry Aldrich (1710), George Smalridge (1719), William Bradshaw (1734), John Conybeare (1756), David Gregory (1767), Thomas Gaisford (1855), Henry White (1934) and Cuthbert Simpson (1969).

All, except the two from Canada (John Lowe and Cuthbert Simpson) and the two happily still with us (John Drury and Christopher Lewis), are in the *Oxford Dictionary of National Biography*.

Christ Church men in the Oxford Dictionary of National Biography

There are over 1,200 Christ Church men in the *ODNB*, and around another 200 men and women who have been associated with the college and cathedral. Just to give an idea of the variety, this is a brief list.

Robert **Chaloner** (1548–1621), educationalist
Richard **Hakluyt** (1552–1616), geographer
Edmund **Gunter** (1581–1626), mathematician
Robert **Gentilis** (1590–1655), translator
Henry **Elsyng** (1606–56), clerk to the House of Commons
Richard **Busby** (1606–95), schoolmaster
John **Locke** (1632–1704), philosopher
Robert **Hooke** (1635–1703), scientist
Sir Richard **Newdigate** (1644–1710), landowner and mining entrepreneur
William **Penn** (1644–1718), founder of Pennsylvania
Richard **Graham** (1648–95), Jacobite conspirator
Sampson **Estwick** (1657–1739), musician
John **Whiteside** (1679–1729), museum curator
John Theophilus **Desaguliers** (1683–1744), scientist and engineer
Charles **Hamilton** (1704–86), landscape gardener
Charles and John **Wesley** (1707–88, 1703–91), founders of Methodism
Laurence **Shirley** (1720–60), murderer
James **Granger** (1723–76), print collector and biographer
George **Colman** (1732–94), playwright and theatre manager
Thomas **Hornsby** (1733–1810), astronomer
John **Parsons** (1742–85), physician and anatomist
Archibald **Acheson** (1776–1849), governor in chief of British North America
Thomas Assheton **Smith** (1776–1858), quarry owner, huntsman, and yachtsman
Charles **Norris** (1779–1858), topographical artist
Philip Barker **Webb** (1793–1854), naturalist
Henry **Herbert** (1800–49), travel writer
Benjamin **Hall** (1802–67), politician whose name is inscribed on Big Ben
George **Payne** (1803–78), racehorse owner and gambler
Robert **Curzon** (1810–73), traveller and manuscript collector
Sir Charles Thomas **Newton** (1816–94), archaeologist
Francis **Buckland** (1826–80), pisciculturist and naturalist
Euseby **Cleaver** (1826–94), promoter of the Irish language
Thomas Littleton **Powys** (1833–96), ornithologist
Sir John **Stainer** (1840–1901), organist and musicologist
Sir Charles Sissmore **Tomes** (1846–1928), dentist
Frederick **Campbell** (1847–1911), railway administrator
Harry **Everard** (1848–1909), golf writer
Sir Henry Maxwell **Lyte** (1848–1940), archivist

Sir Peter Chalmers **Mitchell** (1864–1945), zoologist
John Pius **Boland** (1870–1958), tennis player and Olympic gold medallist
Apsley George Benet **Cherry-Garrard** (1886–1959), polar explorer
Kurt **Hahn** (1886–1974), educationalist
Geoffrey **Dearmer** (1893–1996), writer and radio broadcaster
Philip **Heseltine** (Peter Warlock) (1894–1930), musicologist and composer
Sir Henry 'Chips' **Channon** (1897–1958), diarist
Sir Dick **White** (1906–93), intelligence officer
Wystan Hugh **Auden** (1907–73), poet
Peter **Cazalet** (1907–73), racehorse trainer
Sir Martin **Ryle** (1918–84), Astronomer Royal
Michael Henry **Flanders** (1922–75), lyricist and actor
Donald Ibrahim **Swann** (1923–94), pianist and composer
Alan Kenneth **Clark** (1928–99), diarist
Colin **Matthew** (1941–99), founding editor of the *Oxford DNB*

Plus, of course, 13 Prime Ministers serving a total of 22 terms of office, and 11 Viceroys of India, countless bishops and numerous MPs.

Regius Professors of Divinity

The divinity professorship was annexed to a Christ Church canonry in 1605 by James I. The professors after that date are as follows:

Robert Abbot	1612
John Prideaux	1615
Robert Sanderson	1642
Robert Crosse	1648
Joshua Hoyle	1648
John Conant	1654
Robert Sanderson	1660
William Creed	1661
Richard Allestree	1663
William Jane	1680
John Potter	1707
George Rye	1737
John Fanshawe	1741
Edward Bentham	1763
Benjamin Wheeler	1776

John Randolph	1783
Charles Henry Hall	1807
William Howley	1809
William van Mildert	1813
Frodsham Hodson	1820
Charles Lloyd	1822
Edward Burton	1829
Renn Dickson Hampden	1836
William Jacobson	1848
Robert Payne Smith	1865
James Bowling Mozley	1871
William Ince	1878
Henry Scott Holland	1911
Arthur Headlam	1918
Henry Goudge	1923
Oliver Quick	1939
Leonard Hodgson	1944
Henry Chadwick	1959
Maurice Wiles	1970
Keith Ward	1991
Marilyn McCord Adams	2004

Regius Professors of Ecclesiastical History

Robert Hussey	1842
Arthur Stanley	1856
Walter Shirley	1863
Henry Mansel	1866
William Bright	1868
Charles Bigg	1901
Edward Watson	1908
Claude Jenkins	1934
Stanley Greenslade	1959
John McManners	1972
Peter Hinchliff	1992
Henry Mayr-Harting	1997
Sarah Foot	2007

Regius Professors of Hebrew

The Hebrew professorship was annexed to a canonry at Christ Church in 1630 by Charles I. Professors after that date are as follows:

John Morris	1626
Edward Pococke	1648
Roger Altham	1691
Thomas Hyde	1697
Roger Altham	1702
Robert Clavering	1715
Thomas Hunt	1747
Richard Browne	1774
George Jubb	1780
Benjamin Blayney	1787
Joseph White	1802
Richard Laurence	1814
Alexander Nicoll	1822
Edward Pusey	1828
Samuel Rolles Driver	1882
George Cooke	1914
Herbert Danby	1936
Cuthbert Simpson	1954
William McHardy	1960
James Barr	1978
Hugh Williamson	1992

Regius Professors of Greek

The Greek professorship was founded by Henry VIII in 1541, and attached to Christ Church from its foundation.

John Harpsfield	c.1541
George Etheridge	1547
Giles Lawrence	1551
George Etheridge	1553
Giles Lawrence	1559
John Harmar	1585
Henry Cuffe	1590

John Perin	1597
John Hales	1615
John Harrys	1619
John South	1622
Henry Stringer	1625
John Harmar	1650
Joseph Crowther	1660
William Levinz	1665
Humphrey Hody	1698
Thomas Milles	1705
Edward Thwaytes	1707
Thomas Terry	1712
John Fanshawe	1735
Thomas Shaw	1741
Samuel Dickens	1751
William Sharp	1763
John Randolph	1782
William Jackson	1783
Thomas Gaisford	1811
Benjamin Jowett	1855
Ingram Bywater	1893
Gilbert Murray	1908
E. R. Dodds	1936
Hugh Lloyd-Jones	1960
Peter Parsons	1989
Christopher Pelling	2003

Regius Professors of [Moral and] Pastoral Theology

The pastoral theology professorship was created and attached to Christ Church by Act of Parliament in 1840. It was later renamed the moral and pastoral theology professorship.

Charles Ogilvie	1842
Edward King	1873
Francis Paget	1885
Robert Moberly	1892
Robert Ottley	1903

Kenneth Kirk	1933
Leonard Hodgson	1938
Robert Mortimer	1944
Vigo Demant	1949
Peter Baelz	1972
Oliver O'Donovan	1982
Nigel Biggar	2007

Lady Margaret Professors of Divinity

The Lady Margaret professorship was founded in 1502 by Margaret Countess of Richmond. It was attached to a canonry at Christ Church by Act of Parliament in 1840, although the holders prior to that were often Christ Church men. The holders since 1840 have been:

Godfrey Faussett	1827
Charles Heurtley	1853
William Sanday	1895
Walter Lock	1919
Norman Williams	1927
Frank Cross	1944
John Macquarrie	1970
Rowan Williams	1986
John Webster	1996
George Pattison	2004

The thirty-two clauses of the 1858 Ordinance

1. The two canonries not annexed to professorships or to the archdeaconry would not be refilled once vacant.

2. There were to be 28 Senior Studentships, and 52 Junior Studentships of which 21 would be filled by boys from Westminster School. Of the 31 open Studentships, 7 were to be called Fell Studentships, two Bostock Studentships, and 1 Vernon and 1 Boulter Studentship.

3. Two of the Senior Studentships would be funded by the Lee Trust and called the Dr Lee's Readers in Anatomy and Chemistry. They were to receive not less than £200 p.a. The other Senior Students were also to receive £200 p.a. The

open Junior Studentships would receive £75 p.a., and the Westminster Junior Students between £115 and £125 p.a. The emoluments of the existing Students and those of the two suppressed canonries were to be applied to the new Studentships as soon as they became vacant. Fell's, Boulter's and Bostock's funds were to be applied to the open Junior Studentships. Frewin, Hill, and £1,260 from South's funds were to pay the Junior Westminster Students. Junior Students were not entitled to any income from the Senior Masters' Estate.

4. If funds permitted, once all the above were paid, then the Dean and Chapter were entitled to make up to twelve more Senior Students and up to nine more Junior Studentships.

5. The election of Senior Students was to lie with the Dean, Canons, two Censors and the four senior tutors.

6. Senior Students had to be Anglican, BAs, unmarried, and not disqualified by property or position.

7. Nine of the Senior Studentships should be laymen. Both of the Lee's Readers should be laymen.

8. Senior Students were required to undergo a twelve-month probationary period, and would not be entitled to vote until the end of that period.

9. Senior Students were obliged to resign on marriage.

10. Senior Students owning property or office paying more than £500 p.a. were obliged to resign.

11. Honorary Studentships could be elected by the electors to Senior Studentships.

12. Senior Students appointed to canonries or the headship or fellowship in another college were obliged to resign.

13. Dean, canons, two censors and four senior tutors to make and maintain regulations concerning residence of Senior Students.

14. Holders of Studentships were obliged to take their higher degrees as required or forfeit their Studentship.

15. Senior Students might be deprived for bad conduct.

16. Westminster Junior Students were to be filled on the Wednesday in Rogation Week from boys on the Royal Foundation of the school.

17. The patronage of the Vernon Studentship was to stay the same. Election to the open Junior Studentships rested with the same electors as to the Senior

Studentships. One third of the Junior Studentships was to be in Mathematics or the Physical Sciences.

18. No person was eligible for a Junior Studentship once he had completed eight terms from matriculation.
19. Westminster Junior Studentships were to be tenable for seven years, and open Junior Studentships were to be tenable for five.
20. The whole number was to be filled as quickly as possible as funds permitted, and the present censors, readers, tutors, and lecturers were to be made Senior Students without election.
21. Junior Students were subject to regulations laid down by the dean, canons, two censors and four Senior Tutors.
22. If no candidates for Studentships were available, then elections could be postponed.
23. By-laws could be made and enforced by the dean, canons, and Senior Students.
24. Any question which might arise at any meeting should be decided by vote of all those present.
25. The Dean and Chapter might reduce the number of chaplaincies as they felt appropriate provided there were always a minimum of four, with the emoluments of those not filled to be distributed among the remaining chaplains.
26. The dean and canons were permitted to alter the designation of servitors as they saw fit, and to apply the benefactions of Pauncefort, Gardiner, Frampton, Cotton and Paul to anyone fitting the new designation.
27. The Lord Chancellor had authority to redirect the use of funds if they were too little or too excessive for any purpose to which they were applied.
28. The Dean and Chapter, or dean, canons, censors and senior tutors, to reply to any question from the Visitor.
29. Appeals to the Visitor were available to any member of college, even Junior Students.
30. The Lord Chancellor might disallow any by-law which he felt not in keeping with the Statutes.
31. The words 'Lord Chancellor' meant the Lord High Chancellor of Great Britain, and included the Lord Keeper and the Lords Commissioners for the Custody of the Great Seal. The word 'Tutor' meant a tutor who was a Senior Student.
32. Any member of the House elected before the Ordinance to continue as before, even his emoluments.

Abbreviations and conventions

Abbreviations

Al West	Welch, J., *List of the Queen's Scholars of St Peter's College, Westminster*, (1852)
Bod	Bodleian Library
CCCO	Corpus Christi College Archives
CCL	Christ Church Library
Cen	Censors' papers, Christ Church Archive
CUL	Cambridge University Library
D&C	Dean and Chapter papers, Christ Church Archive
DP	Deanery papers, Christ Church Archive
DY	Documents listed on pp. 241–5 of Denholm-Young (1931)
GB	Governing Body papers, Christ Church Archive
Hearne	Doble, C. E. (ed.), *Remarks and Collections of Thomas Hearne*, (1885–1907)
HMC, *Portland*	Historic Manuscripts Commission, *Report on the manuscripts of His Grace the Duke of Portland, KG, preserved at Welbeck Abbey*
HUO	*History of the University of Oxford*, (8 volumes, 1984–2000)
LP	*Letters and papers, foreign and domestic*
MCA	Merton College Archives
MS Estates	Estates correspondence, Christ Church Archive
OCA	Oriel College Archives
ODNB	*Oxford Dictionary of National Biography*, (2004)
OUA	Oxford University Archives
RA	Royal Archives
S	Steward's Office papers, Christ Church Archive
SOC	Papers of Clubs and Societies, Christ Church Archive
UCA	University College Archives
VCH Oxford	*History of the county of Oxford*

Wood H&A   Gutch, A. (ed.), *History and antiquities of the University of Oxford, in two books, by Anthony à Wood, MA of Merton College*, (1796)
Wood L&T   Clark, A. (ed.), *Life and times of Anthony Wood, antiquary, of Oxford, 1632–1695, described by himself*, 3 vols., (1891–4)

Conventions

All years, even those before 1732, are assumed to start in January.
All archival references, unless otherwise prefixed, are to Christ Church sources.
References to the *Oxford Dictionary of National Biography* are to the name in context unless otherwise indicated.

Monetary values

Using (1) the Retail Price Index and (2) average earnings, the value of £10 compared with its value in 2008 was as follows:

Date	RPI	Average earnings
1550	£2,500	£39,000
1600	£1,500	£20,000
1650	£915	£16,000
1700	£1,400	£17,000
1750	£1,400	£15,000
1800	£550	£8,000
1850	£900	£8,000
1900	£800	£4,000
1950	£250	£760
2000	£13	£14

Figures derived from http://www.measuringworth.com/index.html

Notes

Introduction and acknowledgements

1. Thompson (1900)
2. Hiscock (1946)
3. Trevor-Roper (1950); CCA GB i.b.8, 23. The booklet was first proposed by Trevor-Roper at the Governing Body meeting on 3 May 1950, and is now in its third edition.
4. Bill (1988); Bill & Mason (1970)
5. Caröe (1923); Cook & Mason (1988)
6. Butler (ed.) (2006)
7. In particular: C. S. L. Davies and J. Garnett, *Wadham College* (1994); P. Adams, *Somerville for Women: an Oxford college, 1879–1993* (1996); L. Brockliss (ed.), *Magdalen College* (2009); R. Darwall-Smith, *University College* (2008); C. Hopkins, *Trinity: 450 years of an Oxford college community* (2005); G.H. Martin and J. R. L. Highfield, *A History of Merton College* (1997); Vivian Green, *The Commonwealth of Lincoln College, 1427–1977* (1979); John Jones, *Balliol College: a history* (1988); J. Mordaunt Crook, *Brasenose: the biography of an Oxford College* (2009)

1. Before Christ Church

1. St Frideswide was adopted as the patron saint of the University before 1190, and her feast observed from 1398 – *ODNB*.
2. Blair (1994), 87ff.
3. Boyle (2001), 337–68
4. Blair (1994), 53–4; *ODNB*. Frideswide's story is pictured in a window by Edward Burne-Jones in the cathedral's Latin chapel.
5. Stenton (1953). The shrine, much reconstructed, now stands in the Latin Chapel. Its original site is debated still, although its present position, to which it was moved in 2002, is the likeliest.
6. Thompson (1900), 231; *ODNB*
7. Warner (1924), 228
8. Biddle and Kjølbye-Biddle (1988), 259–63
9. Warner (1924), 183–90
10. Salter (1960), Map SE VI

11. The college which, during the fifteenth century at least, housed a substantial library, stood just outside the gate to St Frideswide's. Its buildings survived into the eighteenth century. Dobson, *HUO*, ii (1992), 539–80; Pantin (1947), v–vii
12. Dobson, *HUO*, ii (1992), 542–4
13. Knowles & Hadcock (1971), 169–70
14. *ODNB*. Using the RPI, this is probably equivalent to over £11 million today. In terms of average earnings, it equates to a phenomenal £135 million.
15. Newman, in Gunn & Lindley (1991), 103–6
16. Gibson (1853), ii, 11, 21
17. BL Cotton Vitellius B V, f.8
18. Thompson (1900), 3
19. Gwyn (1990), note to plate 13. MS Harley 4900, f.18
20. Gibson (1853), ii, 11, 63
21. The public professors were elected by heads of houses from all over the university, and were not permitted to interfere with the administration of the college. Gunn & Lindley (1991), 108; Gibson (1853), ii, 11, 123
22. Gibson (1853), ii, 11, 13–14
23. Brockliss (ed.) (2008), 54–5
24. *ODNB*
25. Similarly at Magdalen College – Brockliss (ed.) (2008), 30–31
26. Gibson (1853), ii, 11, 44–5
27. Gibson (1853), ii, 11, 14–21
28. *ODNB*, on-line edn, May 2005
29. Bowers, in Gunn & Lindley (1991), 197–8
30. Cross, *HUO*, iii, 123–4; Greenslade, *HUO*, iii, 314; Loach, *HUO*, iii, 363–4; Thompson (1900), 7–9; *ODNB*
31. Gibson (1853), ii, 11, 49–53
32. Gibson (1853), ii, 11, 53–5, 62
33. Gibson (1853), ii, 11, 71
34. McConica (ed.), *HUO*, iii (1986), 32
35. Milne & Harvey, 'The building of Cardinal College, Oxford', in *Oxoniensia*, viii, (1943), 137–53; Cotton Vitellius B.V, f.9
36. A library was not built before Wolsey fell.
37. Gibson (1853), ii, 11, 103
38. Newman, in Gunn & Lindley (1991), 109
39. Duncan, *HUO*, iii (1986), 559
40. Thompson (1900), 5; Hammer, *HUO*, iii, 105
41. Milne & Harvey, 'The building of Cardinal College, Oxford', *Oxoniensia*, viii (1943), 137–53; Thompson (1900), 4
42. Remains of the west end of the church under the terrace in Tom Quad were revealed during archaeological excavations
43. Milne & Harvey (1943), 137–53. Thompson (1900), 249–50
44. Harley MS 599, ff.5, 37 and 42
45. The main spit-range in the kitchen could roast forty legs of mutton, or seventy chickens, at the same time. There were originally four fireplaces, and a separate oven

for bread and pastries. It was this latter oven that produced the meringues made famous in Dorothy Sayers's *Gaudy Night*. Jacobs, September 1950
46. Lyte (1886), 447
47. Harvey, *HUO*, ii (1992), 768
48. Newman, *HUO*, iii (1986), 614, 625; Newman, in Gunn & Lindley (1991), 111–12; Lyte (1886), 446; Colvin (1983), 5 and 6
49. Colvin (1983), 3–6
50. Newman, *HUO*, iii (1986), 614–15
51. LP Henry VIII, 4.2, no. 4135
52. Aubrey's drawings, best known for the sketch of the base of the new chapel walls, also show a window which must have been inserted into the north end of the west frontage some time after Wolsey's fall (Colvin (1983), 5). There is a photograph in the archive, taken by Axtell's in 1896, showing the end of Wolsey's construction between the present staircases 6 and 7 (P.TOP.TQ.26).
53. Biddle (1988), 205–10; Thompson (1900), 239. The cloisters had only been restored in 1499. The foundations of the bell-tower have been recreated in the paving around the new fountain, dedicated in June 2008.
54. Youings (1971), 2–28; DY4. Denholm-Young (1931), 214
55. DP iv.b.1, f. 43v
56. Gibson (1853), ii, 11, 109–11, 115–16
57. Hammer, *HUO*, iii (1986), 89. The charter is no longer in the Christ Church archives.
58. Lyte (1886), 449
59. DP iv.b.2. Using the RPI, £5000 equates to around £2.5 million today, or £25 million based on average earnings.
60. Lyte (1886), 479. The vestments and church ornaments were removed, too. William Tresham was sent to the king to ask for some of the white copes to be spared for festival occasions, but he was too late.
61. Gwyn (1990), 612–13; Thompson (1900), 9–10
62. Cross, in *HUO*, iii (1986), 122
63. Lyte (1886), 481
64. Thompson (1900), 10–11; LP Henry VIII, v, 268, no. 577
65. LP Henry VIII, v, 88, no. 185
66. Emden (1974)
67. DY 5
68. Duncan, *HUO*, iii (1986), 342. All the men were of some note, and five warrant entries in the *ODNB*: Cottisford, Croke, Robyns, Tresham and Wakefield.
69. Duncan, *HUO*, iii (1986), 343
70. LP Henry VIII, v, 519, no. 1181
71. Emden; Cross, *HUO*, iii (1986), 131; LP Henry VIII, xiii(I), 196, no. 529 and xiii (I), 334, no 905
72. Gibson (1853), ii, 11, 185–211
73. Probably John Chamber, *ODNB*
74. LP Henry VIII, vi, 183, nos. 399 and 400
75. LP Henry VIII, vi, 326, no. 879
76. LP Henry VIII, v, 156, no. 334

77. *ODNB*; LP Henry VIII, v, 678, no. 1632
78. *ODNB*
79. *ODNB*
80. LP Henry VIII, v, 734, no. 1789; MS Harley 604, f.90v states that the college was worth £703 8s 2½d
81. *Valor Ecclesiasticus*, ii (1814), 250–54
82. Hopkins (2005), 25; pers. comm. with Julian Reid
83. LP Henry VIII, v, 86, no. 173 and 411, no. 872
84. LP Henry VIII, xii (I), 123, no. 261(2)
85. LP Henry VIII, vi, 38, no. 101
86. New College surrendered the site of Peckwater Inn in September 1546.
87. LP Henry VIII, xiii (II), 202, no. 514
88. LP Henry VIII, vii, 400, no. 1026(33); Emden. Buckler left Oxford in 1544 when he was secretary to Katherine Parr. His place as canon of King Henry VIII College was taken by John Leland, librarian and antiquary to Henry VIII. He was knighted by Edward VI at the coronation.
89. The royal visit was cancelled – Parkhurst, John (1511?–75), *ODNB*.
90. Haigh [1996]; iii.b.99
91. xii.b.1, f.10

For 'the keepinge of their horses and cattell and for other occasions': the Meadow

1. MS Estates 126, ff. 16 and 115
2. Bill (1965)
3. D&C i.b.4, f.79
4. MS Estates 126, f.37
5. MS Estates 126, f.1; D&C i.b.2, 227. The famous longhorn cattle grazed on the Meadow from 1987. Archimedes the bull resided in a stall at one end of the barn, and his departure in 2005, with the rest of the herd, was unpopular. A new herd, under the management of a local farmer, arrived in 2009.
6. 1.c.2, 181. There is no record of any payment out of corporate funds, which suggests that the dean and canons paid the £500 out of their own pockets.
7. MS Estates 126, ff.3–11
8. 1.c.2, 183–4
9. D&C i.b.4, f.145
10. MS Estates 126, f.119 and 121 and 202; D&C i.b.4, f.4; D&C i.b.8, f.42v; Maps ChCh M 3 and 5. Earl's Ham, a small island where the Cherwell joined the Thames and part of the site where the boathouses now stand, originally belonged to Brasenose College, until 1665 when it was exchanged for several properties on the High Street so that Brasenose could build its new chapel.
11. Norris was let off the much-needed repairs to the stables and cottages on the condition that Corpus Christi left the fences in good condition at the end of their lease.
12. MS Estates 126, ff.64–73
13. D&C i.b.6, 211

14. MS Estates 126, f.18
15. MS Estates 126, ff.109 and 214
16. MS Estates 126, ff.52–62; Maps ChCh M 6–10. In 1803, designs were drawn up to improve the entrance to the city and the Meadow, including a triumphal arch to be erected in Rose Lane, but the plans never reached fruition. Rose Lane itself was, from 1878, maintained by the Local Board.
17. The disbursement books record some payments to Henry Floyd.
18. MS Estates 126, 219–25
19. xlix.a.1, 42
20. xlix.a.1, 53 & 55, 62 & 64. The construction of the bridge over the Cherwell was also delayed while the channels of the river were widened, the banks strengthened, and Magdalen Bridge itself made broader.
21. MS Estates 126, f.279
22. GB i.b.2, 201. A crossing over the Cherwell to the athletic ground was first considered in February 1877. A year later the Oxford University Athletic Club was given permission to use the ferry.
23. MS Estates 126, f.209
24. *Christ Church 1975, 1977* and *1978*; . GB i.b.14, 166. The trees that had to be taken down were replaced with elms of more resistant strain. London planes were planted in 1978, to be followed by Oriental planes. Christ Church assisted many of the tenant farmers in the replacement of their lost elms, to the tune of £10,000. The first scheme implemented was at Elsfield on the recommendation of the college's agents and the Woodland Management Association, in consultation with the Oxford Preservation Trust and the Countryside Commission.
25. GB i.b.14, 10–14
26. GB i.b.14, 6
27. D&C i.b.6, 22
28. MS Estates 126, ff.19–36; xii.c.258. Vickery was paid 10s. A Mr Roberson, who made most of the inquiries into the robbery, was paid £18, and a watch was put on the Meadow overnight at a cost of 12s.
29. MS Estates 126, f.212
30. MS Estates 126, ff.261–3
31. Newman (1980), 7
32. Sharp (1948), 106
33. For example, *Oxford Mail*, 8 February 1951, 2
34. GB i.b.8, 297. The vice-chancellor's invitation to the 1955 gaudy was rescinded as he was in favour of the road.
35. Newman (1980), 19. At the time, there were 150 Oxford graduates in the House of Commons, including 28 from Christ Church and 4 from Merton College. The presence of Christ Church men in the House of Lords was even stronger.
36. Until 1974, the University had voted representatives on to the city council, and took its turn in the mayoralty.
37. Mercurius Oxoniensis, alias Hugh Trevor-Roper, wrote a series of 'letters' on Oxford matters to his London friend in the style of the late seventeenth century which were published in the *Spectator* between 1968 and 1970. 'How virtue triumphed over

progress', the letter concerning the Meadow Road controversy, was published on 20 December 1968, and reprinted in *The Letters of Mercurius* (1970).
38. *Christ Church 1943/4, 1952, 1955–1968*
39. *Christ Church 1974*
40. Wood L&T, ii, 188
41. MS Estates 126, f.2
42. Maps ChCh M 14. A committee was sent up in May 1868 on the creation of the new Broad Walk from Meadows Building to the river – GB i.b.2, 27.
43. xii.b.24
44. 1.c.2, 221
45. Bompas (1885), 47–8
46. Whately (1866), 38
47. MS Estates 126, f.277
48. MS Estates 126, ff.265 and 271 and 273 and 284
49. GB i.b.7, 493
50. S.xxvi.c.6
51. I am grateful to Christopher Lowe, son of Dean Lowe, for this information.
52. Batey (1989), 27
53. xii.b.75. The turfs cost £12 8s 6d. Bowling greens, rather than alleys, appear to have been popular at the larger colleges. Certainly, Magdalen, Queen's and New College all had them. Bowling alleys were a common feature of larger country houses and royal palaces.
54. *Christ Church, 1954 & 1955*; David Hine, in Butler (ed.) (2006), 117. Captain George Hutchinson MC was Treasurer from 1910 to 1945.
55. The Underwood gates to the Meadow from the Masters' Garden were erected in 1955.
56. Hine, in Butler (ed.) (2006), 116–19; Sladen (2002)
57. GB i.b.2, 361
58. GB i.b.17, 336ff.
59. Ivy-leaved toadflax, or the 'Oxford weed', is said to have been introduced into Oxford from southern Europe in the seventeenth century, carried in on marble sculptures and their packaging. It is virtually unknown in natural habitats in this country. See Mabey (1996), 331.
60. Batey (1989), 143
61. The bitter winter of 1962/3 saw 2 feet of ice form in Mercury. All but four of the fish perished, and necessitated a thorough clean of the pond. £5 10s in cash was found, and the key to Tom Gate which had, apparently, been thrown in in 1947 – *Christ Church 1963*.
62. A proposal was made in 1922 to turf Peckwater Quad, but this was lost by 14 votes to 6. When it was grassed in 1936, it was intended to stand a sundial at the centre as a focal point. In 1978, the surface was changed from gravel to 'Ultrimac', the cost of paving slabs being too high.

2. 'This Royall & Ample Foundation': 1546–53

1. This chapter derives much from the lecture – '1546: Before and after. The making of Christ Church' – given by Dr Christopher Haigh on 2 November 1996 to commemorate the 450th anniversary of the foundation of Christ Church.
2. Dawson (1984), 208–15
3. Cambridge did not need a diocesan seat – both Ely and Norwich were close enough. Trinity College received its charter from the king in December 1546.
4. Henry's plan for his new cathedrals to provide exhibitions for young men to attend university seems to have been transferred to St Frideswide's. Certainly some form of institution functioned during 1545 and 1546 with some of the scholars becoming Students at Christ Church.
5. Trinity College's statutes were formulated soon after Henry's death with a new and full set devised under Elizabeth.
6. D&C vi.b.1
7. McConica (ed.), *HUO*, iii, 33–5
8. DY11, ff.35v and 36
9. DP i.a.1. This volume was compiled retrospectively. Begun by Fell in 1660, much of the work was carried out by Thomas Tanner in 1734/5 – Bod MS Rawl.lett. 30, f.21
10. DP i.a.1, f.13. Richard Smith (Divinity) left Christ Church before October, and Thomas Harding (Hebrew) left in August. Both men favoured the Catholic tradition, Smith becoming professor of theology at Louvain, and chaplain to Mary Tudor – *ODNB*.
11. D&C i.b.1
12. The old prior's lodgings adjoin the Chapter House. Dating in part from the eleventh century, it is one of the oldest continuously inhabited domestic residences in the country.
13. *ODNB*. The chapter book in which the list is written is inscribed on f.vr with Bernard's name, perhaps signifying that he was the first secretary to the chapter.
14. Venn
15. *ODNB*; DP i.a.16, f.9; DP i.a.15, f.70v. John Dyer, a canon of Oseney, was the first choice for the 5th stall in 1546, but he died early in 1547.
16. *ODNB*, and see p. 55
17. The election was moved to Christmas from October sometime in the early 1570s. College officers were also named at this time.
18. D&C i.b.1, ff.3v and 4r
19. D&C i.b.1 ff.4v and 5r
20. xii.b.1. This volume covers only a single term of 1548, but already it is evident that the machinery of the new college is up and running. Not only is everyone being paid, but college incumbents are receiving pensions, the cathedral is being supplied with books and its choristers with surplices. Alms are being distributed, and general expenses are accounted for. The next surviving disbursement book is for the year 1577–8.
21. x(1).c.1
22. D&C i.b.1, f.7v. This is the only occurrence of a mathematics lecturer.
23. Curthoys (1995), 379–95

24. D&C vi.c.4, ff.16–24
25. Richardson (1961), 302
26. Further work on college estates is in preparation.
27. The next-richest college was Magdalen, which had an income of around £1,200.
28. DY11, ff.35v and 36
29. iii.b.99, ff.13–17
30. D&C i.b.2, 299
31. D&C i.b.1, f.iv and ivv. Two versions of this list are written into the first Chapter Book. The *philosophi primi vicenarii* were the second rank of Students. The requirement for bedding is excluded from the second list.
32. x(1).c.1
33. iii.c.1, f.33; iii.c.4, f.39
34. iii.c.4
35. A fother, when applied to lead, is usually reckoned to be 19½ cwt, or just under a ton.
36. iii.c.4, f.13
37. Curthoys (1995), 379–95
38. iii.c.4, ff.55 and 56. Two oxen were stolen in 1547.
39. iii.c.4, f.40 – the official seal cost £4 to make.
40. xiii.b.1, f 12. The house, formerly owned by the college of St Nicholas, by the castle in Wallingford, was purchased by the Dean and Chapter in August 1548 to serve as a place of refuge when Oxford was ridden with pestilence. After 1600 it would appear that the property was leased to tenants for profit. Other colleges did the same. Trinity College, for example, had a house in Garsington – Hopkins (2005) 57 and 58.
41. D&C i.b.1, ff.60v–65; D&C i.b.2, 95
42. BL MS Lansdowne 2, ff.77–8v
43. D&C i.b.1, f.17v; McConica (ed.), *HUO*, iii, 39; *ODNB*
44. McConica (ed.), *HUO*, iii, 41
45. *ODNB*. Both men returned to Oxford, Martyr throughout the remainder of Edward VI's reign until Mary's accession, Tresham from 1553 until his refusal to take Elizabeth's oath of supremacy.
46. *ODNB*
47. *ODNB*
48. Leo Judas's translation of the Psalms was particularly Calvinist, published in Zurich, and probably the choice of Dean Sampson or, possibly, the Dean and Chapter under Edward VI. Thompson (1900), 37–8
49. Ker, *HUO*, iii, 442–4
50. xii.b.1, f.10; McConica (ed.), *HUO*, iii, 443
51. Gibson (1853), ii, 11, 83–5; Williams, *HUO*, iii. 426–7; D&C i.b.2, 230
52. Gibson (1853), ii, 11, 100–102, 59. The sums may not have been exclusively for fabric or clothes, but may have been a general grant towards living expenses.
53. Newman, *HUO*, iii, 629
54. i.b.2, p. 88; *ODNB*

'To perfect the college ...': Christ Church and charity

1. Clark (ed.) (1889), 193–4; Curthoys (1995), 379–95. Wood stated that '...King Henry VIII taking upon him to perfect the college in some sort in its endowment settled here also the number of twenty-four almesmen'.
2. Even some of the men who lived in the almshouse appear to have been married.
3. Although military service is not a stipulated requirement, the tradition is so strong that all the men who currently hold almsmen's patents have at least undergone National Service.
4. lxi.a.11; lxi.a.23; lxi.a.14; lxi.a.24; lxi.a.190; D&C i.b.5, 108; liii.b.1, f.59v
5. OUA Hyp B 17/3. Padgett was admitted in 1547–8 and died in 1569. As members of the university, the almsmen had access to the Chancellor's Court. Several of their wills were proved by the Court.
6. OUA Hyp A/5/66 Registrum Curiae Cancellarii, f.50v
7. DP ii.c.1, f.120. Almost needless to say, Atterbury refuted the charges, but not until July!
8. D&C vi.c.3, f.26
9. John Handley was admitted in the late 1640s, was expelled during the Commonwealth, but returned in 1660 to die in the almshouse in 1698. John Wilkins took Handley's place and remained resident until 1751. John Blundell received his pension from 1749 to 1800.
10. D&C i.b.5, 108; Curthoys (1995), 379–95. Hacker left Christ Church in May, just a month later. Both John Crosier and Christopher Taylor were permitted to stay in the almshouse. Taylor remained for a further 33 years until his death in 1765.
11. MS Estates 142, f.176
12. MS Estates 142, 208–22, 226–8
13. At Winchester, the bedesmen were paid £18, and at Gloucester they received £14 6s, a gown and payment for work around the cathedral which could amount to an extra 10s a week. In Oxford, the inhabitants of Tawney's and Parson's almshouse received £20 a year.
14. GB i.b.2, 173. On 2 June 1875, the Treasurer was authorised to pay £100 extra to the almsmen to persuade them to go. It is unknown whether this was ever paid, and whether the intention was to pay it only to those men still in the almshouse as an extra incentive.
15. MS Estates 142, f.350
16. D&C vi.c.4, f.23v
17. xii.b.1, f.11
18. xii.b.21, f.15; xii.b.45, f.44v
19. xii.b.103, and for example, xii.b.24, f.32v
20. xii.b.104
21. D&C i.b.9, 88
22. xii.b.107 and xii.b.109. Shemuell signed for his £1 in Hebrew script, probably the only example in the archive.
23. xii.b.103
24. D&C i.b.10, 2

25. D&C i.b.10, 98v
26. D&C i.b.10, 54v
27. xii.b.104 and xii.b.107
28. MS Estates 146, ff.41–5
29. MS Estates 146, ff.147–8
30. SOC xx.c.3
31. Rathbone, in Butler (ed.) (2006), 133

3. 'Untyll suche tyme that it shall please the Kynge ...': 1553–1625

1. Loach, *HUO*, iii (1986), 374; Thompson (1900), 18–19; *ODNB*; Bod MS Rawl.B. 407a, f.234
2. *ODNB*; CCL MS 578. Bernard returned to Christ Church and Pyrton on the accession of Elizabeth.
3. Thompson (1900), 22; *ODNB*. No record of this survives in the archive.
4. Loach, *HUO*, iii (1986), 379–80
5. Herts.Tring A & H; MS Estates 35, f.1
6. Thompson, 39–40; D&C i.b.2, 289. A letter in a similar vein was sent from the Lord Chancellor, Stephen Gardiner – MS Harley 7001, f.233.
7. D&C i.b.2, 290
8. D&C i.b.2, 255–9
9. MR iii.c.1/3/1
10. D&C i.b.2, 93
11. x(1).c.3, ff.64v and 65v
12. *ODNB*
13. D&C i.b.2, 218 and 219
14. MS Lansdowne 5, f.4. The members of Christ Church petitioned Leicester to influence the queen in her selection of Sampson as the next dean.
15. *ODNB*
16. McConica (ed.), *HUO*, iii (1986), 38
17. Field (1998), 22
18. Bill (1988), 91–4
19. D&C i.b.1, f. 101v
20. Duke Humfrey's library had been despoiled by the Protestant royal commissioners who formally visited the University in 1549.
21. *ODNB*
22. D&C i.b.2, 220; *ODNB*
23. Thompson (1900), 20
24. D&C i.b.2, 219
25. Williams, *HUO*, iii (1986), 423 and 426
26. D&C i.b.2, 223–33
27. D&C i.b.2, 227
28. liii.b.1. Matters relating to commoners were handled by the sub-dean; matters concerning foundationers (canons, Students, servants, etc.) were dealt with by

chapter. This continued until the change in the constitution in the mid-nineteenth century. Records relating to commoners, other than battels, are generally sparse.

29. D&C i.b.2, 220
30. Williams, *HUO*, iii (1985), 417–18, 428–9
31. D&C i.b.2, 238. Chapter meetings were to be four times a year. A quarter of the annual dividend due to a canon or to the dean would be forfeited for every absence without lawful impediment.
32. D&C i.b.2, 294–5; DP ii.c.1, f.3; Aylmer, in *HUO*, iii (1986), 536–7; 1595–7 were years of terrible harvests.
33. D&C i.b.2, 235–6. Chandence was one of Christ Church's estates on the edge of Oxfordshire near Cumnor.
34. D&C i.b.2, 236
35. McConica, in *HUO*, iii (1986), 648
36. MS Estates 5, f.3
37. x(1).c.14, f.7r
38. x(1).c.13
39. xii.b.20, f.3r
40. xii.b.20, f.3v and 10r
41. Thompson (1900), 28; *ODNB*
42. Durand (1905), 520–28
43. Nichols (1823), 210–11. One of the dead was the cook from Corpus Christi College, who had probably been 'borrowed' to assist with preparations.
44. *ODNB*
45. Elizabeth stayed in Oxford from 22 to 28 September 1592. The battels books record that £20 6s 4½d was spent on food supplies that week, compared with the usual £12 or £13 – x(1).c.28.
46. Thompson (1900), 32
47. Thompson (1900), 42; *ODNB*
48. Hiscock (1946), 170–72
49. Thompson (1900), 33
50. Aylmer, *HUO*, iii (1986), 523–4
51. Hiscock (1946), 176
52. Fletcher, *HUO*, iii (1986), 162, 174–5
53. McConica, *HUO*, iii (1986), 697–701
54. Fauvel, Flood & Wilson (eds.) (2000), 47–50
55. CCL MS 578, letters from Robert Sackville to Philip Sidney
56. Sidney was 12 when he came up to Christ Church, and Montague 13.
57. CCL MS 578
58. Fincham, *HUO*, iv (1997), 183–6; Tyacke, *HUO*, iv (1997), 569ff.
59. Thompson (1900), 34. Ravis was the first dean to have been a Westminster scholar.
60. *ODNB*
61. Thompson (1900), 46–7. King was appointed Bishop of London in 1611, and was buried in St Paul's Cathedral under a gravestone marked simply 'Resurgam'. The stone was famously discovered by Wren after the Great Fire and replaced in the new cathedral as a sign of hope and new beginning.

62. Elliott, *HUO*, iv (1997), 649; Hiscock (1946) 178–80; Nichols, i (1828), 537–63
63. xii.b.49, f.41. The cornets cost 53s.
64. Hiscock (1946), 180; GB i.b.2, 202
65. xii.b.49, f.60; DP ii.c.1, f.6. Of the £105, £93 9s ½d went towards the still-outstanding costs for the building of Peckwater Quad, and the remainder recorded under 'Extraordinary Receipts'.
66. Bancroft, Chancellor of the University between 1608 and 1610, had initiated a programme to tighten up both Oxford's credentials as a bastion of religious orthodoxy and student discipline in general – Fincham, *HUO*, iv (1997), 186–8.
67. D&C i.b.2, 197
68. D&C i.b.2, 201–3
69. D&C i.b.2, 204
70. Fincham, *HUO*, iv (1997), 191–2
71. D&C i.b.2, 313. Although Bandinell was matriculated from Broadgates Hall in March 1619, he did not receive his Studentship until 1621.
72. D&C i.b.2, 321; *ODNB*
73. Fincham, *HUO*, iv (1997), 195
74. Canon commoners appear to have been the early equivalent of Honorary Members of the House. Apart from two made immediately after the Restoration in 1660, most canon commoners were appointed between 1570 and 1635.
75. D&C i.b.2, 305

Aedis Christi: cathedral, college chapel and the choir

1. Much of this material on the cathedral is derived from the four 'Reference files' compiled by Jim Godfrey, verger from 1987, for the use of the cathedral stewards. His research is extraordinary in its scope and accessibility.
2. D&C ix.b.1, 41–3
3. Other 'Civil War' memorials are to William, Viscount Brouncker, gentleman of the Privy Chamber, Sir William Pennyman, Henry Gage's predecessor as governor of Oxford, Lord Chief Justice John Bankes and Lord Keeper Edward Littleton. Villiers's memorial was not erected until *c*.1670.
4. Henry's other cathedrals were at Gloucester, Bristol, Westminster, Peterborough and Chester.
5. Four deans have been Bishop of Oxford: Corbett, John Fell, Paget and Strong. John Howson (bishop 1619–28) had been a Student, Henry Compton (1674–6) and Kenneth Escott Kirk (1937–55) had been canons. Only three bishops have been buried in the cathedral: Robert King, John Fell and Francis Paget.
6. Thomas Goldwell was appointed in 1558 but died before he could take up the office. Hugh Curwen was not appointed until 1567. When he died just a year later, the throne remained empty for another 21 years. John Underhill was bishop from 1589 until 1592, and it was not until 1604 when John Bridges, Dean of Salisbury, was translated to Oxford, that a continuous line of bishops was re-established.
7. *ODNB*; ii.c.1, f.20
8. D&C i.b.7, 477

9. MS Estates 145, 308
10. D&C i.b.2, 223. Compulsory chapel continued until well into the twentieth century, with students, such as Gladstone, employed as 'prick-bills' to log the attendance of their fellows.
11. D&C i.b.5, 259
12. D&C i.b.6, 72 and 230
13. Sandford was a prime mover in the reform of Christ Church's constitution in the 1860s. Kitchin produced the first catalogue of the Library's manuscripts, ironically, in Latin.
14. Thompson (1899), 152–60
15. D&C vii.c.1; Barrett (1993), 337n
16. D&C i.b.7, 623; D&C i.b.9, 17v. The organ keys were repaired in 1821.
17. D&C i.b.8, 50v
18. D&C i.b.6, 103 and D&C i.b.7, 447 and 506. The junior and senior masters were given cloth cushions for their seats. Presumably, the Students had to make do without cushions at all. To make the bowl for the font, the treasurer was given permission to melt down two or three silver tankards.
19. D&C i.b.5, 231; D&C i.b.7, 521 & 601; D&C i.b.9, 32v
20. D&C i.b.9, 16–19v
21. Warner (1924), 40. The verger's accommodation was swept away by Scott's 1870s reordering of the cathedral. The vergers are often some of the longest-serving members of Christ Church: William Francis served the House from 1860 to 1938, as verger from 1867. Jack Holloway was dean's verger from 1946 to 1978, and Edward Evans from 1975 to 2009.
22. Barrett (1993), 111 and 353n. Both the dog-whip and the beer were removed post-haste by Dean Liddell.
23. D&C i.b.5, 104
24. [Danby] (1945)
25. The number of boy choristers was increased to fourteen soon after Liddell's appointment as dean.
26. The yard is known as School Quad. Parts of the law library, once school rooms, have schoolboy graffiti on the walls. The cobbles between School Quad gate and the buttery cellars were laid in 1804 – D&C i.b.8, 38.
27. Barrett (1993), 200 and 204. Dinner in the Chapter House was a relatively modern thing in 1850; certainly in 1817 the boys were eating in Hall.
28. Barrett (1993), 161
29. Corfe was organist from 1846 to 1883.
30. Barrett (1993), 160, 237 and 254
31. *ODNB*. Probably George Dallam, who worked at St George's, Windsor, and St John's College, Oxford, in the early years of the seventeenth century. The lower part of the organ case and screen probably dates from this period. The uppermost portion, above the organ, is a nineteenth-century addition by Scott.
32. *ODNB*
33. DP xv.c.1, f.27

34. Rowntree, *Christ Church 1980/1981*. Repairs to the case were made in the early twentieth century.
35. The vice-chancellor's throne was moved to the Latin Chapel during Liddell's deanery (it was returned in 1962), probably because he held the positions of both dean and vice-chancellor; 24 deans of Christ Church have been vice-chancellor, 21 of those between 1550 and 1700. Liddell was the first since Henry Aldrich.
36. MS Estates 143, ff.158–61. This was part of an Oxford-wide cessation of burials in college chapels, and part of a more national attempt to tighten up burials in cities. A portion of the new burial ground at Oseney, on land given by Christ Church, was allocated to the college. Christ Church can still bury deans and members of their family outside in the garth to the south of the choir.
37. Hopkins (1975), 51. The Friends have helped with many projects, including the restoration of Burne-Jones's Frideswide window, the rare Becket window, and St Frideswide's shrine, along with new lighting, and, most recently, the new glass doors.
38. *The Times*, 6 May 1942

4. 'The present engagement of the greatest part of them in Armes': 1625–88

1. Thompson (1900), 48
2. *ODNB*; DP ii.c.1, f.20
3. Thompson (1900), 49. The royal couple stayed at Merton College on this occasion.
4. Fincham, *HUO*, iv (1997), 202–4
5. DP ii.c.1, ff.8–15
6. D&C i.b.2, 263. The audit house seems to have been used rather like a Senior Common Room, for meals and entertainment.
7. D&C i.b.2, 265
8. D&C i.b.2, 260
9. D&C i.b.2, 204, 241, 371 and 377
10. D&C i.b.2, 401
11. DP ii.c.1, f.28
12. DP ii.c.1, f.30
13. DP ii.c.1, f.25; Porter, *HUO*, iv (1997), 70–71
14. *ODNB*
15. D&C i.b.2, 405; *ODNB*. Lockey was expelled from his Studentship in 1651 for offending the Parliamentary Visitors with the content of one of his sermons.
16. Thompson (1900), 52–3; Wood *H&A*, ii, 408–9
17. DP ii.c.1, f.27
18. Elliott, Jr., *HUO*, iv (1997), 652–3
19. Roy & Reinhart, *HUO*, iv (1997), 689–91; *ODNB*
20. Wood *H&A*, ii, 438–9
21. Roy & Reinhart, *HUO*, iv (1997), 684–5; Wood *H&A*, ii, 440
22. Wood *H&A*, ii, 443
23. Thompson (1900), 65

24. Thompson (1900), 54–5; *ODNB*. The college and cathedral plate was taken by the Crown. John Fell commissioned a complete set of communion plate for the cathedral in 1660.
25. *ODNB*
26. Wood *H&A*, ii, 454–5
27. Roy & Reinhart, *HUO*, iv (1997), 699–700, 706; Roy (ed.) [1963–4], 456
28. Thompson (1900), 56; MCA Liber Rationarius Bursarium, MCR 3.2 There is no record either at Corpus Christi or at Christ Church for the construction of the gateway between these two colleges.
29. liii.b.3, f.110
30. DP ii.c.1, f.32
31. Thompson (1900), 66
32. liii.b.3
33. DP i.a.1
34. D&C ix.b.1
35. DP ii.c.1, f.40 is a circular to all heads of houses asking them for a further £30 per college to be sent to Nathaniel Smith, receiver to their Majesties. Assurance of repayment was to be given, under the Privy Seal, out of the tenths of the diocese.
36. D&C i.b.3, ff.9v–10
37. Roy & Reinhart, *HUO*, iv (1997), 721; *ODNB*. Thomas Edwards, a London minister vehemently against toleration and the Independents, suspected that preaching officers were sent deliberately to Oxford to inculcate the students with the views of the army – *Gangraene*, part 3, 1646, 23 and 131.
38. Dobson (ed.) [1955], 101–2. Nearly 200 men are listed in the Protestation Return for Christ Church, of whom over 60 contrived to be either absent or sick.
39. Bod MS Ballard 9; Roy & Reinhart, *HUO*, iv (1997), 724
40. Samuel Fell died in London, the day after the execution of Charles I, of, it was said, a broken heart.
41. Roy & Reinhart, *HUO*, iv (1997), 724–6; Thompson (1900) 54; *ODNB*
42. Roy & Reinhart, *HUO*, iv (1997), 730
43. *ODNB*. Meade continued to serve Charles I in exile.
44. *Al West*, 112
45. Curthoys (1995), 379–96; D&C i.b.3, 33
46. D&C i.b.3, 1v; CUL MS Mm.1.46, p.133; Bod Add. MS 32094, f.3; *ODNB*
47. A scheme of windows depicting biblical stories was installed in the cathedral during the 1630s, paid for by the gifts of canons and wealthy patrons.
48. D&C i.b.3, 40v; Thompson (1900), 73; Bod MS Rawl.B.407a, f.246. The 'Jonah' window is in the west wall of the north aisle.
49. D&C i.b.3, 39
50. DP ii.c.1, ff.46–8; D&C i.b.3, 52
51. D&C i.b.3, f.1v
52. D&C i.b.3, f.4v. Elections returned to their usual date, close to Christmas, at the end of 1651.
53. DP ii.c.1, ff.43 and 44
54. DP ii.c.1, f.52; D&C i.b.3, 62; Burrows (1881), 358

Notes

55. DP ii.c.1, ff.50 and 66
56. D&C i.b.3, 30, 53 and 64; Thompson (1900), 74–8
57. D&C i.b.3, 16
58. D&C i.b.3, 25 & 61
59. D&C i.b.3, 13 & 43
60. Fell maintained prayer-book services during the Interregnum in 'secret' at Thomas Willis's house in Merton Street, just yards from the back gate to Christ Church.
61. D&C i.b.3, 23, 51, 62–3, 66; Thompson (1900), 76–7
62. D&C i.b.3, 13. It was emphasised that this dispensation was not to become a precedent.
63. D&C i.b.3, 14. MAs of the House were internal honorary degrees, but all four of these men had studied previously at Cambridge
64. D&C i.b.3, 3; 1.c.3, 838. Read remained at Marcham until 1669.
65. D&C i.b.3, 3v
66. D&C i.b.3, 71; MS Estates 44, ff.16–20
67. D&C i.b.3, 70
68. *ODNB*
69. xii.b.104
70. *ODNB*; Bill (1988), 18
71. D&C i.b.3, 101
72. Most of those who had been deprived were either dead or ineligible to return.
73. Bill (1988), 22–5
74. Gouk, *HUO*, iv (1997), 629
75. D&C i.b.3, 103–4; DP ii.c.1, f.68. In 1659, the Students had requested the reinstatement of sermons in Latin.
76. Wood *L&T*, ii, 3 and 195. Berry hung on to his place as a chaplain until 1670 when, either drunk or love-sick, he stabbed himself. Discovered in time by his bedmaker, he recovered, but was sent down. He went to Ireland and somehow managed to procure himself a place in a cathedral there.
77. Wood *L&T*, ii, 3, 96–7; Porter, *HUO*, iv (1997), 71–6
78. D&C i.b.3, 105
79. DP ii.c.1, ff.70 and 71; MS Estates 80, ff.222–66 and D&C i.b.3, 111
80. Wood says that the documents from Cardinal College had been kept in a little study off the Treasury, or in a worm-eaten old chest, lying so neglected, damp, and eaten by rats that few survived in pieces larger than a shilling.
81. xii.b.104 and 105
82. Beddard, *HUO*, iv (1997), 807; Bennett, *HUO*, v (1986), 11
83. *ODNB*
84. Porter, *HUO*, iv (1997), 38n, 39 and 63
85. Thompson (1900), 12; MS Estates 121, f.183
86. D&C i.b.3, 126. Levett appears to have been allowed to return as, in 1666, he was appointed a tutor, and in 1681 became principal of Magdalen Hall. Thomas Ackworth was already a tutor.
87. D&C i.b.3, 128–9. Morison had received his BA in 1664.
88. Fowler (1873), 362. Fowler became Bishop of Gloucester in 1691.

89. de Beer (ed.) (1976), 61–2
90. Wood *L&T*, ii, 2; Elliott, *HUO*, iv (1987), 614; *ODNB*. The play was not only the last to be acted in Christ Church Hall but almost the last to be performed by undergraduates in Oxford until the mid-nineteenth century.
91. D&C i.b.3, 128. A sconce at this time was usually a fine, but came to be a 'punishment' meted out by undergraduates on each other, often requiring the downing of a quantity of ale in one go.
92. D&C i.b.3, 151; DP ii.c.1, f.72; *ODNB*
93. *ODNB*; Fauvel, Flood, & Wilson (eds.) (2000), 80–82
94. *ODNB*
95. *ODNB*
96. DP ii.c.1, f.75; Thompson (1900), 232–4; Wood *L&T*, iii, 11
97. Thompson (1900), 233–4; Cen i.a.2; Martin & Highfield (1997), 216; Green (1979), 275; Hopkins (2005), 149
98. Wood *L&T*, iii, 81
99. Thompson (1900), 83
100. There is no evidence that such an agreement was ever made
101. Thompson (1900), 92–5; D&C vi.c.3, 54–7; DP ii.c.1, ff. 76–85. This system continued until 1869, when Christ Church gave up the privilege.
102. Thompson (1900), 96–7; Uglow (2009), 259; xii.b.106, 113. Lady Castlemaine returned in 1674 to place her son in Christ Church as an undergraduate. The sturgeon, with wine to accompany it, cost £6 18s 6d.
103. Wood *L&T*, ii, 157
104. Crespion became a Gentleman of the Chapel Royal and confessor to the Royal Household.
105. Wood *L&T*, ii, 207–11; D&C xii.b.114
106. Wood *L&T*, ii, 525ff. No expenses are recorded in the disbursement books.
107. Beddard, *HUO*, iv (1997), 889
108. Wood *L&T*, iii, 16ff., 57
109. CCL MS 375; *ODNB*; Thompson (1900), 101–3; D&C i.b.3, 249; Beddard, *HUO*, iv (1997), 900–2
110. Wood *L&T*, iii, 192
111. *ODNB*
112. Bod MS Tanner 30, ff.83v & 93r; Beddard, *Christ Church 1976/1977*. George Hooper was, in 1686, chaplain to the king and rector of St Mary's Lambeth. William Wigan was vicar of Kensington, and became chaplain to William and Mary.
113. Beddard, *HUO*, iv (1997), 917ff.; Darwall-Smith (2008), 208ff.; Thompson (1900), 105; D&C i.b.3, 272–8
114. These numbers vary slightly from those of Thompson who says that there were 46 admissions in 1686 and 11 in 1687. The variations are probably caused by the frequent differences between admission dates and matriculation dates.
115. Bennett, *HUO*, v (1986), 17. Many undergraduates, particularly those from more influential families, were summoned home by anxious parents.
116. Beddard, *HUO*, iv (1997), 932–3
117. Wood *L&T*, iii, 215

118. Wood *L&T*, iii, 223; Bennett, *HUO*, v (1986), 17
119. Usually an occasion for great celebrations, only Magdalen and Christ Church rang bells to acknowledge the birth of Prince James in June 1688.

Christ Church time

1. Caröe (1923), 67–70; Thompson (1900), 230
2. *ODNB*. Tresham, although not a religious radical, definitely had Roman Catholic leanings.
3. Hiscock (1946), 143; xii.b.26, f.16. The number of Students was increased to 101 in 1663 by the Thurston bequest.
4. MS Estates 144, f.12; MS Estates 143, f.2. There is some evidence for yet another recasting in 1626 by Humphrey and James Keene, Hiscock (1946), 145.
5. Wood *L & T*, ii (1892), 497; MS Estates 143, ff.4 20; Hiscock (1946), 148; D&C i.b.5. A bellyard, on the north side of the Great Quadrangle, appears in the Chapter minutes in the eighteenth century.
6. Wood *L&T*, ii, 497
7. Hiscock (1946), 149; MS Estates 144, f.408. In 1953, Tom weighed in at 6 tons 4½ cwt.
8. Sharpe (28 May 1953), 1694–5
9. GB i.b.8, p.166
10. Hiscock (1946), 149; xii.b.69, f.7
11. GB.i.b.2, pp. 99 and 105
12. Hiscock (1946), 149; S.xxxiv.a.2 'B'; D&C ii.b.11, 175
13. S.xxxiv.a.2 'T' and 'G'
14. Letter home by William Spencer Barrett dated 26 January 1936, printed in Butler (ed.) (2006), 145
15. There is no surviving evidence of the sundial on the cathedral, and the one on the Hall has recently been restored. The first recorded keeper of the clock, Mr Wells, was appointed in 1552.
16. *ODNB*
17. MS Estates 143, ff.83–6, 91–9, 135–6
18. MS Estates 143, f.370
19. Vulliamy advised that the increased weight of the pendulum bob from 90 lb to 222 lb was too great.
20. Although Vulliamy stated that the clock was put right daily, other records suggest that it was corrected every Monday morning; Roberts (1814), 8.
21. MS Estates 144, ff.201–15. At the same time as the clock was under repair, while the scaffolding was up, the stonework was repaired or replaced where necessary, and the whole of the tower washed.
22. Lewis, *Christ Church 2008*
23. Howse (1997), 110
24. *ODNB* (2004), online edn, Oct 2006
25. xlix.a., f.90v. Joyce's estimate was £170, Dent's £230, Potts's £275 and Cooke's £300 (although this was fully inclusive of all building work as well).

26. S.xxxiv.a.2 'C'

5. 'With strength of argument and in good order': 1689–1755

1. Thompson (1900), 113–14; *ODNB*
2. D&C i.b.4, f.4
3. D&C i.b.4, f.1
4. Thompson (1900), 112; *ODNB*
5. Admissions had begun to climb during Owen's deanery from a low in the 1640s. During the first decade of Fell's office, admissions reached their pre-nineteenth-century peak of 502. They fell back down in the 1690s, and then began to climb slowly until the 1720s.
6. The usual proportion of gentlemen commoners in an annual intake was between a fifth and a quarter. It was the relative proportions of Students and commoners that dropped. Aldrich's efforts to bring in the talented as well as the wealthy resulted in a huge increase in the number of servitors.
7. Bennett, *HUO*, v (1986), 43; *ODNB*
8. Bennett, *HUO*, v (1986), 38–9; Green, *HUO*, v (1986), 311
9. Bennett, *HUO*, v (1986), 57
10. *ODNB*
11. Bennett, *HUO*, v (1986), 80–81
12. Thompson (1900), 115; *ODNB*. Aldrich was the last Christ Church vice-chancellor until Henry Liddell was elected to the position in 1870.
13. D&C i.b.4, f.15v
14. D&C i.b.4, f.22. Anthony Alsop was a renowned poet – *ODNB*.
15. D&C i.b.4, f.23v
16. D&C i.b.4, f.23v
17. Where these crosses were made is unknown.
18. *ODNB*. Smalridge would go on to become dean. He is described in the Chapter Book as a 'person of unblemished reputation' – D&C i.b.4, f.24
19. D&C i.b.4, f.24v
20. D&C i.b.4, ff.24–7
21. D&C i.b.4, f.90v
22. D&C i.b.5, f.38v. Beaulieu was the son of a French refugee priest who had received his BD from Christ Church in 1685.
23. D&C i.b.4, ff.64v–66
24. D&C i.b.4, f.32v; Thompson (1900), 135
25. D&C i.b.4, f.97. William was probably the son of William Dockwra, who tried to introduce a penny post system to London in the late seventeenth century.
26. D&C i.b.4, ff.115–16, 134v; HMC, *Portland*, vii, 76
27. Hearne, iii, 89; HMC, *Portland*, vii (1901), 24; Edward Harley, later 2nd Earl of Oxford, had matriculated from Christ Church in 1707. William Stratford, canon from 1703, had been chaplain to Edward's father, Robert, who was politically in the ascendant. Much of what we know about Atterbury's deanery comes from Stratford's one-sided and acerbic commentary.

Notes

28. HMC, *Portland*, vii (1901), 49–50
29. Bennett, *HUO*, v (1986), 51ff.
30. *ODNB*; Bennett, *HUO*, v (1986), 88–9. Smalridge was appointed to Atterbury's vacated deanery of Carlisle and to a canonry at Christ Church.
31. Bennett, *HUO*, v (1986), 90
32. HMC, *Portland*, vii, 60–62
33. Hearne, iii, 237–8
34. Bennett, *HUO*, v (1986), 90–92; Bennett (1975), 147
35. Bill (1988), 40–41
36. HMC, *Portland*, vii, 63
37. HMC, *Portland*, vii. 68
38. HMC, *Portland*, vii, 74
39. *ODNB*
40. HMC, *Portland*, vii, 83–4. Stratford was certain that the admission of the new Students was illegal, and that their rights were probably non-existent. The three Westminster Students elected in 1711 were Paul Forester, later a canon of Christ Church; George Wigan, a renowned poet; and Samuel Wesley.
41. *ODNB*; Darwall-Smith, in Brockliss (ed.) (2008), 335–6
42. HMC, *Portland*, vii, 85 and 96. Aldrich was dealt with discreetly by the vice-chancellor. Aldrich, who had already been presented to the rectory of Henley in 1709, just left the university quietly in 1713.
43. Palmer was allocated Peck 6:2.
44. HMC, *Portland*, vii, 89 and 91
45. HMC, *Portland*, vii, 123–38. Brooks had been Chapter Clerk since 1695 and acting auditor since 1708. The first recorded act of the Chapter after Atterbury's departure was to declare and ratify the election of Brooks as Register. The entry was signed by all those who had suffered most under Atterbury: Smalridge, Hammond, Burton, Gastrell and Stratford – D&C i.b.5, f.2v–3.
46. Entry fines were the seven-yearly fees paid for the renewal of a tenancy.
47. The audit was not formally concluded until 27 July 1713 – D&C i.b.5, f.4v. Some of the business of the audit entered by Perrott, including the first attempt to register the 1712 election, was crossed through in the Chapter book – D&C i.b.4, ff.141 and 142. The order for this was given on 23 September 1713 – D&C i.b.5, f.5v.
48. HMC, *Portland*, vii, 140
49. D&C i.b.4, 146; HMC, *Portland*, vii, 148–50
50. HMC, *Portland*, vii, 152–3
51. HMC, *Portland*, vii, 155
52. Smalridge's appointment was not met with universal approval. According to some, his promotion, along with those of his successors, was designed to increase Whig influence in the university. Langford, *HUO*, v (1986), 114
53. D&C i.b.5, f.1
54. Langford, *HUO*, v (1986), 102–6
55. Bennett & Mitchell, *HUO*, v (1986), 96, 164, 188
56. HMC, *Portland*, vii, 155–6

57. *ODNB*. Delaune had a rather scandalous career in Oxford, including the embezzlement of the University Press of around £2,000 during his delegacy.
58. xiii.b.6. In 1719, caution money was £5 for a commoner, £15 for a gentleman commoner and £30 for a nobleman.
59. HMC, *Portland*, vii, 252–4
60. *ODNB*; HMC, *Portland*, vii, 260–62. Mrs Smalridge was granted a pension of £300 per annum by Princess Caroline, and Stratford organised the sale of Smalridge's books and paintings.
61. *ODNB*
62. HMC, *Portland*, vii, 264; *ODNB*
63. Thompson (1900), 146
64. *ODNB*
65. HMC, *Portland*, vii, 321; *ODNB*. Boulter's time in Ireland, where he was renowned as a generous and charitable man, was much more successful than his deanery.
66. HMC, *Portland*, vii, 360–63, 381
67. *Al West*, 289 and <http://www.theclergydatabase.org.uk>, accessed 1 March 2008; D&C i.b.5, 82; Thompson (1900), 149
68. Green, *HUO*, v. (1986), 436–52; Thompson (1900), 149
69. HMC, *Portland*, vii, 382–3
70. *ODNB*
71. HMC, *Portland*, vii, 441
72. D&C i.b.5, 37v and 40. Rules laid down in 1631 were reiterated in 1718. Only in exceptional circumstances, such as the replacement of the dean's privy and outhouses after their demolition to make way for the new library, were private facilities funded by the corporate body.
73. HMC, *Portland*, vii, 466
74. D&C i.b.5, 92 and 93
75. HMC, *Portland*, vii, 273
76. HMC, *Portland*, vii, 276
77. D&C i.b.5, 115; Thompson (1900), 150
78. *ODNB*; online ed. January 2008
79. *ODNB*
80. Thompson (1900), 152
81. D&C i.b.5, 205
82. MS Estates 139, f.4
83. *ODNB*; online edn. January 2008
84. MS Estates 73, f.11
85. D&C i.b.5, 259
86. D&C i.b.5, 237 and 260. Bill (1988); D&C i.b.5, 226 and 263; Watson (2008), 21–2
87. D&C i.b.5, 121 and 167
88. D&C i.b.5, 172
89. D&C i.b.5, 195 and 228
90. D&C i.b.5, 173 and 206. A separate Librarian appointed for the Wake collection by its trustees (the dean, and the regius professors of divinity and Hebrew) in 1759 was

Notes

granted the same privilege of holding a living in conjunction with his position – D&C i.b.6, 50.

91. D&C i.b.5, 252. Both Barnes and Sealy were admonished for riot again in November 1751. Barnes was expelled and Sealy's degree was put back a year. Sealy resigned his Studentship just a month later. Barnes evidently had another shot at education, and went to St Edmund Hall in 1757. He later became chancellor of Exeter diocese, and died in his 88th year in 1820. His son, Frederick, was elected a Student of Christ Church in 1790, and made a canon in 1810, a position he held until his death in 1859.
92. D&C i.b.5, 266
93. D&C i.b.5, 249
94. Bill (1988), 161
95. DP xi.c.1(i); xii.c.180
96. D&C i.b.4, ff.98v–99v
97. Much of the material about education in the late seventeenth and eighteenth centuries is derived from Bill (1988). Bill gives very few footnotes.
98. Records do not survive before 1699, but collections were evidently introduced before this date. There is no sense that the volume which covers the period from 1699 is recording a new method. The collections of noblemen and gentlemen commoners are not recorded until 1774.
99. Bill (1988), 196–7
100. D&C i.b.1, f.iv
101. Bill (1988), 208
102. Thompson (1900), 119
103. Bill (1988), 256–7
104. The King's Library was assembled by George III and given to the nation by George IV. It now forms part of the British Library.
105. Bill (1988), 258–9; Thompson (1900), 119. Alsop produced an edition of Aesop as another New Year book in which he was rather disparaging about Bentley (*Fabularum Aesopicarum delectus* (1698))
106. Bill (1988), 214; li.b.1, f.2v. It was studied by Benjamin Marshall, a Canoneer Student from St Paul's School.
107. D&C i.b.5, f.6; Bill (1988), 215–16
108. D&C i.b.4, f.15v
109. D&C i.b.4, f.98v
110. Bill (1988), 254
111. Volton, *HUO*, v (1986), 575
112. Fauvel, Flood, & Wilson (eds.) (2000), 6. The Savilian professorships of geometry and astronomy were founded in 1619 by Henry Savile, warden of Merton College and provost of Eton.
113. Bill (1988), 263–8
114. *ODNB*; Fauvel, Flood, & Wilson (eds.) (2000), 152; xlviii.b.36
115. Clarke, *HUO*, v (1986), 523. Markham and Jackson also aimed to encourage and enthuse gentlemen commoners and noblemen, those destined to rule, by introducing histories of the classical world in English, and modern history, such as Raleigh.

116. Locke was studied at Christ Church right from the time that the University attempted to suppress his work in 1703. The *Essay on Human Understanding* was only removed from the curriculum under pressure from the growth of classics.
117. Bill (1988), 306
118. Langford, *HUO*, v (1986), 125–7; Ward (1958), 188–92; *A true copy of the poll taken at Oxford, January 31, 1750*
119. Sutherland, *HUO*, v (1986), 133
120. *ODNB*
121. D&C i.b.5, 286. Christ Church had the right of nomination to the principalship of the newly founded Hertford College.

6. 'Learning has been made a duty, a pleasure and even a fashion': 1755–1809

1. Mitchell, *HUO*, v (1986), 1–8; Darwall-Smith (2008), 275–95
2. The annual election from Westminster School was only of four or five boys each year. The Careswell exhibitions did not begin until the mid-eighteenth century, and then only with small numbers.
3. Green, *HUO*, v (1986), 315
4. The West Midlands, for the purpose of this study, includes Gloucestershire, Herefordshire, Shropshire, Staffordshire, Warwickshire and Worcestershire. The counties and countries are grouped as in HUO, iv (1997), 59. In the period 1525–1660, only 0.5 per cent of admissions of known origin came from Ireland, but admissions from Wales were 10 per cent of the total. Around 3 per cent were born abroad in this period, most in the West Indies. Very few, though, were not of British descent.
5. *HUO*, v (1986), 357–8
6. Lee matriculated in 1713. He died on 26 September 1755, just four months after Gregory's installation.
7. D&C i.b.6, 20, 26; Jones (1939), 10
8. Bill (1988), 104–5. The bequest, using the RPI, was worth in the region of £3.5 million today. The building of the Anatomy School was not a specific term of the bequest, but the terms of the will could not be met without it.
9. D&C i.b.6, 127
10. MS Estates 90. The Butlers Marston and Helsthorpe estates in Warwickshire were purchased in 1768.
11. D&C i.b.6, 134, 153. Freind, a Westminster Student in the 1690s, had also been a royal physician.
12. D&C i.b.6, 134, 149, 165, 166
13. For example, *Oxford Journal*, 17 January 1789; *Oxford Journal*, 24 July 1790; *ODNB*
14. Turner, *HUO*, v (1986), 662, 666; Webster, *HUO*, v (1986), 698, 706–7. For example, see D&C i.b.6, 103, 185, 192.
15. Webster, *HUO*, v (1986), 707; *ODNB*. Thomson had been accused of sodomy with a servant boy, and was hounded out of the University in spite of the support of colleagues.

16. D&C i.b.6, 149, 594
17. D&C i.b.7, 594, 625
18. D&C i.b.7, 652
19. D&C i.b.8, 35; MS Estates 127, ff.218–22; D&C i.b.9, 1. Susini (1754–1814) was famed for his extraordinary wax anatomical models. The finest of his models were made for the University of Cagliari between 1803 and 1805.
20. Bill (1988), 271–2
21. Bill (1988), 280
22. D&C i.b.6, 50. This revived requirement seems to have been honoured in the breach, even after 1759. Of the 23 men who were permitted to enter the law-line (move from the standard classical course to one more focused on law) between 1740 and 1800, only one had received his MA beforehand. Nine went on to careers in law.
23. Evans (ed.) (1888), 101–9, 125, 137. A Studentship was initially worth around £20 per annum with another £20 or £30 if the cost of meals and other perks were taken into account.
24. D&C i.b.6, 93; ODNB
25. Bill (1988), 218–19; D&C i.b.6, 194. Both men had been out on the town, and were probably the worse for wear.
26. Couch (ed.) (1892), 231
27. D&C i.b.7, 374; MS Estates 139, 289
28. D&C i.b.6, 58, 238, 239; D&C i.b.7, 344, 421. Chelsum was a favoured Student. In 1759 he had been granted leave of absence to serve as usher at Westminster School. He was granted, in 1777, the curacy of St Thomas's, one of the local Christ Church livings that Students were permitted to hold in conjunction with a Studentship, before being installed at Lathbury in Buckinghamshire, his year of grace commencing on 22 May 1780. He was also praelector theologiae and catechist.
29. D&C i.b.7, 498; ODNB, online edn. January 2008
30. D&C i.b.7, 516; D&C i.b.7, 526. To borrow a manuscript was strictly forbidden in the Library's rules under normal circumstances.
31. D&C i.b.7, 520, 537
32. D&C i.b.7, 664; D&C i.b.8, 23
33. D&C i.b.8, 35, 44v
34. The Students were encouraged to travel. William Burke, in 1760, was appointed secretary in Guadeloupe, and given permission to leave whilst retaining his Studentship. Soley was permitted a second year's absence to study abroad in 1777. In 1778, Nares and Wilmot were permitted to take up commissions in the army.
35. MCA, Blackwell's sales ledgers, volume 1, 1797/8
37. D&C i.b.6, 127. It was not just internal prizes either; the Chancellor's prize for Latin verse was won for three years in succession, between 1779 and 1781, by Christ Church men – Clarke, HUO, v (1986), 520
38. D&C i.b.6, 156; DP xi.c.1 (ii), f.28; MS Estates 120, ff.79–86; ODNB. After appeal, Shipley was allowed to return. He took his BA and MA, and then was given a living, a comfortable distance away, in North Wales.
39. Bill (1988), 184, 186–7, 193. The Boulter exhibitions were often held in conjunction with a Fell exhibition, at least until Jackson's deanery. The combination of the two

prizes made them even more financially attractive. Gentlemen commoners ran up bills of around 4 to 5 shillings.
40. D&C i.b.6, 35
41. D&C i.b.6, 104; *ODNB*; Dunbabin, *HUO*, v (1986), 273. Frewin's bequest was given to provide the Westminster Students with living expenses between their election in the early summer and receipt of their first official stipends six months later after the college election at Christmas.
42. Thompson (1900), 158; D&C i.b.6, 193
43. Thompson (1900), 159
44. D&C i.b.6, 212; D&C i.b.7, 321
45. D&C i.b.7, 366, 368, 451, 454
46. D&C i.b.6, 58, 70, 78, 89. In 1772, the Chapter decreed that up to £20 of the fines collected for bothering the Porter out of hours would be paid directly to the Porter – D&C i.b.6, 226.
47. Green, *HUO*, v (1986), 355
48. D&C i.b.6, 101, 104
49. D&C i.b.6, 58, 61
50. Thompson (1900), 162–3; D&C i.b.6, 179
51. D&C i.b.6, 253, 288. The name of the offender is indeed scratched out of the Chapter Books. It is possible that he was Thomas Hind, who matriculated in 1772 and went on to be a tutor and praelector rhetoricae before being appointed to the college living of Westwell. He is certainly missing from the battels books for the appropriate period.
52. D&C i.b.6, 222, 227; D&C i.b.7, 285, 383, 384, 437, 445; Thompson (1900), 167; D&C i.b.5, 43; Curthoys (1995), 379–95. Scriven and Soley were both hauled before the Chapter again in June 1778 for attacking the Masters' Common Room and threatening the rhetoric reader, and were expelled.
53. D&C i.b.6, 223, 229
54. D&C i.b.6, 199, 208; MS Estates 25, ff.24–35. The bill for the enclosure of Bledington was presented in 1768, and the acts for Butlers Marston and East Garston were passed in 1771.
55. Bill (1988), 187–9; D&C i.b.6, 187
56. D&C i.b.6, 211
57. D&C i.b.6, 219
58. The £1,000 gift of Richard Robinson, the Archbishop of Armagh, for Canterbury Quad was invested in 3 per cent consol annuities (a form of government bond) in 1773, and the following year several thousand pounds' worth of New South Sea annuities purchased for trust funds were sold.
59. D&C i.b.6, 228, 242, 255. The Treasurer was also indemnified against any theft from the Treasury.
60. D&C i.b.6, 224, 226, 232, 235, 240
61. GB i.b.6, 155; D&C i.b.6, 240, 246
62. D&C i.b.6, 265; D&C i.b.7, 370
63. D&C i.b.6, 256
64. D&C i.b.6, 291–5

Notes

65. D&C i.b.7, 494. The Under-Treasurer was also known as the Deputy or Assistant Treasurer.
66. From the beginning of 1821, hours were to be 10 am to 1 pm every day, regardless of the quarter or status. Only tutors were to be granted preferential treatment – D&C i.b.9, 15.
67. D&C i.b.7, 571–2
68. D&C i.b.7, 686; MS Estates 125, f.2. In 1791, the under-treasurer received £20 in salary, an additional £20 under the heading 'half office', and a ten guinea bonus from the Dean and Canons at Christmas, £71 for the administration of the Trust estates, £30 17s from acquittances, and £2 15s as his share of the seal fines.
69. D&C i.b.6, 288; D&C i.b.7, 332
70. D&C i.b.8, 12, 27v
71. D&C i.b.8, 69v
72. D&C i.b.7, 686; Thompson (1900), 178. The Duke of York's visit was the third royal visit during Jackson's deanery. George III had come to Oxford in 1785 and 1786, visiting Christ Church relatively informally.
73. Couch (ed.) (1892), 174–5
74. MS Estates 125, ff.1–8, 15. Senior servants had to have guarantors to ensure that they carried out their duties and were properly responsible for the monies in their charge. Richard Green, for example, was appointed Head Butler in 1803, and gave a bond of £1,000, backed by Revd William West Green of Magdalen Hall and William Fletcher, alderman, that he would pay the Students, chaplains, singing men, choristers and servants all sums due to them, and would preserve the college plate. Forty years later, Henry Grant's bond was £3,000 when he was appointed Head Butler. The size of the bonus indicates just how lucrative these positions could be.
75. D&C i.b.8, 71, 43, 76v, 70
76. D&C i.b.7, 646; D&C i.b.8, 66; MS Estates 146, f.19; xii.c.238; Mitchell, *HUO*, v (1986), 188–90
77. D&C i.b.7, 669
78. D&C i.b.7, 686; D&C i.b.8, 80v
79. *ODNB*, online edn. January 2008; Mitchell, *HUO*, v (1986)
80. *The Times*, 2 July 1793
81. Probably Antonio Bruni (1757–1821), Italian violinist and conductor; Tebaldo Monzani (1762–1839), flautist; Johann Baptist Cramer (1771–1858), pianist and composer; Elizabeth Billington (1768–1818), opera singer; and Anne-Marie Krumpholtz (1744–1824), harpist.
82. Encaenia is the ceremony at which the University of Oxford awards honorary degrees to distinguished men and women and commemorates its benefactors.
83. BL Addit. MS 27591, f.93
84. DP xix.c.1
85. Markham was the youngest of Dean Markham's sons, four of whom came to Christ Church
86. D&C i.b.7, 558; Thompson (1900), 179–80. According to Thompson, the punishment was completely ineffective, and the traditional ride out continued until the railway arrived in Oxford.

87. Harvie, *HUO*, vi (1997), 728
88. Green, *HUO*, v (1986), 465–7
89. Green, *HUO*, v (1986), 607; *ODNB*
90. Green, *HUO*, v (1986), 607–37; Brock, *HUO*, vi (1997), 7
91. Green, *HUO*, v (1986), 331
92. Couch (ed.) (1892), 174
93. Couch (ed.) (1892), 307

7. 'Reading as if my life depended on my diligence': 1809–55

1. xlviiia.45, ff.68–70; Roberts (1814), 70
2. Hurd (2007), 12; Potter (1994), 65. Real tennis had been popular from Tudor times, but it was expensive, and only affordable by the wealthier students. In 1830, an hour's play could cost 14s.
3. xlviii.a.45; *ODNB*
4. *ODNB*
5. Jackson retired after the death of the University Chancellor, Portland. He did not wish to face the anticipated battle between Grenville and Liverpool, knowing that it would cause unrest within Christ Church.
6. *ODNB*
7. *ODNB*; Curthoys, in Butler (ed.) (2006), 90. Twenty-one of these were obtained by undergraduates admitted by Jackson. Nine of the first thirteen firsts awarded in 1808 were to Christ Church men.
8. Thompson (1900), 186; D&C i.b.8, 90v and 99; D&C i.b.9, 2
9. D&C i.b.8, 123; *ODNB*
10. D&C i.b.9, 51
11. xlviii.a.42a, ff.5 and 6; Fauvel, Flood and Wilson (eds.) (2000), 162–3. The algebra book was probably that of the schoolmaster, Charles Butler, *An easy introduction to algebra, to which is prefixed an essay on the uses of mathematics* (1799).
12. xlviii.a.54, f.160 and 55, ff.5 and 105–6
13. Hannabus, *HUO*, vii (2000), 443. Between 1810 and 1820, nearly 30 per cent of those obtaining mathematical honours were from Christ Church.
14. Thompson (1899), 18
15. Gaskell (ed.) (1939), 178 and 179; *ODNB*. Harrison did recover, receiving prizes and accolades.
16. Smith exchanged the deanery of Christ Church with Thomas Gaisford for the 'golden stall' at Durham, so-called because it had an income far higher than most other canonries.
17. Short kept a notebook which he entitled 'History of my pupils' – Cen i.a.4 – in which he recorded not only academic achievements but also character notes and, in some cases, their post-Christ Church careers.
18. *ODNB*; D&C i.b.9, 105v
19. Thompson (1900), 192. The lecture room is now the McKenna Room.
20. Thompson (1900), 193
21. Thompson (1899), 18

Notes

22. *ODNB*
23. Acland (1890), 14. Quotation from *Travels of Carus, Physician to the King of Saxony*.
24. Acland was the second choice as Kidd's replacement. William Page, who was the only Student qualified under the bequest, turned the post down.
25. *ODNB*
26. MS Estates 127, f.427
27. MS Estates 127, ff.431 and 433
28. DP ii.c.2, f.66; Kent (2001), 30
29. From Liddell's testimonial for Acland for Clinical Professorship, 5 October 1857
30. The word palaeontology is first cited, according to the *OED*, in 1836. 'Fossilogy' was used earlier.
31. Edmonds and Douglas (1976)
32. Curthoys, *HUO*, vi (1997), 342
33. Gaisford was not entirely alone; the president of St John's College considered that the honours system had fostered an '*unchristian spirit of emulation*' – Brock, *HUO*, vi (1997), 20.
34. Thompson (1900), 195; Bill & Mason (1970), 24
35. Atlay (1903), 39; Acland, 'Remarks on the extension of education at the University of Oxford in a letter to the Rev W. Jacobson, DD' (1848), 19. Acland regretted the elevation of the class-lists '*into a fetish to which all else must be sacrificed*' but felt that examination was the means by which to make any extension to the curriculum effective.
36. Thompson (1900), 195; Curthoys, *HUO*, vi (1997), 169
37. Bill & Mason, 26
38. Thompson (1900), 188; Ward (1965), 41–2
39. Air XXXV, Act II
40. Couch (1892), 209–10; *ODNB*; Baker (1981), 184–8; Brock, *HUO*, vi (1997), 56–9; Young, in Butler (ed.) (2006), 86–7. The slogan is still *in situ*.
41. The Christ Church Club, later to become the Grillions Club after the hotel in which the club met, was founded to be a neutral meeting ground for those of opposing political views in 1812.
42. Memoir of Sir Thomas Acland by his son (1902), 23; Jenkins (1995), 20
43. Gladstone had begun Christ Church life with rather unsatisfactory rooms in Chaplains' Quad (Foot (ed.) (1968), 204–5), but this was not uncommon. Even noblemen were occasionally put into rooms '*on account of which the servants of the paternal mansion would give a month's warning*', until more suitable accommodation became available – [Arnold] (1867), 144–5. The construction of Meadows Building was designed to alleviate the stress on college rooms.
44. Hawarden letters: W. E. Gladstone to T. Gladstone, 7 December 1829; Matthew, in Butler (ed.) (2006), 89
45. Jenkins (1995), 11
46. Hiscock (1946), 91–2; CCL MS 466; Brock, *HUO*, vi (1997), 41–2. The diary is just for the calendar year 1809.
47. Gaskell (ed.) (1939), 163

48. Gaskell (ed.) (1939), 166–7; Atlay (1903), 33 and 38; Curthoys & Day, *HUO*, vi (1997), 284. The Christ Church Society, or Loder's, was founded in 1814 and held weekly wine parties. The Mitre club (1820–43) was most definitely just for drinking and eating: '*an epicurean oasis where the business of the day was properly concerned with the correct wine and the quality of the dinner*' – Firman (1966), 12 and 13.
49. *Memoirs of Earl Cowper by his wife* (1913), 29–35
50. D&C i.b.8, 91v, 118, 162v. College decrees had always stipulated that only the head porter could keep a dog in college.
51. Events like the vandalism to Mercury, committed by a gentleman commoner rather than a Student, were not recorded in the Chapter minutes. Mercury had suffered at least once before, in 1773, when he was pulled down and then hung by the neck on Canon Edward Bentham's door – Bod. MS Top. Oxon. D.247, f.38v.
52. *ODNB*
53. D&C i.b.8, 174
54. Cen i.a.4, 133–4. Charles and his older brother, Arthur, both migrated to Trinity College, Cambridge. Short recorded that he was sad to see the older boy go.
55. D&C i.b.9, 48. Page's life after 1825 appears to have been both exemplary and dull.
56. D&C i.b.9, 48 and 56v
57. D&C i.b.9, 56–7v
58. D&C i.b.8, 97
59. D&C i.b.9, 14v, 17v, and 26v; Cen i.a.4, 42. On his return from rustication at the beginning of Hilary term 1822, Borough was found guilty of a serious disturbance in which he made a bonfire in the centre of Peckwater Quad with doors and '*other combustible materials*'. It signified the end of his Studentship. Bonfires in Peckwater seem to have been a fairly regular occurrence; William Cother was accused of a similar offence in May 1831 – D&C i.b.9, 119 – and there was the famous fire in which the Library statues were burnt in 1870. So regular were they, one made it into *Christ Church Days*, the 1867 novel by Frederick Arnold, described as just a 'lark'.
60. Curthoys and Day, *HUO*, vi (1997), 279
61. W. F. Hook correspondence, in a private collection and copied, with permission, by the Archivist, E. G. W. Bill.
62. Gaskell (ed.) (1939), 164
63. Hiscock (1946), 94. Astley had also run up debts of £400, and reckoned that he knew less when he left Oxford than he did when he arrived.
64. D&C i.b.10, 110.
65. Gaskell (ed.) (1939), 161 and 189. Gaskell was determined to go down without a debt unpaid – '*It was the boast of Augustus that he found Rome brick, and that he left her marble, but how much more glorious will be my boast, when I shall be able to say that I found bills abundant, and that I left them scarce; that I found them unpaid, and left them paid; that I found them a two-edged sword in the hands of tradesmen and their shop-boys, and [left] them a shaft against their recurrence and a shield against oppression.*'
66. [Arnold] (1867), 229–34
67. D&C i.b.8, 166. Cleaver was the son of Euseby Cleaver, the Archbishop of Dublin.
68. D&C i.b.8, 178v

69. DP xi.c.1. There was no reliable witness to Hampden's alleged misconduct, and so counsel recommended that his word should be taken as truth.
70. D&C i.b.10, 146v and 147
71. D&C i.b.10,163
72. DP xi.c.1 (iii). Hampden senior was unpopular among the traditionalists in the University for advocating the abolition of subscription to the Thirty-nine Articles and the admission of non-conformists. He was not afraid to draw a direct connection between his theology and political reform – *ODNB*.
73. Curthoys & Day, *HUO*, vi (1997), 277
74. Thompson (1900), 260–64; Curthoys & Day, *HUO*, vi (1997), 273–4
75. I am grateful to Terry Morahan of Belfast for sharing his research on early competitive rowing.
76. Plate 53 *HUO*, vi (1997); Frost [1989]
77. The prominence of Christ Church in these early Varsity races caused the dark blue of the House to be adopted for Oxford.
78. Parkhouse, in Butler (ed.) (2006), 127
79. Curthoys & Day, *HUO*, vi (1997), 275
80. Gaskell (ed.) (1939), 160. Of the 41 undergraduate gentlemen commoners listed in the 1830 *University Calendar*, 23 were from Eton.
81. English (1991), 15–32
82. Thompson (1900), 187
83. *ODNB*. Short came up from Westminster School in 1809. He left Oxford after Peel's defeat in the University election of 1829, having supported him vigorously.
84. *The Times*, 16 June 1814
85. Thompson (1900), 188; D&C i.b.8, 146v
86. DP ii.c.2, f.47
87. Roe had matriculated in 1806. He became a barrister, King's Counsel of the Duchy of Lancaster, and then police magistrate first at Marlborough Street and then at Bow Street. He was knighted in 1832.
88. MS Estates 146, ff.48–11; DP ii.c.2, f.42. The total loss was £805 17s 3d.
89. Thompson (1900), 193; D&C i.b.8, 16
90. Couch (1892), 316; Parsons, in Butler (ed.) (2006), 104
91. D&C i.b.10, 93
92. MS Estates 125, ff.252 and 276; *The Times*, 4 November 1846; *Manchester Guardian*, 11 November 1846
93. Thompson (1900), 194
94. *ODNB*
95. Thompson (1900), 197. Henry Liddell, soon to be Gaisford's successor in the Deanery, was appointed a commissioner, his acceptance of which must have been a blow to Gaisford.
96. Thompson (1900), 217
97. Curthoys, *HUO*, vi (1997), 352
98. Ward, *HUO*, vi (1997), 318 and 320
99. Curthoys, in Butler (ed.) (2006), 91
100. Jenkins (1995), 117; Bill & Mason (1970), 33

101. Servitors no longer had to perform menial tasks to pay for their board and lodging. The rebuilding of Chaplains' Quad and Fell's Building would provide the necessary accommodation.
102. Thompson (1900), 198–9
103. Bill & Mason (1970), 34. The 'outsiders' were Sir John Coleridge and G. H. S. Johnson.
104. Scholarships attached to specific schools could be continued.
105. Thompson (1900), 197 and 199; D&C i.b.10, 151. The canons felt that '*mere intellectual merit*' should not be the sole reason for election to a Studentship, and the requirement of previous residence had allowed for the assessment of character before the final decision was made.
106. Bill & Mason (1970), 36. *ODNB*
107. *ODNB*. Wade was a Utilitarian journalist who published, between 1820 and 1835, his pamphlets *The Black Book* and *The Extraordinary Black Book*, which revealed the wealth of the Church and its incumbents.
108. Barrett (1993), 5 and 13
109. There were three further reports: the third, in May 1836, established the Commission as a permanent body, the fourth, in June 1836, proposed alterations to benefices, and a fifth was prepared in draft but not signed owing to the death of William IV.
110. Barrett (1993), xv and 409n. By 1867, the only cathedrals which had not commuted their property for a grant from the Ecclesiastical Commissioners were Christ Church, Hereford and Manchester.
111. Barrett (1993), 227
112. *Ecclesiastical Duties and Revenues Bill. Memorial of the Dean and Chapter of Christ Church, Oxford.* Copy in DP ii.c.2, f.51
113. The other two were the Established Church Act 1836, and the Pluralities and Residence Act 1838.
114. Barrett (1993), 15 and 16
115. Bill & Mason (1970), 36–7
116. Thompson (1900), 215–18
117. Westminster Students were elected in May or June, but not formally elected to their Studentships until Christmas Eve. They were, however, expected to reside during the Michaelmas term, and were treated as Students from the beginning.
118. Thompson (1900), 217. The Latin prayer book was substituted by an English one in 1861. Prick-bills were appointed from among the junior freshmen to mark the names of those attending chapel and report the names of absentees.
119. [Arnold] (1867), 5. Although a novel, *Christ Church Days* is set accurately in the last years before the Christ Church Ordinance. Its author, Frederick Arnold, came up to Christ Church in 1856. He became editor of the *Literary Gazette*.
120. Responsions was a name describing the first of the three examinations once required for an academic degree at the University of Oxford. It was nicknamed the 'Little-Go' and was generally taken by students prior to or shortly after matriculation, allowing the University to verify the quality of the students in the absence of standardised school examinations. It was abolished in 1960.
121. [Arnold] (1967), 125–7. Charley had exercises set by one coach, and then gave them to another to be answered!

122. The canons only dined on High Table at gaudy dinners.

'Water coming to the house of office': the plumbing

1. MS Estates 144, f.4
2. MS Estates 144, f.10; *VCH Oxford*, iv (1979), 354. Christ Church, with six other colleges and St Mary Hall, paid between 10s and £1 per annum for water from the conduit.
3. MS Estates 144, ff.6 and 8
4. MS Estates 144, f.11
5. xlix.a.1, f.105
6. MS Estates 144, f.30
7. MS Estates 144, f.160; D&C i.b.9, f.60v
8. D&C i.b.9, 107
9. xlix.a.1, f.105
10. MS Estates 138, ff.122–30; Hibbert (ed.) (1988), 494. The improvement of the water supply to Christ Church was part and parcel of improvements to supply city-wide. New reservoirs were constructed, new pipes laid – largely through the energy of Sir Henry Acland – and, by 1884, every house in Oxford was connected to mains water.
11. *Christ Church 1958*
12. *Christ Church 1959*. The increase in summer schools and conferences encouraged the 'en-suiting' of most rooms. Most recently, the refurbishment of Blue Boar Quad has seen the inclusion of pods with shower, toilet and basin in every room.
13. MS Estates 144, f.222
14. MS Estates 121, f.219
15. Hibbert (ed.) (1988), 461 and 168
16. MS Estates 144, f.287; GB i.b.2, 67
17. GB i.b.2, 276; xlix.a.1, f.47
18. GB i.b.2, 289
19. MS Estates 130, f.295
20. GB i.b.2, 289
21. MS Estates 130, ff.297–9; MS Estates 128, f.21; GB i.b.2, 286, 289
22. MS Estates 128, ff.24–47
23. GB i.b.3, 186. Works on the drains north of the Great Quadrangle were not to be carried out if there was a serious outbreak of cholera and if the dean was advised 'by competent authority' that the work ought to be stopped.
24. MS Estates 130, ff.74–172v; GB i.b.3, 166
25. GB i.b.12, 43

8. 'To conduce the welfare and usefulness of Christ Church': 1855–98

1. *ODNB*; Thompson (1899), 134–5
2. Much of the following on the Ordinance of 1858 and the Christ Church Oxford Act 1867 is derived from Bill & Mason (1970). A useful short summary of the reforms of the nineteenth century can be found by Curthoys, in Butler (ed.) (2006), 90–93

3. Jacobson was known as a reserved and cautious man with a well-developed sense of right and duty.
4. In 1690, Thomas Wood, Bishop of Coventry and Lichfield, bequeathed property in St Ives, Huntingdonshire, and £3,000 for the maintenance of the Senior Masters and Junior Students at Christ Church. The estate at Chatteris, Cambridgeshire, was purchased, and the revenues from the Senior Masters' Estate distributed proportionately by seniority.
5. Bill & Mason (1970), 193–5; MS Estates 127, ff.32–8
6. MS Estates 117, ff.40–42
7. MS Estates 117, ff.45–50
8. MS Estates 117, f.51. All but Jacobson signed this document.
9. Bill & Mason (1970), 61–2
10. D&C i.b.10, f.175v
11. This obsession with being a member of the House is misleading. Of the 44 deans of Christ Church from 1546 to the present day, only 25 have been Housemen.
12. The second unattached canonry was suppressed on the death of Jelf in 1871. The redistribution of its funds did not take place until March 1874 – GB i.b.2, 147.
13. According to Thompson, Luke was devoted to Christ Church.
14. Blore was also the only gremial member of Christ Church to be elected in this way before the passing of the Christ Church Act in 1867.
15. Although the Board was able to elect tutors, the dean and canons could still act independently in some cases; in 1861, as trustees under Dr Lee's will, the Lee's reader in law and modern history was appointed without any reference to the Electoral Board at all. The board was abolished in 1891.
16. RA VIC/MAIN/Z/445/28. All letters from the Royal Archive are cited with the permission of Her Majesty Queen Elizabeth II.
17. Richard Jelf was principal of King's College, London, from 1844 to 1868.
18. RA VIC/MAIN/ Z/443/82 and 84
19. RA VIC/MAIN/Z/1 & 21. Fisher was elected to a Studentship in 1845, and was appointed a tutor in 1851. He was appointed private secretary and keeper of the privy seal to the Prince of Wales in 1861.
20. RA VIC/MAIN/Z/445/33
21. RA VIC/MAIN/Z/445/20 and 44
22. RA VIC/MAIN/Z/446/5
23. RA VIC/MAIN/Z/265/16–18
24. Evidence would suggest that the friendship was mutual. Legend has it that Leopold named one of his daughters after Alice Liddell, although correspondence in the Royal Archives shows that the child was in fact named after the prince's sister who had died in 1878 and with whom he had been very close. I am grateful to Pamela Clark, Registrar of the Royal Archives, for this information. Alice Liddell named one of her sons Leopold, more usually known as Rex.
25. Bill & Mason (1970), 103, n.1. The dean and canons had in fact often been very generous, both with large benefactions and donations from private funds benefiting both college and incumbents.

26. Gordon objected, too, to the move of the Senior Students to High Table which, he said, 'gave the appearance of a proper position without the reality and I hate shams.'
27. Prout, of course, Charles Sandford, Thomas Vere Bayne, Charles Dodgson, Augustus Harcourt, William Church, George Blore, Charles Hoole, Charles Bigg, Charles Martin, Robert Brodie, Thomas Chamberlain, Richard Meux Benson, Henry Parry Liddon and Henry Thompson. Vere Bayne kept minutes of all the meetings of the Students, beginning on 18 February 1865 until 10 December 1868 – CCL MS 449.
28. Bill & Mason (1970), 107 and 115
29. The cost of college life was occasionally cited as a reason for Student debt.
30. Walter Jr. had matriculated in 1864.
31. Curthoys, *HUO*, vii (2000), 145. The appointment of a steward was Christ Church's response to a general overhaul of college catering across the university. The choice of the title 'steward' rather than 'domestic bursar' is interesting. Whether deliberately or not, the Chapter chose the term used for the position at Cardinal College.
32. The Dean presided over the meeting. His formal appearance in the Common Room – the Senior Students' domain – was unprecedented. Faussett was both Steward and Treasurer from 1868 until 1880.
33. Between 1855 and early 1868, the government changed three times.
34. The original plan was that the Chapter would select one, the Students another, and the third be decided by the two men so chosen. Milman also thought that Christ Church should be divided in two, with the revenues divided between the capitular body, under the dean and canons, and the educational establishment, under the Dean and Students.
35. Mason, *HUO*, vii (2000), 226
36. Bill & Mason (1970), 176
37. Mansel declined to sign the canons' letter as he had not been present at or involved with any of the negotiations and debates. *ODNB*.
38. The only debate was in the House of Lords over clause 28, which dealt with the abolition of ranks of undergraduates. Lord Bute assumed, wrongly, that the clause was abolishing the admittance of noblemen to Christ Church altogether.
39. GB i.b.2, pp. 2 &3. The minutes, taken by Bayne, record that three committees were set up, the seal fixed to the leases of properties in Kentish Town, the steward requested the audit of his accounts, and that Sandford proposed referees be made honorary Students.
40. GB i.b.2, 87. This was not passed by Governing Body until 1871, probably as more of a practical decision than a political one.
41. These comprised a Library Committee, College Officers Committee, a committee on Senior Students, a Cathedral Services Committee, a Portraits Committee, a Cathedral Restoration committee, a Committee on Unattached Students, another on the residence for the Censors' servant, and one to discuss the creation of a new Broad Walk between Meadows Building and the river. GB i.b.2, 2–30
42. Harvie, *HUO*, vi (1997), 723–30
43. Curthoys, in Butler (ed.) (2006), 90–93; Thompson (1900), 207. It was under the 1882 statutes, ratified on 3 May 1882, that the Senior Students became Students (divided into Official and Ordinary Students), and the Junior Students became

scholars. A committee was first set up in 1870 to discuss the celibacy of Senior Students – GB i.b.2, 66. Shute was the first Student to be re-elected after marriage. It was he who promoted the one-to-one tutorial, still a novelty in the 1880s, but a system that would come to epitomise an Oxford education in the twentieth century. Students still had to request permission to marry until the 1960s.

44. MS Estates 130, f.140
45. MS Estates 134, f.25; GB i.b.3, p.14
46. MS Estates 134, ff.27–38
47. Harvie, *HUO*, vii (2000) 69 and 73; Dodgson, Remarks on Report of Finance Committee [March 1886]; Wakeling (ed.), vii (2004), 26 and 262, and 4n; CCL MS 536/1; GB i.b.3, 29 and 34; MS Estates 134; MS Estates 135; MS Estates 139
48. GB i.b.2, 12, 38 & 43. The term 'servitor' was replaced by 'exhibitioner' on 16 December 1867.
49. Honey & Curthoys, *HUO*, vii (2000), 550
50. Honey & Curthoys, *HUO*, vii (2000), 567
51. The fourth-century statute of Aphrodite and Eros was bequeathed to Christ Church by Alexander Mackenzie in 1813. All the statues show evidence of burning, and Aphrodite was cracked into several pieces.
52. *The Times*, 18 May 1870
53. GB i.b.2, 73–4
54. Hiscock (1946), 97–101; Mason, *HUO*, vii (2000), 221–2, 225; DP v.c.1; *The Times*, 24 May 1870
55. *The Times*, 4 December 1893
56. The Blenheim row probably caused Sampson to suffer a breakdown – Bod MS Top Oxon.d.278, f.163v.
57. Mason, *HUO*, vii (2000), 227. The incident prompted another spate of correspondence in *The Times*. One letter suggested that if the behaviour of the rich and aristocratic young men was to be accepted and even feted, then how was it possible to 'reproach the lower classes for their strikes, their violence, or their indifference to authority'? Another letter suggested that the dean was trying too hard to foster an environment of scholarship in a college that contained a number of 'rich men who never learnt to work at school and who will not work in Oxford', and that his punishments were too severe. Correspondence did not die down until Paget himself wrote to *The Times* saying that he felt that he had been lenient, and that the perpetrators had received a far lesser sentence than they would have done had the action taken place outside college.
58. Curthoys, *HUO*, vii (2000), 123–4
59. DP v.a.2
60. GB i.b.2, 30 and 76. More rooms in college were set aside as tutorial rooms. In 1868, Peck 8:1 was converted into a tutor's room and then, in 1870, two more sets of rooms.
61. The collections were transferred on long-term loan, and Christ Church men would be free to use them as before. MS Estates 127, f.455v. Kent (2001); Howarth, *HUO*, vii (2000), 462–4.

Notes

62. The possibility of a Lee's Readership in physics was put to committee on 28 April 1869 and approved in November of that year. Reinhold, from Merton College, was elected on 18 December.
63. GB i.b.2, 96
64. Howarth, *HUO*, vii (2000), 463. The numbers taking honours in chemistry also doubled, from 54 to over 100.
65. Balliol, Magdalen, Trinity and Wadham Colleges were the other four. There were only thirteen teaching scientists in the colleges. Howarth, *HUO*, vii (2000), 491.
66. Stubbs was made an honorary Student in 1878 at the same time as Samuel Rawson Gardiner, another eminent historian who was overlooked by Gaisford – Mason, *HUO*, vii (2000), 229.
67. Soffer, *HUO*, vii (2000), 366–9
68. DP ii.c.3; GB i.b.2, 105. High Table was set aside for members of Governing Body only in December 1871
69. GB i.b.2, 311; Brock, and Mason, *HUO*, vii (2000), 58 and 222. Lord Salisbury, squarely on Pusey's side, sent his sons to University College, rather than Christ Church. His efforts to protect the boys from such heresies backfired when Macan was appointed to a fellowship at University College, eventually becoming its Master in 1906.
70. UCA UC:MA43/J1/1; GB i.b.3, 356. Macan kept a diary recording the events of 1881/2. Some time later he was nominated to a lectureship in Greek History, but the Electoral Board decided again not to appoint him.
71. GB i.b.2, 90 and 94
72. i.b.2, 78
73. GB i.b.2, 278 and 299 and 300
74. GB i.b.2, 305. There were evidently functions before these: an engraving of a British Medical Association dinner in the Hall was published in the *Illustrated London News* in 1868.
75. S xxvii.c.1/32
76. Curthoys, *HUO*, vii (2000), 145
77. S xxxiii.c.1
78. Henry Grant had been butler at Christ Church since 1850. He was not replaced. The staff were reorganised so that there was a bailiff, buttery clerk, steward's clerk, and the Sub-Treasurer who was to be seen as the senior college servant. £300 per annum was saved in wages.
79. GB i.b.2, 241
80. GB i.b.2, 247
81. Acland held both posts simultaneously. The present manciple, or steward's accountant, is the successor to the junior steward.
82. GB i.b.2, 248
83. S xxxii.c.1. A notice dated 4 November 1881 stated 'that the accounts of the Treasurer should be kept wholly separate, and that there should be no running account between the two offices after 25 December next'.
84. Christ Church went Head in Torpids in 1907, in the 1908 VIIIs, and both Torpids and VIIIs in 1909.

85. Parkhouse, in Butler (ed.) (2006), 127–31
86. Potter (1994), 95
87. Jones, *HUO*, vii (2000), 525. In the 1950s, the Christ Church beagles were amalgamated with New College. There were Christ Church point-to-point races at least until the First World War – xx.c.1.
88. Rugby, cricket, beagling, rowing and football were all sufficiently organised by the late nineteenth century to have regular team pictures taken. There are also early records for athletics, cricket and lawn tennis.
89. Jones, *HUO*, vii (2000), 520 and 539. The 1880 match was said to have been attended by 45,000 spectators.
90. The cricket ground prior to this date was near the railway station.
91. SOC v.a.12
92. Jones, *HUO*, vii (2000), 536; Parkhouse, in Butler (ed.) (2006), 127–31; *Christ Church 1975*
93. GB i.b.3, 99; SOC xx.c.1
94. University College established its JCR more formally in 1889, Brasenose in 1887. Magdalen was quicker, refounding its JCR in 1867 from an earlier, less controlled club for the demies. Corpus had shut down its first JCR in 1852, and was the last to redress the situation, in the 1890s. New College had a JCR from the 1680s and Pembroke College from 1794 – Curthoys, *HUO*, vii (2000), 150–51. The JCR had the first telephone to be linked to the outside world, from 1895. The Porter's Lodge did not get an outside connection until 1920.
95. No doubt helped by Dean Liddell's appointment as vice-chancellor in 1870.
96. SOC xvi.c.1; Hiscock (1946), 188–94
97. Bod MS Top Oxon.b.128
98. Howarth, *HUO*, vii, 639
99. Symonds, *HUO*, vii (2000), 708 & 710; Hight (1937), 161–71
100. Rathbone, in Butler (ed.) (2006), 132–3. The mission was renamed and re-created in the 1930s under the leadership of John Arkell (ChCh 1928).
101. Ockwell and Pollins, *HUO*, vii (2000), 669; *ODNB*; Report by Mackinder to the Governing Body of Christ Church for the year 1895/6, in GB xvii.c.1. The college was formally incorporated on New Year's Day 1895.
102. GB i.b.2, 53, 55 and 17 November 1869. Probably 'Mrs Pott's cottage', now the Clerk of Work's offices. Soon after the creation of the servants' reading room, the choir school was given the building in exchange for a room in Meadows Building until the new school facilities were constructed.
103. Curthoys, *HUO*, vii (2000), 148–9
104. The Reading Room collection was reabsorbed into the main Library in 1932, and the room became the Law Library for the next forty years.
105. GB i.b.2, 357; Hiscock (1946), 107–10; Library Records 72. It was under J. G. Barrington-Ward that the Library began to be more of a resource of all members of college.
106. GB i.b.2, 41 and 70
107. GB i.b.2, 260
108. DP v.a.3, vii and viii

'More like some fine castle, or great palace, than a college ...': the buildings

1. Work in progress.
2. D&C i.b.2, 125
3. Bodleian Library ME Wood F.28, ff.169–70
4. MS Bod1.13, f.5v; Newman, *HUO*, iii (1986), 614
5. Bodleian Library ME Wood F.28, ff.169–70; xii.b.24, f.74v; xii.b.25, ff.15v and 16; MS Estates 142, f.1
6. *ODNB*
7. Salter (1960), 221 and 260
8. D&C i.b.2, 151; Thompson (1900), 115–17
9. Sturdy et al. (1961/2); D&C i.b.2, 277; xii.b.25 and 29
10. D&C i.b.2, 149
11. *ODNB*; Bussby (1967); Thompson (1900), 63; xi.b.35, ff.79–85; Hiscock (1946), 213
12. Girouard, in Butler (ed.) (2006), 49–51; Hiscock (1946), 207–8; Thompson (1900), 234–5; Tyack (1998), 112–14
13. Beddard, *Christ Church 1976–1977*
14. *The Antiquarian Repertory*, ii (1779), 52
15. Wood *L&T*, ii (1892), 176; Thompson (1900), 89; xii.b.113; MS Estates 126, f.309; xxxiii.b.11, f.10
16. CCL MS 376; Caröe (1923); Newman, *HUO*, iv (1997), 171–2; MS Estates 143, ff.2–29; Tyack (1998), 142; White (2007), 107; Colvin (1995); MS Estates 144, f.14
17. The main quadrangle was occasionally called Tom Quad after the construction of the Tower, but not habitually until the 1970s.
18. Colvin, *HUO*, v (1986), 832; Tyack (1998), 142–3; Thompson (1900), 116; xxxiii.b.15; Bill, 'The rebuilding ...'
19. *ODNB*
20. Hiscock (1946), 18; D&C i.b.5, 9 and 10; Chichester (1977), 7. A gallery had been installed in the old library to accommodate Aldrich's collections.
21. HMC, *Portland*, iii, 217
22. Hiscock (1946), 53; CCL Library Building Accounts, f.10v
23. Bodleian MS Top.Oxon.d.287, f.34v
24. D&C i.b.6, 8; CCL Library Building Accounts, ff.23–8
25. MS Estates 127, ff.17–52
26. MS Estates 127, ff.28–58; Cook & Mason (eds.) (1988); xii.c.213; D&C i.b.7
27. *ODNB*
28. Thompson (1900), 159–60; MS Estates 127
29. Hiscock (1946), 74; MS Estates 144, f.25; D&C i.b.6, 296; D&C i.b.7, 321; xii.c.14; D&C i.b.6, 226
30. DP ix.b.1, 80 and 72; D&C i.b.6, 280; Thompson (1900), 165–6; xxiii.b.3; MS Estates 144, f.24; D&C i.b.7, 451 and 454
31. During the eighteenth century, the Hall roof was replaced after a fire, and its doorway redesigned. The Buttery was also refurbished.

32. Thompson (1900), 231; D&C i.b.8, 78v; MS Estates 144, f.147ff.
33. Tyack (1998), 227; Colvin (1983), 141–2; MS Estates 126, f.312; GB i.b.2, 89
34. Maintenance had been undertaken on the cathedral, almshouse, Library and Tom Tower.
35. *Report of George Gilbert Scott, Esq., R.A. on the Cathedral of Christ Church, Oxford*, 3 June 1869; Thompson (1899), 157; xlix.a.1; DP vii.c.1; Pevsner (1979), 188
36. xlix.a.1; Howell, *HUO*, vii (2000), 747 and 751. The tower was restored in the 1970s.
37. The Hall glass was replaced again with a scheme by Reyntiens in 1980.
38. MS Estates 144, ff.360–8
39. GB i.b.6, 18, 139 and 145; GB i.b.8, 46, 116, 119, 237, 416–17, 452, etc.
40. Tyack (1998), 313–14
41. St Aldates Quad and the Liddell Building in Iffley Road were constructed in the 1980s and 1990s, the latter with the co-operation of Corpus Christi College.
42. The Law Library was refurbished in 2003.

9. 'Half arsenal, half hotel': twentieth-century Christ Church

1. The 1899/1900 *Annual Report* is the first known report for old members. They were, for at least three decades, very short and perfunctory affairs, recording new appointments to the Governing Body and lectureships, the successes of old members, but only to the highest positions such as senior Cabinet posts, and occasional news.
2. Two undergraduate members were killed in South Africa that year: George Watson and Calverley Hancock.
3. In 1905, the Rhodes scholars included one from Jamaica, and one from Germany.
4. Masterman (1975), 146–53
5. Names include Courage, Sandeman, Hoare, Mavrogordato, Baring, Horlick and Metaxa. Strong, *Collegas discipulos amicos salutat abiturus Thomas B. Strong, decanus*.
6. Brock, *HUO*, vii (2000), 806–7. The other two colleges under consideration were New College, which the Archbishop of York had told Derby was full of 'trouble', and Magdalen College, which won the day.
7. Wheeler (2001), 34
8. Dodds (1977), 32
9. *Christ Church 1912–1913* and *1913–1914*
10. *Christ Church, October 1914 – October 1915*. The six senior members were Lt. C. D. Fisher, RNVR; Major A. K. Slessor, Ox & Bucks Light Infantry; 2nd Lt. R. H. Dundas, Black Watch; 2nd Lt. K. G. Feiling, Black Watch; Capt. G. T. Hutchinson, Oxfordshire Yeomanry; A. E. J. Rawlinson, chaplain to the forces. A. T. Carter was engaged in legal work at the Treasury, and J. Murray served in the Munitions Ministry.
11. Masterman (1975), 86; Dodds (1977), 37
12. Dodds (1977), 44
13. S.xxxiii.c.1
14. *Christ Church, October 1914 – October 1915*
15. *Christ Church Roll of Service* (1920); http://www.cwgc.org/ (accessed 13 October 2009). Christy, aged 35, was part of the Great Retreat from Mons, and received the

DSO. Bertie was killed in action at Hooge, on the front line of the Salient, on 8 May 1915; he had not even formally matriculated.
16. Masterman (1975), 115 and 144
17. Strong, *Collegas discipulos amicos salutat abiturus Thomas B. Strong, decanus* [1920]
18. Baynes had been elected to his Studentship in 1873.
19. GB xv.c.3
20. GB i.b.5, pp. 236–348; GB i.b.6, p.6; *Christ Church* 1924–8
21. Temple went on to be archbishop of both York (1929) and Canterbury (1942).
22. Hopkins (1975)
23. Masterman (1975), 177–8
24. SOC.xxiii.c.1–4. Davies was J. M. Barrie's foster son. He and Buxton were Barrie's 'Lost boys', and there was speculation at the time that the men had died in a suicide pact. There is no evidence to suggest that their deaths were anything more than a tragic accident.
25. *ODNB*
26. The 1922 Everest expedition was the first serious attempt to reach the summit, and the first to use bottled oxygen. Strutt (ChCh 1893) was the deputy expedition leader and Longstaff (ChCh 1894) one of the medical team. The expedition members received a medal for Alpinism at the 1924 Olympics. Jacob (ChCh 1922) played rugby for Oxford and for England, and was immortalised in 1924 on an F. & J. Smith's cigarette card.
27. The statutes were under constant revision from the late nineteenth century and into the twentieth. Most of the alterations were relatively minor, or to take account of changes such as the final suppression of the seventh canonry, for example.
28. [Arnold] (1867), 8
29. *Cherwell*, 20 June 1925, 195–8
30. *Cherwell*, 20 June 1925, 189. There had been a concert on 23 May at which all the music performed was by Christ Church musicians from Tudor times to the present – DP xix.c.2.
31. Marius B. Winter's band was the first dance band to perform on British radio from Marconi House on 26 March 1923. Vincent Lopez was a pianist and prominent band-leader in New York from 1917 into the 1950s. His orchestra was the first dance band to perform live on American radio, in 1921.
32. SOC xx.c.1
33. SOC xxiii.a.4. Murray, already an MA from Melbourne University and ordained when he came to Christ Church on a Lucas Tooth Scholarship, became Australia's youngest bishop.
34. *The Times*, 25 June 1925; DP xix.c.2
35. Smith (1992), 56–66
36. SOC xxiii.a.4; Shuffrey, in Butler (ed.) (2006), 144–5. Plus-fours were all the rage, but were not permitted in Hall at dinner time. There is speculation that this is why Oxford bags became so popular, as they could be pulled on over the plus-fours.
37. Harrison, *HUO*, viii (1994), 106

38. Christopher Mayhew had been president in Hilary term 1937, Bill Shebbeare in Trinity 1936, and Ian Harvey in Hilary term 1936. Between 1823 and Trinity term 2009, Christ Church had 83 presidents.
39. CCL MS 554
40. Harrison, *HUO*, viii (1994), 389. Christ Church, with All Souls College, were centres for conservative discussion. Keith Feiling and Robert Blake established the history of British Conservatism as an accepted subject for academic study.
41. Driberg (1979), 70–73
42. SOC xxiii.c.111
43. Dodds (1977), 130
44. Ceadel, 'The myths of King and Country', in *The Times*, 9 February 1983. Ceadel argues that the critics misinterpreted what was no more than a student debate, confusing, perhaps deliberately, a dislike of jingoism and war in principle with a lack of national pride.
45. Lindemann's 'rescues' were independently organised, pre-empting the establishment of the Academic Assistance Council in 1933 – Morrell (1997), 269–70.
46. Einstein was aware of the negative feelings. In a poem which he left for Robert Dundas, whose rooms he used, he wrote 'Grumble: why's this creature staying, with his pipe and piano playing? Why should this barbarian roam? Could he not have stopped at home?' Translation by J. B. Leishman, quoted in Butler (ed.) (2006), 138.
47. *Christ Church 1935–6*
48. DP xx.c.1
49. Grenville, in Butler (ed.) (2006) 136–7; *Christ Church, 1935/6*
50. Lee/8 – a memorandum by Dr P. W. Kent dated 14 July 1994.
51. Masterman (1975), 179–80; Hopkins (1975), 47
52. *Christ Church 1938/9*
53. Cen v.c.26; GB i.b.5, 384–8
54. The subject was raised again in 1969 when Charles Stuart penned a private list of those he thought likely to vote for separation. These were Gilbert Ryle, Patrick Gordon-Walker, A. J. 'Freddy' Ayer, C. Dillwyn, Eric Dodds, E. W. Gray, Roy Harrod, Denys Page and Carl Collie.
55. Some of the paintings were later taken to the New Bodleian Library.
56. GB i.b.5, 403
57. Williams, in Butler (ed.) (2006), 150
58. When the war finished, the problems continued for some time as students returned and new ones arrived before many of the staff came back.
59. Sisman (2010), 77–91
60. This research was published in 1947 as *The Last Days of Hitler*.
61. Howard (2006) and in Butler (ed.) (2006), 152–3
62. Kent (2001), 39–42
63. Wright, in Butler (ed.) (2006), 140–41. Bell, Eden, Portal and Cecil were all elected to Honorary Studentships. There is an altar in the cathedral dedicated to Bell's memory.
64. *Christ Church 1947/8*
65. DP xix.c.2

66. The part of Katherine of Aragon was taken by Barbara Clegg, later scriptwriter for radio and television including *Crossroads, The Chrysalids* and *Dr Who*. Halfway down the cast-list, as 2nd gentleman, was Norman Painting, best known as Phil Archer.
67. Law, in Butler (ed.) (2006), 174
68. *Christ Church 1947–8 and 1959*; Kent, 1994
69. The collection of the seventeenth-century diarist John Evelyn was presented to Christ Church, on deposit, by a descendant, C. J. A. Evelyn, in 1949. The printed works were sold in 1976. The manuscripts and ephemera were moved to the British Library, and the administrative documents to the Surrey Record Office, in 1994.
70. Trevor-Roper's booklet went into a third edition in the 1985, and is given to all undergraduates at college matriculation.
71. *Christ Church 1951*
72. *Christ Church 1954–1956*; Sladen, in Butler (2006), 161–3
73. Roche, *HUO*, viii (1994), 251–89. Many branches of natural science could be studied under the umbrellas of other schools. Metallurgy, for example, was part of the chemistry school until 1968, and engineering part of physics until the 1980s.
74. Wheeler (2001)
75. Dodds (1977), 27
76. Ayer (1977), 76
77. Smith (1992), 60
78. Venables (1967), 88; *ODNB*. John Wing's memoir in *Christ Church 1996* suggests that he escaped as soon as possible and hoped never to repeat the experience!
79. Ayer (1977), 81
80. Hugh Trevor-Roper [*Christ Church 1977*]; *ODNB*. Between 1919 and 1940, Christ Church received 33 firsts.
81. Masterman (1975), 181
82. *Christ Church 1969*; 'Cuthbert Simpson: a note', in *Bulletin of the General Theological Seminary*, lv (5), November 1969, 23–7
83. SOC xxiv.c.8. Peter Rooley, as president of the JCR, launched a petition to stop the reduction of the grassed area of Tom Quad and the parking of cars there, having seen markers being placed in the grass which were designed to show how the changes would work; 225 junior members signed the petition and then, under cover of darkness, removed all the pegs and sent them to the Senior Censor with the petition. According to Richard Hamer, the marking of the quad was actually an attempt by one member of the Governing Body to show how horrible the proposed changes would be.
84. GB i.b.13, 190. At the same time as consultation was increasing within college, the changes in local government in 1974 meant that the University lost its seats on the city council.
85. MR iii.c.1/3/6. Dean Williams had been horrified to discover that 20 per cent of places at Christ Church were taken by sons of old members, even allowing for the few who were turned down because their entrance examination results were terrible. At Magdalen, he commented, being the son of an old member was almost guaranteed to lose a candidate a place, as the college was trying to turn itself into a 'reading college with a parade of firsts'.

86. Thomas, *HUO* (1994), 192–4 and 214. In 1965, 71 per cent of Christ Church's undergraduates had been educated at independent schools compared with only 25 per cent at The Queen's College.
87. The total number of schools and universities which contributed to the junior membership of Christ Church was around 160.
88. *Christ Church 1964*
89. GB i.b.9, 706; i.b.22, 76. The Tutorship for Admissions was supplemented in 1990 when an Admissions Officer was appointed specifically to liaise with schools.
90. In the first 25 years of the DPhil, nearly half of the recipients were overseas students. The degree was popularised by American Rhodes Scholars. J. G. Darwin, *HUO*, viii (1994), 616.
91. Harrison, *HUO*, viii (1994), 89
92. Thomas, *HUO*, viii (1994), 210–11
93. One particular scout, Humphreys, was recalled with affection: 'He didn't need to be told that I was rather out of my depth, but simply made the sort of suggestions which were appropriate from time to time' – Kerslake, in Butler (ed.) (2006), 145.
94. One of the arguments put forward to Governing Body in support of a GCR was that there had been such an establishment before in the form of a Bachelors' Common Room around the time of the battle of Trafalgar! The first of the new breed of graduate, or middle, common rooms was founded at Lincoln College in 1958 – Thomas, *HUO*, viii (1994), 211.
95. Balsdon (1957), 190. Not for the first time was Christ Church's odd constitution used as an excuse not to do something. Of course, now the possibility of a female dean is real.
96. *Christ Church, 1964*. This vote was passed 23:8, and another, to ask for permission for women to dine in Hall, by 33:23. It was 1975 before the first college became mixed.
97. Brock, *HUO*, viii (1994), 747–8
98. Merton College followed the example of the other men's colleges in October 1979, and Oriel College was the last to admit women, in 1985. Only two of the women's colleges then remained single-sex: St Hilda's and Somerville.
99. Pallot, in Butler (ed.) (2006), 198–200. Four years after Dr Pallot's election, she was still the only female member of Governing Body. There were 4 female lecturers out of 21. By the start of the academic year 2006, there were 12 female Students, of whom all but Dr Pallot and Dr Andreyev (1987) had been appointed within the previous decade, and 17 lecturers out of 45. The 'noughties' saw the arrival of the first female canons.
100. *Christ Church 1978*
101. Dobson, Butler (ed.) (2006), 186
102. *ODNB*
103. SOC Dacre 1/1/T, 3 September 1974
104. Canon Demant, in his address at Simpson's funeral on 6 July 1969, said that 'to my mind, zeal in the handling of college and cathedral affairs was Cuthbert Simpson's outstanding characteristic'.
105. GB i.b.2, 292 and 296
106. GB i.b.14, 198

107. Brock, *HUO*, viii (1994), 740. Within ten years of the publication of the Franks Report, four-fifths of contributions came from the seven best-endowed colleges (Christ Church, St John's, All Souls, Merton, Magdalen, Nuffield and Queen's).
108. In addition to new science honour schools, combined subjects had appeared like Engineering and Economics (1963), Physics and Philosophy (1968), and Maths and Philosophy (1968). PPE, or modern Greats, had first appeared in 1947, Geography in 1928, but Fine Art did not become a full honours subject until 1977. Biology and Engineering were not stand-alone subjects until even later.

10. 'Through all the vicissitudes of English history': Conclusion

1. Strong [1920]

Bibliography

Acland, H., *Oxford and Modern Medicine* (1890)
Anon., 'Cuthbert Simpson: a note', in *Bulletin of the General Theological Seminary*, lv (5), November 1969
Architectural Review, vol. cxlv, no. 886 (April 1968), 269–72
[Arnold, Frederick], *Christ Church Days. An Oxford story*, 2 vols (1867)
Atlay, J. B., *Sir Henry Wentworth Acland, Bart. KCB, FRS, Regius Professor of Medicine in the University of Oxford: a memoir* (1903)
Ayer, A. J., *Part of My Life* (1977)
Baker, William J., *Beyond Port and Prejudice: Charles Lloyd of Oxford, 1784–1829* (1981)
Balsdon, Dacre, *Oxford Life* (1957)
Barrett, Philip, *Barchester: English cathedral life in the nineteenth century* (1993)
Batey, Mavis, *The Historic Gardens of Oxford and Cambridge* (1989)
Beal, Peter, *Parnassus Biceps* (1990)
Beddard, R. A., 'Christ Church under John Fell,' in a supplement to *Christ Church 1976/77*
Beer, E. S. de (ed.), *The Correspondence of John Locke*, vol. 1 (1976)
Bendall, S., *Dictionary of Land Surveyors and Local Map-makers of Great Britain and Ireland, 1530–1850*, 2 vols (1997)
Bennett, G. V., *The Tory Crisis in Church and State, 1688–1730* (1975)
Biddle, M. and Kjølbye-Biddle, B., 'An early medieval floor-tile from St Frideswide's minster', in *Oxoniensia*, liii (1988), 259–63
Biddle, Martin, 'Wolsey's bell-tower', in *Oxoniensia*, liii (1988), 205–10
Bill, E. G. W., *Christ Church Meadow* (1965)
Bill, E. G. W., 'The rebuilding of Peckwater Quadrangle at Christ Church' (unpublished, undated paper)
Bill, E. G. W., *Education at Christ Church, Oxford, 1660–1800* (1988)
Bill, E. G. W. and Mason, J. F. A., *Christ Church and Reform, 1850–1867* (1970)
Blair, J., 'St Frideswide reconsidered', in *Oxoniensia*, lii (1987), 71–127
Blair, J., *Anglo-Saxon Oxfordshire* (1994)
Bompas, George C., *Life of Frank Buckland* (1885)
Boyle, A. et al., 'Excavations in Christ Church cathedral graveyard, Oxford', in *Oxoniensia*, lxvi (2001), 337–68
Brock, M. G. and Curthoys, M. C., *History of the University of Oxford. Vol. VI: Nineteenth-century Oxford, Part 1* (1997)

Bibliography

Brock, M. G. and Curthoys, M. C., *History of the University of Oxford.* Vol. VII: *Nineteenth-century Oxford, Part 2* (2000)

Brockliss, L. W. B. (ed.), *Magdalen College, Oxford: a history* (2008)

Brown, Helen, 'The Zodiacal coins of Jahangir', in *The Ashmolean*, iii (1983)

Burrows, Montagu (ed.), *The Register of the Visitors of the University of Oxford from AD 1647 to AD 1658* (1881)

Bussby, F., 'Brian Duppa, Bishop of Winchester, 1660–1662' in *Winchester Cathedral Record* (1967)

Butler, C. (ed.), *Christ Church, Oxford: a portrait of the House* (2006)

Caröe, W. D., *'Tom Tower', Christ Church, Oxford* (1923)

Catto, J. and Evans, T. A. R., *History of the University of Oxford.* Vol. II: *Late medieval Oxford* (1992)

Chichester, Morna, *Christ Church Library, c. 1562–1976* [unpublished dissertation, 1977]

Clark, A. (ed.), *Life and Times of Anthony Wood, Antiquary, of Oxford, 1632–1695, Described by Himself*, 3 vols (1891–4)

Clark, A. (ed), *'Survey of the Antiquities of the City of Oxford', composed in 1661–6, by Anthony Wood*, 2 vols (1887–90)

Cook, J. and Mason, J. F. A. (eds.), *The Building Accounts of Christ Church Library, 1716–1779* (1988)

Colvin, H., *Unbuilt Oxford* (1983)

Colvin, H., *A Biographical Dictionary of British Architects, 1600–1840* (2008)

Couch, Lilian M. Quiller (ed.), *Reminiscences of Oxford by Oxford men, 1559–1850* (1892)

Crossley, A. (ed.), *History of the County of Oxford, iv: the city of Oxford* [VCH] (1979)

Curthoys, J., 'To perfect the college ... – the Christ Church Almsmen 1546–1888', in *Oxoniensia*, lx (1995), 379–95

[Danby, Herbert], *Notes on the Chapter Fund, 1869–1944* (1945), printed for private circulation to the Governing Body

Darwall-Smith, Robin, *A History of University College, Oxford* (2008)

Davenport-Hines, Richard, *Letters from Oxford: Hugh Trevor-Roper to Bernard Berenson* (2006)

Dawson, J. E. A., 'The foundation of Christ Church, Oxford and Trinity College, Cambridge in 1546', in *Bulletin of the Institute of Historical Research*, lvii (1984), 208–15

Demant, V. A., *In Memoriam: Cuthbert Aikman Simpson, DD*, sermon preached in the cathedral on 6 July 1969

Denholm-Young, N., *Cartulary of the Medieval Archives of Christ Church* (1931)

Doble, C. E. (ed.), *Remarks and Collections of Thomas Hearne* (1885–1907)

Dobson, Christopher S. A. (ed.), *Oxfordshire Protestation Returns, 1641–2* [1955]

Dodds, E. R., *Missing Persons: an autobiography* (1977)

Dodgson, C. L., *The New Belfry at Christ Church* (1873)

Driberg, Tom, *Ruling Passions* (1979)

Dunbabin, J. P. D., 'Oxford and Cambridge college finances, 1871–1913', in *Economic History Review*, xxviii (1975), 631–47

Durand, W. Y., 'Palaemon and Arcyte, Progne, Marcus Geminus, and the theatre in which they were acted, as described by John Bereblock (1566)', in *Proceedings of the Modern Language Association of America*, xx, 1905, 520–28

Edmonds, J. M. and Douglas, J. A., 'William Buckland, FRS (1784–1856) and an Oxford geological lecture, 1823', in *Notes and Records of the Royal Society of London*, xxx (2) (1976)

Emden, A. B., *A Biographical Register of the University of Oxford, A.D. 1501 to 1540* (1974)

English, Barbara, 'The education of the landed elite in England, c. 1815 – c. 1870', in *Journal of Educational Administration and History*, xxiii (1) (1991), 15–32

Evans, Margaret (ed.), *Letters of Richard Radcliffe and John James of Queen's College, Oxford, 1755–83* (1888)

Fauvel, John, Flood, Raymond, and Wilson, Robin (eds.), *Oxford Figures: 800 years of the mathematical sciences* (2000)

Field, John, *The King's Nurseries: the story of Westminster School* (1998)

Firman, Catharine K., 'The Mitre Club, 1820–1843', in *American Oxonian*, liii (1) (1966)

Foot, M. R. D. (ed.), *Gladstone Diaries*, vol. 1, *1825–1832* (1968)

Foster, Joseph, *Alumni Oxonienses, 1500–1714* (4 vols, 1891)

Foster, Joseph, *Alumni Oxonienses, 1715–1886* (4 vols, 1888)

Foster, Joseph, *Oxford Men, 1880–1892* (1893)

Foster, Joseph, *Oxford Men and their Colleges* (1893)

Fowler, Thomas, *A History of Corpus Christi College* (1873)

Frost, Richard, *Christ Church Boat Club: a short history* [1989]

Gardiner, R. B. (ed.), *The Registers of Wadham College, part 2. 1719–1871* (1895)

Gaskell, Charles Milnes (ed.), *An Eton Boy: being the letters of James Milnes Gaskell from Eton and Oxford 1820–1830* (1939)

Gibson, Strickland, *Statutes of the Colleges of Oxford* (1853)

Green, S. J. D. and Horden, Peregrine (eds.), *All Souls under the* Ancien Régime: *politics, learning, and the arts, c. 1600–1850* (2007)

Green, Vivian, *The Commonwealth of Lincoln College, 1427–1977* (1979)

Gunn S. J. and Lindley, P. G. (eds), *Cardinal Wolsey: church, state, and art* (1991)

Gutch, A. (ed.), *History and Antiquities of the University of Oxford, in Two Books, by Anthony à Wood, MA of Merton College* (1796)

Gwyn, Peter, *The King's Cardinal: the rise and fall of Thomas Wolsey* (1990)

Haigh, C. A., '1546, Before and after; the making of Christ Church' (unpublished lecture given to celebrate the 450th anniversary of the foundation of Christ Church, 1996)

Halfpenny, Eric, 'The Christ Church trophies', in *Galpin Society Journal*, xxviii (1975)

Harrison, Brian (ed.), *History of the University of Oxford.* Vol. VIII: *The twentieth century* (1994)

Harvey, John H., 'The building works and architects of Cardinal Wolsey', in *Journal of the British Archaeological Association*, viii (1943), 48–59

Heard, Kate, 'Christ Church, Oxford, and the English Reformation, 1546–1576' (unpublished undergraduate thesis, 1998)

Hibbert, C. (ed), *Encyclopaedia of Oxford* (1988)

Hight, G., 'Origin and inception of the Canterbury settlement', in *Report of the Australian and New Zealand Association for the Advancement of Science*, xxiii (1937)

Hiscock, W. G., *A Christ Church Miscellany: new chapters on the architects, craftsmen, statuary, plate, bells, furniture, clocks, plays, the Library, and other buildings* (1946)

Bibliography

Historic Manuscripts Commission, *Report on the Manuscripts of His Grace the Duke of Portland, KG, Preserved at Welbeck Abbey*, vii (1901)
Hopkins, C., *Trinity: four hundred years of an Oxford college community* (2005)
Hopkins, C. H. G., *Bishop A. T. P. Williams* (1975)
Howard, Michael, *Captain-Professor: a life in war and peace* (2006)
Howse, Derek, *Greenwich Time and the Longitude* (1997)
Hurd, Douglas, *Robert Peel: a biography* (2007)
Ingram, James, *Memorials of Oxford*, vol. 1 (1837)
Jacob, E. F., *St Frideswide: the patron saint of Oxford* (1953)
Jacobs, M., 'Christ Church kitchens', in *Institutional Management Association Journal*, September 1950
Jenkins, Roy, *Gladstone* (1995)
Jones, E. Alfred, *Catalogue of the plate of Christ Church Oxford* (1939)
Jones, John, *Balliol College: a history* (1997)
Kent, P. W., 'Michael Foster and his legacy to higher education', in *Oxford Magazine* (4th week, Michaelmas term, 1994)
Kent, P. W., *Some Scientists in the Life of Christ Church*, Oxford (2001)
Ker, N. R., 'Oxford college libraries in the sixteenth century', in *Bodleian Library Record*, vi (3) (January 1959)
Knowles, D. and Hadcock, R. Neville, *Medieval Religious Houses: England and Wales* (1971)
Lane-Poole, Stanley, 'The cabinet of oriental coins in the library of Christ Church, Oxford', in *Numismatic Chronicle* (1886)
Law, Brian R., *Building Oxford's Heritage: Symm and Company from 1815* (1998)
Lowe, J., *Handbook to the Cathedral Church of Christ in Oxford* (1949)
Lyte, H. C. Maxwell, *A History of the University of Oxford from the Earliest Times to the Year 1530* (1886)
Mabey, Richard, *Flora Britannica* (1996)
Machin, G. I. T., *Politics and the Churches in Great Britain, 1832–1868* (1977)
Martin, G. H. and Highfield, J. R. L., *A History of Merton College, Oxford* (1997)
Mason, J. F. A., *Christ Church Common Room and its Possessions* (unpublished paper, February 1991)
Mason, J. F. A., 'Pink v. white: the redecoration of the Upper Library in 1964–5', in *Christ Church Library Newsletter*, vol. 2, issue 3 (Trinity 2006)
Masterman, J. C., *On the Chariot Wheel: an autobiography* (1975)
McConica, J. (ed.), *History of the University of Oxford. Vol. III: The collegiate university* (1986)
Milne, J. G. and Harvey, J. H., 'The building of Cardinal College, Oxford', in *Oxoniensia*, viii (1943), 137–53
Morgan, Paul, *Oxford Libraries outside the Bodleian: a guide* (1980)
Morrell, Jack, *Science at Oxford, 1914–1939: transforming an arts university* (1997)
Morris, James, *Oxford* (1965)
Muller, Max, *My Autobiography* (1901)
Neild, Robert, *The Financial History of Trinity College, Cambridge* (2008)
Newman, Roland, *The Road and Christ Church Meadow: the Oxford inner relief road controversy, 1923–74. A study of the relationship between central and local government* (1980)

Nichols, John, *The Progresses and Public Processions of Queen Elizabeth* ... (1823)
Nichols, John, *Progresses, Processions, and Magnificent Festivities of King James the First, his Royal Consort, Family, and Court* (1823)
Oakeshott, W. F. (ed.), *Oxford Stone Restored: the work of the Oxford Historic Buildings Fund, 1957–1974* (1975)
Oxford Dictionary of National Biography (2004). (If the article has been updated in the on-line version, this has been recorded in the notes.)
Pantin, W. A., 'Before Wolsey', in H. R. Trevor-Roper (ed.), *Essays in British History presented to Sir Keith Feiling* (1964)
Pantin, W. A., *Canterbury College Oxford*, vols i and iv (1947 and 1985)
Pevsner, N., *Oxfordshire* (1979)
Port, M. H., *Six Hundred New Churches: a study of the Church Building Commission, 1818–1856, and its church building activities* (1961)
Postles, D., 'The foundation of Oseney Abbey', in *Bulletin of the Institute of Historical Research*, liii, no. 128 (November 1980), 242–4
Potter, Jeremy, *Tennis and Oxford* (1994)
RCHM, *An Inventory of the Historical Monuments in the City of Oxford* (1939)
Rex, Richard, *Henry VIII and the English Reformation* (2006)
Richardson, W. C., *History of the Court of Augmentations, 1536–1554* (1961)
Rickard, R. L. (ed.), *The Progress Notes of Warden Woodward round the Oxfordshire estates of New College, Oxford, 1659–1675* [1945]
Roberts, B. C., *Letters and Miscellaneous Papers* (printed but not published, 1814, Bod 270, c. 396)
Rowntree, Diana, 'Oxford College barges', in *Architectural Review* (July 1956)
Rowntree, John, 'The organs of Christ Church cathedral' (printed as a supplement to the Annual Report, *Christ Church 1980/1981*)
Rowse, A. L., *Oxford in the History of the Nation* (1975)
Roy, Ian (ed.), *The Royal Ordnance papers, 1642–1646* [1963–4]
Salter, H. E., *Survey of Oxford*, vol. 1 (1960)
Scott, G. G., *Report of George Gilbert Scott, Esq., R. A. on the cathedral of Christ Church, Oxford, 3 June 1869*, printed for private circulation only
Sharp, Thomas, *Oxford Replanned* (1948)
Sharpe, Frederick, 'Re-hanging Great Tom', in *Country Life* (28 May 1953)
Shaw, Watkins, *The Succession of Organists* (1991)
Sisman, Adam, *Hugh Trevor-Roper: the biography* (2010)
Sladen, C., 'The Masters' Garden mystery', in *Christ Church Matters*, 10 (Michaelmas 2002)
Smith, Henry, *The Impersonal Autobiography of an Economist: how you appear to me* (1992)
Stenton, F., *St Frideswide and Her Times* (1953)
Strong, T. B., *Collegas discipulos amicos salutat abiturus Thomas B. Strong, decanus*. A speech delivered by Dean Strong to the House in Hall on 18 June 1920 just before his departure from Oxford for the bishopric of Ripon. Unpublished.
Sturdy, D., Rouse, E. Clive, and Cole, J. C., 'The painted roof of the Old Library, Christ Church', in *Oxoniensia*, xxvi and xxvii (1961/2)
Sutherland, L. S. and Mitchell, L. G. (eds.), *History of the University of Oxford. Vol. V: The eighteenth century* (1986)

Bibliography

Swinstead, J. Howard, *Christ Church Cathedral School, Oxford: register of choristers, probationers, masters, precentors, organists from 1837–1900* (1900)
Thalmann, Jacqueline (ed.), *40 years of Christ Church Picture Gallery* (2008)
Thompson, H. L., *Henry George Liddell, DD, Dean of Christ Church, Oxford: a memoir* (1899)
Thompson, H. L., *Christ Church* (1900)
Trevor-Roper, Hugh, *Christ Church Oxford: the portrait of a college* (1950)
Trevor-Roper, Hugh, *Keith Feiling: memorial tribute, Christ Church, 22 October 1977* (later printed in *Christ Church 1977*)
A True Copy of the Poll taken at Oxford January 31, 1750
Tyack, G., *Oxford: an architectural guide* (1998)
Tyacke, N. (ed.), *History of the University of Oxford*. Vol. IV: *Seventeenth-century Oxford* (1997)
Uglow, Jenny, *A Gambling Man: Charles II and the Restoration, 1660–1670* (2009)
Valor Ecclesiasticus, ii (1814)
Venables, Roger, *'D': portrait of a don* (1967)
Venn, J. and Venn, J. A., *Alumni Cantabrigienses. Part 1: from the earliest times to 1751* (4 vols, 1922)
Wakeling, E. (ed.), *Lewis Carroll's Diaries* (1993–2005)
Wakeling, E. (comp.), *Oxford Pamphlets, Leaflets, and Circulars of Charles Lutwidge Dodgson* (1993)
Ward, G. R. M., *Foundation Statutes of Bishop Fox for Corpus Christi College in the University of Oxford, AD 1517. Now first translated into English, with a life of the founder* (1843)
Ward, W. R., *Georgian Oxford: University politics in the eighteenth century* (1958)
Ward, W. R., *Victorian Oxford* (1965)
Warner, S. A., *Oxford Cathedral* (1924)
Watson, Nigel, *Independent Vision: a history of the Portsmouth Grammar School* (2008)
Weeks, James, 'The architects of Christ Church library', in *Architectural History*, 48 (2005), 107–38
Weinstock, M., *Hearth Tax Returns, Oxfordshire, 1665* (1940)
Welch, J., *List of the Queen's Scholars of St Peter's College, Westminster* (1852)
Whately, E. Jane, *Life and Correspondence of Richard Whately*, i (1866)
Wheeler, Sara, *Cherry: a life of Apsley Cherry-Garrard* (2001)
White, R., 'Wren's architectural projects in Oxford', in Green and Horden (eds.), *All Souls under the* Ancien Régime: *politics, learning, and the arts, c. 1600–1850* (2007)
Wright, Abraham, *Parnassus Biceps* (1656)
Youings, Joyce, *The Dissolution of the Monasteries* (1971)

Index

Figures in *italics* indicate captions; colour plates are indicated by 'Pl.' 'ChCh' is an abbreviation for Christ Church, Oxford.

2nd South Midland Mounted Brigade 300
15th/19th the King's Royal Hussars 66
20th Hussars 299
68th Regiment of Light Infantry 57
'101' chime 134, *134*, 135, 137, 314
1867 Act (Christ Church, Oxford, Act) 245, 274

Abbot, Charles 210
Abbots Wood, South Stoke, Oxfordshire 114
Abingdon, Oxfordshire 49, 52
Abingdon abbey 22
Abingdon Road, Oxford 32, 216
Ackermann, Rudolph Pl.
Ackworth, Thomas 120
Acland, Arthur 273, 274
Acland, Henry Wentworth 208, 209, 213, 214, 269, 270
Act Supper 111
Addenbrook, John 145–6
Adderley, James 276
Adderley, Ralph 281
Adkins, William 23–4, 26
Admiralty Computing Service 316
Adrianus of Tyre 168
Aeneid (Virgil) 80
Aeschylus 203
Aesop 168
Aglionby, George 99
Airay, Henry 82
Aitkin, P. H. 297
Akehurst, Alexander 182
Alasco, Prince, of Siradia (Sieradz) 79
Alba (a pastoral) 83
Albert, Prince Consort 251
Aldrich, Charles 151, 168

Aldrich, Dean Henry 94, 129, 131, 138–42, *139*, *142*, 145, 147–52, 157, 165–8, 170, 282, 287, 288, 297, Pl.
  Artis Logicae Compendium 172
  Logic 184
Aldrichian professorship of chemistry 207
Algar, Prince of Leicester 1–2
Alington, Cyril 311
All Souls College, Oxford 44, 130, 202, 311
Allestree, Richard 103, 115, 117, 118, *118*, 120, 121, 127, 130, 285, 294
Allestree Library 283
Allotment Association 299
almshouse 57, 59, *59*, 60, 61, *63*
almsmen 57–62, *59*, *63*, 109, 190
Alsop, Anthony 143, 169
Altham, Roger 150
Amadas, Robert 14, 15
Ambler, John 275
Amending Act (1856) 241
Amhurst, Nicholas: *Terrae-filius* 198
Ampleforth College 322
Amsterdam 64
Anderson, J. G. C. 298–9
Angel, Andrea 299
Anglican church 64
Anglicanism 111, 158, 198, 263
'Animadversiones' 280
Anne, Queen 83, 127, 140–41, 148, 155, 175
Annesley, George 112, *112*, 113
Annual Reports 30, 293, 299, 307, 312, 314, 318, 322, 323, 325
Anonym debating society 276
Anstice, Robert 217
Aphrodite and Eros statue 266
Apollonius Rhodius 182
Aristotelian
  logic 81, 171–2
  principles 55, 174
Aristotle 166

Index

Arkwright, Godfrey 297
Arlington, Henry Bennet, 1st Earl of 117
Armer, Sir Frederick 31
Arminianism 101
Armistice (1918) 300–301, *300*
Armistice Day 135
Arnold, Frederick 304
Artari, Giuseppe Pl.
Ashley, Lord 129
Ashmolean Museum 314, 317
   anatomy room 180
   mineral collections 209
Astley, Jacob 217
Astley, John 280
Atherton, George 115
athletics 275, 296, 318, 319
Atkins, Alderman 69
Atterbury, Charles 184
Atterbury, Dean Francis ix, 58, 147–54, *148*, 156, 169, 170, 175, 187
Atterbury, Lewis 114, 141, 288
Attwood (maniple) 194
Auden, W. H. 35, 320
Audit House 60, 184
Awdry, John 255–6
Axtell, Alfred *250*
Ayer, A. J. 'Freddy' 320

Bach, Johann Sebastian 94
Bacon, Francis 201
Badcock, Benjamin 26
Bagot, Dean Lewis 155, 177, 181, 186, 190, 198, 199, 217
Bagshaw, Henry 117
Bailey, Arthur 258
Baldwin, Stanley 310–11
Baldwin, Thomas 27
Balliol College, Oxford 11, 31, 183, 246, 249, 264, 265, 273, 274, 307
balloon flights 34
Bampton, Oxfordshire 2, 124
Banbury, Oxfordshire 102
Bandinell, James 85
Banister, William 119
banking 190–91
Banks, Robert 45, 47
Banting (cathedral guide) 194
Barford, Warwickshire *278*
Baring, Henry Bingham *206*
Barings Bank *206*
Barnes, Frederick 202, 209, 210, 221, 240, 248, 249

Barnes, Ralph 164
Barrow, Dr 187
Barton, Philip 186
Batey, Keith and Mavis 316
Bath and Wells diocese 61
Bathurst, Charles 202, 203
Bathurst, Ralph 126
Bathurst, William Hiley 203
battels bills 74, 193, 218, 272–3, 275
Bayly, Francis 155
Baynes, R. E. 270, 301
Bazalgette, Joseph 236
beagling 274–5, *296*
Beats (prisoner) 224
Beaulieu, George 146
Beaumont, Edward 54
Beaumont, T. W. 318
Bedford, Samuel 118
Bell, George 316
Belsyre, Alexander 44, 47, 51, 52, 53
Benbow, Robert 17
Benedictine monasteries 5
Bennet, John 193
Bennet, John, junior 193
Bennet, Thomas 119
Bennett, Richard 281
Benolt, Thomas 4
Benson, Robert 261
Benthall, Richard 37
Bentley, Richard 168, 169, 170
Bereblock, John *78*, 79
Berkeley, John 119
Berkeley, Maurice 100
Berkshire 22, 24
Bernard, Sir Francis 184
Bernard, Thomas 44–5, 67–8, 78
Bernard College 68
Berry, Richard 116
Bertie, Second Lieutenant N. M. K. 299
Best, John (later Bishop of Carlisle) 16
Best and Sons 237
Bethell, Lord 219
Beveridge, William 31
Bible, the 8, 9, 55, 73, 82, 90, 145, 151, 174
Bill, Geoffrey xi, 174
Billings, John 94
Billington, Mrs 196
Binsey, Oxfordshire 99, 154
Birkenhead, F. E. Smith, 1st Earl of 302, 310
Blackett, Hugh 281
Blackstone, James 183
Blackwell's stationer's shop, Oxford 183

397

Bledington, Gloucestershire 190
Blenheim Palace 221, 267
'Blenheim Row' (1893) 267–8, Pl.
Bletchley Park, Buckinghamshire 316
Blithman, John 70
Blore, George 249, 261
Blücher, Gebhard von 221
Blue Boar Lane, Oxford 291
Blue Boar Quadrangle 292, 321, 322, 327
'Blue Book' 226
Blues and Royals 66
Board of Agriculture 265
Board of Health 235–6
boat clubs 27, 28, 220, 275, 318, 319
Bodington, William 58
Bodleian Library, Oxford 83, 102, 127, 297
Bodleian Schools Quadrangle 180
Boer War 34, 293
Boland, John Pius 274
Bold, Henry 117
bookbinders 55
booksellers 55–6
Boote, Robert 77
Borenius, Tancred 297
Borough, Edward 216
Borough, Mr (organ repairer) 94
Borrett, R. V. 38–9, *319*
Bossom, Charles 28
Bostock, John 124
Bostock exhibition 243
Botanic Gardens 28, 34
Le Boucq, Jacques Pl.
Boughton, Northamptonshire 82
Boulter, Dean Hugh 131, 156–7, 159, 185
Boulter exhibition 243
Bourton-on-the-Water, Gloucestershire 124
Boyle, Charles, 4th Earl of Orrery 141, 143, 147, 168–9, *169*, 170, *181*, 288
Boyle, Courtenay 279
Boyle, Edward 316
Boyle, John 143
Boyle, Robert 122
Bracegirdle (usher at King Henry VIII College) 21
Bradley, E. H. 29
Bradshaw, Dean William 157, 158–60, 184, 186
Brahms, Johannes: *Rinaldo* 276
Brasenose College, Oxford 120, 198, 220–1, 278, 298, 314
Brassard, John 58
Bread and Butter Row 256–7, 272

Bresson, John 58
Brewer Street, Oxford 92, 93, 302
Brickland, Thomas 57
Bristol
  bishopric of 156, 157, 176
  blitz refugees 315
  deanery of 70
Bristol cathedral foundation 229
British Council 318
Broad Walk, Oxford 23, 24, 28, 30, 32, 33, 302
Broadgates Hall 56, 80
Broderick, Warden 29
Brodie, Robert 236, 261
Brodrick, John 189
Brooke, Henry 31
Brooks, John 150, 152, *153*, 154
Brown, Anthony 106
Brown, Matthew 109
Brown, T. E. 226
Browne, Mary 144, 145
Bruarne, Thomas 45
Bruni, Signor 196
Bruton, Edward 27
Buchanan report: *Traffic in Towns* 31
Buckhurst, Thomas Sackville, Lord 74, 75, 82
Buckland, Frank 34, *35*, 213
Buckland, William 207, 209, 213, 214, 249
Buckler, Walter 20
Bull, John 61, 202, 203, 240, 248, 249
Bullingdon Club 268, 275
Bulstrode Park, Buckinghamshire 196
Burgesdichius: *Institutiones Metaphysicae* 173
Burgess (of Corpus Christi) 183
Burne-Jones, Sir Edward 290
Burras, Mr (director of Botanic Gardens) 28, 29
Burton, Dr 221
Burton, Edward 249
Burton, Francis 203
Burton, Robert 288
Burton, Thomas 150, 151
burying the censor 187, 188
Busby, Richard 124, 125, 172, 174, 181
Buste, John 81, 82
Butler, Bishop 88
Butler, Charles 204
Butler, Professor Christopher, ed.: *Portrait* xii
Butlers Marston, Warwickshire 190
Button, Ralph 109, 115
Buxton, John 213
Buxton, Rupert 303

Index

Calcutta cathedral 137
Calfhill, James 47, 68
Cam River 66
Cambridge Apostles 212
Cambridge University 82, 220
Camperdown, battle of 195
Candelar, John 21
Canner, Thomas 16, 17, 18
Canning, Charles 205
Canning, George 210
canon commoners 86, 128
canonries, suppression of 240, 241, 244, 246
canons
  Augustinian 3
  Cardinal College 5, 6, 10, 15, 46
  and Cathedrals Act 230–31
  Christ Church *see under* Christ Church, Oxford
  of the first order 6
  honorary 89, 231
  King Henry VIII College 16–21, 282
  non-residentiary 231
  petty (of the second order) 6
  residentiary 89
Canterbury, Kent 19
Canterbury, Archbishop of 120
Canterbury Association 277
Canterbury Cathedral 230
Canterbury College, Oxford 3, 19, 40, 45, 48, 56, 131, 289
Canterbury Gate 127, 303, Pl.
Canterbury Lodge 234
Canterbury Quadrangle 19, 186, 199, 212, 214, 234, 289, 304, 320, Pl.
Cardinal Club 276, 277
Cardinal College, Oxford 55
  canons 5, 6, 10, 15, 46
  chapel 87
  chaplains 7
  charter of privileges 14
  college buildings 10–12, 87
  college treasures 14–15
  constitution 5, 43
  daily life 9–10
  dean 6, 14
  Erasmian teaching 9
  feeder schools 4–5, 15
  founded (1525) 57, 304
  humanism 4
  library 10
  location 5
  property 13–14, *13*, 15–16
  staff 8–9, 15
  statutes 5, 6, 7, *7*, 9, 14, 15, 47, 53, 54
  student behaviour 9
  suppression of 15–16
  Taverner becomes organist and choirmaster 7–8
Careswell, Edward 160, *161*, 162
Careswell bequest 160–61, 162, 178, 216, 245
Carew, Dean George 69–70
Carey, William 218
Carey benefaction 243
Carfax, Oxford 83
Carfax conduit 233, 235
Carnsew, Richard and William 80
Caröe, W. D. xi–xii, *286*, 294
Carpenter, William 114
Carter, Robert 16, 17, 18
Carter, Thomas 84, *84*
Cartwright, William 102
Carus (physician to the King of Saxony) 207–8
Cassington, Oxfordshire 99, 315
Castle Hotel 320
Castlemaine, Lady 127
cathedral bodies, reform of 229
Cathedral Church of Christ in Oxford 41–2
Cathedral Garden 36
Cathedrals Act *see* Ecclesiastical Duties and Revenues Act
Cathedrals Commission 61, 91, 229
Catherine of Aragon 2, 3, 12
Catherine of Braganza 126–7
'Catholic question' 210–11
Catholicism 55, 64, 71, 130, 131
caution money 156, 163, 191, 218, 311
Caversham, Berkshire 162
Cecil, Lord Robert 316
Cecil, William, Lord Burghley 75
Censor Theologiae 17, 73, 166, 255
censors, role of 329–30
Censorship Theologiae 74, 166
Chadwick, Dean Henry 324, 325, 326
Challoner, Dr Penelope 326
Challoner divinity lectures 89
Chaloner, Robert 161
Chamber, Dr 17, 18
Chamberlain, Thomas 261
Champernowne, Amyas 281
Chandence 'home' farm (Chandlings), Berkshire 25, 99

Chantries Act (1545) 40
Chapel Royal, Windsor 70, 94
chaplains 5, 7, 10, 16, 17, 43, 46, 70, 83, 89, 91, 92, 116, 163, 165, 183, 193, 226, 243, 261, 272, 300
Chaplain's Quad 187, 234, 285, 286, 289–90
Chapter Books 43, 46, 54, 62, 70, 71, 72, 84, 92, 131, 138, 142, 143, *144*, 154, 176, 180, 192, 203
Chapter Clerk 24, 119, 152, 154, 193, 219
Chapter Fund 90–91
Chapter House 3, 12, 19, 88, 90, 91, 260, 262, 263, 291
Charity Commission 61, 62
Charles I, King 97–8, 100, 101, *101*, 102, 104, *104*, 107, 108, 109, 197
Charles II, King 59–60, 103, *112*, 115, 117, 122, 126–7, *128*, 131, 284
Charles Edward Stuart, Prince, the Young Pretender 164
Charlton, Andrew 160
Charterhouse School 162, 191, 265, 322
Chatteris, Cambridgeshire 162
Chelsum, James 183
Cheltenham, Gloucestershire 213
Cherry-Garrard, Apsley 296, 320, 321
Cherwell 304
Cherwell Bridge 28
Cherwell River 23, 26–9, 33, 34
Chester, bishoprics of 141
Chester, Charles 107–8
Chinnery, George 201, *202*, 203, 204, 207
choir, choirboys, choristers 5, 7, 8, 16, 17, 21, 43, 46, 83, 90–94, 98, 116, 193, 226, 294, 298, 300, *300*, 301
choir school 91–3, 302, 321
choirmaster 7
cholera 235
Christ Church Choral Society 212
Christ Church, Oxford
   admission (1691–1710) 140
   Anatomy School 174, 175, 180, 186, 207, 208, 269, 288, 292, 304, 318
   buildings and architecture 119, 141, *142*, 186, 187, 282–92
   canons 43–5, *44*, 48, 56, 71, 88, 91–2, 111, 115, 116, 126, 130, 131, 132, 149, 150, 151, 154, 194, 229, 230, 243, 244, 247, 252–3, 257–8, 262–3, 271, 283–4
   capitular estates administration 230

charity 57–66, 194–5
Charter of Dotation 47, 53
college seals 262
college servants 46–7, 193–4, 195, 272, 277, 318
Common Room 125, 234, 236, 257, 298
Common Room Smoking Room 298
conference trade 328–9
constitution 90, 165, 229, 230, 238, *239*, 250, 252, 255, 257, 259, 263, 268, 271, 278, 293, 310, 313, 323, 324, 332
the dean 5, 43, *44*, 49, 56, 58, 69, 71, 75, 82, 83, 91–2, 113, 116, 119, 129, 142, 157, 164, 184, 187, 247, 260, 310, 327
debate over split between college and cathedral 312–14, 326–7, 332
earliest representation of 78
education 53–5, 65–6, 80–81, 113–14, 122–3, *123*, 165–75, *169*, 177–85, 198–9, 200, 201–10, 268–70, 294–6, 303
electricity installed 291, 294
endowment 19, 21, 22, *41*, 47–8, 332
examination statutes 198–9, 201
fan tracery 107
financial matters 48, 51–3, 102, 107, 119, 185–6, 190–95, 230, 264–5, 292
first professors 43, *44*, 45, 54–5, 85
food 49–51, *51*, 74–7, 93, 127, 194, 196–7, *197*, 226, 273, 298–9, 306, 317, 320
foundation charter (1546) 42, *42*, 47, 126
founded (1546) 5, 21, 41, *41*, 42, *42*, 88
gardens 35–8
Graduate Common Room 322, 323, 324
Junior Common Room 275, 306, 320, 321, 322, 324
laboratory 269–70, 291, 310, 318
lack of patental guidance 228
Law Library 292, 318
lecture theatre 292
Library xii, 2, 55, 72–3, 120, 129, 141, 146, *181*, 183, 184, 186, 194, 199, 226, 233, 235, 265, 266, 276, 278–9, *280*, 283, *284*, 288, 289, 291–2, 314, 318, 320, 321, 328
losses in two world wars 299, 316
and 'Merton Mall' 31, 32
modernisation 319–20
museum 208, 269, 291

Index

new honours school in natural science (1840s) 208
oath-taking 49
office staff 327–8
origins of ChCh men 177–8, *178*
overcrowding 199–200
picture gallery 292, 318, 321
postgraduate study 323–4
presence in Convocation 140
presence of the Court 104, 105–7, 127
Prime Ministers *223*
quadrangles 38–9
quatercentenary celebrations (1925) 304, *305*, 306, 308, 317
river bank charges 27–8
sanitation and water supply 233–7
Senior Common Room 37, 211, 219, 260, 292, 314, 320, 324
sits back from University politics 155
statutes 42, 43, 49, 69, 71, 137, 198–9, 201, 228, 261–3, 283
support for the Whigs 175
tercentenary celebrations (1846) 225
theft from the Treasury 222, 224–5
Union officials 307
unique joint foundation of college and cathedral xii, 41, 88, 247, 264, 310, 333
and women 116, 218–19, 237, 324–6, 332
at its zenith 202
Christ Church Cathedral, Oxford 35, 56, 67
 the bells 133–5, *134*
 built of soft local stone 96
 Charles II's intervention on canons' preaching 126
 clocks in 135–6
 costs and funding 90–91
 during the First World War 299–301, *300*
 founded (1542) 40
 Frideswide window 290
 inventory 69
 Latin chapel 87, 89, 161, 189
 Liber Vitae and memorial tablets 301–2
 location 56
 Lucy chapel 87
 Military Chapel 95
 the organ 90, 94–5, 110
 Scott's plans 290–91
 services 88–89, 93, 94, 95, 231, 276, 321
 sundial on 135
 'tunnel' to *290*, 291, 317

unique joint foundation of college and cathedral xii
Christ Church Days (Frederick Arnold) 218, 231
Christ Church, Oxford, Act 1867 245, 274
Christ Church (Oxford) Mission, Poplar, east London 277, 318
Christ Church Private Fire Brigade 319, *319*
Christy, Stephen 299
Church, the 174
 Parliament attacks 102
 regularisation by Henry I 3
Church, William 249, 261
Church Assembly 314
Church Revenues Commission 229–30
Cicero *171*
City of Birmingham Symphony Orchestra 66
City Water Works 235
Clarendon, Edward Hyde, 1st Earl of
 History of the Rebellion 203
 The Life of Edward, Earl of Clarendon 203
Clarendon Laboratory 310
Clarke, Jeremiah 114
Clarke, John 8
Classis system 166, 167, 168, 170, *171*
Cleaver, Henry 218
Clerk of Works' office 93
Clerke, Canon Charles 240, 243, 244, 248, 249, 261
Cleveland Commission 264, 265
Clinton, Henry Fynes 182–3
Clive, Lewis 310
clocks 135–7, *136*
clubs 275, 276, 281
Cluff, Mr (chef) 196–7
Co-operative Congress (1882) 272
Coalbrookdale, Shropshire 27
Codrington, Christopher 119
Coke, Henry 11
Coldstream Guards 306, 316
Coleman, Mr 65
Coleridge, John and Paul Pl.
Coleridge, John Taylor 259
collections 155, 166, 167, 172, 182, 209, 281
College Histories series xi
Collie, Carl Howard 310, 316
Colman, George 194
Colman (student) 199–200
Commemoration speech 162, 185, 272
Commemoration Week 34, 272, 276–7, 304

Committee for Public Revenue 59
Committee on the Headship of Christ Church 313–14
commoners xiii, 43, 46, 56, 60, 71, 74, 86, 99, 107, 140, 163, 164, 183, 203, 207, 225
   canon 86, 128
   and collections 167
   gentlemen 45, 113, 119, 139, 140, 167, 177, 189, 191, 194, 218, 221, 240
Commonwealth (1649–53) 23, 94, 109, *110*, 111, 115, 117, 118, 119, 122, 174
Communist Party 308
Consolidated (or Amalgamated) Clubs 275
Convocation 140, 199, 211
Convocation of Canterbury 140
Conybeare, Dean John 141, 160, 161, 163, 164–5, 175–6, 179
Cook, Jean xii
Cooke, A. H. 316
Cooke, R. G. 318
Cooks Corporation 102
Copley, John Singleton 184
Copyhold Commissioners 263
Corbett, Dean Richard 83, 88, 97, 98
Corfe, Charles 94
Corne, William 204, 210
Cornish, Henry 115
Corpus Christi College, Oxford 4, 5, *7*, 9, 18, 19, 22, 26, 27, 31, 36, 37, 40, 44, 80, 82, 103, 105, 121, 127, 183, 209, 213, 221, 236, 249, 309
   constitution 43
Corro, Antonio del 74
Cottisford, John 16
Cotton, Edward 124
Cotton exhibition 243
Counting House 106
Court of Arches 120
Court of Augmentations 43, 47
Court of Common Pleas 24
Cowley, Oxfordshire 165, 298
Cowley Lands 23
Cowper, Francis 214
Cox, Dean Richard 21, 40, 41, 42, 52, 54, 67, 68
Cramer, John 202
Cramer, Mr (performer) 196
Cranmer, Archbishop Thomas 17, 45, 68
Cratford, Edward 54
Creed, William 115
Crespion, Stephen 127

cricket 220, 275, 296, 318
Crimean War 57
Croft, John 316
Croke, Canon Richard 16, 18, 19
Crompton, William 114
Cromwell, Oliver 111, 112, *112*, 114
Cromwell, Thomas 12, 15, 17, 18, 19
Crook, Mr (lawyer) 24
Crossman, Anthony 32
Crozier, John 60
Cubitt, Sir William 236
Cuddesdon, Oxfordshire 207
Curtius Rufus, Quintus 183
Curtoppe, James 47
Curwen, Richard 16
Cutteslowe, Oxford 190

Dallam, Thomas 94
Dampmartin, Catherine 2, 67, 68, 73
Dandalo, Signor 64, 65
Daniel, Samuel: *Arcadia* 83
Darby, Michael 133
Daubeny, Charles 207, 208, 209
Daventry priory 19
Davies, Robert 119
Davis, John 187
Day, Thomas 44
de Burgo, Nicholas 16
de la Pole family 4
de Ros, William Lennox Lascelles Fitzgerald 220
Deadman's Walk 32
Deane, Thomas *250*, 289–90
Declaration of Indulgence (1687) 131–2
Delaune, William 156
Demosthenes 183
Denbigh pauper lunatic asylum 674
Denne, Vincent 114
Derby, Lord 256, 296
Desaguliers, John Theophilus 175
Development Office 327, 328
Devereux, William 113
Devick, Henry 86
Devonshire, William Cavendish, Duke of 157
Dillwyn, Colin 313
disbursement books, disbursements 46, 53, 56, 62, 63, *65*, 195
discipuli 46, 143
Dissolution of the Monasteries 3, *41*
Dixon, H. B. 269
Dixon, Mr (Timber Yard lessee) 26
Dockwra, William 146

Index

Dod, Benjamin 143
Dodds, Eric 297, 320
Dodgson, Charles Lutwidge (Lewis Carroll) 227, 236, 252, 261, 265, 266, 271, 280, 293
   Alice in Wonderland 256, 266
   Through the Looking Glass 266
Dolben, John 115, 117, 118, *118*, 119, 130, 294
doles of meat 64–5
Domus (college funds) 243
Donne (lecturer) 47
Donnington Bridge 32
Dorset, Edward Sackville, Earl of 97
'Double-Cross system' 316
Dowdeswell, Edward 249
Dowdeswell, John 216
Downing, Mr (engineer) 235
Dramatic Society 319
dress 9, 29, 56, 73, 83, 98, 113, 251, 265, 306
Driberg, Tom 308
Dry, Thomas 217
Dudden, Holmes 311
Dunbavin, Nathaniel 114
Duncan, Admiral 195
Dundas, R. H. 30, 308, 320, 321
Duppa, Dean Brian 88, 90, 97, 98, 284
Durham
   bishopric of 311
   deanery of 205
   diocese 6
Durham Cathedral 215, 229
Dutch elm disease 28

E. Dent & Co. 137
Eagle Foundries (Oxford and Birmingham) 27
Earl's Ham 26, 29, Pl.
East Garston, Berkshire 190
Easthampstead living 245, 248, 249
Ecclesiastical Commission, Commissioners 89, 253, 313, 333
Ecclesiastical Duties and Revenues Act (1840) (Cathedrals Act) 230, 240
Ecclesiastical Duties and Revenues Commission 229
Eden, Anthony (later 1st Earl of Avon) 303, 316
Edgehill, battle of (1642) 103
Education Act (1944) 329
Edward VI, King 17, 42, 43, 55, 67, 68, 69, 133

Edward VII, King (and as Prince of Wales) 135, 251, 294
Edward VIII, King (as Prince of Wales) 296
Edwards, William 275
Eedes, Francis 117
Eedes, Richard 75
Egerton, Henry 156
Egerton, Philip 212
VIIIs 275
Einstein, Albert 308, *309*
Elcock (lecturer) 47
Electoral Board 249–50, 261, 271
Eliot, T. S. 316
Elizabeth, Queen (later the Queen Mother) 305
Elizabeth I, Queen 58, 69, 70, 71–2, 75, 78, *78*, 79, 82
Elizabeth II, Queen 135, 292
Ellis, William 122
Elmsley, Peter 215
Encaenia 196
English Civil War (1642–51) 23, 27, 34, 58–9, 87, 103–9, 111, 114, 332
Ephraim Ward's Flying Stage Wagons 196
Essay Club (the WEG) 212–13
Essex, Earl of 75, 103
Esson, William 269
Etheridge, George 45, 55, 67
Ethicae Compendium 173
Eton College, Etonians 4, 212, 218, 221, 265, 274, 275, 311, 322
Eucharist, the 55
Euclid 172, 181, *181*, 183, 188, 213, 231, 280
Euripides 203
Eustachius: *Ethics 171*, 173
Evans, Major-General 57
Eveleigh, John 198
Evelyn Collection 318
Evening Standard 322
Everest, Mount 303
Exeter, bishoprics of 141
Exeter College, Oxford 160, 204, 220, 249
exhibitioners 21
Eynsham, Oxfordshire 124, 133, 162
Eynsham abbey 48

Faulkner, J. (chef) 225, 273–4
Faussett, Robert Godfrey 249, 257, 260, 261, 264, 265, 266, 274
Faussett (Treasurer) 62
Feiling, Keith 316, 321

Fell, Dean John ix, 12, 28, 32, 38, 108, 115, 117–21, *118*, 123–7, 129, 130, 138, 139, 147, 149, 166, 167–8, 174, 282, 285, 286, *290*, 291, 294, 321
Fell, Margaret 108
Fell, Dean Samuel 103, 105–9, 118, 233, 284–5, Pl.
Fell and Hill trust 124
Fell estates 186
Fell exhibition 243
Fell Oration 170
Fell Tower *239*, 291, 318, Pl.
Fell Trust 162
Fell's Buildings 183, 187, 286, 289–90
fencing 318
Ferrand, William 281
Finance Committee 263
First World War 34–5, 38, 92, 95, 291, 294, *295*, 297–301, 317
Fisher, Charles 299
Fisher, Herbert 251
Fleet prison, London 55
Fletcher, W. A. (Flea) 274
flooding 22–3, 28
Floyd, Henry 27
Folly Bridge 235
football 296, 316
Foreign Office 317
Forte, Lord 292
Foster, Michael 313, 314, 318, 320
Foulkes, Robert 109
Founder's Prayers 306
Fowler, Edward 121
Fowler, John 292
Fox-Strangways, Giles (Baron Stavordale) 281
Foxe, John 14, 80
  Acts and Monuments (*Book of Martyrs*) 73
Fraenkel, Eduard 309
Frampton, Robert, Bishop of Gloucester 162
Frampton exhibition 243
Frampton Trust 162
France, post-revolutionary 195
Francis, Thomas 47
Francis, William 311–12
Franco, Solomon 64
Franks Commission 333
Franks report 329
Frederick, Prince of Denmark 33
Frederick, Prince of Wales 179
Freind, John 180, 288
French revolution 198
French wars 21, 40

Frewen, Accepted 97
Frewin, Richard 186, 266
Frewin Hall, New Inn Hall Street, Oxford 251
Frideswide, St 1–2, 73, Pl.
Friends of the Cathedral 36, 95
Frisius, Gemma 80
Froschauer, Christopher 55
Frye, Mother 63
Furnivall, Dorothy 77
Furnivall, John *51*, 77–8

Gager, William 79–80
  Rivales 80
Gaisford, Helen (née Douglas) 215
Gaisford, Dean Thomas 94, 204, 206, 207, 209, 210, 215, 216, 220, 225–7, 231, 238, 240, 266, 270
Galpin, James 24
Galton, Thomas 24
Gardiner, Richard 103, 115, 124, 127, 285
Gardiner, Stephen 15
Gardiner exhibition 243
Gardiner-Hill, P. F. 318
Garrard, Henry 112–13, *112*
Garsington, Oxfordshire 161
Gaskell, James 205, 213–14, 217
Gastrell, Francis 152
Gates, William 58
gaudies 116, 185, 195, 225, 264, 272, 293, 294, 298, 327
Gaudy Oration 170
Geale, Richard 108–9
General Strike (1926) 307–8
Gentleman, David Pl.
gentlemen commoners 45, 113, 119, 139, 167, 177, 189, 191, 194, 218, 221, 240
George I, King 155, 156
George III, King 195
George IV, King (as Prince Regent) 221
George V, King 135, 296, *305*, 306
George VI, King 135
German Academic Exchange Service (DAAD) 318
Gibbon, Edward 177, 182
Gibbs, George 281
Gibson, Edmund, Bishop of Lincoln 159
Gielgud, Sir John 35
Giffard, Hardinge, 1st Earl of Halsbury 260
Gill and Ward 27
Gilpin, Bernard 55
Gladstone, William Ewart 204, 205, 212–13, *223*, 227–8, 230, 241, 245, 251

Index

Glanville, Philippa 14
Godley, John Robert 277
Godwin, Dean Thomas 78
golf 296, 318
Gondomar (Spanish ambassador) 83
Gooch, Thomas *284*
Goodenough, Dr 216
Goodman, Christopher 54
Goodwin, Colonel 102
Goodwin, Edward 222–4
Goodwin, Dean William 83, 84, 97, 98
Gordon, Osborne 228–9, 231, 240, 245, 248, 252, 254, 257
Gore, Mr 56
Goudge, Henry 313
Governing Body 28, 29, 32, 36, 45, 62, 66, 88, 91, 92, 137, 190, 209, 228, 236, 237, 241, 243, 245, 247, 254, 255, 259, 260, 261, 262–7, 272–5, 279, 292, 297, 302, *309*, 313, 314, 322, 325, 326, 328, 329, 330
Grace, Michael 316
Graham, George 143
Grand Union Canal 66
Grant, Henry 273
Grant Bailey, Samuel 313, 314
Gray (ChCh Treasurer) 32
Gray, Eric 318
Great Bowden, Leicestershire 114
Great Quadrangle, Christ Church (Tom Quad) 12, 16, 32, 35, 36, 38, 44, 56, 66, 79, 102, 104–5, 108, 119, 127, 213, 214, 235, 236, 248, *267*, 268, *280*, 282, 285, 286, *290*, 291, 306, 314, Pl.
Great Tom 40, 133, 134–5, *134*, 149, 194, 268, 286, 328
'Greats' 295
Green Dragon pub, Oxford 22
Greenwich Mean Time *136*, 137
Gregory, Dean David 172, 174, 175, 177, 179–80, *181*, 182, 186, 190
Gregory, George 190
Grenville, George *223*
Grenville, William, 1st Baron 221
Gresham College 109
Gresley, Richard 216, 220
Gresley, William 220
Greville, Fulke 85
Griffiths, E. R. 236–7
Grimthorpe, Lord 137
Gristie, Mary 144
Grosvenor, John 180

Grotius, Hugh: *De veritate religionis Christianae* 174
Guise, General John 266, 288
Gunter, Edmund 122
Guy's Hospital, London 207

Hacker, Robert 60
Hall, Anna (née Byng) 217
Hall, Dean Charles Henry 202, 209, 210, 211, 214, 215, 217, 221, 225
Halley, Edmond 123
Hamilton, James, Duke of 155–6
Hammond, Dr John 151, 152
Hampden, John 218
Hampden, Renn Dickson, Bishop of Hereford 218, 219, 249
Hampton Court conference (1604) 82
Hannes, Edward 119
Hanwell, Richard 175
Harbin, Henry 191
Harcourt, Augustus Vernon 248, *250*, 251, 254, 257, 260, 261, 269–70, 324
Harcourt, Simon, Earl 148, 149, 151, 152, 175
Hardie, Frank 308
Hardie report 322, 329
Hardinge (student being punished) 280–81
Hardwicke, Earl of 165
Harley, Edward 147, 150
Harley, Robert 147, 175
Harrington, James 138
Harrison, A. R. W. 322
Harrison, Benjamin 204–5
Harrison report 322, 329
Harrod, Roy 308, 313, 320
Harrow School 265, 322
Harrowby, Lord 255
'hashish' club 297
Hassall, Arthur 270
Hastings, John 16, 18
Hatley, John 16
Hatton, Christopher 74
Haverford College 294
Hawkes (under-butler) 113
Hay, Canon 184
Haynes, William 43–4
Head of the River 274, 296, *296*, 303
Headmasters' Conference 272, 329
Hearne, Thomas 147
Heaton, Dean Eric 326, 327
Hebdomadal Board 226
Hebdomadal Council 97

Heber, Reginald 202
Henley regatta 220
Henrietta Maria, Queen 97
Henry, Prince of Wales 83
Henry I, King 3
Henry VI, King 4
Henry VIII, King 3, 14, 15, 17, 20, 21, 22, 40–44, 47, 48, 57, 67, 85, 87–8, 102, 230, 304, *305*, 311
Hephaestion 225
Herbert Morrell Cup *319*
Herodotus 188
Hertford College, Oxford 176, 198
Hether, Mr 56
Heurtley, Charles 240, 249
Hibbert Trust lecture 271
Hickman, Mr 235
Higden, Dean John 6, 15–18
High Laver, Essex 194
High Street, Oxford 2, 30, 235
Hill, 'Hooky' 318, *319*
Hill, Canon Richard 124
Hillier and Sons 38
Hinksey, Oxfordshire 235
Hinksey conduit 233
Hinksey Hill 235
Hiscock, W. G. xi, 80
   Christ Church Miscellany 317
History of the University of Oxford xiii
Hitler, Adolf 316
Hoare, Mr (giraffe skeleton donor) 208
Hodges, Nathaniel 109
Hodgson, Leonard 313
Hodson, Christopher 133
Hogg, Quintin 307
Hoggar (engineer) 236
Holford, Lady 162, 190, 191
Holford Trust 162, 190, 191
Holland, Canon Henry Scott 298
Holland, John 156
Holmes, Robert 183
Holwell, William 89
'Holy Club' 158
Home Guard 35
Home Office 310
Homer 171
Hook, Dr 216, 217
Hook, Walter 216–17
Hook, W. F. 215
Hooke, Robert 122, 175
   A description of helioscopes 123
   Micrographia 122

Hooker, Thomas 216
Hoole, Charles 261
Hooper, Dr 129
Hopkins, Clare xii
House of Commons 179, 261, 307
House of Lords 31, 316
Howard, Michael 316
Howe, Richard 117
Howson, John 82
Hoyle, Joshua 109
Hudson (cook) 114
Hudson, John 23, 61
Hume, John 187
Humphreys, Hanbury 191
Hunt, George 191
Hunt, George Ward 255, 259
hunting 220, 274, *296*
Hus, John 8
Hussey, Robert 219, 246
Hussey, William 269
Hutchinson, George 37, 38
Hyde, Judge Edward (later Lord Chief Justice) 24

Iffley lock 220
Iffley Road, Oxford 32, 92
   sports ground 28
Ince, Dr 92
influenza pandemic (1918) 300–301
Inglis, Robert 211–12
Interregnum 117
Invincible, HMS 299
Ipswich School, Suffolk 4, 15
Iris Garden 38
Irish potato famine 64
Isle of Man, internment on 310

Jackson (bridge designer) 28
Jackson, Dean Cyril 177, 186–7, 197, 198, 201–2, 203–4, 210, 215, 217, 225, 281
Jackson, Samuel 117
Jackson, William 183
Jacob, Herbert Percy 303
Jacobitism 164
Jacobson, William 240, 248, 249, 256
Jacobson family 33
Jacobstahl, Paul 309–10
Jacoby, Felix 310
James, Richard 164
James, Dean William 74, 75, 79
James I, King 82, 83, 85–6, 97
James II, King (and as Prince) 103, 127, 129, 130, 131, 132, 138, 139, 332

Index

Jane, William 89, 141
Jekyll, Gertrude 38
Jelf, Richard 89, 91, 240, 249, 251, 271
Jenkins, Canon Claude 36, 37
Jenkinson, David 52
Jenkinson, Richard 155
Jesus College, Oxford 220, 311
Jones, Colonel Samuel 109
Jones (servitor) 183–4
Jonson, William 11
Joyce of Whitchurch 137
Judas, Leo 55
junior members: defined xiii
Jutland, battle of 299

Kapurthala, Maharajah of 296
Kean, Charles 3
Keene, Henry 288–9
Keene, Richard 133
Keill, John 174, 175
Kelly, John 180
Kempster, Christopher 286
Kennedy, Ludovic 317
Kent, Dr Paul 323
Kentish Town, London 162
Keys, Richard 90
Kidd, Professor John 207, 208, 209
Killcanon, Oxford 36–7, 135, *136*, 285, 314, Pl.
Killigrew, Henry 100
Kimber, John 189–90
King, Dean John 82, 83
King, John (almsman) 57
King, John (auditor) 118
King, One 98
King, Edward 23
King Henry VIII College, Oxford 55, 88
 canons 16–21, 282
 the dean 16, 17, 18, 20, 21
 foundation charter (1532) 16
 income 19
 property re-granted to ChCh 47
 staff 21
 statutes 16–17, 18, 19, 53
 surrendered to the Crown (1545) 21
King's College, Cambridge 4, 11, 37, 44
King's College, London 64
King's Library 168
Kirkland Cave, Yorkshire 209
Kirton, John 33
Kitchin, George (later Dean of Durham) 89
Knox, Vicesimus 198

Krumpholtz, Madame 196

La Ferté 299
Labour government, fall of (1931) 308
Lady Margaret professorship 37, 55, 85, 241, 261
Lambeth Palace, London xi, 37, 260
Lamprey, Thomas 165
Land Commission 265
Langley, Henry 109, 115
Langley, Oxfordshire 83
Langton chest 17
Latimer, Hugh 17
Laud, Archbishop William 97, 100, 101, 167, 227, 284
Laudian Code (1636) 97–8
Lavie (Chapter Clerk) 219
Law, Edward 215
Law Library 292, 318
lawn tennis 274
Lawrence Phelps and Associates 94
lay clerks 5, 17, 43, 46, 58, 91, 92, 300
Lee, Matthew 174–5, 179, 185, 249, 288
Lee, Sarah 179
Lee bequest 172, 174, 179, 180, 181, *181*, 182, 185, 207, 208, 243
Lee Certamen 179
Lee's Readers 249–50, 261, 270, 301, 310, 324
Leicester, Robert Dudley, Earl of 70, 73, 74
Leigh, Lord Thomas 120
Leighton, Edward 16, 17, 18
Leighton, Francis 276
Lely, Peter *118*
Leopold, Prince 251–2
Letters Patent 68
Levett, William 120
Lewis, Charles 57
Lewis, Dean Christopher ix–x
Ley, Dr Henry George 306
Library ceiling Pl.
Library fund 159
Liddell, Alice 252
Liddell, Dean Henry George 12, 33, 87, 94, 204, 205, 207, 231–2, 238–48, *239*, 251, 256, 266–7, 268, 270, 282, 290, *290*, 291, 311, 321, Pl.
Liddell, Mrs 276
Liddell family 33, 276
Liddon, Henry Parry 254, 266
Lincoln College, Oxford 158, 201, 219, 249
Lincoln diocese 6, 20, 87

Lindemann, Frederick (later Lord Cherwell) 308–9, 310, 316
Lithuanian churches 64
Little Tom 149
Littlemore priory 19
Liverpool, Lord 217
Livy 218
Lizeron (chef) 196
Llandaff 215
Llewelyn Davies, Michael 303
Lloyd, Charles (tutor) 204, 209, 210–11
Lloyd, Charles Harford (organist) 94
Lloyd, Thomas 160
Lloyd George, David 302, 310
Locke, John 117, 121, 128–9, *128*, 194
   Essay on Human Understanding 173
Lockey, Thomas 100
Loder's Club 214, 265, 276, 317
Loggan, David 32, 36, 37, 135
   Oxonia illustrata 285
London, Dr John 11, 18
London bridge 233
London Works, Birmingham 27
Longden, Robert 320
Longley, Archbishop Charles 202, 255, 259
Longstaff, Tom 303
Lopez, Vincent 304
Lord Chancellor 4, 148, 160, 165, 219, 302
Lord Williams's School, Thame 118
Lovyns, John 11
Lowe, Dean John 92, 312, 314, 321, 327, 329
Lowe, Robert 108
Lower, Richard 111, 122, 175
Ludford, Edward Taylor 187
Luke, George 248, 249
Luther, Martin 8
Lutherans 8

Macan, Reginald 271
Macclesfield, Earl of 175
Macey, Thomas 27
Mackenzie, Alexander 281
Mackinder, Halford 277
Maclaurin, Colin: *Treatise on Algebra* 181, 188
Madan, Falconer 278
Maddox (associate of James Rose) 224
Madeira 244
Magdalen Bridge 23, 30, 31
Magdalen College, Oxford 4, 6, 7, 9, 13, 17, 18, 55–56, 80, 83, 94, 103, 130, 140, 151, 157, 208, 241, 249, 265

Magdalen College School 30, 91, 92
Magdalen Hall (now Hertford College) 249
Mansel, Canon Henry 261
Marburg University 310
Marcham, Oxfordshire 114
Marjoribanks, Edward 266
Markham, David 190
Markham, Osborn 197–8
Markham, Dean William 167, 172, 177, 181, 182, 187, 188, 190, 199
Marlborough, Charles Spencer, 3rd Duke of 175
Marlborough, John Spencer, 1st Duke of 141, 150
Marlborough College 265
Marlborough Street police station, London 225
Marshall, Dean Richard 54, 68, 69
Martin, Charles 261
Martin, Thomas 117
Mary, Queen 306
Mary II, Queen ix
Mary Tudor 17, 54, 67, 68–69, 70, *70*, 133, 332
Mason, Chancellor John 69
Mason, Dr John xi, xii
Massey, Dean John 130–31, 132, 138, 154, 287
Masterman, J. C. 294, 297, 301, 308, 311, 316, 325
Masters' Garden 37–8
matriculation statute (1581) 283
Matthew, Dean Tobie (later Archbishop of York) 73, 79
Maurice of the Palatinate, Prince 103
Mayne, Jasper 115
Meade, Robert 108
Meadow, the
   Atterbury's demand 153–4
   Bennett's plan of Pl.
   flooding 23
   management of 25–8, 190
   'Merton Mall' 30–32
   popular for leisure 32, 34
   protection of 29
   revenues 99
   and sanitation 236
   Shire Lake runs through 22
   Son et Lumière (1968) 35, 333
   swan-upping 34
   trees 28–9, 32–3
   trials over 23–5, *25*
   in war 34–5, 299

Index

Meadow Building 38, 187, 235, 237, *239*, *250*, 290, 314, 320
Meadow Gate 35, 302, 314, 328
Mecklenburg, Prince of 221
Medici, Cosimo de, Duke of Tuscany 127
Melanchthon, Philipp 8
Melbourne, Lord 229
Melton, prebend of 18
Memorial Garden 30, 38, 292, 302, Pl.
Mercia 1
Mercurius Oxoniensis 32
Mercury 38–9, 124, 137, 215, 234, 285–6, 289, *290*, 304, 318
Mermaid club 276
Merton College, Oxford 17, 20, 22, 23, 26, 29, 31, 102, 103, 105, 121, 127, 130, 133, 156, 326
Merton Field 26, 30, 34, 93, 236
Merton Grange 27
'Merton Mall' 30–32
Merton Meadow 26, 29–30, 34
Methodists 158
Metternich, Prince Klemens von 221
MI5 316
MI6 316
Michael, St 95
Michelangelo 288
Military School of Education 298
Millham Bridge 23
Mills, Cecil *278*
Mills, Dr 107
Mills, John 115
Milman, Arthur 258, 259
Ministry of Production 316
Mitford, William: *History of Greece* 184
Moderations 231
Modius, Marcus 266
Monck, George 114
Monmouth, Duke of 35, 127, 129
Montacute, Elizabeth 22
Montague, Edward 82
Monzani, Signor 196
More, Sir Thomas 15
Morison, Alexander 120–21
Morley, Dean George (later Bishop of Worcester) 114–17, 119
Morris, George 281
Morris, James (now Jan) 35, 333
Morris, John 124, 174, 288
Mrs Pott's cottage 93
Mullens, Reverend 203–4
Mumford, Lewis 32

Murray, Charles 306–7
Mylls, Richard 98
Myres, J. N. L. 313

Napleton, John 198
Naseby, battle of (1645) 107
Nash, Richard 162, 272
Nash bequest 162, 185
Nazism 309, 310, 316
New (artist) 35, 36, 37
New College, Oxford 4, 11, 18, 19, 40, 44, 48, 71, 133, 265, 324
'New Interest' camp 175
New Library xii, 72, 183, 186, 199, *284*, Pl.
New Year gift book 167–9, *169*
New Zealand, ChCh bid to establish a new colony in (1850) 277
Newdigate, Richard 119, 175
Newry, Francis Needham, Lord *267*
Newton, Sir Isaac 201, 204
    Principia 270
Newton, Richard 198
Nicholson, Otho 233, 283
noblemen 45, 119–20, 139, 140, 141, 167, 177, 191, 194, 240, 270–71
Noel, Mr Justice 24
Nondescripts 275, 317, 318
Norfolk, Duke of 15
Norris, James 26
Norris, John 58
North Commission 333
North Hinksey 233
Norwich diocese 6
Nowell, Laurence 47, 55
Nuneham 221
Nuneham Courtenay 197

Oakeley 225
Oakley, Frederick 200
Obolensky, Prince Sergius 296
Oecolampadius (Johannes Hussgen) 8
Officer Training Corps 277, 315
Ogilvie, Charles 240, 248, 249
Okell, William 120
Old Library 38, 141, 186, 206, 235, 286, 314
Oliver, Dean John 18, 19
Olympic Games (1896) 274
Ordinance (1858) 216, 242, 245, 247–9, 252–6
organists 7, 8, 66, 91, 93, 94, 186, 294, 300–301, *300*, 306

Oriel College, Oxford 43, 120, 198, 226, 236, 249, 265, 270, 326
Oseney, Oxfordshire 21, 233
Oseney abbey, Oxfordshire 3, 22, 33, 40, *41*, 43, 44, 48, 49, 52, 133, *134*, 283
Oseney Cathedral, Oxford 20–21, 47, 88
Oseney Mill *234*
Ottery St Mary, Devon 124
Otway, Thomas 119
Ouse River 66
Oval House (previously Popular Mission in the East End) 66
Owen, Dean John 111, 114, 115
Oxford
   400th anniversary of diocese's foundation (1942) 95
   anger against the power of the gown in 102
   anti-Protestant opinion in 67
   archdeaconry of 262
   bicycles in 30
   bishopric of 215
   diocese of 87
   foundation of the new see (1542) 20
   the name 1
   proposed military academy *100*
   removal of defences (1642) 102–3
   rioting outbreaks (1714–17) 155
   settlement of 1
Oxford, Bishop of 124, 129–30
Oxford, Reverend 3
Oxford Act (1854) 228, 238, 240, 242
Oxford and Cambridge Commission 333
Oxford and District Fire Brigades Competition 319
Oxford castle jail 64–5, *65*, 225
Oxford Dictionary of National Biography xiii, 332
'Oxford Eye' 34
Oxford Journal 180
Oxford Local Examinations Delegacy 277
Oxford Magazine 299
Oxford Mission, Calcutta 277
Oxford Society of Change Ringers 66
'Oxford' time 137
Oxford Town Hall 83
Oxford Tutors' Association 216, 245
Oxford Union 37
Oxford University 82
   Aristotelian and humanist principles 55
   and Catholicism 101–2, 131, 139
   celebrates William of Orange's arrival 132
   Congregation 32
   financial support for Charles I 102
   insufficient library provision 277–8
   reform of statutes 97
   Royal Commission (1850) 227–30
   statutes 126, 227
   term dates 73
   Tory Oxford 140, 175
   Wolsey as benefactor 4
Oxford University Musical Club 272
Oxford University Press 119, 125, 168, 172, 183
Oxford University Volunteer Corps 277, *278*
Oxford Volunteers 195
'Oxford weed' 38
Oxfordshire 22, 24, 48
Oxfordshire and Buckinghamshire Light Infantry 95, 298
Oxley, James 281

Padgett, Nicholas 58
Page, Cyril 216
Page, Denys 316, 317
Page, Miss (ex-college secretary) 37
Paget, Arthur 197–8
Paget, Dean Francis (later Bishop of Oxford) 267, 268, 277, 294
Pakenham, Frank 308
Pallot, Judith 326
Palmer, Sir Roundell 259, 261
Palmer, Samuel 151–2
Palmer, Thomas 283
Pappus 183
Paris riots (1968) 321
Parker, Matthew 40
Parker, Archdeacon Samuel 130, 132
Parkinson-Fortescue, Chichester 257
Parks Road, Oxford 269
Parliamentary Visitors 108, 109, 111, 112, 113, 116, 122
Parson, John (of Balliol) 183
Parsons, John (medical faculty Student) 180
Paul, Prince, of Serbia 296
Paul, Rachel 124
Paul, St 188
Paul exhibition 243
Pauncefort, Edward 162
Pauncefort exhibition 243
Pauncefort Trust 162
Paviland, near Swansea 209
Payne Smith, Canon Robert 61, 256, 261, 277
Peace of Paris (1814) 221

Index

Pearson, Bishop John: Exposition on the Creed *171*, 174
Peascod Street, Windsor 124
Peckwater Inn, Oxford 11, 19, 40, 44, 48, 56, 141, 283
Peckwater Quadrangle 11, 37, 39, 84, 109, 115, *139*, 141, *142*, 150, 151, 152, 186, 191, 214, 216, 221, 234, 237, 268, 287–8, 289, 303, 304, 306, 320, Pl.
Peel, Sir Robert 201, *202*, 210–11, 229
Peele, George 80
Pegge, Christopher 180–81
Pelling, John 146
Pemberton, William 164
Pembroke, Philip Herbert, 4th Earl of 108, 151
Pembroke College, Oxford 56, 61, *63*, 109, 265, 311, 314
Penn, William 119, 294
Penrose, Thomas 187
Pension Fund 264
Pepys, Kenelm (Lord Cottenham) 281
Pepys, William Weller 182
Percival, John 120
Perrin, William 172
Perrott, Charles 152
Perry, Thomas 27
Pert, Paul 106
Peterhouse, Cambridge 325
Pett, Dr 183
Pett, Phineas 222–4
Pettingal, Thomas 183
Phalaris 168
   Epistles 168–9, *169*, 170
Phalaris affair 147
Philharmonic Society 276
philosophi 45–6, 54, 143
Philothespians 276
Phipps, Sir Charles 251
Physic Garden 27
Pickhaver, William 234
Piedmont, students of 64, *65*
Pindar 204
'Pink Lunch' 308
Pitt, William, the Younger 196
plague 76, 77, 82, 97, 107, 109, 117, 127
Plan socialist magazine 308
Plank (Frederick Roe's chief assistant) 224
plays 34, 36, 69, *70*, 79, 80, 83, 100, 101, 121, 182, 219, 276, 319
Pococke, Edward 37, 109, 115, 123
Pococke Garden 37, 135

Pole, Cardinal Reginald 67, 69
Portal, Charles 316
Porter's Lodge 135, 193
Portland, William Cavendish-Bentinck, 3rd Duke of 196, *197*
Portsmouth Grammar School 322
Potter, John 141, 150, 151, 156
Potts of Leeds 137
Powell and Moya 291, 292
Poynter, John 115
Poynton, A. B. 320
Prance, Basil *250*
Prayer Book rebellion (1549) 55
Price, Bartholomew 265
Princeton University 309, *309*
Priory House 37, 38, 44, 67
   garden 36, 37, 38, 109
Pritchard, Charles 60
Privy Council 127
Prout, Thomas 248, 249, 252–5, 257–62, 271
Pruern, George 279
Public Inquiry (1953) 30
Puckering, Sir John 74
Puritanism 85, 110
Pusey, Edward 240, 248, 249, 260, 271, Pl.
Pyrton church 68
Pyrton rectory, Oxfordshire 45

Queen Anne's Bounty 162
Queen's College, Oxford 82

Radcliffe, Anthony 109, 115, 141, 287
Radcliffe Camera 221
Radge (Head Porter) 194
Radio Security Service 316
Rainolds, John 80, 82
RAMC Territorials 310
Ramsbury estate 186
Randolph, John 183
Ravis, Dean Thomas 75, 82, 283
Rawlins, Mr 234
Read, Mr (vicar of Marcham) 114
Reading, Berkshire 277
real tennis 274
Red Cross 300
Redman, Henry 11
Referees' Award 260
Reform Act (1832) 229
Reinhold, A. W. 270
Reliquiae Diluvianae 209
Responsions 231, 266

Restoration (1660) 109, *112*, 114, 117, 128, *128*, 134, 172, 174
Reynolds, Dean Edward 108, 111, 114
Reynolds, Sir Joshua 184
Rhodes, Richard: *Flora's Vagaries* 121
Rhodes Scholars 294, 297, 312, 321
Richardson, John 146, 161–3
Ridley, Nicholas 17
Rieger 95
Rigaud, Stephen 209
Riley, John Pl.
Roberts, James 90
Roberts, Thomas Pl.
Robertson, Abraham 183
Robertson, Robert 281
Robinson, Rev. Henry L. xi
Robinson, Richard 289
Robyns, John 16
Rochester, bishopric of 153
Rochester cathedral 182
Roe, Frederick Adair 224
Rogers (Censor) 47
Rogers, Christopher 115
Romans 1
Roper, John 16, 20
Rose, James 224
Rose Place, Oxford 22
Rosebery, Archibald Primrose, Lord *223*
Rostherne living, Cheshire 71
Rotterdam 64
Roubillac, Louis-François 129
Rowell's 136
rowing 220–21, 274, 275, *296*, 318
Rowley, John 143
Roxburgh, Lord 86
Royal Air Force (RAF) 315, 316
Royal Assent 261
Royal Commission on ecclesiastical revenues and patronage 215, 226
Royal Flying Corps 298
Royal Naval Volunteer Reserves 316
Royal Navy 195
Royal Society 122, *123*, 174
rugby 296, 303, 318
Rugby School 265
Runcibles 318
Rupert of the Rhine, Prince 103
Ruskin, John 216, 245, 251
Russell, Alexander 310
Russell, Richard 114, 115
Russell government (1847) 226
Rutton, William 197–8

Ryle, Gilbert 308, 312, 313, 316, 320
Ryle, Martin 316

Sacheverell, Henry 151
Sackville, Robert 81, 82
Sadler, James 34
Sadler, Michael 277
St Alban Hall 20
St Aldates 10, 24, 30, 36, 47, 57, 61, 67, 235, 294, 302
St Aldates Quadrangle 327
St Anne's College 37
St Ebbe's parish 103
St Edmund Hall, Oxford 249
St Frideswide, shrine of 20, 87, 90
St Frideswide's Mead, Oxford 22
St Frideswide's priory, Oxford 1–3, 5, 10, 11, 13, 21, 24, 26, 36, 40, *284*, Pl.
  cartulary 2
  Chapter House 3, 12
  property 13, *13*, 19, 22
St Frideswide's priory church 2, 11, 41–2, 56, 87
St Hilda's College 30
St John's College 44, *78*, 83, 198
St Mary Hall 183, 236, 249
St Michael's parish, Oxford 190
St Paul's Cathedral, London 215, 258, 286
St Peter's parochial school 27
St Thomas's parish, Oxford 22, 133
Salisbury, Earl of 22, 263
Salter (rusticated student) 216
Salwey, Herbert 256, 261
Sampson, Dean Thomas 70, 71, 73, 74
Sampson (senior censor) 267, 268
Sancroft, Archbishop 129
Sandford, Charles W. (later Bishop of Gibraltar) 89, 210, 238, 249, 254, 257, 258, 260, 261, 293
Sandford Lock 236
Sandford Weir 303
Sandhurst (Royal Military Academy) 66
Sandwyche, William 19
Sandys, Duncan 30–31
Sarum rite 17
Saunders, A. P. 207
Sawkins, Charles 197
Saxons 1
Sayers, Henry 93
Schmidt, Dr Wolfgang 317–18
Schola anatomica 180
School Quadrangle 93

Index

Schoolmaster Studentships 323
Scots Wars 40, 101
Scott, Sir George Gilbert 87, 95, 135, 290–91
Scott, John 58
Scott, Robert 205, *239*
Scott, Robert Falcon 296
Scriven, John 189
Scullion, The (painting by John Riley) Pl.
Sealy, William 164
Second World War 34–5, 92, 96, 135, 291, 308, 310, 314–16, *315*
secularisation 326, 327
Segary, William 115
Senhouse, Humphrey 275
Senior Masters' Estate 240
servitors 45, 63, 98, 109, 116, 119, 120, 124, 130, 140, 159, 183–4, 232, 270, 275
Sestrière 318
Sex Discrimination Act 325
Seymour, Lord Webb 185
Shadwell, John 261
Shakespeare, William 80, 184, 276
  Henry VIII 3, 317
Sharp, Thomas: *Oxford Replanned* 30
Sheard, Mr (tenement dweller) 27
Sheldonian Theatre, Oxford 125, 196, 221
Shelter 66
Shemuell, Beta 64
Sheppard, Fleetwood 122
Sherlock, William 188
Shipley, William: *Comparative Observations on Two of the Poems ... in a late Certamen* 185
Shire Lake 22, 23, Pl.
Shirley, Walter 256, 257, 261
Short, Thomas Vowler 202, 205–6, *206*, 221
Shotover, Oxfordshire 149
'Show Sunday' 34
Showell (deputy Head Porter) 194
Shreve, John Pl.
Shropshire 160, *161*, 162, 178
Siam, Crown Prince (later King) of 296, 302
Siddall, Henry 45, 47
Sidney, Philip 81, 82
Sidney, Robert 81, 82
'Siga' chambers 191
Silsby, Thomas 114
Simpson, Dean Cuthbert 92, 321, 324, 327
skiing 318
Skippon, Major General 109
smallpox 125
Smallwell, Edward, Bishop of Oxford 196

Smalridge, Dean George xii, 141, 143–4, 145, 148, 154–6, 157, 166, 167, 169, 170, 174, 177, 179
Smith, Father Bernard 94
Smith, Henry 306, 308, 320–21
Smith, Dean Samuel 209, 215–16, 224, 225
Smith, Sebastian 115
Soddy, Frederick 303
Soley, John 189
Sollomans, Mr (a fence) 224
Sonnenschein, Teulon *250*
Sonning, Berkshire 11
Sophocles 203, 218
Souter, Mr 136
South, Dr Robert 129–30, 162, 288
South Sea annuities 186
South Trust 162
Southwell, Sir Richard 47
Southwell minster 194
Spalding, Augustine 143–5, *144*
Spanish Civil War 310
Spectator 214
Spelsbury, vicar of 124
sport 274–5, 296–7, *296*, 303, 318–19
Spycer, Henry 16
Staffordshire 160, *161*, 162
Stainer, John 94
Standing Orders and Bye-laws Committee 262
Standlake, Oxfordshire 124
Staniforth, Thomas 220
Stanley, A. P. 246, 251
Starr, Samuel 84, *84*
Staunton, William 11
Stephens, William 180
Steward's Office 36, 272, 274, 327–8
Stewart, John 271
Still, Arthur 281
Stockwell Mead, Oxford 22, 24
Stormont, Lord 184
Strabo 183
Strasbourg Protestants 64
Stratford, Canon William 147, 150–55, 157, 159, 161, 162, 288
Stratford Trust 161, 162
Strawberry Hill, Twickenham, Middlesex 3
Strong, Sampson Pl.
Strong, Dean Thomas Banks (later Bishop of Ripon) 294, *295*, 296, 297–8, 301, 302, 307, 310, 331–2
Strutt, Edward 303
Stuart, Charles 316

Stubbs, William 226, 270
Student Emeritus 318
Students (*alumni*)
    admissions (1691–1710) 140
    behaviour 56, 73–4, 97–8, 113, 120–22,
        142–6, 163–5, 187–90, 197–8,
        214–20, 265–8, 279–81
    Canoneer Students 71, 199, 205
    and Commission's Fourteen Points 242–3,
        245
    complaints about 54
    declining quality 209
    dispute over bread issue 74–7, 86
    in English Civil War 105
    equivalent of Fellows in other colleges xiii,
        45
    and exhibitioners 21
    expulsion and restoration of some after
        Visitation 108–9, 115–16
    Faculty Students 71
    first Students at ChCh 43, *44*, 45–6
    funding of Studentships 240
    official journeys abroad 99–100, 112–13,
        112
    over two centuries of discontent 99
    permitted to marry 263
    petition (1641) 99
    proposals of 245–6, 247, 254–5
    ranks 45–6, 111
    recreation 99
    requirements 49, *50*
    role of 230–31
    Thurston Students 71
    Vernon Students 71, 242
    Westminster *see* Westminster Students
Suarez, Francisco: *Disputationes Metaphysicae*
    146
Suez crisis (1956) 31
Sugworth 49
Sumervil (prisoner) 224
Susini, Signor Clementi 181
swan-upping 33, 34
swans 33–4, *33*, 39
Swinney, John 189
Symm, Joshua *250*
Symm's 237, *250*
Syrian earthquakes (1823) 64

T. Cooke & Son 137
Tatham, Edward 201
Tattersall, James 207
Tattershall, Lincolnshire 8

Taunton Commission 265
Taverner, John 7–8
Taylor, Christopher 60
Taylor, F. A. 320
Temple, John 109
Temple, William 169, 302
    Essay on Ancient and Modern Learning 168
Tenison, Archbishop 141
Terry, Thomas 155, 158, 159, 186
Tests Act (1871) 263
Thame River 66
Thames Conservancy 39, 236
Thames River 1, 2, 22, 23, 26, 28, 29, 33,
    66, *112*
theologiae (senior men|) 45, 54
Thirty-Nine Articles 89, 161, 174, 198, 199
Thompson, Rev. Henry L. xi, xiii, 131, 157,
    187, 225, 227, 230–31, 260, 261, 293
Thomson, William 180, 183
Thucydides 218
Thurston, William 120
Thurston bequest 120, *134*
Tickford priory 19
Timber Yard 26, 27, 190
Times, The 221, 252, 256, 257, 266, 306, 325
Timms (porter) 265
Tioglath Pileser (bear cub) 34, *35*
Tom Gate 62, *63*, 235, 301, 328
Tom Tower xii, 12, 38, 119, 123, 134, *134*,
    149, *286*, 303, 328, Pl.
Tom Tower Clock 39, 120, 135, 136–7, 314
Tonbridge School 198
Torald's Ham, Oxford 22
Torpids 275, 303
Torporley, Nathaniel 122
    Diclides coelometricae 81
Torporley, Thomas 71
Torrington, Viscount 217
tourism 328
Town Planning Committee 30
Townesend, William 287
Toynbee, Philip 307
Tractarian principles 277
Treasury 36, 186, 192, 193, 211, 222, 224,
    262, 274, 278, 328
Treasury Committee 262
Trelawney, Jonathan, Bishop of Winchester
    129
Tresham, William 15, 16, 17, 18, 21, 44, 55
Trevor, Thomas 119
Trevor-Roper, Hugh xi, *315*, 316, 318, 321,
    325, 326, 329, 332

Index

Trill Mill, Oxford 22, 302
Trill Mill stream 22–3, 236
Tring rectory 68
Trinity College, Cambridge 40, 41, 57, 72, 221, 259, 307, 329
Trinity College, Oxford xii, 19, 126, 226, 270, 318
trusts 124, 160–62
Tubbs sisters 23
TUC (Trades Union Congress) 308
Tunstall, Cuthbert 80
Turner, Sir Edward 175
Turner, Peter 122
Tutor for Admissions 323
Tutor for Graduates 324
Tutorial Fund 254, 264
Tutors' Book 322
Twenty Committee 316
Twenty debating society 276, 317
Twistleton, Edward 259
Tyburn 109
typhus 107

Ufford earls of Suffolk 4
University Boat Club 28, 303
University Boat Race, first (1829) 220
University Church of St Mary the Virgin, Oxford 83, 126
University College, Oxford 79, 109, 130, 177, 236, 249, 265, 297
University Commission (1850) 210, 226–30, 238–9, 240, 244, 246, 252, 253, 254, 255, 260
  Fourteen Points 242–3, 247
University Commission (1877) 263
University Labour Club 308
University of Aberdeen 64
University of Toronto 312
University Officer Training Corps 35
University Rifle Volunteers 35
Upper Library Pl.

Valor Ecclesiasticus 18–19
van Linge, Abraham 110, 284
van Linge, Bernard 284
Vansittart, Nicholas, Baron Bexley 210
Varsity Pairs 275
VE Day 135
Venables family 71
Vere Bayne, Thomas xiii, 62, 236, 246–7, 249, 257, 258, 261, 266, 271, 272, 293, 328

Vermigli, Peter Martyr 2, 36, 45, 54–5, 67
Vesal 207
Vickery, Mr (Bow Street runner) 29
Victoria Foundry, Derby 27
Victoria, Queen 134, 135, 251
Villiers, William, Visdcount Grandison 87
Vincent, Thomas 115, 117
Virgil *171*
Visitor role 79
Vulliamy, Benjamin 136–7

Wade, John: *Black Book* 229
Wadham College, Oxford 208
Wadsworth, Captain James 110
Wagers Club 318
Wainwright, John 155
Wake, William, Archbishop of Canterbury 141, 160, 288
Wakefield, Robert 16
Walker, Obadiah 130, 131, 132
Walker, Patrick Gordon 308
Walker, Robert 208
Wall, John 115
Wallingford Castle *76*, 77, 78
  chapel of St Nicholas *76*
  St Nicholas's college 77
Wallingford, Oxfordshire 52, 53
Wallis, John (a City Justice) 145
Wallis, John (Savilian professor of geometry) 171
Walpole, Horace 3
Walter, John 256
Walton, Sir William 294, 298, 300
Ward, Isaiah 122
Ward, Samuel 114
Warren, Thomas 197–8
Warrigals 275, 318
Warwick gaol 225
Warwickshire 179–80
Waterloo, battle of 222
Watson, Richard 183
Watson, Steven 322
Webb, Philip Barker 203
Weekes, Emme 103
Wellesley, Charles 215–16
Wellington, Arthur Wellesley, 1st Duke of 216
Wells, Edward 138
Wesley, Charles 158
Wesley, John 158
Wessex 1
Westburn, John 133

415

Westfaling, Herbert 233
Westminster, dean of 72, 75, 121
Westminster, deanery of 153
Westminster School 6, 71–2, 84, 125, 172, 174, 182, 199, 206, 221, *239*, 322
Westminster Students 71, 72, 124, 147, 162, 168, 174, 179, 182, 186, 197, 207, 217, 218, 231, 242, 246, 289, 294
Westminster supper 197
Westphaling, Herbert 54
Westwell rectory 215
Wetherell, Nathan 177
Wetwang, Yorkshire 17
Whateley, Arthur 258
Whately, Richard 34
Wheeler, Thomas 224
White, Dick 316
White, Dean Henry Julian 302–3, 310, 327
White, John 82
White, John Meadows 219
White, Joseph Blanco 211
White, Sir Thomas 68, 69
Whitgift, Archbishop 74, 75
Whittingham, William 56, 67
Wigan, William 127, 129
Wiles, Maurice 316
Wilkins, John 59
Wilkins (under-butler) 113
Wilkinson, Henry 110, 115
Willen, Buckinghamshire 124
William III, King ix, 127, 130, 132
Williams, Dean Alwyn Terrell Petre (later Bishop of Durham) 95, 311, 312, 327
Williams, Henry 16, 18
Williams (servitor) 183–4
Williams, William *287*
Willis, Henry 94
Willis, Thomas 122, 175
Willoughby, Mr (of Eynsham) 133
Winchester Cathedral 230
Winchester College 4, 71, 265, 311, 322
Winter, Marius B. 304
Wirksworth, Derbyshire 209
Witney, Oxfordshire 18
Wodehouse, P. G. 311
Wolsey, Cardinal Thomas 21, 43, 45, 54, 56, 79, 116, 283, 285, 286, 332, Pl.
　arms of 4, 5
　benefactor of Oxford University 4
　and Cardinal College property 13, 47–8
　cardinal's hat 3
　charged with praemunire 15
　and college treasures 14, 15
　considers building a new chapel 11
　death 15
　falls from power (1529) 12, 18, 19, 282, *305*
　founds Cardinal College 4–5, 57, 87, 304
　and Higden 6
　influence and income 4
　interest in education 4, 9
　origins 4, 13
　reforms 3
　and Taverner 7–8
Wolsey debating society 276
Wolsey Tower 135, *239*, *290*, 291
women undergraduates Pl.
Wood, Anthony 32, 101, 116, 125–6, 130
　The History and Antiquities of the University of Oxford 285
Wood, Thomas, Bishop of Coventry and Lichfield 162
Wood, Sir William Page 259
Wood Trust 162
Woodcock, Dr Henry 222, 249
Woodroffe, Benjamin 117, 138, 146–7
Woodside Ironworks, Dudley 27
Woodstock, Oxfordshire 83, 133
Woodward, Thomas 143
Woolwich, London 299
Worcester 215, 233
Worcester College, Oxford 331
Wordsworth, Charles 220
Wordsworth, John 303
Workers' Educational Association 277, 294
Worshipful Company of Feltmakers 3
Wortley Montagu, Edward 128, 167
Wren, Sir Christopher 119, 123, 286, *286*
Wriothesley, Thomas 4
Wyche, Sir Peter 87, 106
Wyche, William 106
Wykeham, William 4
Wykyns, John 58

Xenophon 172, 183
Xylander 183

Yeomanry 299
York, Archbishop of 17–18
York, Duchess of 127
York, Duke of 127–8, 194, 221
York diocese 6

Zurich (Zwingli) bible 55